GROWING OLD IN AMERICA

ISSN 1538-6686

GROWING OLD IN AMERICA

Barbara Wexler

INFORMATION PLUS® REFERENCE SERIES
Formerly Published by Information Plus, Wylie, Texas

GALE
CENGAGE Learning·

Farmington Hills, Mich • San Francisco • New York • Waterville, Maine
Meriden, Conn • Mason, Ohio • Chicago

GALE
CENGAGE Learning®

Growing Old in America

Barbara Wexler

Kepos Media, Inc.: Steven Long and Janice Jorgensen, Series Editors

Project Editors: Tracie Moy, Laura Avery

Rights Acquisition and Management: Ashley Maynard, Amanda Kopczynski

Composition: Evi Abou-El-Seoud, Mary Beth Trimper

Manufacturing: Rita Wimberley

For product information and technology assistance, contact us at
Gale Customer Support, 1-800-877-4253.
For permission to use material from this text or product,
submit all requests online at **www.cengage.com/permissions.**
Further permissions questions can be e-mailed to
permissionrequest@cengage.com

Cover photograph: © Robert Kneschke/Shutterstock.com.

Gale
27500 Drake Rd.
Farmington Hills, MI 48331-3535

ISBN-13: 978-0-7876-5103-9 (set)
ISBN-13: 978-1-5730-2669-7

ISSN 1538-6686

This title is also available as an e-book.
ISBN-13: 978-1-5730-2709-0 (set)
Contact your Gale sales representative for ordering information.

Printed in the United States of America
1 2 3 4 5   20 19 18 17 16

TABLE OF CONTENTS

of health care reform legislation on older adults. The challenges of long-term care are highlighted along with in-home services that enable older adults to remain in the community.

delves into the types of frauds that are perpetrated against the older population, domestic and institutional abuse, and mistreatment.

PREFACE

Growing Old in America is part of the *Information Plus Reference Series*. The purpose of each volume of the series is to present the latest facts on a topic of pressing concern in modern American life. These topics include the most controversial and studied social issues of the 21st century: abortion, capital punishment, crime, the environment, health care, immigration, national security, social welfare, weight, women, youth, and many more. Although this series is written for high school and undergraduate students, it is an excellent resource for anyone in need of factual information on current affairs.

By presenting the facts, it is the intention of Gale, Cengage Learning, to provide its readers with everything they need to reach an informed opinion on current issues. To that end, there is a particular emphasis in this series on the presentation of scientific studies, surveys, and statistics. These data are generally presented in the form of tables, charts, and other graphics placed within the text of each book. Every graphic is directly referred to and carefully explained in the text. The source of each graphic is presented within the graphic itself. The data used in these graphics are drawn from the most reputable and reliable sources, such as from the various branches of the U.S. government and from private organizations and associations. Every effort has been made to secure the most recent information available. Readers should bear in mind that many major studies take years to conduct and that additional years often pass before the data from these studies are made available to the public. Therefore, in many cases the most recent information available in 2016 is dated from 2013 or 2014. Older statistics are sometimes presented as well if they are landmark studies or of particular interest and no more-recent data are available.

Although statistics are a major focus of the *Information Plus Reference Series*, they are by no means its only content. Each book also presents the widely held positions and important ideas that shape how the book's subject is discussed in the United States. These positions are explained in detail and, where possible, in the words of their proponents. Some of the other material to be found in these books includes historical background, descriptions of major events related to the subject, relevant laws and court cases, and examples of how these issues play out in American life. Some books also feature primary documents or have pro and con debate sections that provide the words and opinions of prominent Americans on both sides of a controversial topic. All material is presented in an evenhanded and unbiased manner; readers will never be encouraged to accept one view of an issue over another.

HOW TO USE THIS BOOK

The percentage of Americans over the age of 65 years has increased over the past century, and will continue to increase as children born during the mid-20th-century baby boom age. This book explores the current condition of aging in the United States. Included is a general overview on growing old in the United States, the economic status of older people, the Social Security program, Medicare and Medicaid, the living arrangements of older adults, working and retirement, and the education levels and political behavior of older Americans. Physical and mental health problems, drug and alcohol abuse, care for older adults, and crime and victimization of older adults are also covered.

Growing Old in America consists of 11 chapters and three appendixes. Each chapter is devoted to a particular aspect of aging. For a summary of the information that is covered in each chapter, please see the synopses that are provided in the Table of Contents. Chapters generally begin with an overview of the basic facts and background information on the chapter's topic, then proceed to examine subtopics of particular interest. For example, Chapter 3: Living Arrangements of the Older Population begins by explaining that the majority of older adults live independently in the community—less than 4% of people aged 65 years and older live in nursing homes. This is followed by a discussion of multigenerational households, homelessness, long-term care, supportive housing, assisted living, and other residential alternatives. The chapter concludes with a discussion of the housing challenges faced by older adults and adaptations that can help them remain safely in their home rather than relocating to alternative housing. Readers can find their way through a chapter by looking for the section and subsection headings, which are clearly set off from the text. They can also refer to the book's extensive Index if they already know what they are looking for.

Statistical Information

The tables and figures featured throughout *Growing Old in America* will be of particular use to readers in learning about this issue. These tables and figures represent an extensive collection of the most recent and important statistics on growing old and related issues—for example, graphics cover the living arrangements of older adults, the marital status of older Americans, chronic health conditions, crimes against older Americans, national health expenditures, health insurance coverage, and the percentage of workers with retirement plan benefits. Gale, Cengage Learning, believes that making this information available to readers is the most important way to fulfill the goal of this book: to help readers understand the issues and controversies surrounding growing old in the United States and to reach their own conclusions.

Each table or figure has a unique identifier appearing above it for ease of identification and reference. Titles for the tables and figures explain their purpose. At the end of each table or figure, the original source of the data is provided.

To help readers understand these often complicated statistics, all tables and figures are explained in the text. References in the text direct readers to the relevant statistics. Furthermore, the contents of all tables and figures are fully indexed. Please see the opening section of the Index at the back of this volume for a description of how to find tables and figures within it.

Appendixes

Besides the main body text and images, *Growing Old in America* has three appendixes. The first is the Important Names and Addresses directory. Here, readers will find contact information for a number of government and private organizations that can provide further information on growing old. The second appendix is the Resources section, which can also assist readers in conducting their own research. In this section, the author and editors of *Growing Old in America* describe some of the sources that were most useful during the compilation of this book. The final appendix is the detailed Index. It has been greatly expanded from previous editions and should make it even easier to find specific topics in this book.

COMMENTS AND SUGGESTIONS

The editors of the *Information Plus Reference Series* welcome your feedback on *Growing Old in America*. Please direct all correspondence to:

Editors
Information Plus Reference Series
27500 Drake Rd.
Farmington Hills, MI 48331-3535

CHAPTER 1
OLDER AMERICANS: A DIVERSE AND GROWING POPULATION

Old age is the most unexpected of all the things that happen to a man.

—Leon Trotsky

THE U.S. POPULATION GROWS OLDER

The U.S. population is aging. Throughout the second half of the 20th century and the first two decades of the 21st century the country's older population (adults aged 65 years and older) increased significantly. According to the Administration on Aging (AoA), the number of adults age 65 and older increased by 7.6 million from 2002 to 44.7 million in 2013 (the most recent year for which comprehensive data were available as of August 2015), which represented 14.1% of the total U.S. population. In *The Next Four Decades—The Older Population in the United States: 2010 to 2050* (May 2010, http://www.census.gov/prod/2010pubs/p25-1138.pdf), Grayson K. Vincent and Victoria A. Velkoff of the U.S. Census Bureau project that by 2030 one out of five U.S. residents will be aged 65 years and older and that by 2050 the population of people aged 65 years and older will number 88.5 million. Table 1.1 shows projected growth in the population of older adults between 2010 and 2050. Older adults will make up an increasing percentage of the total U.S. population, growing from 13% in 2010 to 20.2% in 2050.

The Census Bureau observes that throughout the world, the growth in the population of older adults will outpace the growth of any other segment of the population. Figure 1.1 compares the percentages of young children (aged five years and younger) and adults aged 65 years and older of the global population between 1950 and 2050. It reveals a steady decline in the percentage of children and a sharp increase in the percentage of older adults between 2000 and 2050. Figure 1.2 shows how the percentage of the oldest older adults (people aged 80 years and older) is expected to increase. For example, in the United States, as a percentage of all people age 65 and older, the percentage of those aged

80 years and older is projected to increase by six percentage points between 2008 and 2040, from 29.5% to 35.5%.

Fewer children per family and longer life spans have shifted the proportion of older adults in the population. Growth in the population segment of older adults in the United States, often called "the graying of America," is considered to be one of the most significant issues facing the country in the 21st century. The swelling population of people aged 65 years and older affects every aspect of society—challenging policy makers, health care providers, employers, families, and others to meet the needs of older Americans.

Many of the findings and statistics cited in this chapter are drawn from data collected by the following federal entities: the AoA; Agency for Healthcare Research and Quality; Census Bureau; Centers for Medicare and Medicaid Services; Employee Benefits Security Administration; National Center for Health Statistics; National Institute on Aging; Office of Research, Evaluation, and Statistics; Office of Statistical and Science Policy; Office of the Assistant Secretary for Planning and Evaluation (U.S. Department of Health and Human Services); Substance Abuse and Mental Health Services Administration; U.S. Bureau of Labor Statistics; U.S. Department of Housing and Urban Development; U.S. Department of Veterans Affairs; and the U.S. Environmental Protection Agency. These organizations are dedicated to encouraging cooperation and collaboration among federal agencies to improve the quality and utility of data on the aging population. Other data are drawn from the AoA's *Profile of Older Americans: 2014* (2015, http://www.aoa.acl.gov/Aging_Statistics/Profile/2014/docs/2014-Profile.pdf).

To understand the aging of the U.S. population, it is important to not only consider the current population of older adults but also to look at how the older population will fare over time. To anticipate the needs of this growing segment of society, policy makers, planners,

TABLE 1.1

Projected U.S. population by age, 2010–50

[Number in thousands]

Age	2010	2020	2030	2040	2050
Number					
Total	310,233	341,387	373,504	405,655	439,010
Under 20 years	84,150	90,703	97,682	104,616	112,940
20 to 64 years	185,854	195,880	203,729	219,801	237,523
65 years and over	40,229	54,804	72,092	81,238	88,547
65 to 69 years	12,261	17,861	20,381	18,989	21,543
70 to 74 years	9,202	14,452	18,404	17,906	18,570
75 to 79 years	7,282	9,656	14,390	16,771	15,964
80 to 84 years	5,733	6,239	10,173	13,375	13,429
85 to 89 years	3,650	3,817	5,383	8,450	10,303
90 years and over	2,101	2,780	3,362	5,748	8,738
Percent					
Total	100.0	100.0	100.0	100.0	100.0
Under 20 years	27.1	26.6	26.2	25.8	25.7
20 to 64 years	59.9	57.4	54.5	54.2	54.1
65 years and over	13.0	16.1	19.3	20.0	20.2
65 to 69 years	4.0	5.2	5.5	4.7	4.9
70 to 74 years	3.0	4.2	4.9	4.4	4.2
75 to 79 years	2.3	2.8	3.9	4.1	3.6
80 to 84 years	1.8	1.8	2.7	3.3	3.1
85 to 89 years	1.2	1.1	1.4	2.1	2.3
90 years and over	0.7	0.8	0.9	1.4	2.0

SOURCE: Grayson K. Vincent and Victoria A. Velkoff, "Appendix Table A-1. Projections and Distribution of the Total Population by Age for the United States: 2010 to 2050," in *The Next Four Decades—The Older Population in the United States: 2010 to 2050*, U.S. Census Bureau, May 2010, http://www.census.gov/prod/2010pubs/p25-1138.pdf (accessed February 17, 2015)

and researchers rely on projections and population estimates. Population estimates and projections are made at different times and are based on different assumptions. Therefore, it is not surprising to find considerable variation in the statistics cited by different agencies and investigators. This chapter contains estimates and projections of demographic changes from several different sources, and as a result there is some variability in the data presented.

HOW DO POPULATIONS AGE?

Unlike individuals, populations can age or become younger. There are key indicators of the age structure of a given population. Populations age or grow younger because of changes in fertility (birthrates expressed as the number of births per 1,000 population per year) and/or mortality (death rates expressed as the number of deaths per 1,000 population per year) or in response to migration (people entering or leaving the population).

The aging of the United States in the early 21st century resulted from changes in fertility and mortality that occurred over the past century. Such shifts in birthrates and death rates are called demographic transitions. Generally, population aging is primarily a response to long-term declines in fertility, and declining fertility is the basic cause of the aging of the U.S. population. Reduced infant and child mortality, chiefly as a result of public health measures, fueled the decline in the fertility rate; that is, the increased survival of children

prompted families to have fewer offspring. The birth of fewer babies resulted in fewer young people.

According to the Central Intelligence Agency (CIA), in *The World Factbook: United States* (July 30, 2015, https://www.cia.gov/library/publications/the-world-factbook/geos/us.html), in 2015 the total fertility rate in the United States was an estimated 1.87 children born per woman. This rate is sharply lower than the fertility rates between 1946 and 1964, following the end of World War II (1939–1945). Victorious soldiers returning home after the war were eager to start families, and this was facilitated by the relatively prosperous postwar economy.

Census Bureau statistics indicate that during this period, which came to be known as the baby boom, U.S. fertility rates exploded, at one point approaching four children born per woman. People born during the baby boom (1946–1964) became known as baby boomers, and it is this cohort (a group of individuals that shares a common characteristic such as birth years and is studied over time) that is responsible for the tremendous increase projected in the number of people aged 65 years and older, and especially aged 65 to 74 years. The older adult segment of the population is expected to swell until 2030, as the baby boom cohort completes its transition from middle age to old age. In 2033 for the first time the population of adults age 65 and older will outnumber the population age 18 and younger.

FIGURE 1.1

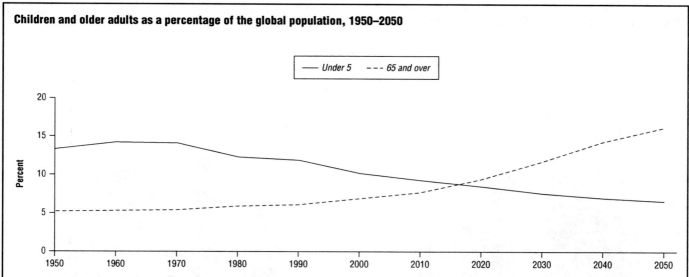

Children and older adults as a percentage of the global population, 1950–2050

Under 5 - - - 65 and over

SOURCE: Kevin Kinsella and Wan He, "Figure 2-1. Young Children and Older People as a Percentage of Global Population: 1950 to 2050," in *An Aging World: 2008*, U.S. Census Bureau, 2009, http://www.census.gov/prod/2009pubs/p95-09-1.pdf (accessed February 17, 2015). Data from the United Nations Department of Economic and Social Affairs.

FIGURE 1.2

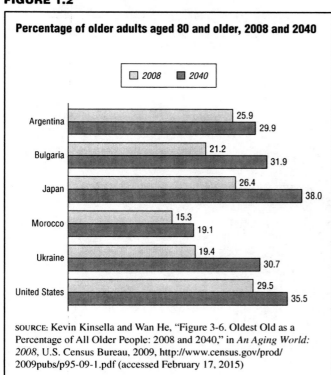

Percentage of older adults aged 80 and older, 2008 and 2040

☐ 2008   ■ 2040

	2008	2040
Argentina	25.9	29.9
Bulgaria	21.2	31.9
Japan	26.4	38.0
Morocco	15.3	19.1
Ukraine	19.4	30.7
United States	29.5	35.5

SOURCE: Kevin Kinsella and Wan He, "Figure 3-6. Oldest Old as a Percentage of All Older People: 2008 and 2040," in *An Aging World: 2008*, U.S. Census Bureau, 2009, http://www.census.gov/prod/2009pubs/p95-09-1.pdf (accessed February 17, 2015)

The decline in death rates, especially at the older ages, has also contributed to the increase in the number of older adults. The death rates of older adults began to decrease during the late 1960s and continued to decline through the first decade of the 21st century. Advances in medical care have produced declining death rates for all three of the leading causes of death: heart disease, malignancies (cancer), and cerebrovascular diseases that cause strokes. Kenneth

D. Kochanek et al. report in "Mortality in the United States, 2013" (*NCHS Data Brief*, no. 178, December 2014) that the age-adjusted death rate in the United States reached an all-time low of 731.9 deaths per 100,000 population in 2013.

Projections of an increasing proportion of older adults between 2015 and 2030 are based on three assumptions: historic low fertility and the prospect of continuing low fertility until 2030, aging of the baby boom cohort, and continued declines in mortality at older ages and low mortality until 2030. Demographers (those who study population statistics) expect that when the entire baby boom generation has attained age 65 (or older) in 2030, the proportion of older people in the U.S. population will stabilize. Figure 1.3 shows how the baby boomers will be a smaller proportion of the population, decreasing from about 25% of the population in 2012 to 0.6% in 2060.

DEFINING OLD AGE

Forty is the old age of youth; fifty the youth of old age.

—Victor Hugo

When does old age begin? The challenge of defining old age is reflected in the terminology that is used to describe adults aged 50 years and older: for example, middle aged, elder, elderly, older, aged, mature, or senior. The AARP (formerly the American Association of Retired Persons), a national advocacy organization for older adults, invites people to join its ranks at age 50. Many retailers offer senior discounts to people aged 50 or 55 years and older, and federal entitlement programs such as Medicare (a medical insurance program for older adults and people with disabilities) extend benefits to people at age 65, while Social Security (a program that

FIGURE 1.3

Baby boomers' contribution to the U.S. population in 2012, 2035, and 2060

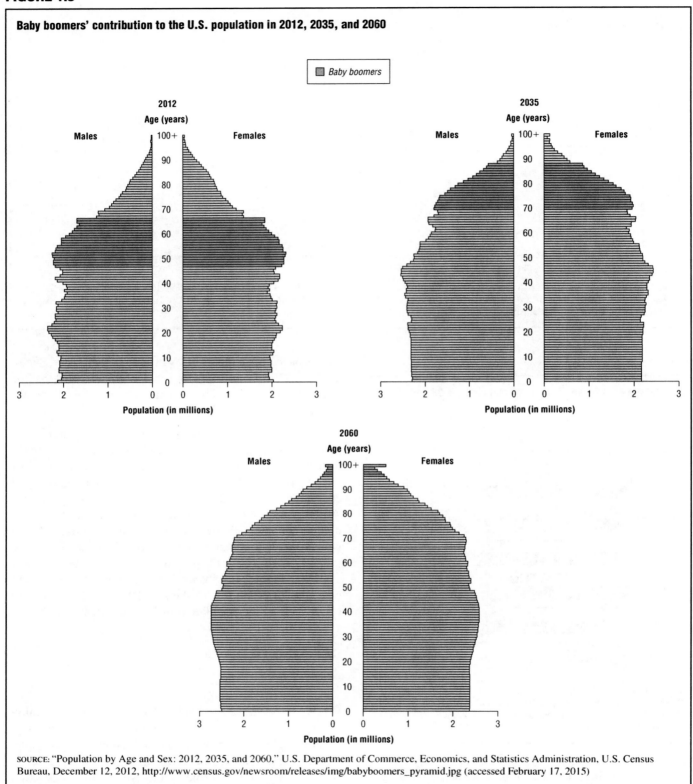

SOURCE: "Population by Age and Sex: 2012, 2035, and 2060," U.S. Department of Commerce, Economics, and Statistics Administration, U.S. Census Bureau, December 12, 2012, http://www.census.gov/newsroom/releases/img/babyboomers_pyramid.jpg (accessed February 17, 2015)

provides retirement income and health care for older adults) benefits may begin as early as age 62. Despite these varying definitions, in this text, unless otherwise specified, the term *older adults* refers to people aged 65 years and older.

Gerontology (the field of study that considers the social, psychological, and biological aspects of aging) distinguishes three groups of older adults: the young-old are those aged 65 to 74 years, the middle-old includes those aged 75 to 84 years, and

FIGURE 1.4

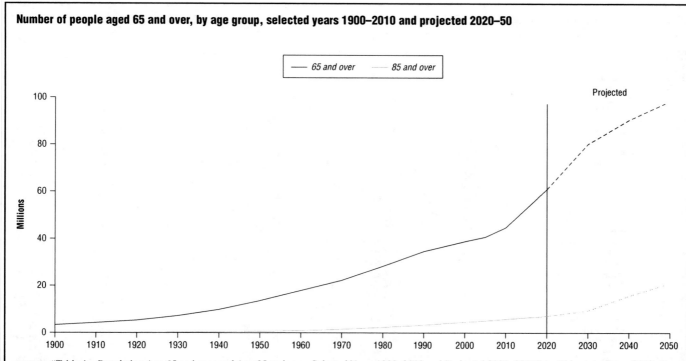

Number of people aged 65 and over, by age group, selected years 1900–2010 and projected 2020–50

— 65 and over   ⋯⋯ 85 and over

SOURCE: "Table 1a. Population Age 65 and over and Age 85 and over, Selected Years 1900–2010 and Projected 2020–2050," in *Older Americans 2012: Key Indicators of Well-Being*, Federal Interagency Forum on Aging-Related Statistics, June 2012, http://www.agingstats.gov/main_site/data/2012_documents/docs/entirechartbook.pdf (accessed February 17, 2015)

the oldest-old are those age 85 years and older. Figure 1.4 shows that in the United States the oldest segment of older adults, the oldest-old, grew from just over 100,000 people in 1900 to 5.5 million in 2010 and is projected to increase to 19 million by 2050.

LIFE EXPECTANCY

Life expectancy (the anticipated average length of life) has increased dramatically since 1900, when the average age of death for men and women combined was 47.3 years. The Centers for Disease Control and Prevention (April 2015, http://www.cdc.gov/nchs/fastats/life-expectancy.htm) reports that life expectancy rose to 78.8 years in 2013. Most projections see life expectancy continuing to rise. According to the CIA, in *World Factbook: United States*, the life expectancy of a baby born in the United States in 2015 was 77.3 years for males and 82 years for females.

Some researchers, however, caution that the historic trend of increasing longevity has ended, with life expectancy at birth beginning to decline as a direct result of the obesity epidemic in the United States. For example, James A. Greenberg of Brooklyn College estimates in "Obesity and Early Mortality in the United States" (*Obesity*, vol. 21, no. 2, February 2013) that the rise in obesity in the United States may slow or even reverse the long-term trend of increasing life expectancy. Greenberg bases

his projections on an analysis of the body mass index (a number that shows body weight adjusted for height) and finds that obesity reduces life expectancy by 9.4 years.

Global Life Expectancy

The more developed regions of the world have lower death rates than the less developed regions and, as such, have higher life expectancies. In *World Factbook*, the CIA observes that some nations more than doubled their life expectancy during the 20th century. In 2014 the projected life expectancy at birth in Monaco was 89.6 years, and it was at least 79 years in many developed countries. (See Table 1.2.) Many less-developed countries have also seen a steady increase in life expectancy, except for countries in Africa that have been hard hit by the human immunodeficiency virus (HIV)/acquired immunodeficiency syndrome (AIDS) epidemic. Table 1.2 shows the ranks of the top-50 countries in terms of life expectancy in 2014. The United States is number 42.

Table 1.3 shows the ranks of the 30 countries with the lowest estimates of life expectancy in 2014. South Africa at 49.6 years and Chad at 49.4 years had the lowest life expectancy. Nazrul Islam Mondal and Mahendran Shitan explain in "Relative Importance of Demographic, Socioeconomic and Health Factors on Life Expectancy in Low- and Lower-Middle-Income

TABLE 1.2

Estimated life expectancy at birth by country, 2014

Rank	Country	Years	Date of information
1	Monaco	89.57	2014 est.
2	Macau	84.48	2014 est.
3	Japan	84.46	2014 est.
4	Singapore	84.38	2014 est.
5	San Marino	83.18	2014 est.
6	Hong Kong	82.78	2014 est.
7	Andorra	82.65	2014 est.
8	Switzerland	82.39	2014 est.
9	Guernsey	82.39	2014 est.
10	Australia	82.07	2014 est.
11	Italy	82.03	2014 est.
12	Sweden	81.89	2014 est.
13	Liechtenstein	81.68	2014 est.
14	Canada	81.67	2014 est.
15	France	81.66	2014 est.
16	Jersey	81.66	2014 est.
17	Norway	81.60	2014 est.
18	Spain	81.47	2014 est.
19	Israel	81.28	2014 est.
20	Iceland	81.22	2014 est.
21	Anguilla	81.20	2014 est.
22	Netherlands	81.12	2014 est.
23	Bermuda	81.04	2014 est.
24	Cayman Islands	81.02	2014 est.
25	Isle of Man	80.98	2014 est.
26	New Zealand	80.93	2014 est.
27	Ireland	80.56	2014 est.
28	Germany	80.44	2014 est.
29	United Kingdom	80.42	2014 est.
30	Greece	80.30	2014 est.
31	Saint Pierre and Miquelon	80.26	2014 est.
32	Austria	80.17	2014 est.
33	Malta	80.11	2014 est.
34	Faroe Islands	80.11	2014 est.
35	European Union	80.02	2014 est.
36	Luxembourg	80.01	2014 est.
37	Belgium	79.92	2014 est.
38	Taiwan	79.84	2014 est.
39	Korea, South	79.80	2014 est.
40	Virgin Islands	79.75	2014 est.
41	Finland	79.69	2014 est.
42	United States	79.56	2014 est.
43	Turks and Caicos Islands	79.55	2014 est.
44	Wallis and Futuna	79.42	2014 est.
45	Saint Helena, Ascension, and Tristan da Cunha	79.21	2014 est.
46	Gibraltar	79.13	2014 est.
47	Denmark	79.09	2014 est.
48	Puerto Rico	79.09	2014 est.
49	Portugal	79.01	2014 est.
50	Guam	78.82	2014 est.

SOURCE: Adapted from "Country Comparison: Life Expectancy at Birth," in *The World Factbook*, Central Intelligence Agency, 2014, https://www.cia.gov/library/publications/the-world-factbook/rankorder/2102rank.html (accessed February 18, 2015)

TABLE 1.3

Countries with lowest estimated life expectancy at birth, 2014

Rank	Country	Years	Date of information
194	Malawi	59.99	2014 est.
195	Guinea	59.60	2014 est.
196	Burundi	59.55	2014 est.
197	Rwanda	59.26	2014 est.
198	Congo, Republic of the	58.52	2014 est.
199	Liberia	58.21	2014 est.
200	Cote d'Ivoire	58.01	2014 est.
201	Sierra Leone	57.39	2014 est.
202	Cameroon	57.35	2014 est.
203	Congo, Democratic Republic of the	56.54	2014 est.
204	Zimbabwe	55.68	2014 est.
205	Angola	55.29	2014 est.
206	Mali	54.95	2014 est.
207	Burkina Faso	54.78	2014 est.
208	Niger	54.74	2014 est.
209	Uganda	54.46	2014 est.
210	Botswana	54.06	2014 est.
211	Lesotho	52.65	2014 est.
212	Nigeria	52.62	2014 est.
213	Mozambique	52.60	2014 est.
214	Gabon	52.06	2014 est.
215	Namibia	51.85	2014 est.
216	Zambia	51.83	2014 est.
217	Somalia	51.58	2014 est.
218	Central African Republic	51.35	2014 est.
219	Swaziland	50.54	2014 est.
220	Afghanistan	50.49	2014 est.
221	Guinea-Bissau	49.87	2014 est.
222	South Africa	49.56	2014 est.
223	Chad	49.44	2014 est.

SOURCE: Adapted from "Country Comparison: Life Expectancy at Birth," in *The World Factbook*, Central Intelligence Agency, 2014, https://www.cia.gov/library/publications/the-world-factbook/rankorder/2102rank.html (accessed February 18, 2015)

Countries" (*Journal of Epidemiology*, vol. 24, no. 2, March 2014) that many factors contribute to lower life expectancy in developing countries. Chief among them are poverty, inadequate medical care, lack of education, and HIV prevalence.

OLDER ADULTS IN THE UNITED STATES

According to U.S. Census estimates, in 2020 there will be an estimated 56.4 million people aged 65 years and older living in the United States. (See Table 1.4.) The young-old (aged 65 to 74 years) will account for 59%

(33 million) of the population age 65 and older. The 16.6 million people aged 75 to 84 years will make up 29.5% of the older adult population, and 12% (6.7 million) will be the oldest-old (aged 85 years and older).

By 2030 the number of young-old is projected to rise to 39.2 million, the middle-old will be nearing 25.8 million, and the oldest-old will be 9.1 million. (See Table 1.4.) Older women are expected to outnumber older men. Longer female life expectancy, combined with the fact that men often marry younger women, contributes to a higher proportion of older women living alone (widowed or unmarried).

The Oldest-Old

The AoA states in *Profile of Older Americans: 2014* that in 2013 adults who reached "age 65 had an average life expectancy of an additional 19.3 years (20.5 years for females and 17.9 years for males)." The population aged 85 years and older is projected to grow from 6.3 million in 2015 to 7.5 million in 2025, a 19% increase in that decade. (See Table 1.4.)

Some researchers believe death rates at older ages will decline more rapidly than is reflected in Census Bureau projections, which will result in even faster

TABLE 1.4

Projections of the population by age and sex, 2015–60

[Resident population as of July 1. Numbers in thousands.]

Sex and age	2015	2020	2025	2030	2035	2040	2045	2050	2055	2060
Both sexes	**321,369**	**334,503**	**347,335**	**359,402**	**370,338**	**380,219**	**389,394**	**398,328**	**407,412**	**416,795**
Under 5 years	19,965	20,568	21,010	21,178	21,268	21,471	21,775	22,147	22,499	22,778
5 to 9 years	20,463	20,274	20,889	21,347	21,529	21,632	21,845	22,158	22,536	22,894
10 to 14 years	20,590	20,735	20,555	21,182	21,650	21,842	21,952	22,171	22,489	22,871
15 to 19 years	21,092	21,048	21,219	21,060	21,706	22,190	22,395	22,516	22,743	23,067
20 to 24 years	22,740	22,059	22,077	22,299	22,183	22,866	23,383	23,615	23,757	23,999
25 to 29 years	22,473	23,722	23,103	23,179	23,450	23,377	24,098	24,646	24,903	25,065
30 to 34 years	21,659	23,168	24,450	23,878	23,995	24,302	24,259	25,004	25,572	25,845
35 to 39 years	20,346	22,060	23,586	24,898	24,360	24,507	24,838	24,813	25,572	26,151
40 to 44 years	20,178	20,568	22,291	23,840	25,176	24,668	24,840	25,190	25,180	25,949
45 to 49 years	20,817	20,204	20,613	22,351	23,919	25,274	24,798	24,995	25,363	25,368
50 to 54 years	22,312	20,638	20,063	20,506	22,257	23,844	25,219	24,781	25,006	25,395
55 to 59 years	21,811	21,879	20,294	19,777	20,260	22,023	23,629	25,023	24,633	24,893
60 to 64 years	19,093	21,141	21,265	19,799	19,351	19,880	21,653	23,275	24,689	24,357
65 to 69 years	16,094	18,194	20,202	20,397	19,071	18,704	19,283	21,054	22,686	24,112
70 to 74 years	11,500	14,882	16,891	18,830	19,091	17,940	17,664	18,294	20,039	21,662
75 to 79 years	8,126	10,112	13,154	15,013	16,819	17,143	16,212	16,042	16,717	18,393
80 to 84 years	5,806	6,527	8,191	10,737	12,343	13,924	14,294	13,634	13,574	14,274
85 to 89 years	3,875	3,964	4,521	5,747	7,622	8,867	10,114	10,492	10,137	10,184
90 to 94 years	1,859	2,024	2,114	2,464	3,192	4,320	5,127	5,951	6,275	6,184
95 to 99 years	498	649	728	782	940	1,254	1,751	2,141	2,550	2,752
100 years and over	72	89	119	138	154	193	267	387	493	604
Median age (years)	37.8	38.5	39.3	40.1	41.0	41.6	42.0	42.4	42.7	43.0
Male	**158,345**	**165,036**	**171,489**	**177,528**	**183,030**	**188,093**	**192,919**	**197,727**	**202,671**	**207,764**
Under 5 years	10,211	10,520	10,747	10,833	10,879	10,983	11,138	11,329	11,509	11,652
5 to 9 years	10,448	10,360	10,676	10,910	11,003	11,055	11,164	11,325	11,519	11,702
10 to 14 years	10,513	10,584	10,500	10,821	11,061	11,158	11,215	11,327	11,490	11,685
15 to 19 years	10,796	10,749	10,835	10,762	11,093	11,341	11,446	11,508	11,624	11,790
20 to 24 years	11,678	11,300	11,290	11,404	11,354	11,706	11,972	12,091	12,165	12,289
25 to 29 years	11,447	12,161	11,818	11,841	11,982	11,956	12,327	12,609	12,742	12,825
30 to 34 years	10,906	11,781	12,510	12,194	12,241	12,402	12,392	12,776	13,069	13,210
35 to 39 years	10,181	11,099	11,979	12,725	12,430	12,494	12,669	12,670	13,062	13,361
40 to 44 years	10,025	10,272	11,193	12,086	12,845	12,569	12,648	12,834	12,843	13,241
45 to 49 years	10,324	10,010	10,266	11,194	12,097	12,869	12,612	12,706	12,903	12,921
50 to 54 years	10,955	10,182	9,889	10,165	11,100	12,013	12,796	12,564	12,675	12,885
55 to 59 years	10,601	10,651	9,929	9,672	9,969	10,911	11,833	12,627	12,426	12,560
60 to 64 years	9,131	10,147	10,229	9,578	9,362	9,685	10,631	11,559	12,364	12,201
65 to 69 years	7,612	8,567	9,556	9,676	9,105	8,936	9,285	10,227	11,157	11,967
70 to 74 years	5,306	6,900	7,804	8,747	8,901	8,426	8,309	8,683	9,604	10,523
75 to 79 years	3,615	4,538	5,938	6,760	7,623	7,808	7,447	7,388	7,780	8,655
80 to 84 years	2,417	2,783	3,529	4,660	5,351	6,087	6,289	6,062	6,060	6,454
85 to 89 years	1,448	1,545	1,808	2,327	3,115	3,626	4,181	4,374	4,284	4,330
90 to 94 years	591	686	749	897	1,178	1,612	1,919	2,258	2,407	2,414
95 to 99 years	128	181	216	243	299	405	572	703	851	931
100 years and over	14	20	29	35	41	52	73	106	137	170
Median age (years)	36.5	37.3	38.0	39.0	39.8	40.4	40.8	41.3	41.6	42.0
Female	**163,024**	**169,467**	**175,846**	**181,874**	**187,308**	**192,126**	**196,476**	**200,601**	**204,741**	**209,031**
Under 5 years	9,755	10,047	10,264	10,346	10,389	10,488	10,637	10,818	10,990	11,127
5 to 9 years	10,015	9,914	10,214	10,437	10,526	10,576	10,680	10,833	11,018	11,192
10 to 14 years	10,076	10,150	10,055	10,361	10,590	10,683	10,737	10,844	10,999	11,185
15 to 19 years	10,297	10,299	10,384	10,298	10,613	10,849	10,949	11,008	11,119	11,277
20 to 24 years	11,062	10,759	10,787	10,895	10,828	11,160	11,411	11,523	11,592	11,711
25 to 29 years	11,026	11,561	11,284	11,338	11,468	11,421	11,770	12,037	12,161	12,240
30 to 34 years	10,753	11,387	11,940	11,683	11,755	11,901	11,868	12,228	12,504	12,635
35 to 39 years	10,166	10,961	11,607	12,173	11,929	12,013	12,169	12,144	12,510	12,790
40 to 44 years	10,153	10,296	11,098	11,755	12,330	12,098	12,192	12,356	12,338	12,708
45 to 49 years	10,493	10,195	10,347	11,157	11,822	12,405	12,186	12,289	12,460	12,447
50 to 54 years	11,356	10,456	10,174	10,342	11,157	11,831	12,423	12,217	12,331	12,509
55 to 59 years	11,210	11,228	10,365	10,106	10,291	11,112	11,795	12,396	12,207	12,333
60 to 64 years	9,962	10,993	11,036	10,221	9,989	10,195	11,022	11,715	12,325	12,156
65 to 69 years	8,482	9,626	10,646	10,721	9,967	9,768	9,997	10,827	11,528	12,145
70 to 74 years	6,193	7,982	9,088	10,083	10,189	9,514	9,355	9,611	10,435	11,139
75 to 79 years	4,512	5,574	7,216	8,253	9,196	9,335	8,765	8,654	8,937	9,738
80 to 84 years	3,389	3,744	4,662	6,076	6,992	7,837	8,005	7,572	7,514	7,820
85 to 89 years	2,427	2,420	2,713	3,420	4,507	5,241	5,933	6,118	5,853	5,854
90 to 94 years	1,268	1,337	1,365	1,567	2,014	2,708	3,208	3,693	3,867	3,770
95 to 99 years	370	468	511	540	640	849	1,179	1,438	1,698	1,821
100 years and over	58	69	91	103	114	141	194	280	356	434
Median age (years)	39.2	39.8	40.6	41.4	42.3	42.9	43.3	43.6	43.8	44.1

SOURCE: "Table 9. Projections of the Population by Age and Sex for the United States: 2015 to 2060," in *2014 National Population Projections Summary Tables*, U.S. Census Bureau, Population Division, December 2014, https://www.census.gov/population/projections/data/national/2014/summarytables.html (accessed February 18, 2015)

growth of this population segment. The Census Bureau reports that among the oldest-old, women dramatically outnumber men; in 2020 there will be nearly twice as many women aged 85 years and older than men. (See Table 1.4.)

Centenarians

During the first half of the 21st century the United States will experience a centenarian boom. Living to age 100 and older is no longer a rarity. The chances of living to age 100 have increased by 40% since 1900. The centenarian population more than doubled during the 1980s. In 2015 about 72,000 Americans were age 100 or older. (See Table 1.4.) By 2060 that number is expected to increase to 604,000.

As the numbers and percentages of all older adults increase, the shape of the U.S. population pyramid (also called the age structure diagram), which graphically displays the projected population by age, will change. Figure 1.5 shows how the projected population age distribution in 2030 and 2050 differs from the distribution in 2012.

According to Guinness World Records (2013, http://www.guinnessworldrecords.com/records-5000/oldest-person), the oldest verified age attained by a human is 122 years and 164 days. Guinness World Records relies on the Gerontology Research Group (GRG), which tracks supercentenarians (people aged 110 years and older) throughout the world. The GRG reports (http://www.grg.org/Adams/E.HTM) that as of December 2013, it had validated 68 living supercentenarians: 65 women and 3 men. By the following November, the number of validated cases had jumped nearly 18% to 80: 78 females and 2 males. The GRG notes, however, that it is likely that many additional cases are unverified, and estimates there may be as many as 300 to 450 living supercentenarians worldwide as of 2015. For the United States, the estimate is 60 to 75.

On March 5, 2015, Misao Okawa, the oldest person in the world, celebrated her 117th birthday. In "Yes, 5 People Born in the 1800s Are Still with Us" (USAToday.com, January 22, 2015), Matthew Diebel recounts Okawa's advice about how to live a long life: "Eat and sleep and you will live a long time." She died on April 1, 2015.

Racial and Ethnic Diversity

The older population is becoming more ethnically and racially diverse, although at a slower pace than the overall population of the United States. In 2012 non-Hispanic whites made up approximately 79% of the older population, with African Americans (9%), Hispanics (7%), and Asian Americans (4%) composing smaller segments. (See Table 1.5.) By 2060 the composition of the older population is projected to be more racially and ethnically diverse: 56% will be non-Hispanic white, 21% Hispanic, 13% African American, and 8% Asian American. Although the older population is projected to increase among African Americans, Asian Americans, and Hispanics, the proportion of the older population that is Hispanic is projected to grow the most dramatically, from 7% in 2012 to 21% in 2060. (See Table 1.5.)

Marital Status

As in previous years, in 2014 older men were much more likely than older women to be married. Seven out of 10 (72%) men age 65 and older were married, compared with 46% of women in the same age group. (See Table 1.6.)

As older women outnumber older men in all age groups, it is not surprising that there are more widows than widowers. In 2014 more than three times as many women as men age 65 and older were widowed—35% of women, compared with 11% of men. (See Table 1.6.) Just 11% of older adults were divorced, whereas an even smaller proportion (4%) had never married.

Foreign-Born Older Adults

Karen Zeigler and Steven A. Camarota of the Center for Immigration Studies report in *U.S. Immigrant Population Record 41.3 Million in 2013* (September 2014, http://cis.org/immigrant-population-record-2013) that in 2013 the nation's foreign-born population numbered 41.3 million, accounting for an estimated 13.1% of the total U.S. population.

According to the Population Reference Bureau, in "Elderly Immigrants in the United States" (October 2013, http://www.prb.org/Publications/Reports/2013/us-elderly-immigrants.aspx), the foreign-born population of adults age 65 and older grew 70%, from 2.7 million in 1990 to 4.6 million in 2010. This growth is occurring

FIGURE 1.5

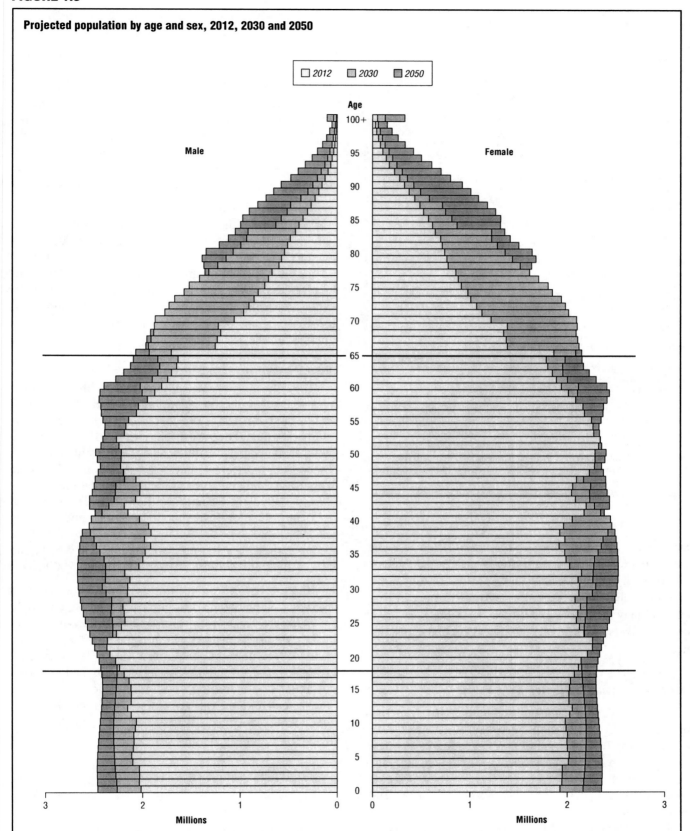

Projected population by age and sex, 2012, 2030 and 2050

☐ 2012 ▨ 2030 ▨ 2050

Age

Male

Female

Millions

Millions

SOURCE: Jennifer M. Ortman, Victoria A. Velkoff, and Howard Hogan, "Figure 2. Age and Sex Structure of the Population for the United States: 2012, 2030, and 2050," in "An Aging Nation: The Older Population in the United States," *Current Population Reports*, U.S. Census Bureau, May 2014, http://www.census.gov/prod/2014pubs/p25-1140.pdf (accessed February 20, 2015)

TABLE 1.5

Projected distribution of older adults by race and Hispanic origin, selected years 2012–60

[Numbers in thousands]

Age, race, and Hispanic origin[a]	2012	2020	2030	2040	2050	2060
			Percent			
65 years and over	100.0	100.0	100.0	100.0	100.0	100.0
One race	99.2	99.1	98.9	98.6	98.2	97.6
White	86.0	84.3	82.2	79.9	77.3	74.7
Non-Hispanic white	79.3	76.4	72.3	66.7	60.9	55.9
Black	8.8	9.7	10.7	11.5	12.3	13.4
American Indian and Alaska Native	0.6	0.7	0.9	1.0	1.2	1.3
Asian	3.8	4.3	4.8	5.9	7.1	7.9
Native Hawaiian and other Pacific Islander	0.1	0.1	0.2	0.2	0.3	0.3
Two or more races	0.8	0.9	1.1	1.4	1.8	2.4
Race alone or in combination[b]						
White	86.6	85.0	83.2	81.1	78.9	76.8
Black	9.0	9.9	11.0	12.0	12.9	14.4
American Indian and Alaska Native	1.1	1.3	1.5	1.7	1.9	2.1
Asian	4.0	4.6	5.2	6.4	7.8	8.8
Native Hawaiian and other Pacific Islander	0.2	0.2	0.3	0.4	0.5	0.5
Hispanic	7.3	8.6	11.0	14.7	18.4	21.2
Non-Hispanic	92.7	91.4	89.0	85.3	81.6	78.8

[a]Hispanics may be of any race.
[b]In combination means in combination with one or more other races. The sum of the five race groups adds to more than the total population, and 100 percent, because individuals may report more than one race.
Note: Responses of "some other race" from the 2010 Census are modified.

SOURCE: Adapted from Jennifer M. Ortman, Victoria A. Velkoff, and Howard Hogan, "Appendix Table A-2. Projections and Distribution of the Older Population by Selected Age Groups, Race, and Hispanic Origin for the United States: 2012 to 2060," in "An Aging Nation: The Older Population in the United States," *Current Population Reports*, U.S. Census Bureau, May 2014, http://www.census.gov/prod/2014pubs/p25-1140.pdf (accessed February 20, 2015)

because the long-term foreign-born population is aging, and some older adults are arriving in the United States to reunite with family already here. The latter group may face more challenges because they may not speak English, and may lack work experience. Late-life immigrants are more likely to be female, widowed, and have physical limitations.

WHERE OLDER AMERICANS LIVE

In *A Profile of Older Americans: 2014*, the AoA reports that in 2013 adults aged 65 years and older accounted for 15% or more of the population in 19 states. The proportion of the population aged 65 years and older varied by state. Florida had the largest proportion of older adults, with 18.7% of the total, followed by Maine (17.7%), West Virginia (17.3%), Pennsylvania (16.4%), Vermont (16.4%), Montana (16.2%), Delaware (15.9%), Hawaii (15.6%), Iowa (15.6%), Oregon (15.5%), Rhode Island (15.5%), Arizona (15.4%), Arkansas (15.4%), New Hampshire (15.4%), Connecticut (15.2%), South Carolina (15.2%), Ohio (15.1%), Michigan (15%), and Missouri

(15%). Figure 1.6 displays people aged 65 years and older as a percentage of total population by state in 2013.

In 20 states—Alaska (61.7%), Nevada (50.7%), Colorado (46.8%), Georgia (44.4%), Arizona (43.2%), Idaho (43.1%), South Carolina (43.1%), Utah (40%), Washington (38.2%), North Carolina (38.1%), Delaware (37.8%), Texas (36.7%), New Mexico (36.2%), Oregon (33.7%), Virginia (33.3%), New Hampshire (33%), Montana (31.5%), Tennessee (31%), Wyoming (30.5%), and Hawaii (30.3%)—the population aged 65 years and older increased by 30% or more between 2003 and 2013. Figure 1.7 shows growth in the older population by state between 2003 and 2013.

The AoA indicates that in 2013, 81% of older adults lived in metropolitan areas. About half (54%) of these individuals lived outside of cities, and more than one-quarter (27%) were city dwellers. Approximately 19% of older adults lived in nonmetropolitan areas. Older adults relocate less often than any other age group. Of older adults who changed residence between 2013 and 2014, just 19% moved out of state; the vast majority (81%) remained in the same state.

Older Americans Are More Religious

The Pew Forum on Religion and Public Life indicates in *Millennials in Adulthood* (March 2014, http://www.pewsocialtrends.org/2014/03/07/millennials-in-adulthood) that older Americans tend to be more religious than younger Americans. Consistent with this observation is the fact that older adults are also more likely to say they believe in God. Survey data reveal that 74% of the Silent Generation (born between 1925 and 1945) and 73% of baby boomers (born between 1946 and 1964) said they believe in God compared with 69% of Generation Xers (born between 1965 and 1980), and 58% of millennials (born between 1981 and 2000).

In *Majority Still Says Religion Can Answer Today's Problems* (June 27, 2014, http://www.gallup.com/poll/171998/majority-says-religion-answer-today-problems.aspx), Frank Newport of the Gallup Organization reports that Gallup poll data reveal that older Americans are among the most religious age groups and observes that about two-thirds (62%) of adults age 65 and older believe that religion can answer today's problems compared with less than half (48%) of younger adults between the ages of 18 and 29.

ENJOYMENT OF OLDER AGE

Getting old isn't nearly as bad as people think it will be. Nor is it quite as good.

—Pew Research Center, "Growing Old in America: Expectations vs. Reality" (June 29, 2009)

In view of the myriad difficulties and challenges facing older adults, including ill health, inadequate financial resources, and the loss of friends and loved ones, it seems natural to

TABLE 1.6

Marital status of persons by age and sex, 2014

[Numbers in thousands, except for percentages. Data are based on the Current Population Survey, 2014 Annual Social and Economic Supplement (CPS ASEC) sample of 98,000 addresses.]

All races	Total Number	Married spouse present Number	Married spouse absent Number	Widowed Number	Divorced Number	Separated Number	Never married Number	Total Percent	Married spouse present Percent	Married spouse absent Percent	Widowed Percent	Divorced Percent	Separated Percent	Never married Percent
Both sexes														
Total 15+	252,224	123,700	3,494	14,274	25,343	5,391	80,022	100.0	49.0	1.4	5.7	10.0	2.1	31.7
15–17 years	12,920	26	77	13	19	66	12,718	100.0	0.2	0.6	0.1	0.1	0.5	98.4
18–19 years	7,877	126	50	2	28	60	7,611	100.0	1.6	0.6	0.0	0.4	0.8	96.6
20–24 years	22,255	2,339	158	21	195	278	19,264	100.0	10.5	0.7	0.1	0.9	1.2	86.6
25–29 years	21,446	6,886	355	61	714	401	13,029	100.0	32.1	1.7	0.3	3.3	1.9	60.8
30–34 years	20,960	11,196	295	66	1,331	497	7,574	100.0	53.4	1.4	0.3	6.3	2.4	36.1
35–39 years	19,399	11,812	357	118	1,961	577	4,575	100.0	60.9	1.8	0.6	10.1	3.0	23.6
40–44 years	20,377	12,798	416	216	2,690	716	3,540	100.0	62.8	2.0	1.1	13.2	3.5	17.4
45–49 years	20,661	13,477	331	288	3,053	681	2,831	100.0	65.2	1.6	1.4	14.8	3.3	13.7
50–54 years	22,339	14,164	339	577	3,569	675	3,016	100.0	63.4	1.5	2.6	16.0	3.0	13.5
55–64 years	39,532	25,367	581	1,941	6,720	996	3,926	100.0	64.2	1.5	4.9	17.0	2.5	9.9
65–74 years	25,787	16,842	278	3,489	3,614	331	1,232	100.0	65.3	1.1	13.5	14.0	1.3	4.8
75–84 years	13,427	7,043	179	4,442	1,160	89	514	100.0	52.5	1.3	33.1	8.6	0.7	3.8
85+ years	5,246	1,625	80	3,038	288	23	191	100.0	31.0	1.5	57.9	5.5	0.4	3.6
15–17 years	12,920	26	77	13	19	66	12,718	100.0	0.2	0.6	0.1	0.1	0.5	98.4
18+ years	239,304	123,674	3,417	14,260	25,324	5,325	67,304	100.0	51.7	1.4	6.0	10.6	2.2	28.1
15–64 years	207,765	98,190	2,957	3,304	20,282	4,947	78,085	100.0	47.3	1.4	1.6	9.8	2.4	37.6
65+ years	44,459	25,510	537	10,970	5,061	444	1,937	100.0	57.4	1.2	24.7	11.4	1.0	4.4
Male														
Total 15+	122,353	61,850	1,777	3,059	10,729	2,226	42,711	100.0	50.6	1.5	2.5	8.8	1.8	34.9
15–17 years	6,528	14	56	7	7	34	6,409	100.0	0.2	0.9	0.1	0.1	0.5	98.2
18–19 years	4,053	33	22	—	14	21	3,962	100.0	0.8	0.6	—	0.4	0.5	97.8
20–24 years	11,227	859	70	4	59	134	10,101	100.0	7.6	0.6	0.0	0.5	1.2	90.0
25–29 years	10,816	2,911	177	12	291	114	7,311	100.0	26.9	1.6	0.1	2.7	1.1	67.6
30–34 years	10,370	5,229	151	16	562	165	4,246	100.0	50.4	1.5	0.2	5.4	1.6	40.9
35–39 years	9,555	5,709	207	27	869	246	2,497	100.0	59.8	2.2	0.3	9.1	2.6	26.1
40–44 years	10,035	6,229	236	68	1,224	290	1,988	100.0	62.1	2.4	0.7	12.2	2.9	19.8
45–49 years	10,145	6,736	173	83	1,331	302	1,520	100.0	66.4	1.7	0.8	13.1	3.0	15.0
50–54 years	10,906	7,007	155	130	1,582	295	1,736	100.0	64.2	1.4	1.2	14.5	2.7	15.9
55–64 years	18,996	12,911	271	458	2,855	427	2,073	100.0	68.0	1.4	2.4	15.0	2.2	10.9
65–74 years	12,069	9,025	140	760	1,421	136	586	100.0	74.8	1.2	6.3	11.8	1.1	4.9
75–84 years	5,755	4,107	91	867	417	52	221	100.0	71.4	1.6	15.1	7.2	0.9	3.8
85+ years	1,898	1,079	27	627	96	9	59	100.0	56.8	1.4	33.1	5.1	0.5	3.1
15–17 years	6,528	14	56	7	7	34	6,409	100.0	0.2	0.9	0.1	0.1	0.5	98.2
18+ years	115,825	61,836	1,721	3,052	10,722	2,192	36,302	100.0	53.4	1.5	2.6	9.3	1.9	31.3
15–64 years	102,631	47,639	1,518	805	8,795	2,029	41,844	100.0	46.4	1.5	0.8	8.6	2.0	40.8
65+ years	19,722	14,212	258	2,254	1,934	197	867	100.0	72.1	1.3	11.4	9.8	1.0	4.4
Female														
Total 15+	129,871	61,850	1,717	11,214	14,614	3,165	37,311	100.0	47.6	1.3	8.6	11.3	2.4	28.7
15–17 years	6,391	12	21	6	12	32	6,309	100.0	0.2	0.3	0.1	0.2	0.5	98.7
18–19 years	3,824	92	27	2	14	40	3,649	100.0	2.4	0.7	0.0	0.4	1.0	95.4
20–24 years	11,028	1,481	88	17	136	144	9,162	100.0	13.4	0.8	0.2	1.2	1.3	83.1
25–29 years	10,629	3,974	177	49	423	286	5,718	100.0	37.4	1.7	0.5	4.0	2.7	53.8
30–34 years	10,590	5,967	144	50	768	332	3,328	100.0	56.3	1.4	0.5	7.3	3.1	31.4
35–39 years	9,844	6,102	150	91	1,092	330	2,078	100.0	62.0	1.5	0.9	11.1	3.4	21.1
40–44 years	10,342	6,569	180	149	1,466	426	1,552	100.0	63.5	1.7	1.4	14.2	4.1	15.0
45–49 years	10,516	6,741	158	205	1,722	379	1,311	100.0	64.1	1.5	1.9	16.4	3.6	12.5
50–54 years	11,433	7,157	184	447	1,987	379	1,280	100.0	62.6	1.6	3.9	17.4	3.3	11.2
55–64 years	20,536	12,456	309	1,483	3,866	569	1,853	100.0	60.7	1.5	7.2	18.8	2.8	9.0
65–74 years	13,718	7,817	138	2,729	2,193	195	646	100.0	57.0	1.0	19.9	16.0	1.4	4.7
75–84 years	7,671	2,935	88	3,575	743	37	292	100.0	38.3	1.1	46.6	9.7	0.5	3.8
85+ years	3,348	547	53	2,411	192	14	132	100.0	16.3	1.6	72.0	5.7	0.4	3.9
15–17 years	6,391	12	21	6	12	32	6,309	100.0	0.2	0.3	0.1	0.2	0.5	98.7
18+ years	123,480	61,838	1,696	11,208	14,602	3,133	31,002	100.0	50.1	1.4	9.1	11.8	2.5	25.1
15–64 years	105,134	50,551	1,439	2,499	11,486	2,918	36,241	100.0	48.1	1.4	2.4	10.9	2.8	34.5
65+ years	24,737	11,299	278	8,715	3,127	247	1,070	100.0	45.7	1.1	35.2	12.6	1.0	4.3

Note: Prior to 2001, this table included group quarters people.
Dash (—) = represents or rounds to zero.

source: "Table A1. Marital Status Of People 15 Years and over, by Age, Sex, Personal Earnings, Race, and Hispanic Origin: 2014," in *America's Families and Living Arrangements: 2014: Adults (A Table Series)*, U.S. Census Bureau, Population Division, October 2014, http://www.census.gov/hhes/families/data/cps2014A.html (accessed April 17, 2015)

FIGURE 1.6

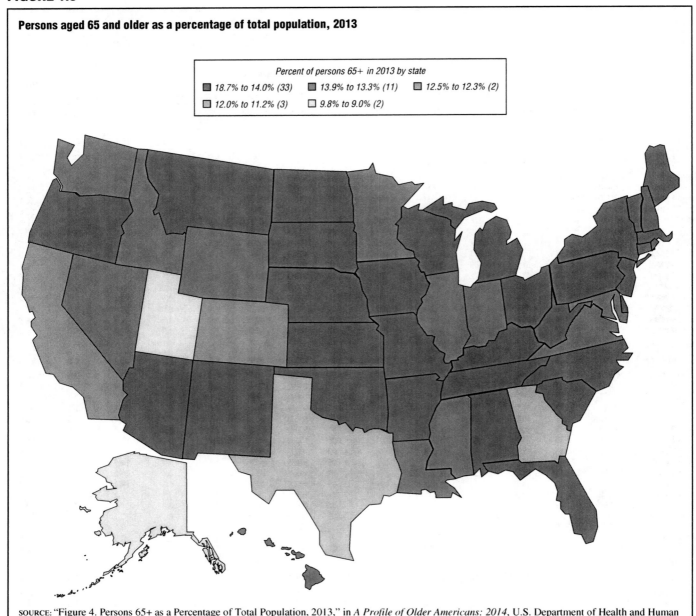

Persons aged 65 and older as a percentage of total population, 2013

Percent of persons 65+ in 2013 by state

- 18.7% to 14.0% (33)
- 13.9% to 13.3% (11)
- 12.5% to 12.3% (2)
- 12.0% to 11.2% (3)
- 9.8% to 9.0% (2)

SOURCE: "Figure 4. Persons 65+ as a Percentage of Total Population, 2013," in *A Profile of Older Americans: 2014*, U.S. Department of Health and Human Services, Administration on Aging, May 2015, http://www.aoa.acl.gov/Aging_Statistics/Profile/2014/docs/2014-Profile.pdf (accessed April 28, 2015)

assume that advancing age will be associated with less over-all happiness and more worry. However, several studies refute this premise. Researchers find less worry among older adults than anticipated and note the ability of older adults to adapt to their changing life conditions.

In "Trends in Psychological Well-Being" (April 2013, http://www.norc.org/PDFs/GSS%20Reports/Trends%20in %20sychological%20Well-Being_Final.pdf), Tom W. Smith and Jaesok Son of the independent research organization NORC at the University of Chicago report that happiness generally increases with advancing age. Nearly 40% of Americans age 65 and older describe themselves as "very happy" compared with 33% of those aged 35 to 49 years.

In "The Real Roots of Midlife Crisis" (Atlantic.com, November 17, 2014), Jonathan Rauch explains that research-ers have described happiness and age as a U-shaped curve with life satisfaction falling until it bottoms out during the late 40s or early 50s and then rising with age until the last years of life. The observed increase in happiness may be attributed to fewer responsibilities (child-rearing respon-sibilities are over, careers peak), and older adults tend to become more realistic in terms of their expectations of themselves and others.

In "Why Elders Smile" (NYTimes.com, December 4, 2014), David Brooks suggests that older adults are more relaxed, in part because they do not have to worry

FIGURE 1.7

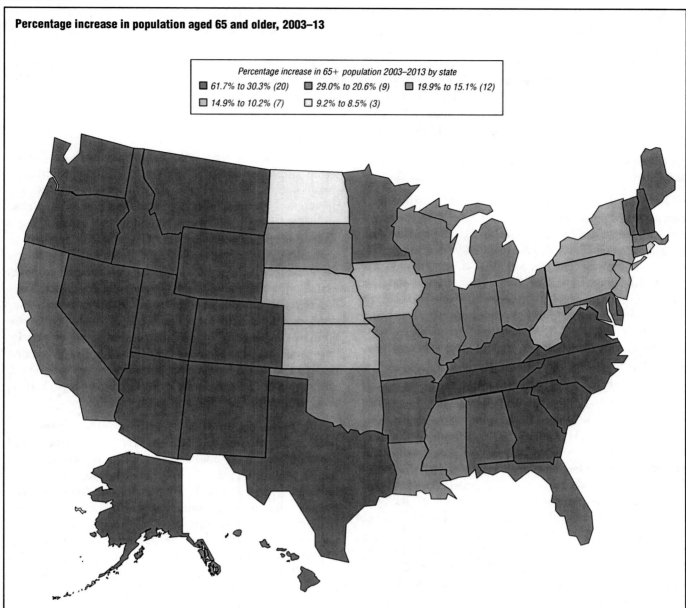

Percentage increase in population aged 65 and older, 2003–13

Percentage increase in 65+ population 2003–2013 by state

■ 61.7% to 30.3% (20)　■ 29.0% to 20.6% (9)　■ 19.9% to 15.1% (12)

□ 14.9% to 10.2% (7)　□ 9.2% to 8.5% (3)

SOURCE: "Figure 5. Percent Increase in Population Age 65+, 2003 to 2013," in *A Profile of Older Americans: 2014*, U.S. Department of Health and Human Services, Administration on Aging, May 2015, http://www.aoa.acl.gov/Aging_Statistics/Profile/2014/docs/2014-Profile.pdf (accessed April 28, 2015)

about the future and are better able to enjoy the present. They are more adept at managing life's challenges and have mastered many life skills. Older adults also have perspective and recognize that "most setbacks are not the end of the world," and their experience and empathy enables them to more accurately predict how events will unfold, closing the gap between expectations and reality.

Amit Bhattacharjee and Cassie Mogilner suggest in "Emotion Regulation in Older Age" (*Happiness from Ordinary and Extraordinary Experiences*, vol. 41, no. 1, June 2014) that older people seem better able than younger people to be happy with ordinary experiences such as seeing plants thriving in the garden or watching a movie. The researchers conclude, "young people actively looking to define themselves find it particularly rewarding to accumulate extraordinary experiences that mark their progression through life milestones.... Once people grow older and have established a better sense of who they are, the experiences they view as self-defining are just as likely to include the routine events that reveal how they like to spend their time."

Perceptions of Aging Influence Longevity and Happiness

Becca R. Levy et al. report in the landmark study "Longevity Increased by Positive Self-Perceptions of

Aging" (*Journal of Personality and Social Psychology*, vol. 83, no. 2, August 2002) that older people with more positive self-perceptions of aging lived 7.5 years longer than those with less positive self-perceptions of aging, even after taking into account other factors, including age, gender, socioeconomic status, loneliness, and overall health. Analyzing data from the 660 participants aged 50 years and older in the Ohio Longitudinal Study of Aging and Retirement, the researchers compared mortality rates with responses made 23 years earlier by the participants. The responses included agreeing or disagreeing with statements such as "As you get older, you are less useful."

Levy et al. assert, "The effect of more positive self-perceptions of aging on survival is greater than the physiological measures of low systolic blood pressure and cholesterol, each of which is associated with a longer life span of 4 years or less.... [It] is also greater than the independent contribution of lower body mass index, no history of smoking, and a tendency to exercise; each of these factors has been found to contribute between 1 and 3 years of added life." They conclude that negative self-perceptions can diminish life expectancy, whereas positive self-perceptions can prolong it.

In "The Power of Positive Emotions: It's a Matter of Life or Death—Subjective Well-Being and Longevity over 28 Years in a General Population" (*Health Psychology*, vol. 29, no. 1, January 2010), Jingping Xu and Robert E. Roberts analyze 28 years of data from 6,856 subjects to determine whether happiness and life satisfaction are related to longevity. The researchers find that the subjective assessment of well-being, which includes positive feelings and life satisfaction, predicted a lower risk of mortality in the population. Xu and Roberts explain that "positive emotions broaden our attention and action span, down-regulate ('undo') what negative feelings do to us, and build enduring psychological, physical, and social resources that we can draw upon when needed, thus promote health and longevity."

Andrew Steptoe and Jane Wardle of the University College London report in "Positive Affect Measured Using Ecological Momentary Assessment and Survival in Older Men and Women" (*Proceedings of the National Academy of Sciences*, vol. 108, no. 45, November 8, 2011), a study of more than 3,800 people aged 52 to 79 years, that those who said they were happiest had a 35% chance of living longer than those who said they felt least happy. The researchers conclude that their findings "provide further reason to target the positive well-being of older people. In addition to addressing the health status and material circumstances of older people, efforts to improve affective states may have beneficial health consequences."

Research conducted by Kerry A. Sargent-Cox, Kaarin J. Anstey, and Mary A. Luszcz and reported in "Longitudinal Change of Self-Perceptions of Aging and Mortality" (*Journals of Gerontology: Series B*, vol. 69, no. 2, February 18, 2013) confirms that how people view and interpret age-related changes influences their future health. Those who perceive age-related changes negatively are less likely to adapt well to these changes and as a result, are more vulnerable to declining health.

ATTITUDES ABOUT AGING

People of all ages hold beliefs and attitudes about aging and older adults. Even young children can distinguish age differences, and they display attitudes that appear to be characteristic of their generation. Because attitudes strongly influence behavior and because more Americans reach older ages than ever before, interaction with older people and deeply held beliefs about growing old are likely influenced by cultural and societal attitudes about aging and older adults. The availability, accessibility, adequacy, and acceptability of health care and other services intended to meet the needs of older people are similarly influenced by the attitudes of younger people. The prevailing attitudes and opinions of political leaders, decision makers, health and human services personnel, and taxpayers are particularly important in shaping policies, programs, services, and public sentiment.

In many countries and cultures, older people are held in high esteem. Their wisdom, experience, and contributions to the community are highly valued. Older adults are respected in some cases because they have endured and persevered in harsh living conditions and because they have accumulated wisdom and knowledge that younger generations need to survive and carry on the traditions of their culture. Examples outlined in "7 Cultures That Celebrate Aging and Respect Their Elders" (HuffingtonPost.com, February 25, 2014) include China, Greece, India, Korea, and many Native American cultures.

In other cultures, older adults may be viewed as draining valuable or scarce resources. A person's worth may be measured in terms of income (the flow of money earned through employment, interest on investments, and other sources) and the amount of accumulated wealth. When older adults retire from full-time employment, they may lose status because they are no longer working, earning money, and "contributing" to society. When an individual's sense of self-worth and identity is closely bound to employment or occupation, retirement from the workforce can make him or her feel worthless. In "The Liberation of Growing Old" (NYTimes.com, January 3, 2015), Anne Karpf discusses such social attitudes and notes that with many older adults remaining in the workforce or providing child care for working parents, "age can no longer be neatly correlated with economic activity."

Stereotypes Fuel Worries of Older Adults

Although people of all ages worry about the future, for older adults aging may signify a future threat to their health and well-being, diminished social status, a loss of power, and the possibility of a loss of control over their life. Researchers posit that social stereotypes, such as media portrayals of older adults as weak and helpless and of old age as a time of hardship, loss, and pain, have a powerful influence on attitudes and may be another source of worry for older adults. They contend that the image of a tragic old age can create worries about having a tragic old age. Worse still, the negative image of old age can become a self-fulfilling prophecy, thereby confirming negative stereotypes and promoting ageism (discrimination or unfair treatment based on age).

For example, in "Expectations about Memory Change across the Life Span Are Impacted by Aging Stereotypes" (*Psychology and Aging*, vol. 24, no. 1, March 2009), Tara T. Lineweaver, Andrea K. Berger, and Christopher Hertzog interviewed 373 people, in three different age groups, to assess their thoughts about memory throughout the adult life span. They were asked to rate the memory of different older adults, who were described as having positive or negative personality traits. Consistent with previous research, the study subjects believed that memory declines with advancing age. Furthermore, they rated adults described as having positive personality traits with having better memory ability and less age-related memory loss than those described as having negative personality traits. Another important finding was that the older subjects were more strongly influenced by the personality descriptions than the younger subjects.

Gabriel A. Radvansky, Nicholas A. Lynchard, and William von Hippel confirm in "Aging and Stereotype Suppression" (*Aging, Neuropsychology, and Cognition*, vol. 16, no. 1, January 2009) that older adults are more likely than younger adults to believe and use stereotyping information, even when they do not intend to judge people based on stereotypes. Furthermore, older adults have trouble changing or modifying their interpretation of a situation, even when it becomes apparent that their initial interpretation was incorrect. The researchers aver that although older adults may be more susceptible to the influence of stereotypes, this effect can be prevented, or minimized, by providing them with clear information that contradicts stereotyping information.

In "Association between Positive Age Stereotypes and Recovery from Disability in Older Persons" (*Journal of the American Medical Association*, vol. 308, no. 19, November 21, 2012), Becca R. Levy et al. note that older adults who hold positive views of aging such as wisdom, accomplishment, and satisfaction are 44% more likely to fully recover from potentially disabling illnesses than

those who hold negative stereotypes of aging. The researchers also find that older adults who view growing old as becoming helpless, useless, or unappreciated are less likely to seek preventive medical care and more likely to suffer from physical problems and memory loss.

Stereotypes about aging and older adults have become more negative over time. In "Increasing Negativity of Age Stereotypes across 200 Years: Evidence from a Database of 400 Million Words" (*PLOS One*, February 12, 2015), Reuben Ng et al. report that in 1880, age stereotypes reversed from positive to negative. The researchers attribute the medicalization of aging and the growing proportion of the population over the age of 65 as factors responsible for the rise in negative age stereotypes.

Baby Boomers Challenge Stereotypes

Since their inception, baby boomers have left their mark on every U.S. institution. As teenagers and young adults, they created and championed a unique blend of music, pop culture, and political activism. They have witnessed remarkable technological and medical advancements during their lifetime and have come to expect, and even loudly demand, solutions to health and social problems.

As the baby boomers join the ranks of older Americans, they are fomenting a cultural revolution. The boomers approaching age 65 are not content to be regarded as "old." Accustomed to freedom and independence, they want to be recognized and treated as individuals rather than as stereotypes. Overall, the aging boomers are better educated, healthier, and wealthier than any other older adult cohort in history. They are living longer, and many are redefining old age by reinventing retirement, continuing to pursue health, and challenging the public's perception of what it is to be old.

Although baby boomers are living longer than previous generations, they are not necessarily healthier in their 60s. Dana E. King et al. report in "The Status of Baby Boomers' Health in the United States: The Healthiest Generation?" (*Journal of the American Medical Association Internal Medicine*, vol. 173, no. 5, March 11, 2013) that boomers suffer from more chronic diseases than past generations. They are more likely to be obese and to suffer from high blood pressure and high cholesterol (factors that are associated with increased risk of disease). Compared with their predecessors, they are more likely to be disabled, exercise less frequently, and consume more alcohol. According to King et al., one positive aspect is that fewer boomers have smoked cigarettes and, therefore, fewer suffer from smoking-related illnesses such as emphysema. Still, fewer describe themselves as in "excellent" health—just 13.2%, compared with 32% of the previous generation.

Along with the image of baby boomers as being healthy and fit, other stereotypes persist. For example, in "Aging America and the Boomer Wars" (*Gerontologist*, vol. 48, no. 6, December 2008), Harry R. Moody, the director of the Office of Academic Affairs for AARP, describes the polarizing stereotypes of the baby boomers. On one side are people who characterize boomers as selfish, materialistic, whining, and greedy—people who will consume all available resources with no thought to future generations. On the other side are those who view boomers as idealistic advocates of social activism and community service. Moody cautions that these opposing stereotypes should be avoided to prevent "oversimplified polarities and to appreciate the power that public discourse and media images can have in shaping our thinking about generational change in an aging society."

In "Sixty-Five Isn't What It Used to Be: Changes and Trends in the Perceptions of Older Adults" (*International Social Science Review*, vol. 88, no. 3, 2014), Mari Plikuhn, Ashlee Niehaus, and Rebecca D. Reeves find that perceptions of older adults' loneliness and poor health have been increasingly less negative among both adults aged 18 to 64 years and adults age 65 and older. The researchers opine that "a growing understanding of issues faced by older adults has led to a more realistic and positive view of the older years and a decline in negative stereotypes often associated with aging." The researchers credit the dramatic decline in negative perceptions of older adults and many common stereotypes in large part to the increasingly positive portrayal of older adults in the media and changing social attitudes about aging.

CHAPTER 2
THE ECONOMICS OF GROWING OLD IN THE UNITED STATES

Security was attained in the earlier days through the interdependence of members of families upon each other and of the families within a small community upon each other. The complexities of great communities and of organized industry make less real these simple means of security. Therefore, we are compelled to employ the active interest of the Nation as a whole through government in order to encourage a greater security for each individual who composes it . . . . This seeking for a greater measure of welfare and happiness does not indicate a change in values. It is rather a return to values lost in the course of our economic development and expansion.

—Franklin D. Roosevelt, Message of the President to Congress, June 8, 1934

The economic status of older Americans (defined as those aged 65 years and older) is more varied than that of any other age group. Although some older adults are well off, most others have limited resources. As a whole, the older U.S. population has a lower economic status than the overall adult population. During retirement most people rely on Social Security and are supplemented by pensions and assets. Some must also depend on Supplemental Security Income (SSI), a federal assistance program administered by the U.S. Social Security Administration (SSA) that guarantees a minimum level of income for needy older, blind, and/or disabled individuals. It acts as a safety net for individuals who have little or no Social Security or other income and limited resources.

With fixed incomes and sharply limited potential to improve their incomes through employment, many older people become vulnerable to circumstances such as the loss of a spouse, prolonged illness, or even economic variations such as inflation or recession that further compromise their financial well-being, sometimes plunging them into poverty. One common scenario is a couple that has planned well for retirement but then runs through all their assets to pay the health care costs of a long-term illness. When the ill partner dies, the surviving spouse is left impoverished. Another example is retirees who discover, as many people did during the latter half of the first decade of the 21st century, that their retirement accounts had lost more than half of their value.

Some older adults may want to return to work, but their prospects are uncertain. The Great Recession (which lasted from late 2007 to mid-2009) resulted in historically high rates of unemployment across all age groups. Those rates declined after 2009. In 2010 employment growth resumed, and by December 2014 the labor force participation rate for Americans age 55 and older was higher than at the start of the recession. In a February 6, 2015, press release, the U.S. Bureau of Labor Statistics (BLS) reports that although the overall unemployment rate slowly declined to 5.7% in January 2015 from 6.6% in January 2014, unemployment among older workers declined very slightly during the same period (to 4.1% from 4.6%). Sara E. Rix of the AARP Public Policy Institute observes in "The Employment Situation, December 2014: Unemployment Rate for Older Workers Lowest since 2008" (January 2015, http://www.aarp.org/content/dam/aarp/ppi/2015/the-employment-situation-december-2014-AARP-ppi-econ-sec.pdf) that the average length of unemployment for older jobseekers was 54.3 weeks, and more than half of older jobseekers had experienced long-term unemployment of 27 weeks or longer since the Great Recession. About one-third of all workers experienced an extended layoff of that duration in 2014.

THE ECONOMIC WELL-BEING OF OLDER ADULTS

There are two important measures of an individual's or household's economic well-being. One is income, defined as the flow of money earned through employment, interest on investments, and other sources. The other is asset accumulation or wealth, which is the economic resources (property or other material possessions) owned by an individual or household.

TABLE 2.1

Income-to-poverty ratio by age group, 2013

[Sums in thousands]

	Totals		Income-to-poverty ratio in 2013							
			Below 100%		100% to below 200%		200% to below 400%		400% and above	
	Persons		Persons		Persons		Persons		Persons	
	Sum	PCT	Sum	PCT	Sum	PCT	Sum	PCT	Sum	PCT
Totals	312,965	100.0%	45,318	14.5%	60,706	19.4%	93,887	30.0%	113,054	36.1%
Age										
0 to 17	73,625	100.0%	14,659	19.9%	16,705	22.7%	21,556	29.3%	20,705	28.1%
18 to 64	194,833	100.0%	26,429	13.6%	33,482	17.2%	57,629	29.6%	77,293	39.7%
65 to 80+	44,508	100.0%	4,231	9.5%	10,518	23.6%	14,702	33.0%	15,056	33.8%

SOURCE: "Income-to-Poverty Ratio, by Age Group, 2013 (Sums in Thousands)," in *Current Population Survey (CPS): CPS Table Creator*, U.S. Census Bureau, 2014, http://www.census.gov/cps/data/cpstablecreator.html (accessed April 29, 2015)

Income Distribution

According to data from the U.S. Census 2014 Current Population Survey Annual Social and Economic Supplement (2014, http://www.census.gov/cps/data/cpstablecreator.html), in 2013, 9.5% of the older population (4.2 million older adults) lived below 100% of the poverty threshold, up from 8.9% in 2010. (See Table 2.1.) Poverty thresholds are the dollar amounts the U.S. Census Bureau uses to determine poverty status. If an individual or couple's income is less than half the poverty threshold then they are below 50% of poverty; less than the threshold itself, they are in poverty (below 100% of poverty). In 2013 the poverty threshold for a person age 65 or older was $11,173 and for two older adults, it was $14,095.

According to the Administration on Aging (AoA), in *A Profile of Older Americans: 2014* (2015, http://www.aoa.acl.gov/Aging_Statistics/Profile/2014/docs/2014-Profile.pdf), the median reported income for all older adults in 2013 was $29,327 for males and $16,301 for females. Figure 2.1 shows the distribution of income among older adults. Households headed by people aged 65 years and older had a median income of $51,486 in 2013, whereas the individual median income for older adults was $21,225. About half (52%) of households headed by an older adult had incomes of $50,000 or more, and 6% had incomes less than $15,000. The AoA further reports that median household income for older adults in 2013 was highest for non-Hispanic whites ($53,821), followed by Asian Americans ($53,179), African Americans ($41,336), and Hispanics ($35,981).

Sources of Income

Unlike younger adults, who derive most of their income from employment, older adults rely on a variety of sources of income to meet their expenses. Since the 1960s Social Security has provided the largest share of income for older Americans. In 2012 Social Security benefits were a major source of income, providing at least 50% of total income reported for 65% of older adult beneficiaries. (See Figure 2.2.) For 47% of unmarried beneficiaries and 22% of beneficiary couples over the age of 65 years in 2012, Social Security accounted for 90% of total income.

The AoA explains in *Profile of Older Americans: 2014* that the income for most older adults comes from four sources. In 2012 Social Security accounted for 35%, earnings provided 34%, pensions contributed 17%, asset income accounted for 11%, and other sources added 3% of income for older adults. (See Figure 2.3.)

Pension Funds

Historically, many large employers, along with most local and state governments and the federal government, offered pension plans for retirement. In the United States American Express established the first private pension plan (an employer-run retirement program) in 1875. General Motors Corporation provided the first modern plan during the 1940s.

Employers are not required to provide pensions, and pension plans do not have to include all workers; they may exclude certain jobs and/or individuals. Before 1976 pension plans could require an employee to work a lifetime for one company before becoming eligible for pension benefits. As required by the Employee Retirement Income Security Act (ERISA) of 1974, starting in 1976 an employee became eligible after 10 years of service. By 2000 most plans required five years of work before an employee became vested (eligible for benefits). In companies that offer pension plans, employees are eligible to begin receiving benefits when they retire or leave the company if they have worked for the requisite number of years and/or have reached the specified eligibility age.

DEFINED BENEFIT PLANS AND DEFINED CONTRIBUTION PLANS. There are two principal types of pension

FIGURE 2.1

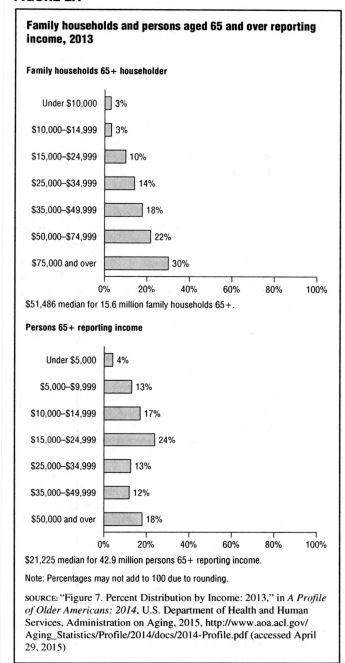

Family households and persons aged 65 and over reporting income, 2013

Family households 65+ householder

Under $10,000 — 3%
$10,000–$14,999 — 3%
$15,000–$24,999 — 10%
$25,000–$34,999 — 14%
$35,000–$49,999 — 18%
$50,000–$74,999 — 22%
$75,000 and over — 30%

$51,486 median for 15.6 million family households 65+.

Persons 65+ reporting income

Under $5,000 — 4%
$5,000–$9,999 — 13%
$10,000–$14,999 — 17%
$15,000–$24,999 — 24%
$25,000–$34,999 — 13%
$35,000–$49,999 — 12%
$50,000 and over — 18%

$21,225 median for 42.9 million persons 65+ reporting income.

Note: Percentages may not add to 100 due to rounding.

SOURCE: "Figure 7. Percent Distribution by Income: 2013," in *A Profile of Older Americans: 2014*, U.S. Department of Health and Human Services, Administration on Aging, 2015, http://www.aoa.acl.gov/Aging_Statistics/Profile/2014/docs/2014-Profile.pdf (accessed April 29, 2015)

FIGURE 2.2

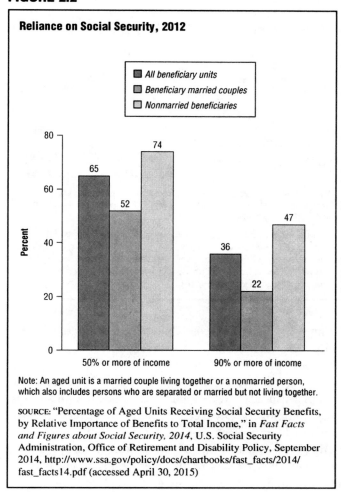

Reliance on Social Security, 2012

Legend:
- All beneficiary units
- Beneficiary married couples
- Nonmarried beneficiaries

50% or more of income: 65, 52, 74
90% or more of income: 36, 22, 47

Note: An aged unit is a married couple living together or a nonmarried person, which also includes persons who are separated or married but not living together.

SOURCE: "Percentage of Aged Units Receiving Social Security Benefits, by Relative Importance of Benefits to Total Income," in *Fast Facts and Figures about Social Security, 2014*, U.S. Social Security Administration, Office of Retirement and Disability Policy, September 2014, http://www.ssa.gov/policy/docs/chartbooks/fast_facts/2014/fast_facts14.pdf (accessed April 30, 2015)

plans: defined benefit plans and defined contribution plans. As described earlier, defined benefit plans promise employees a specified monthly benefit at retirement. A defined benefit plan may stipulate the promised benefit as an exact dollar amount, such as $100 per month at retirement. More often, however, benefits are calculated using a plan formula that considers both salary and service—for example, 1% of the average salary for the last five years of employment multiplied by years of service with the employer.

A defined contribution plan does not promise employees a specific amount of benefits at retirement. Instead, the employee and/or employer contribute to a plan account, sometimes at a set rate, such as 5% of earnings annually. Generally, these contributions are invested on the employee's behalf, and the amount of future benefits varies depending on investment earnings.

An example of a defined contribution plan is the 401(k) plan. This plan allows employees to defer receiving a portion of their salary, which is contributed on their behalf to the plan. Income taxes are deferred until the money is withdrawn at retirement. In some instances employers match employee contributions. Created in 1978, these plans were named for section 401(k) of the Internal Revenue Code.

According to Don McNay, in "Why the Decrease in Unions and Defined Benefit Retirement Plans Hurts Us All" (HuffingtonPost.com, October 29, 2014), in 2011 just 14% of U.S. private-sector workers had a pension plan that provides a defined benefit, down from 38% in 1979. Although participation in defined benefit plans has declined, participation in defined contribution plans that grow in response to employer and worker contributions has increased. The BLS notes in the press release

FIGURE 2.3

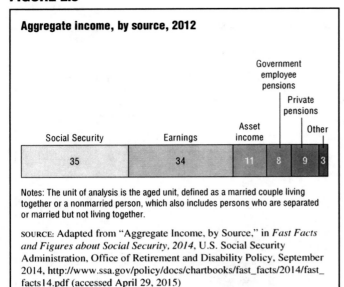

Aggregate income, by source, 2012

Government
employee
pensions

Private
pensions

Social Security	Earnings	Asset income		Other	
35	34	11	8	9	3

Notes: The unit of analysis is the aged unit, defined as a married couple living together or a nonmarried person, which also includes persons who are separated or married but not living together.

SOURCE: Adapted from "Aggregate Income, by Source," in *Fast Facts and Figures about Social Security, 2014*, U.S. Social Security Administration, Office of Retirement and Disability Policy, September 2014, http://www.ssa.gov/policy/docs/chartbooks/fast_facts/2014/fast_facts14.pdf (accessed April 29, 2015)

"Employee Benefits in the United States—March 2014" (July 25, 2014, http://www.bls.gov/news.release/pdf/ebs2.pdf) that 48% of full-time workers in the private sector participated in defined benefit or defined contribution plans in 2014. (See Table 2.2.) Since the mid-1990s many employers have converted their defined benefit plans to hybrid plans that incorporate elements of both defined benefit and defined contribution plans. For example, cash balance plans are based on defined contributions of pay credits (based on an employee's compensation rate) and interest credits that are deposited annually by the employer into an account, the balance of which serves as the defined benefit.

PRIVATE AND PUBLIC PENSIONS. The SSA reports in *Fast Facts and Figures about Social Security, 2014* (September 2014, http://www.ssa.gov/policy/docs/chartbooks/fast_facts/2014/fast_facts14.pdf) that the proportion of older adults' income from pensions has grown rapidly since the 1960s, with private pensions tripling by 2012. (See Figure 2.4.) During the same period the proportion of people receiving government employee pensions increased to 14% in 2012 from 9% in 1962. The proportion of older adults with income from assets, the second-most-common source of income after Social Security, in 2012 (51%) was comparable to but slightly lower than in 1962 (54%). The proportion of older adults with earned income declined more notably to 28% in 2012 from 36% in 1962.

Unlike Social Security and many public plans, most private pension plans do not provide automatic cost-of-living adjustments. Without these adjustments many retirees' incomes and purchasing power erode. Military, government, and Railroad Retirement pensioners are more likely to receive cost-of-living increases than are pensioners in the private sector.

FEDERAL PENSION LAWS. Pension plan funds are often invested in stocks and bonds, much as banks invest their depositors' money. When the investment choice is a good one, the company makes a profit on the money in the fund; bad investments result in losses. During the early 1970s several major plans were terminated before they accumulated sufficient assets to pay employees and their beneficiaries retirement benefits. These asset-poor plans were unable to make good on their promises, leaving retirees without benefits despite their years of service.

To protect retirement plan participants and their beneficiaries from these catastrophic losses, ERISA was passed in 1974. ERISA established a new set of rules for participation, added mandatory and quicker vesting schedules, fixed minimum funding standards, and set standards of conduct for administering plans and handling plan assets. It also required the disclosure of plan information, established a system for insuring the payment of pension benefits, and created the Pension Benefit Guaranty Corporation, a federal corporation, to provide uninterrupted benefit payments when pension plans are terminated.

The Retirement Equity Act of 1984 requires pension plans to pay a survivor's benefit to the spouse of a deceased vested plan participant. Before 1984 some spouses received no benefits unless the employee was near retirement age at the time of death. Under the 1984 law, pension vesting begins at age 21, or after five years of being on the job, and employees who have a break in employment for reasons such as maternity leave do not lose any time already accumulated.

PENSION FUNDS DECLINE. Because both private and public pension funds are invested in the stock market, many suffered serious losses in response to the Great Recession and its aftereffects, which were still felt in 2015. According to John W. Ehrhardt, Zorast Wadia, and Alan Perry, in the *Milliman 2015 Pension Funding Study* (April 2015, http://us.milliman.com/uploadedFiles/insight/2015/2015-corporate-pension-funding-study.pdf), the 100 largest corporate (defined benefit) pension plans suffered a $131.3 billion loss of funded status in 2014, as even robust stock market returns were unable to compensate for past market downturns, unrealistic financial projections, a spike in the number of retirees, and benefit increases made during better times.

The losses in funding sustained during and after the recession, along with the funding requirements by the Pension Protection Act of 2006, which provides significant tax incentives to enhance and protect retirement savings for millions of Americans, combined to create a growing pension fund deficit. Ehrhardt, Wadia, and Perry note that annual contributions declined to $39.8 billion from $44.2 billion in 2013 and that the deficit increased to $82 billion between 2009 and the end of 2014.

TABLE 2.2

Percentage of private and public sector workers with retirement plan benefits, 2014

[All workers = 100 percent]

Characteristics	Civilian[a]			Private industry			State and local government		
	Access	Participation	Take-up rate	Access	Participation	Take-up rate	Access	Participation	Take-up rate
All workers	**68**	**53**	**78**	**65**	**48**	**75**	**89**	**81**	**91**
Worker characteristics									
Management, professional, and related	83	71	86	80	67	84	92	83	90
Management, business, and financial	85	75	88	84	74	87	—	—	—
Professional and related	82	70	85	77	63	82	92	83	90
Teachers	86	76	89	—	—	—	91	82	90
Primary, secondary, and special education school teachers	95	86	90	—	—	—	99	90	91
Registered nurses	79	65	83	—	—	—	—	—	—
Service	44	29	65	38	21	56	84	76	91
Protective service	79	61	77	62	28	45	91	85	93
Sales and office	71	52	74	69	49	71	89	82	92
Sales and related	67	39	59	67	39	59	—	—	—
Office and administrative support	73	59	81	70	56	79	90	83	92
Natural resources, construction, and maintenance	70	56	81	67	53	79	95	86	90
Construction, extraction, farming, fishing, and forestry	64	51	80	60	47	78	—	—	—
Installation, maintenance, and repair	75	60	81	73	58	80	—	—	—
Production, transportation, and material moving	71	54	76	70	53	75	85	74	87
Production	75	59	79	75	59	78	—	—	—
Transportation and material moving	67	49	73	65	47	72	—	—	—
Full time	78	64	81	74	58	79	99	90	91
Part time	37	21	56	37	19	52	38	33	86
Union	94	86	91	92	83	91	97	89	92
Nonunion	64	48	74	62	45	72	83	74	89
Average wage within the following categories[b]:									
Lowest 25 percent	41	22	53	38	18	48	73	66	90
Lowest 10 percent	29	12	41	27	11	39	59	52	89
Second 25 percent	70	52	75	67	47	71	93	84	91
Third 25 percent	81	67	83	76	62	81	95	86	91
Highest 25 percent	88	79	89	85	75	88	98	89	91
Highest 10 percent	90	81	90	88	79	89	98	90	92
Establishment characteristics									
Goods-producing industries	76	62	82	76	62	82	—	—	—
Service-providing industries	67	52	77	63	46	73	89	81	91
Education and health services	77	63	82	69	53	77	90	81	90
Educational services	87	77	89	72	61	85	91	81	90
Elementary and secondary schools	91	81	89	—	—	—	92	83	90
Junior colleges, colleges, and universities	87	76	88	89	78	88	86	76	88
Health care and social assistance	70	54	77	69	52	76	89	79	89
Hospitals	90	78	86	—	—	—	95	83	87
Public administration	91	84	92	—	—	—	91	84	92
1 to 99 workers	51	36	71	50	35	70	77	69	89
1 to 49 workers	46	33	72	45	32	71	68	60	87
50 to 99 workers	65	45	70	63	43	68	90	81	90
100 workers or more	85	69	81	82	64	78	91	83	91
100 to 499 workers	79	58	74	78	55	71	88	80	92
500 workers or more	90	79	88	89	77	86	92	84	91
Geographic areas									
Northeast	68	55	82	64	51	80	90	81	91
New England	66	53	80	63	49	77	86	80	93
Middle Atlantic	68	56	82	64	52	81	91	82	90
South	69	51	75	65	46	71	91	80	89
South Atlantic	69	52	75	65	47	72	91	80	88
East South Central	70	52	74	64	45	70	92	80	87
West South Central	68	50	74	64	44	69	89	81	91
Midwest	72	57	78	70	53	76	87	80	92
East North Central	71	56	78	69	52	75	84	78	92
West North Central	74	59	79	71	54	76	91	83	91
West	64	51	79	60	45	75	90	83	93
Mountain	63	46	74	59	42	71	88	76	86
Pacific	65	53	81	60	46	77	91	86	95

TABLE 2.2

Percentage of private and public sector workers with retirement plan benefits, 2014 [CONTINUED]

[All workers = 100 percent]

aIncludes workers in the private nonfarm economy except those in private households, and workers in the public sector, except the federal government.
bSurveyed occupations are classified into wage categories based on the average wage for the occupation, which may include workers with earnings both above and below the threshold. The categories were formed using percentile estimates generated using Employer Costs for Employee Compensation (ECEC) data for March 2014.
Note: Dash indicates no workers in this category or data did not meet publication criteria.

SOURCE: "Table 1. Retirement Benefits: Access, Participation, and Take-Up Rates, National Compensation Survey, March 2014," in *Employee Benefits in the United States—March 2014*, U.S. Bureau of Labor Statistics, July 2014, http://www.bls.gov/news.release/pdf/ebs2.pdf (accessed April 29, 2015)

FIGURE 2.4

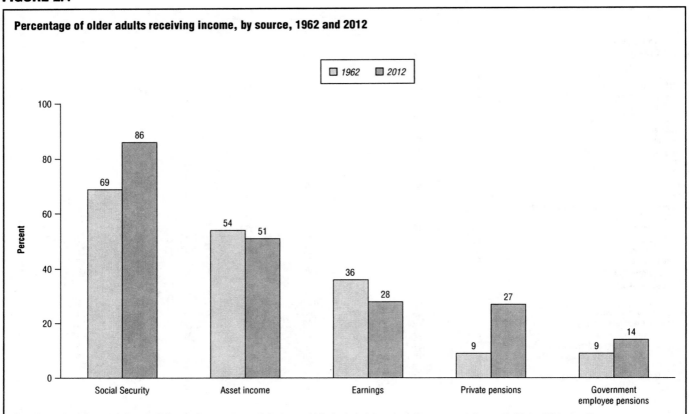

Percentage of older adults receiving income, by source, 1962 and 2012

Note: An aged unit is a married couple living together or a nonmarried person, which also includes persons who are separated or married but not living together.

SOURCE: "Percentage of Aged Units Receiving Income, by Source," in *Fast Facts and Figures about Social Security, 2014*, U.S. Social Security Administration, Office of Retirement and Disability Policy, September 2014, http://www.ssa.gov/policy/docs/chartbooks/fast_facts/2014/fast_facts14.pdf (accessed April 30, 2015)

Further, at the close of 2014, in an effort to assist some of the country's most distressed pension plans, Congress passed a measure permitting benefits of current retirees to be reduced. The legislation reversed four decades of federal law that protected benefits already earned from cuts. In "Pension Plans, Once Inviolable Promises to Employees, Are Getting Cut" (WashingtonPost.com, February 9, 2015), Michael A. Fletcher observes that even though no plans had yet cut benefits to retirees already receiving benefits, several planned to reduce benefits for current employees and new hires. Fletcher reports that advocates for retirement security view this legislation as "an assault on retirees' pensions."

There have also been several instances of alleged pension fraud. For example, Jacob Gershman reports in "Former Detroit Treasurer and Two Others Convicted of Pension Fraud" (WSJ.com, December 8, 2014) that in 2014 the former treasurer of Detroit, Michigan, and two of the city's pension officials were convicted of defrauding retirees of nearly $100 million by accepting bribes and kickbacks in exchange for their votes on investment decisions.

In 2014 federal regulators accused the state of Kansas of misleading investors about the health of its public employee pension fund. In "U.S. Settles with Kansas over Alleged Pension Fraud" (CJOnline.com, August 11,

2014), Roxana Hegeman describes the settlement of this case by the U.S. Securities and Exchange Commission (SEC). The SEC asserted, "Kansas failed to adequately disclose its multi-billion-dollar pension liability in bond offering documents, leaving investors with an incomplete picture of the state's finances and its ability to repay the bonds amid competing strains on the state budget."

Another instance of pension fraud involved the California Public Employees' Retirement System (CalPERS), the country's largest public pension fund. In "Police: Man in Pension Fraud Appears to Have Killed Himself" (NYTimes.com, January 14, 2015), the Associated Press reports that Alfred Villalobos, defendant at the center of the CalPERS bribery scandal who was slated to go to trial in February 2015, appeared to have committed suicide. Villalobos was accused of bribing a former chief executive of CalPERS to make investments that benefited Villalobos's clients.

Personal Savings

One of the most effective ways to prepare for retirement is to save for it. In the issue brief *The 2015 Retirement Confidence Survey: Having a Retirement Savings Plan a Key Factor in Americans' Retirement Confidence* (April 2015, http://www.ebri.org/pdf/briefspdf/EBRI_IB_413_Apr15_RCS-2015.pdf), Ruth Helman et al. report on the results of the 2015 Retirement Confidence Survey (RCS). They report that 22% of Americans are very confident and 36% are somewhat confident that they will have enough money to live comfortably in retirement. These percentages are up from the record lows reported in 2009, when just 13% of Americans felt very confident that they would be comfortable in retirement. The most confident workers are those that participate in retirement plans.

The 2015 RCS finds that U.S. workers have saved very little for retirement. Helman et al. indicate that in 2015, 57% of workers reported having total savings and investments, excluding the value of their homes, of less than $25,000, and 28% said they have saved less than $1,000 for retirement. Because this level of savings will render them woefully unprepared for retirement, 13% of workers plan to postpone retirement, 10% say they never plan to retire, and 67% of workers are planning to supplement their income by working for pay in retirement.

One popular way to save for retirement is to contribute to individual retirement plans. Individuals fund these retirement plans themselves. The money that they contribute can be tax deductible, the plans' earnings are not taxed, and contributors determine how the money is invested. Since 1974 one of the major types of individual retirement plans has been the individual retirement account (or individual retirement arrangement; IRA).

IRAs fall into several different categories, but the two most common types are traditional IRAs (deductible and nondeductible) and Roth IRAs. A variety of factors determine which kind of IRA best serves an individual's needs. Profit-sharing plans for the self-employed (formerly called Keogh plans) are another type of individual retirement plan.

The 2015 RCS finds that workers believe their retirement income will come from a variety of sources. According to Helman et al., 46% of American workers anticipate that their retirement income will primarily come from an employer-sponsored retirement savings plan, 31% said Social Security will be a major source of retirement income, 27% will receive a traditional pension, 28% will rely heavily on their IRAs, 23% will rely on personal savings and investments, and 16% said employment will be their major source of retirement income.

NET WORTH

Because the economic well-being of households depends on income and wealth, assessment of income alone is not the best measure of older adults' financial health. To draw a more complete economic profile of the older population, it is necessary to evaluate older households in terms of measures of wealth, such as home equity, savings, and other assets and liabilities. For example, a household may be in the top one-fifth of income distribution but be saddled with a large amount of debt.

Net worth is a measure of economic valuation and an indicator of financial security that is obtained by subtracting total liabilities from total assets. Greater net worth enables individuals and households to weather financial challenges such as illness, disability, job loss, divorce, widowhood, or general economic downturns.

Data from the U.S. Census Bureau *Survey of Income and Program Participation* reveal that the median net worth of households headed by adults aged 65 years and older increased to $170,516 in 2011 from $146,205 in 2000, with the largest increase among adults between the ages of 65 and 69. (See Table 2.3.) The Federal Reserve Board conducts a Survey of Consumer Finances every three years. The 2013 survey (vol. 100, no. 4, September 2014, http://www.federalreserve.gov/pubs/bulletin/2014/pdf/scf14.pdf) reports that from 2010 to 2013 nearly all age groups experienced declines in median income. The median net worth of American families also declined from 2010 to 2013 except in families headed by people aged 44 years or younger and those headed by older adults aged 65 to 74 years. (See Table 2.4.)

Christopher S. Rugaber observes in "Household Net Worth Reaches Record $83 Trillion" (Associated Press, March 12, 2015) that even though higher stock prices and

TABLE 2.3

Net worth by age of householder, 2000 and 2011

Characteristic	Total 2000	Total 2011	First quintile 2000	First quintile 2011	Second quintile 2000	Second quintile 2011	Third quintile 2000	Third quintile 2011	Fourth quintile 2000	Fourth quintile 2011	Fifth quintile 2000	Fifth quintile 2011
Total	73,874	68,828	−905	−6,029	14,319	7,263	73,911	68,839	187,552	205,985	569,375	630,754
Less than 35 years	9,765	6,676	−11,971	−22,646	469	0	9,792	6,682	38,381	33,477	150,095	153,616
35 to 44 years	59,689	35,000	−2,683	−14,700	11,822	4,058	59,774	35,000	150,022	128,430	435,731	448,824
45 to 54 years	111,867	84,542	0	−5,991	36,439	12,175	11,867	84,542	239,931	228,708	654,893	654,229
55 to 64 years	150,866	143,964	378	0	54,257	39,057	150,866	144,200	339,142	333,750	932,347	889,867
65 years and over	146,205	170,516	1,341	400	67,067	68,783	146,428	171,135	287,447	344,870	741,210	899,608
65 to 69 years	154,226	194,226	1,341	100	71,761	62,284	154,464	194,500	325,199	410,191	855,769	1,028,949
70 to 74 years	161,027	181,078	1,341	15	72,164	70,151	161,845	181,609	315,615	370,060	776,553	1,054,468
75 and over	134,535	155,714	1,341	972	61,031	70,584	134,804	155,714	254,485	302,916	654,909	770,397

Note: Quintile is the portion of a frequency distribution containing one-fifth of the total sample. Each quintile represents 20 percent, or one-fifth, of all households. Median net worth statistics within quintiles of the net worth distribution are at the 10th, 30th, 50th, 70th, and 90th percentiles.

SOURCE: Marina Vornovitsky, Alfred Gottschalck, and Adam Smith, "Table A1. Median Household Net Worth, by Net Worth Quintiles and Age of the Householder: 2000 and 2011," in *Distribution of Household Wealth in the U.S.: 2000 to 2011*, U.S. Census Bureau, 2015, http://www.census.gov/people/ wealth/files/Wealth%20distribution%202000%20to%202011.pdf (accessed May 4, 2015)

improved home values increased Americans' net worth during the last quarter of 2014, most Americans did not benefit because wealth "remains concentrated among richer families."

Older Adults Are Hard Hit by Low Interest Rates

According to the article "6 Ways Low Interest Rates Hurt Retirees" (FiscalTimes.com, June 10, 2013), maintaining low interest rates stimulates some sectors of the economy but actually harms retirees and others on fixed incomes. Low interest rates mean older adults are not earning the steady returns on savings they did just a decade ago. In 2006 the rate was 5.25%; in April 2015 it was 1.5%.

Low interest rates also limit the use of annuities (investments designed to grow and ultimately pay its owner a specific amount for a fixed period or the owner's life) to generate income since the monthly income from a fixed annuity is based on the interest rate at the time of purchase. Similarly, they limit the growth of assets in pension funds, many of which are drastically underfunded. Low interest rates also have been blamed for rising premiums for long-term care insurance (insurance that covers nursing home care, assisted living, and adult day care).

POVERTY

Poverty rates are measures of the economic viability of populations. Poverty standards were originally based on the "economy food plan," which was developed by the U.S. Department of Agriculture (USDA) during the 1960s. The plan calculated the cost of a minimally adequate household food budget for different types of households by age of householder. Because USDA surveys showed that the average family spent one-third of its income on food, it was determined that a household with an income three times the amount needed for food was living fairly comfortably. In 1963 the poverty level was calculated by simply multiplying the cost of a minimally adequate food budget by three. Later, the U.S. Census Bureau began comparing family income before taxes with a set of poverty thresholds that vary based on family size and composition and are adjusted annually for inflation using the consumer price index (CPI; a measure of the average change in consumer prices over time in a fixed market basket of goods and services).

According to figures shown in Table 2.5, the poverty rate of adults aged 65 years and older (9.5%) in 2013 represented 4.2 million older adults living in poverty. The rates recorded in 2013 for 18- to 64-year-olds (13.6%) and children under the age of 18 years (19.9%) both exceeded that of older adults. Census Bureau data reveal that in 1959 the poverty rate for people aged 65 years and older was 35%, well above the rates for the other age groups. (See Figure 2.5.) The lowest level of poverty in the older population occurred in 2011, when the rate fell to 8.7%.

Poverty Thresholds Are Lower for Older Adults

The Census Bureau measures need for assistance using poverty thresholds (specific dollar amounts that determine poverty status). Each individual or family is assigned one of 48 possible poverty thresholds. Thresholds vary according to family size and the ages of the members. The thresholds do not vary geographically, and they are updated annually for inflation using the CPI.

One assumption used to determine poverty thresholds is that healthy older adults have lower nutritional requirements than younger people, so they require less money for food. This assumption has resulted in different

TABLE 2.4

Family net worth by age and other characteristics, 2010 and 2013

[Thousands of 2013 dollars except as noted]

Family characteristic	Median net worth 2010	Median net worth 2013	Percent change 2010–13	Mean net worth 2010	Mean net worth 2013	Percent change 2010–13
All families	82.8	81.2	−2	534.5	534.6	0
	(2.6)	(2.8)		(10.0)	(9.3)	
Percentile of usual income						
Less than 20	7.3	6.4	−12	81.8	64.6	−21
20–39.9	31.0	27.9	−10	134.7	113.1	−16
40–59.9	66.6	55.4	−17	189.5	164.8	−13
60–79.9	138.6	161.3	16	306.8	350.9	14
80–89.9	321.7	287.9	−11	645.0	631.4	−2
90–100	1,275.7	1,125.9	−12	3,274.6	3,327.3	2
Age of head (years)						
Less than 35	10.0	10.4	4	70.0	75.5	8
35–44	45.2	46.7	3	233.0	347.2	49
45–54	126.3	105.3	−17	614.1	530.1	−14
55–64	192.3	165.9	−14	943.6	798.4	−15
65–74	221.5	232.1	5	909.2	1,057.0	16
75 or more	232.3	194.8	−16	726.5	645.2	−11
Education of head						
No high school diploma	17.2	17.2	0	118.6	108.3	−9
High school diploma	60.7	52.5	−14	233.8	199.6	−15
Some college	54.5	46.9	−14	291.7	317.9	9
College degree	209.2	219.4	5	1,047.8	1,031.6	−2
Race or ethnicity of respondent						
White non-Hispanic	139.9	142.0	2	701.4	705.9	1
Nonwhite or Hispanic	21.9	18.1	−17	188.5	183.9	−2
Housing status						
Owner	187.0	195.4	4	764.6	783.0	2
Renter or other	5.4	5.4	0	61.3	70.3	15
Percentile of net worth						
Less than 25	*	*	NA	−13.7	−13.4	2
25–49.9	34.5	31.3	−9	38.2	35.9	−6
50–74.9	168.5	168.1	0	181.0	177.7	−2
75–89.9	517.3	505.8	−2	565.7	546.2	−3
90–100	1,997.8	1,871.8	−6	3,982.8	4,024.8	1

*Less than 0.05 ($50).
NA = Not applicable.
Note: Net worth is the difference between families' gross assets and their liabilities.

SOURCE: Jesse Bricker et al., "Table 2. Family Median and Mean Net Worth, by Selected Characteristics of Families, 2010 and 2013 Surveys," in *Changes in U.S. Family Finances from 2010 to 2013: Evidence from the Survey of Consumer Finances*, vol. 100, no. 4, September 2014, http://www.federalreserve.gov/pubs/bulletin/2014/pdf/scf14.pdf (accessed May 4, 2015)

poverty thresholds for both the young and old. For example, in 2014 the poverty threshold for a single person under the age of 65 years was $12,316, as opposed to $11,354 for a person aged 65 years or older. (See Table 2.6.) The 2014 poverty threshold for two people including a householder under the age of 65 years was $15,853, compared with $14,309 for two people including a householder aged 65 years or older.

This method of defining poverty fails to take into account the special financial and health challenges that older adults may face. For example, no household costs other than food are counted, although older adults spend a much greater percentage of their income on health care than younger people do. Also, the dollars allocated for food consider only the nutritional needs of healthy older adults; many are in poor health and may require more costly special diets or nutritional supplements.

WELL-OFF OLDER ADULTS

More older Americans live comfortably in the 21st century than at any other time in history. Many of those in their mid-70s and 80s were born during the Great Depression (1929–1939). The enforced Depression-era frugality taught their families to economize and save. During the 1950s and 1960s, their peak earning years, they enjoyed a period of unprecedented economic expansion. Since then, many have raised their children, paid off their home mortgages, invested wisely, and become eligible to receive Social Security payments.

TABLE 2.5

People in poverty, by selected characteristics, 2012 and 2013

[Numbers in thousands, percentage points as appropriate. People as of March of the following year.]

Characteristic	2012			2013			Change in poverty (2013 less 2012)[b]	
		Below poverty			Below poverty			
	Total	Number	Percent	Total	Number	Percent	Number	Percent
People								
Total	310,648	46,496	15.0	312,965	45,318	14.5	−1,178	−0.5
Family status								
In families	252,863	33,198	13.1	254,988	31,530	12.4	−1,669	−0.8
Householder	80,944	9,520	11.8	81,217	9,130	11.2	−390	−0.5
Related children under age 18	72,545	15,437	21.3	72,573	14,142	19.5	−1,295	−1.8
Related children under age 6	23,604	5,769	24.4	23,585	5,231	22.2	−538	−2.3
In unrelated subfamilies	1,599	740	46.3	1,413	608	43.0	−132	−3.3
Reference person	641	278	43.3	595	246	41.3	−32	−2.0
Children under age 18	855	440	51.4	714	340	47.7	−99	−3.7
Unrelated individuals	56,185	12,558	22.4	56,564	13,181	23.3	623	1.0
Race[c] and Hispanic origin								
White	242,147	30,816	12.7	243,085	29,936	12.3	−880	−0.4
White, not Hispanic	195,112	18,940	9.7	195,167	18,796	9.6	−144	−0.1
Black	40,125	10,911	27.2	40,615	11,041	27.2	130	g
Asian	16,417	1,921	11.7	17,063	1,785	10.5	−136	−1.2
Hispanic (any race)	53,105	13,616	25.6	54,145	12,744	23.5	−871	−2.1
Sex								
Male	152,058	20,656	13.6	153,361	20,119	13.1	−537	−0.5
Female	158,590	25,840	16.3	159,605	25,199	15.8	−641	−0.5
Age								
Under age 18	73,719	16,073	21.8	73,625	14,659	19.9	−1,415	−1.9
Aged 18 to 64	193,642	26,497	13.7	194,833	26,429	13.6	−68	−0.1
Aged 65 and older	43,287	3,926	9.1	44,508	4,231	9.5	305	0.4
Nativity								
Native born	270,570	38,803	14.3	271,968	37,921	13.9	−882	−0.4
Foreign born	40,078	7,693	19.2	40,997	7,397	18.0	−296	−1.2
Naturalized citizen	18,193	2,252	12.4	19,147	2,425	12.7	173	0.3
Not a citizen	21,885	5,441	24.9	21,850	4,972	22.8	−469	−2.1
Region								
Northeast	55,050	7,490	13.6	55,478	7,046	12.7	−444	−0.9
Midwest	66,337	8,851	13.3	66,785	8,590	12.9	−261	−0.5
South	115,957	19,106	16.5	116,961	18,870	16.1	−236	−0.3
West	73,303	11,049	15.1	73,742	10,812	14.7	−237	−0.4
Residence								
Inside metropolitan statistical areas	262,949	38,033	14.5	265,915	37,746	14.2	−287	−0.3
Inside principal cities	101,225	19,934	19.7	102,149	19,530	19.1	−404	−0.6
Outside principal cities	161,724	18,099	11.2	163,767	18,217	11.1	118	−0.1
Outside metropolitan statistical areas[d]	47,698	8,463	17.7	47,050	7,572	16.1	−891	−1.6
Work experience								
Total, aged 18 to 64	193,642	26,497	13.7	194,833	26,429	13.6	−68	−0.1
All workers	145,814	10,672	7.3	146,252	10,736	7.3	64	g
Worked full-time, year-round	98,715	2,867	2.9	100,855	2,771	2.7	−96	−0.2
Less than full-time, year-round	47,099	7,805	16.6	45,397	7,965	17.5	160	1.0
Did not work at least 1 week	47,828	15,825	33.1	48,581	15,693	32.3	−132	−0.8
Disability status[e]								
Total, aged 18 to 64	193,642	26,497	13.7	194,833	26,429	13.6	−68	−0.1
With a disability	14,996	4,257	28.4	15,098	4,352	28.8	95	0.4
With no disability	177,727	22,189	12.5	178,761	22,023	12.3	−166	−0.2

Although these factors have contributed to a more favorable economic status for this cohort (a group of individuals that shares a common characteristic such as birth years and is studied over time) of older adults than they would have otherwise enjoyed, most older people are not wealthy. The AoA reports that in 2012, households headed by adults age 65 and older had a median income of $48,957.

It should also be noted that even well-off older adults were affected by the recession. Gaobo Pang, Peng Xia, and Jin Xu of Tower Watson explain in "Household Balance Sheets of Older Americans Mirror Economic Booms and Busts" (March 13, 2015, http://www.towers watson.com/en-US/Insights/Newsletters/Americas/insider/2015/03/household-balance-sheets-of-older-americans-mirror-economic-booms-and-busts) that between 2001 and

TABLE 2.5

People in poverty, by selected characteristics, 2012 and 2013 [CONTINUED]

[Numbers in thousands, percentage points as appropriate. People as of March of the following year.]

aData are based on the Current Population Survey: Annual Social and Economic Supplement (CPS ASEC) sample of 68,000 addresses. The 2014 CPS ASEC included redesigned questions for income and health insurance coverage. All of the approximately 98,000 addresses were eligible to receive the redesigned set of health insurance coverage questions. The redesigned income questions were implemented to a subsample of these 98,000 addresses using a probability split panel design. Approximately 68,000 addresses were eligible to receive a set of income questions similar to those used in the 2013 CPS ASEC and the remaining 30,000 addresses were eligible to receive the redesigned income questions. The source of the 2013 data for this table is the portion of the CPS ASEC sample which received the income questions consistent with the 2013 CPS ASEC, approximately 68,000 addresses.
bDetails may not sum to totals because of rounding.
cFederal surveys now give respondents the option of reporting more than one race. Therefore, two basic ways of defining a race group are possible. A group such as Asian may be defined as those who reported Asian and no other race (the race-alone or single-race concept) or as those who reported Asian regardless of whether they also reported another race (the race-alone-or-in-combination concept). This table shows data using the first approach (race alone). The use of the single-race population does not imply that it is the preferred method of presenting or analyzing data. The Census Bureau uses a variety of approaches. Information on people who reported more than one race, such as white *and* American Indian and Alaska Native or Asian *and* black or African American, is available from Census 2010 through American FactFinder. About 2.9 percent of people reported more than one race in Census 2010. Data for American Indians and Alaska Natives, Native Hawaiians and other Pacific Islanders, and those reporting two or more races are not shown separately.
dThe "outside metropolitan statistical areas" category includes both micropolitan statistical areas and territory outside of metropolitan and micropolitan statistical areas.
eThe sum of those with and without a disability does not equal the total because disability status is not defined for individuals in the armed forces.
fRepresents or rounds to zero.

SOURCE: Carmen DeNavas-Walt and Bernadette D. Proctor, "Table 3. People in Poverty by Selected Characteristics: 2012 and 2013," in *Income and Poverty in the United States: 2013*, U.S. Census Bureau, September 2014, http://www.census.gov/content/dam/Census/library/publications/2014/demo/p60-249.pdf (accessed May 4, 2015)

FIGURE 2.5

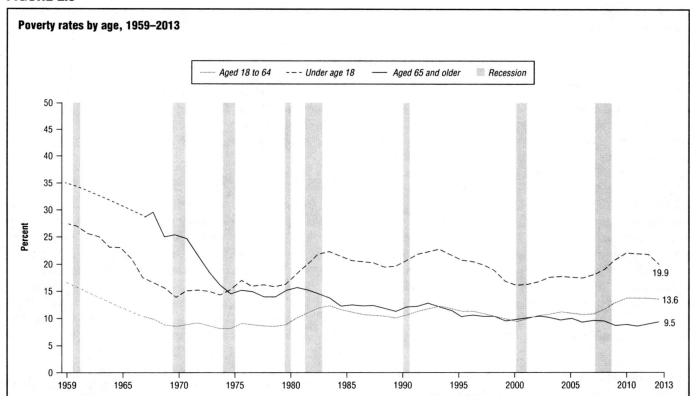

Poverty rates by age, 1959–2013

Note: The data points are placed at the midpoints of the respective years. Data for people aged 18 to 64 and 65 and older are not available from 1960 to 1965.

SOURCE: Carmen DeNavas-Walt and Bernadette D. Proctor, "Figure 5. Poverty Rates by Age: 1959 to 2013," in *Income and Poverty in the United States: 2013*, U.S. Census Bureau, September 2014, http://www.census.gov/content/dam/Census/library/publications/2014/demo/p60-249.pdf (accessed May 4, 2015)

2013 non-retirement assets declined. Reflecting the economic trends in the larger, national economy, older adults' total net worth averaged 7.3 times their earnings in 2001 and 8.6 times earnings in 2004 but decreased to 6.8 times earnings in 2013.

Older adults' responses to economic uncertainty vary. In *Assessing the Impact of Severe Economic Recession on the Elderly: Summary of a Workshop* (2011), Malay Majmundar observes that older adults who reduced their consumption and spending in response to

TABLE 2.6

Poverty thresholds, by size of family and number of related children under 18, 2014

Size of family unit	Related children under 18 years								
	None	One	Two	Three	Four	Five	Six	Seven	Eight or more
One person (unrelated individual)									
Under 65 years	12,316								
65 years and over	11,354								
Two people									
Householder under 65 years	15,853	16,317							
Householder 65 years and over	14,309	16,256							
Three people	18,518	19,055	19,073						
Four people	24,418	24,817	24,008	24,091					
Five people	29,447	29,875	28,960	28,252	27,820				
Six people	33,869	34,004	33,303	32,631	31,633	31,041			
Seven people	38,971	39,214	38,375	37,791	36,701	35,431	34,036		
Eight people	43,586	43,970	43,179	42,485	41,501	40,252	38,953	38,622	
Nine people or more	52,430	52,685	51,984	51,396	50,430	49,101	47,899	47,601	45,768

SOURCE: Poverty Thresholds for 2012 by Size of Family and Number of Related Children under 18 Years, in *Poverty Thresholds*, U.S. Census Bureau, 2014, https://www.census.gov/hhes/www/poverty/data/threshld/ (accessed May 4, 2015)

the recession, especially those who vividly remember the toll of the Great Depression, may remain fearful even when the economy recovers and may continue to limit their spending.

CONSUMER EXPENSES

On average, older households spend less than younger households because they generally have less money to spend, fewer dependents to support, and different needs and values. The BLS notes that in 2013–14 the annual per capita expenditure for people aged 65 to 74 years was $48,006, whereas those aged 75 years and older spent just $35,342. (See Table 2.7.) Those under the age of 25 years were the only group with a smaller expenditure, spending $31,771 per capita annually. The greatest amounts were spent on housing (including utilities), food, transportation, and health care. Not surprisingly, older adults spend more on health care than any other age group, both in actual dollars and as a percentage of expenditures.

Per Capita Household Expenditures

Most older adult households contain fewer people than younger households. Although larger households, in general, cost more to feed, operate, and maintain, they are less expensive on a per capita basis. Home maintenance, such as replacing a roof or major appliance, costs the same for any household, but in larger households the per capita cost is lower. Purchasing small quantities of food for one or two people may be almost as costly as buying in bulk for a larger household. Because older adults often have limited transportation and mobility, they may be forced to buy food and other necessities at small neighborhood stores that generally charge more than supermarkets and warehouse stores. Larger households may also benefit from multiple incomes.

High energy costs also cause older adults physical and financial hardship, prompting some to suffer extreme heat and cold in their home. Programs such as the Low Income Home Energy Assistance Program (2015, http:// www.acf.hhs.gov/programs/ocs/liheap), which is operated by the U.S. Department of Health and Human Services' Administration for Children and Families, attempt to prevent older adults from suffering from a lack of heat in their home. The program assists eligible households to meet their home energy needs.

AGING CONSUMERS: A GROWING MARKET

Older adults have proven to be a lucrative market for many products. Many older adults are working beyond retirement, and these older workers may prove to be an untapped market for advertisers, affecting a number of consumer sectors. Older adults are redefining aging; only a minority of Americans expects to retire as their parents did. Older adults are now more likely to continue working, and working out, rather than retiring to the shuffleboard court or the rocking chair on the front porch. As a result, they are considered an important market for an expanding array of products, such as specialty foods, drinks, anti-aging cosmetics, and over-the-counter and prescription drugs, as well as products that are traditionally marketed to older adults, such as health and life insurance plans and burial plots.

Examples of other products and services marketed to older adults include devices that help them remain in their homes safely and comfortably, allowing them to "age in place." In "How to Profit from Aging Baby Boomers" (USNews.com, June 27, 2014), Dave Bernard explains that along with products and services to help older adults maintain their independence, companies that

TABLE 2.7

Average annual expenditures and characteristics, by age group, June 2013–June 2014

Item	All consumer units	Under 25 years	25–34 years	35–44 years	45–54 years	55–64 years	65 years and older	65–74 years	75 years and older
Number of consumer units (in thousands)	126,420	8,390	20,597	21,633	24,061	23,065	28,673	16,489	12,184
Consumer unit characteristics:									
Income before taxes									
Mean	$64,432	$30,129	$58,609	$80,218	$82,149	$73,634	$44,473	$52,604	$33,470
Income after taxes									
Mean	56,437	28,583	52,581	69,685	69,902	62,369	41,292	48,056	32,140
Age of reference person	50.2	21.6	29.8	39.6	49.8	59.3	74.1	68.7	81.5
Average number in consumer unit:									
People	2.5	2.1	2.8	3.3	2.7	2.1	1.8	1.9	1.6
Children under 18	0.6	0.4	1.0	1.4	0.6	0.2	0.1	0.1	*
Adults 65 and older	0.4	*	*	*	0.1	0.1	1.4	1.4	1.3
Earners	1.3	1.3	1.5	1.6	1.7	1.3	0.5	0.7	0.2
Vehicles	1.8	1.1	1.6	1.9	2.2	2.1	1.7	1.9	1.3
Percent distribution:									
Reference person:									
Men	48	50	48	47	48	50	46	51	39
Women	52	50	52	53	52	50	54	49	61
Housing tenure:									
Homeowner	63	14	40	60	69	78	80	81	80
With mortgage	37	8	32	50	50	43	24	31	13
Without mortgage	26	6	7	10	19	35	57	50	67
Renter	37	86	60	40	31	22	20	19	20
Race of reference person:									
Black or African-American	13	12	13	15	15	12	9	10	8
White, Asian, and all other races	87	88	87	85	85	88	91	90	92
Hispanic or Latino origin of reference person:									
Hispanic or Latino	13	19	17	19	12	8	6	7	6
Not Hispanic or Latino	87	81	83	81	88	92	94	93	94
Education of reference person:									
Elementary (1–8)	4	3	3	4	4	4	7	4	10
High school (9–12)	33	30	27	29	33	33	40	37	45
College	63	67	70	68	63	62	53	58	45
Never attended and other	*	*	*	*	*	*	*	*	*
At least one vehicle owned or leased	87	65	88	90	90	90	85	91	78
Average annual expenditures:									
Mean	$51,933	$31,771	$47,738	$60,045	$62,627	$55,758	$42,557	$48,006	$35,342
Food									
Mean	6,665	4,681	6,364	7,833	8,056	6,710	5,314	6,179	4,220
Share	12.8	14.7	13.3	13.0	12.9	12.0	12.5	12.9	11.9
Food at home									
Mean	4,003	2,494	3,657	4,585	4,777	4,199	3,411	3,854	2,854
Share	7.7	7.9	7.7	7.6	7.6	7.5	8.0	8.0	8.1
Cereals and bakery products									
Mean	534	337	472	621	633	538	478	522	423
Share	1.0	1.1	1.0	1.0	1.0	1.0	1.1	1.1	1.2
Cereals and cereal products									
Mean	180	126	172	218	213	177	144	164	118
Share	0.3	0.4	0.4	0.4	0.3	0.3	0.3	0.3	0.3
Bakery products									
Mean	354	211	300	403	420	361	334	357	305
Share	0.7	0.7	0.6	0.7	0.7	0.6	0.8	0.7	0.9

*Value is too small to display.

SOURCE: "Table 1300. Age of Reference Person: Annual Expenditure Means, Shares, Standard Errors, and Coefficient of Variation, Consumer Expenditure Survey, 3rd Quarter 2013 through 2nd Quarter 2014," in *Consumer Expenditures Midyear Average*, U.S. Department of Labor, U.S. Bureau of Labor Statistics, April 2, 2015, http://www.bls.gov/cex/22014/midyear/age.pdf (accessed May 4, 2015)

offer travel and recreation services, lifelong learning, and smart technology are targeting older adult consumers.

Baby Boomers: The Emerging "Silver" Market

The aging baby boomers (people born between 1946 and 1964) have been dubbed "zoomers" to reflect the generation's active lifestyle. Market researchers believe the sheer size of the soon-to-be silver-haired boomer cohort and its history of self-indulgence, coupled with considerable purchasing power, ensure that this group will contain the most voracious older consumers ever.

The information in this section was drawn from the Boomer Project (2015, http://boomerproject.com), an organization that determines how this generation thinks, feels, and responds to marketing and advertising messages. Included among the insights that the Boomer Project research reveals are the following:

- Boomers at age 50 perceive themselves as 12 years younger, and they expect to live 35 more years. They consider themselves to be in early "middle age" and view 72 as the onset of old age. Boomers have created the "longevity climate"—by delaying retirement they have more money to spend during their longer lives.

- Boomers reject any and all age-related labels to describe themselves. They do not want to be called "seniors," "aged," or even "boomers," and they do not want to be compared with their parents' generation or any previous cohort of older adults.

- Boomers over the age of 50 do not want to reverse or stop the signs of aging, they simply want to postpone or slow the process. They are intent on seeking health rather than youth. Feeling younger is as important as looking younger for boomers eager to age "on their own terms." Boomers are avid participants in the growing number of health clubs, fitness centers, and wellness programs.

- Boomers want more time, which means that services that offer them free time to pursue work and leisure activities are likely to be in great demand. Examples of these include cleaning, home maintenance, and gardening services.

- Boomers are becoming less interested in material possessions and more interested in gaining a variety of experiences. Rather than embracing the premise that "he who has the most toys wins," boomers believe "he who chalks up the most experiences wins."

- Once dubbed the "me generation," boomers operate on the premise that they are entitled to special treatment, not because they have earned it by virtue of age, but simply because they deserve it. They want products and services that are relevant to them personally. Boomers also lead the "age of responsible consumerism" and are budget conscious, purchasing smaller homes and limiting holiday spending. They remain motivated to fulfill their own needs, whether these needs are for community, adventure, or a spiritual life.

- Boomers are life-long learners and a "wired" generation—learning, connecting, and communicating online and via social networks. Continuing education classes and opportunities to learn and enrich their lives through travel are important to this generation.

- Boomers are still interested in promoting social change. The generation known for protesting the Vietnam War (1954–1975) and questioning authority and traditional American social mores continues to support global and local humanitarian and environmental action.

- Boomers do not want to relocate to traditional retirement enclaves and communities. Instead, they prefer to age in place, remaining in their own homes rather than relocating to assisted living facilities or other supportive housing. Having witnessed the institutionalization of their parents in nursing homes and in other assisted living facilities, boomers are intent on remaining in their home, and in the community, for as long as they can.

In *Four Ways to Market to Baby Boomers in 2015* (MagicOnline.com, January 4, 2015), Macala Wright observes that with an annual disposable income of $2.4 trillion, boomers constitute a sizable market, about one-quarter of the U.S. population. Wright reports that boomers are tech savvy and use social media (19 million are on Facebook), but she also notes that boomers use and value traditional marketing such as print and direct mail. Wright asserts that marketers can capitalize on boomers' desire to remain young and vital, and advises marketers to depict them and speak to them as though they are intelligent, accomplished, and confident.

John H. Fleming of the Gallup Organization reports in *Baby Boomers Are Opening Their Wallets* (January 30, 2015, http://www.gallup.com/businessjournal/181367/baby-boomers-opening-wallets.aspx) that boomers' daily spending mirrored the global financial climate, dropping from $114 per day in February 2008 to $55 per day in March 2009 and then returning to about $100 per day in November 2014. Fleming also points out that older boomers (ages 59 to 68) report spending more than younger boomers (ages 50 to 58), likely because they no longer have as many financial responsibilities such as mortgages or college tuition, and they are spending more on products and services they want as opposed to only those they need.

SOCIAL SECURITY

We can never insure one hundred percent of the population against one hundred percent of the hazards and vicissitudes of life, but we have tried to frame a law which will give some measure of protection to the average citizen and to his family against the loss of a job and against poverty-ridden old age.

—President Franklin D. Roosevelt, on signing the Social Security Act, August 14, 1935

Social Security is a social insurance program that is funded through a dedicated payroll tax. It is also known as Old-Age, Survivors, and Disability Insurance (OASDI), which describes its three major classes of beneficiaries.

During the Great Depression poverty among the older population escalated. In 1934 more than half of older adults lacked sufficient income. Although 30 states had some form of an old-age pension program in place, by 1935 these programs were unable to meet the growing need. Just 3% of the older population received benefits under these state plans, and the average benefit amount was about $0.65 per day.

As advocated by President Franklin D. Roosevelt (1882–1945), social insurance would solve the problem of economic security for older adults by creating a work-related, contributory system in which workers would provide for their own future economic security through taxes paid while employed. By the time the Social Security Act was signed into law by President Roosevelt in August 1935, 34 nations were already operating some form of a social insurance program (government-sponsored efforts to provide for the economic well-being of a nation's citizens).

According to the SSA, in "Social Security Basic Facts" (April 2, 2015, http://www.ssa.gov/pressoffice/basicfact.htm), in 2014 more than nine out of 10 people aged 65 years and older received OASDI. Retired workers and their dependents accounted for about three-quarters (74%) of total benefits paid, whereas survivors of deceased workers accounted for 10% of the total, and disabled workers and their dependents rounded out the total with 16% of benefits paid. An estimated 95% (165 million) of the U.S. workforce was covered by Social Security.

Although Social Security was not initially intended as a full pension, 22% of married older adults and 47% of unmarried older adults relied almost exclusively (for 90% or more of their income) on the program in 2012. (See Figure 2.2.) In "We Need to Expand the Most Effective Anti-poverty Program in America" (January 22, 2015, http://billmoyers.com/2015/01/22/need-expand-effective-anti-poverty-program-america), Alex Lawson of Moyers & Company observes that programs such as Social Security were created to reduce the probability that Americans would fall into poverty during old age. Without it, 44% of older adults would be living in poverty, compared with the current 9%.

Social Security benefits are funded through the Federal Insurance Contributions Act (FICA), which provides that a mandatory tax be withheld from workers' earnings and be matched by their employers. (Self-employed workers pay both the employer and employee shares of FICA taxes.) When covered workers retire (or are disabled), they draw benefits that are based on the amount they contributed to the fund. The amount of the benefit is directly related to the duration of employment and earnings; that is, people who have worked longer and earned higher wages receive larger benefits.

Workers can retire as early as age 62 and receive reduced Social Security benefits, or they can wait until full retirement age and receive full benefits. Until 2003 the full retirement age was 65, but beginning that year it began to increase gradually, such that for people born in 1960 or later, retirement age will be 67. A special credit is given to people who delay retirement beyond their full retirement age. This credit, which is a percentage added to the Social Security benefit, varies depending on the retiree's date of birth. Workers who reached full retirement age in 2008 or later can receive a credit of 8% per year.

Table 2.8 shows the relationship between earnings and Social Security benefits. It shows the average indexed monthly earnings (AIME; this is an amount that summarizes a worker's earnings) and the corresponding benefit amounts. Delaying retirement to age 70 yields the highest ratio of retirement benefits to the AIME.

Benefits and Beneficiaries

The SSA indicates in "Social Security Basic Facts" that in 2014 the program paid benefits to more than 59 million people. The majority were older adults (40.9 million retired workers and their dependents), along with 6.2 million survivors of deceased workers and 10.9 million disabled workers and their dependents. According to the SSA, in *Annual Statistical Supplement to the Social Security Bulletin, 2014* (April 2015, http://www.ssa.gov/policy/docs/statcomps/supplement/2014/supplement14.pdf), 163.2 million people with earnings covered by Social Security paid payroll taxes in 2013. Social Security income in 2013 was an estimated $726 billion from workers and employers. Table 2.9 shows the number of beneficiaries of all the OASDI programs as well as the average monthly benefits that were paid in December 2013, the most recent month for which data were available as of August 2015.

Social Security Amendments of 1977

Ever since 1940, the year that Americans began receiving Social Security checks, monthly retirement benefits have steadily increased, but during the 1970s they soared. Legislation enacted in 1973 provided for automatic cost-of-living adjustments (COLAs) that were intended to prevent inflation from eroding Social Security benefits. The average benefit was indexed (annually adjusted) to keep pace with inflation as reflected by the CPI. COLAs were 9.9% in 1979 and peaked at 14.3% the following year. (See Table 2.10.) These increases threatened the continued financial viability of the entire system and prompted policy makers to reconsider the COLA formula.

Some legislators believed that indexing vastly overcompensated for inflation, causing relative benefit levels to rise higher than at any previous time in the history of the program. In an attempt to prevent future Social Security benefits from rising to what many considered excessive

TABLE 2.8

Benefit amount for worker with maximum-taxable earnings, 2015

	Worker with steady earnings at the maximum level since age 22								
	Retirement at age 62[a]			Retirement at age 65[b]			Retirement at age 70[c]		
Retirement in Jan.		Monthly benefits			Monthly benefits			Monthly benefits	
	AIME	At age 62	In 2015	AIME	At age 65	In 2015	AIME	At age 70	In 2015
1987	$2,205	$666	$1,435	$2,009	$789	$1,699	$1,725	$1,056	$2,275
1988	2,311	691	1,428	2,139	838	1,732	1,859	1,080	2,232
1989	2,490	739	1,468	2,287	899	1,787	2,000	1,063	2,113
1990	2,648	780	1,480	2,417	975	1,850	2,154	1,085	2,059
1991	2,792	815	1,468	2,531	1,022	1,841	2,332	1,163	2,095
1992	2,978	860	1,493	2,716	1,088	1,890	2,470	1,231	2,138
1993	3,154	899	1,517	2,878	1,128	1,903	2,605	1,289	2,173
1994	3,384	954	1,568	3,024	1,147	1,885	2,758	1,358	2,232
1995	3,493	972	1,554	3,219	1,199	1,917	2,896	1,474	2,356
1996	3,657	1,006	1,568	3,402	1,248	1,946	3,012	1,501	2,339
1997	3,877	1,056	1,600	3,634	1,326	2,009	3,189	1,609	2,438
1998	4,144	1,117	1,657	3,750	1,342	1,991	3,348	1,648	2,444
1999	4,463	1,191	1,745	3,926	1,373	2,010	3,496	1,684	2,466
2000	4,775	1,248	1,783	4,161	1,435	2,050	3,707	1,752	2,504
2001	5,126	1,314	1,814	4,440	1,538	2,123	3,912	1,879	2,593
2002	5,499	1,382	1,860	4,770	1,660	2,234	4,165	1,988	2,675
2003	5,729	1,412	1,873	5,099	1,721	2,284	4,321	2,045	2,714
2004	5,892	1,422	1,849	5,457	1,784	2,319	4,532	2,111	2,744
2005	6,137	1,452	1,838	5,827	1,874	2,372	4,786	2,252	2,850
2006	6,515	1,530	1,861	6,058	1,961	2,385	5,072	2,420	2,943
2007	6,852	1,598	1,881	6,229	1,998	2,352	5,406	2,672	3,145
2008	7,260	1,682	1,935	6,479	2,030	2,336	5,733	2,794	3,215
2009	7,685	1,769	1,924	6,861	2,172	2,362	6,090	3,054	3,321
2010	7,949	1,820	1,979	7,189	2,191	2,383	6,450	3,119	3,392
2011	7,928	1,803	1,961	7,579	2,249	2,446	6,683	3,193	3,472
2012	8,199	1,855	1,948	7,973	2,310	2,425	6,852	3,266	3,428
2013	8,539	1,923	1,985	8,230	2,414	2,492	7,095	3,350	3,458
2014	8,890	1,992	2,026	8,229	2,431	2,473	7,452	3,425	3,483
2015	9,066	2,025	2,025	8,479	2,452	2,452	7,747	3,501	3,501

[a]Retirement at age 62 is assumed here to be at exact age 62 and 1 month. Such early retirement results in a reduced monthly benefit.
[b]Retirement at age 65 is assumed to be at exact age 65 and 0 months. For retirement in 2003 and later, the monthly benefit is reduced for early retirement. (For people born before 1938, age 65 is the normal retirement age. Normal retirement age will gradually increase to age 67.)
[c]Retirement at age 70 maximizes the effect of delayed retirement credits.
Notes: The initial benefit amounts shown assume retirement in January of the stated year, with maximum-taxable earnings since age 22. Benefits in 2015 reflect subsequent automatic benefit increases (if any). Average Indexed Monthly Earnings (AIME) are shown, reflecting an amount that summarizes a person's earnings, and the corresponding monthly benefit amounts. Retirement at age 70 produces the highest ratio of retirement benefit to AIME.
Initial monthly benefits paid at ages 65 and 70 in 2000–2001 were slightly lower than the amounts shown above because such initial benefits were partially based on a cost-of-living adjustment (COLA) for December 1999 that was originally determined as 2.4 percent based on the consumer price indexes (CPIs) published by the Bureau of Labor Statistics. Pursuant to Public Law 106–554, however, this COLA is effectively now 2.5 percent, and the above figures reflect the benefit change required by this legislation.

SOURCE: "Worker with Steady Earnings at the Maximum Level since Age 22," in *Workers with Maximum-Taxable Earnings*, U.S. Social Security Administration, Office of the Chief Actuary, 2015, http://www.socialsecurity.gov/OACT/COLA/examplemax.html (accessed May 30, 2015)

levels, Congress passed the Social Security Amendments of 1977 to restructure the benefit plan and design more realistic formulas for benefits. Along with redefining COLAs, the 1977 amendments raised the payroll tax slightly, increased the wage base, and reduced benefits.

There were no COLAs in 2010 and 2011. In 2012, however, it was 3.6%. Between 2013 and 2015 it ranged from 1.5% to 1.7%. Table 2.10 shows how this COLA increase translated into SSI payments between 1975 and 2015.

The Earnings Test

Legislation enacted on January 1, 2000, changed the way in which the amount that beneficiaries could earn while also receiving retirement or survivors benefits was determined. The retirement earnings test applies only to people younger than normal retirement age, which ranges from age 65 to 67, depending on year of birth. Social Security withholds benefits if annual retirement earnings exceed a certain level, called a retirement earnings test exempt amount, for people who have not yet attained normal retirement age. These exempt amounts generally increase annually with increases in the national average wage index.

Table 2.11 shows the exempt amounts between 2000 and 2015. One dollar in Social Security benefits is withheld for every $2 of earnings more than the lower exempt amount. Similarly, $1 in benefits is withheld for every $3 of earnings more than the higher exempt amount.

SUPPLEMENTAL SECURITY INCOME

SSI is designed to provide monthly cash payments to older, blind, and/or disabled people who have low

TABLE 2.9

Number and average monthly benefit, by type of benefit and sex, December 2013

Type of benefit	All		Male		Female	
	Number	Average monthly benefit (dollars)	Number	Average monthly benefit (dollars)	Number	Average monthly benefit (dollars)
Total, OASDI	57,978,610	1,182.24	26,249,286	1,338.09	31,729,324	1,053.30
OASI	46,992,611	1,225.75	20,624,280	1,400.56	26,368,331	1,089.02
Retirement benefits	40,803,634	1,247.53	19,515,822	1,433.05	21,287,812	1,077.46
Retired workers	37,892,659	1,293.83	19,099,298	1,451.27	18,793,361	1,133.83
Spouses of retired workers	2,285,636	648.33	84,476	474.22	2,201,160	655.01
Children of retired workers	625,339	632.14	332,048	628.58	293,291	636.17
Survivor benefits	6,188,977	1,082.16	1,108,458	828.69	5,080,519	1,137.46
Children of deceased workers	1,898,904	813.80	996,882	812.56	902,022	815.18
Widowed mothers and fathers	149,778	917.69	11,931	787.66	137,847	928.94
Nondisabled widow(er)s	3,881,676	1,244.00	83,568	1,084.19	3,798,108	1,247.51
Disabled widow(er)s	257,248	716.79	15,902	526.48	241,346	729.33
Parents of deceased workers	1,371	1,094.20	175	997.37	1,196	1,108.37
DI	10,985,999	996.09	5,625,006	1,109.05	5,360,993	877.56
Disabled workers	8,940,950	1,146.42	4,642,134	1,271.42	4,298,816	1,011.44
Spouses of disabled workers	156,672	307.90	8,468	282.69	148,204	309.34
Children of disabled workers	1,888,377	341.38	974,404	342.66	913,973	340.02

OASDI = Old Age Survivors and Disability Insurance.
OASI = Old Age Survivors Insurance.
DI = Disability Insurance.

SOURCE: "Table 5.A1. Number and Average Monthly Benefit, by Type of Benefit and Sex, December 2013," in *Annual Statistical Supplement to the Social Security Bulletin, 2014*, U.S. Social Security Administration, April 2015, http://www.ssa.gov/policy/docs/statcomps/supplement/2014/supplement14.pdf (accessed May 4, 2015)

incomes. Although SSI is administered by the SSA, unlike Social Security benefits, SSI benefits are not based on prior work, and the funds come from general tax revenues rather than from Social Security taxes.

In 1972 Congress passed the legislation establishing SSI to replace several state-administered programs and to provide a uniform federal benefit based on uniform eligibility standards. Although SSI is a federal program, some states provide a supplement to the federal benefit.

In "SSI Federally Administered Payments" (April 2015, http://www.ssa.gov/policy/docs/statcomps/ssi_monthly/2015-03/table02.pdf), the SSA reports that of the 8.4 million people receiving SSI benefits in March 2015, more than 2.1 million were aged 65 years and older. (See Table 2.12.) Although payments vary by age group, the average monthly benefit received by older adults in March 2015 was $432.59. (See Table 2.13.)

WHAT LIES AHEAD FOR SOCIAL SECURITY?

The Social Security program faces long-range financing challenges that, if unresolved, threaten its solvency (the ability to meet financial obligations on time) in the coming decades. Historically, the program collected more money than it has had to pay out. However, according to the program's trustees, in *The 2015 Annual Report of the Board of Trustees of the Federal Old-Age and Survivors Insurance and Federal Disability Insurance Trust Funds* (July 22, 2015, http://www.ssa.gov/oact/tr/2015/tr2015.pdf), since 2010 Social Security expenditures

have exceeded the non-interest income of its combined trust funds.

According to the trustees, the OASDI trust funds will be depleted in 2034, leaving Social Security unable to pay scheduled benefits in full to older adult retirees and their beneficiaries. The trustees urge immediate action, observing that solvency of the combined OASDI trust funds for the next 75 years could be restored if policy makers increase the combined payroll tax rate and reduce scheduled benefits.

To a large extent, demographic changes precipitated this crisis. Social Security is a "pay-as-you-go" program, with the contributions of active workers paying the retirement benefits of those currently retired. The program is solvent at this time because the number of employees contributing to the system is sufficient. The earliest wave of baby boomers is still in the workforce and at its peak earning years. The large cohort of boomers is funding the smaller cohort of retirees born during the low birthrate cycle of the Great Depression. As a result, there are still fewer retirees depleting funds than there are workers contributing. The trustees note that when monthly Social Security benefits began in 1940, a man aged 65 could expect to live an average of about 12.7 additional years; by 2025 a typical 65-year-old man is likely to live on average another 20 years. (See Table 2.14.)

Saving Social Security

There are three basic ways to resolve Social Security's financial problems: raise taxes, cut benefits, or make

TABLE 2.10

TABLE 2.11

Social Security Income federal payment amounts, 1975–2015

Year	COLAª	Eligible individual	Eligible couple
1975	8.0%	$157.70	$236.60
1976	6.4%	167.80	251.80
1977	5.9%	177.80	266.70
1978	6.5%	189.40	284.10
1979	9.9%	208.20	312.30
1980	14.3%	238.00	357.00
1981	11.2%	264.70	397.00
1982	7.4%	284.30	426.40
1983	7.0%ᵇ	304.30	456.40
1984	3.5%	314.00	472.00
1985	3.5%	325.00	488.00
1986	3.1%	336.00	504.00
1987	1.3%	340.00	510.00
1988	4.2%	354.00	532.00
1989	4.0%	368.00	553.00
1990	4.7%	386.00	579.00
1991	5.4%	407.00	610.00
1992	3.7%	422.00	633.00
1993	3.0%	434.00	652.00
1994	2.6%	446.00	669.00
1995	2.8%	458.00	687.00
1996	2.6%	470.00	705.00
1997	2.9%	484.00	726.00
1998	2.1%	494.00	741.00
1999	1.3%	500.00	751.00
2000	2.5%	513.00	769.00
2001	3.5%	531.00	796.00
2002	2.6%	545.00	817.00
2003	1.4%	552.00	829.00
2004	2.1%	564.00	846.00
2005	2.7%	579.00	869.00
2006	4.1%	603.00	904.00
2007	3.3%	623.00	934.00
2008	2.3%	637.00	956.00
2009	5.8%	674.00	1,011.00
2010	0.0%	674.00	1,011.00
2011	0.0%	674.00	1,011.00
2012	3.6%	698.00	1,048.00
2013	1.7%	710.00	1,066.00
2014	1.5%	721.00	1,082.00
2015	1.7%	733.00	1,100.00

ªCost-of-living adjustment.
ᵇThe increase effective for July 1983 was a legislated increase.
ᶜOriginally determined as 2.4 percent based on consumer priced indexes (CPIs) published by the Bureau of Labor Statistics. Pursuant to Public Law 106-554, however, the COLA is effectively now 2.5 percent.

SOURCE: "SSI Monthly Payment Amounts, 1975–2015," in *SSI Federal Payment Amounts*, U.S. Social Security Administration, Office of the Chief Actuary, 2015 http://www.socialsecurity.gov/OACT/COLA/SSIamts.html (accessed May 4, 2015)

Annual retirement earnings test exempt amounts, 2000–15

Year	Lower amountª	Higher amountᵇ
2000	$10,080	$17,000
2001	10,680	25,000
2002	11,280	30,000
2003	11,520	30,720
2004	11,640	31,080
2005	12,000	31,800
2006	12,480	33,240
2007	12,960	34,440
2008	13,560	36,120
2009	14,160	37,680
2010	14,160	37,680
2011	14,160	37,680
2012	14,640	38,880
2013	15,120	40,080
2014	15,480	41,400
2015	15,720	41,880

ªApplies in years before the year of attaining the normal retirement age (NRA).
ᵇApplies in the year of attaining NRA, for months prior to such attainment.
Note: From 1983–1999 the higher exempt amounts applied at ages 65 through 69, as shown in our historical series of exempt amounts.

SOURCE: "Annual Retirement Earnings Test Exempt Amounts," in *Exempt Amounts under the Earnings Test*, U.S. Social Security Administration, Office of the Chief Actuary, 2015, http://www.ssa.gov/oact/cola/rtea.html (accessed May 5, 2015)

- Reducing initial benefits to retirees

- Raising the retirement age (already slated to rise from 65 to 67 by 2027)

- Lowering COLAs

- Limiting benefits based on beneficiaries' other income and assets

Other possible ways to reform Social Security include means testing, which would reduce benefits to workers if their wealth exceeded a predetermined threshold, permitting the federal government to invest a portion of the funds that enter the Social Security system in an effort to grow these funds, and helping people to save money in other ways such that they do not rely as heavily on Social Security in retirement.

Ensuring the Long-Term Solvency of Social Security

Protecting Social Security is vitally important to the nation's retirees and aging baby boomers who will soon retire, but attempts to reform the program have not gained much support in Congress. On March 12, 2015, Senator Bernie Sanders (1941–; I-VT) introduced the Social Security Expansion Act (S. 731). The law would increase the insurance amount for eligible beneficiaries, compute COLAs using the consumer price index for elderly consumers, and increase the special minimum insurance amount for lifetime low earners based on years in the workforce. The bill was immediately referred to committee, where it languished as of August 2015.

Social Security taxes earn more by investing the money. It is most likely that restoring Social Security's long-term financial balance will require a combination of increased revenues and reduced expenditures. The ways to increase revenues include:

- Increasing Social Security payroll taxes

- Investing trust funds in securities with potentially higher yields than the government bonds in which they are currently invested

- Increasing income taxes on Social Security benefits

The ways to reduce expenditures include:

TABLE 2.12

Supplemental Security Income recipients by eligibility category and age, March 2014–March 2015

Month	Total	Eligibility category		Age		
		Aged	Blind and disabled	Under 18	18–64	65 or older
2014						
March	8,388,050	1,161,260	7,226,790	1,319,374	4,949,322	2,119,354
April	8,414,517	1,163,594	7,250,923	1,323,639	4,966,908	2,123,970
May	8,383,570	1,161,836	7,221,734	1,312,342	4,949,231	2,121,997
June	8,410,441	1,164,339	7,246,102	1,320,491	4,962,127	2,127,823
July	8,389,419	1,164,012	7,225,407	1,310,859	4,949,117	2,129,443
August	8,386,962	1,165,624	7,221,338	1,303,077	4,949,221	2,134,664
September	8,413,757	1,167,587	7,246,170	1,308,532	4,965,134	2,140,091
October	8,345,875	1,157,121	7,188,754	1,293,745	4,928,625	2,123,505
November	8,362,879	1,159,272	7,203,607	1,302,319	4,932,149	2,128,411
December	8,335,704	1,151,940	7,183,764	1,299,761	4,913,072	2,122,871
2015						
January	8,326,316	1,154,159	7,172,157	1,288,489	4,910,947	2,126,880
February	8,339,656	1,154,070	7,185,586	1,295,001	4,915,729	2,128,926
March	8,352,303	1,153,562	7,198,741	1,295,518	4,926,759	2,130,026

Note: Data are for the end of the specified month.

SOURCE: "Table 2. Recipients, by Eligibility Category and Age, March 2014–March 2015," in *SSI Monthly Statistics, March 2015*, U.S. Social Security Administration, Office of the Chief Actuary, April 2015, http://www.ssa.gov/policy/docs/statcomps/ssi_monthly/2015-03/table02.pdf (accessed May 4, 2015)

On March 17, 2015, Representative John Larson (1948—; D-CT) introduced the Social Security 2100 Act (H.R. 1391), an analogous bill in the U.S. House of Representatives. Besides the provisions of S. 731, H.R. 1391 would increase the gross income threshold for taxation of Social Security benefits to $50,000 from $25,000 for single taxpayers and to $100,000 from $32,000 for married taxpayers filing joint returns beginning in 2016. It also would impose the employment tax on all wage income above $400,000, effective in 2016, and incrementally increase employment and self-employment taxes up to 15.3% in 2084. This bill also was referred to committee, where it remained as of August 2015.

AMERICANS ARE CONCERNED ABOUT CHANGES TO SOCIAL SECURITY. Americans are not completely confident that they will receive Social Security benefits when they retire. Nonetheless, Jeffrey M. Jones of the Gallup Organization reports in *More U.S. Nonretirees Expect to Rely on Social Security* (April 29, 2015, http://www.gallup.com/poll/182921/nonretirees-expect-rely-social-security.aspx) that a Gallup survey in 2015 finds that more than one-third (36%) of workers said they expect Social Security to be a major source of their retirement funds. Older workers with lower household incomes were more likely to anticipate relying on Social Security as a major source of retirement funds. Nearly half of workers age 55 and older and those with annual household income less than $30,000 expected to rely on Social Security.

Workers' expectations of the role that Social Security will play in their retirement varies with income. Just 23% of people earning $75,000 or more per year say Social Security will be a major source of their retirement funds, whereas 35% of people earning between $30,000 and less than $75,000 and 41% of people earning less than $30,000 expect to rely heavily on Social Security. As reported by Jones, in 2014–15, more employees of all ages and incomes anticipated that Social Security would be a major source of retirement income than had in 2005–06.

TABLE 2.13

Average monthly Supplemental Security Income payment, by eligibility category, age, and source of payment, March 2014–March 2015

[In dollars]

| Month | Total | Eligibility category | | Age | | |
		Aged	Blind and disabled	Under 18	18–64	65 or older
2014			**All sources**			
March	534.96	421.75	553.16	636.98	552.76	429.96
April	536.61	422.13	555.00	644.74	553.34	430.25
May	536.75	422.34	555.20	645.76	553.58	430.44
June	535.88	422.16	554.17	642.77	552.77	430.34
July	534.49	422.09	552.63	637.43	552.21	430.22
August	536.14	422.56	554.50	645.00	553.12	430.60
September	535.21	422.51	553.40	640.39	552.72	430.55
October	531.75	417.94	550.12	639.01	549.72	425.09
November	532.06	418.12	550.42	640.01	549.74	425.23
December	532.08	419.80	550.09	633.23	550.92	426.65
2015						
January	541.46	424.69	560.28	654.00	559.35	432.25
February	539.61	423.34	558.26	647.56	557.97	431.37
March	540.12	424.95	558.61	646.17	558.83	432.59
			Federal payments			
2014						
March	516.00	383.50	536.49	628.80	535.44	395.47
April	517.68	383.84	538.37	636.58	536.04	395.73
May	517.84	384.08	538.58	637.63	536.30	395.96
June	516.96	383.87	537.56	634.62	535.51	395.84
July	515.54	383.78	535.99	629.27	534.97	395.73
August	517.21	384.26	537.89	636.85	535.89	396.13
September	516.27	384.21	536.77	632.24	535.49	396.09
October	516.27	384.24	536.86	632.45	535.92	396.13
November	516.60	384.40	537.19	633.46	535.95	396.28
December	516.62	386.32	536.81	626.69	537.09	397.86
2015						
January	526.06	391.11	547.08	647.39	545.60	403.46
February	524.19	389.70	545.05	640.96	544.22	402.54
March	524.67	391.27	545.37	639.57	545.07	403.75
			State supplementation			
2014						
March	121.47	130.61	118.55	48.38	129.15	131.45
April	121.48	130.65	118.57	48.37	129.17	131.47
May	121.52	130.60	118.62	48.35	129.19	131.43
June	121.40	130.53	118.48	48.28	129.04	131.39
July	121.37	130.49	118.45	48.27	128.96	131.33
August	121.41	130.57	118.47	48.20	128.95	131.39
September	121.38	130.58	118.43	48.14	128.92	131.40
October	141.50	147.31	139.37	62.26	150.23	149.25
November	141.44	147.33	139.28	62.11	150.21	149.27
December	141.55	147.53	139.37	62.15	150.31	149.44
2015						
January	141.50	147.36	139.35	62.16	150.23	149.30
February	141.32	147.19	139.18	62.08	150.08	149.19
March	141.42	147.35	139.25	62.13	150.15	149.28

SSI = Supplemental Security Income.
Note: Data are for the end of the specified month and exclude retroactive payments.

SOURCE: "Table 7. Average Monthly Payment, by Eligibility Category, Age, and Source of Payment, March 2014–March 2014," in *SSI Monthly Statistics, March 2015*, U.S. Social Security Administration, Office of Policy, April 2015, http://www.ssa.gov/policy/docs/statcomps/ssi_monthly/2015-03/table07.pdf (accessed May 4, 2015)

TABLE 2.14

Life expectancy at birth and at age 65, selected years 1940–2090[a]

Calendar year	Intermediate				Low-cost				High-cost			
	At birth[b]		At age 65[c]		At birth[b]		At age 65[c]		At birth[b]		At age 65[c]	
	Male	Female	Male	Female	Male	Female	Male	Female	Male	Female	Male	Female
1940	70.6	76.7	12.7	14.7	70.4	76.5	12.7	14.7	70.8	77.0	12.7	14.7
1945	72.4	78.4	13.0	15.4	72.1	78.1	13.0	15.4	72.8	78.9	13.0	15.4
1950	73.7	79.8	13.1	16.2	73.2	79.3	13.1	16.2	74.3	80.4	13.1	16.2
1955	74.4	80.4	13.1	16.7	73.8	79.7	13.1	16.7	75.2	81.2	13.1	16.7
1960	75.2	80.9	13.2	17.4	74.3	80.0	13.2	17.4	76.1	81.9	13.2	17.4
1965	76.1	81.5	13.5	18.0	75.1	80.4	13.5	18.0	77.3	82.6	13.5	18.0
1970	77.3	82.3	13.8	18.5	76.0	81.1	13.8	18.5	78.8	83.7	13.8	18.5
1975	78.2	83.0	14.2	18.7	76.8	81.7	14.2	18.7	79.9	84.6	14.2	18.7
1980	79.1	83.7	14.7	18.8	77.4	82.1	14.7	18.8	81.1	85.5	14.7	18.8
1985	79.8	84.2	15.4	19.1	77.9	82.5	15.4	19.1	82.0	86.2	15.4	19.1
1990	80.5	84.8	16.1	19.5	78.4	82.9	16.1	19.4	82.9	86.9	16.1	19.5
1995	81.2	85.3	16.8	19.8	78.9	83.3	16.8	19.7	83.8	87.5	16.9	20.0
2000	81.8	85.7	17.6	20.3	79.3	83.6	17.5	20.1	84.5	88.1	17.8	20.5
2001	81.9	85.8	17.8	20.4	79.3	83.6	17.6	20.2	84.6	88.2	18.0	20.7
2002	81.9	85.9	17.9	20.5	79.4	83.6	17.7	20.3	84.7	88.3	18.2	20.8
2003	82.0	86.0	18.1	20.6	79.4	83.7	17.9	20.4	84.9	88.4	18.3	20.9
2004	82.1	86.0	18.2	20.7	79.5	83.7	18.0	20.4	85.0	88.5	18.5	21.1
2005	82.2	86.1	18.3	20.8	79.6	83.8	18.0	20.5	85.1	88.6	18.6	21.2
2006	82.3	86.2	18.4	20.9	79.6	83.8	18.1	20.6	85.3	88.7	18.8	21.3
2007	82.4	86.2	18.6	21.0	79.7	83.9	18.2	20.6	85.4	88.8	19.0	21.4
2008	82.5	86.3	18.7	21.1	79.7	83.9	18.3	20.7	85.5	88.9	19.1	21.5
2009	82.6	86.4	18.8	21.2	79.8	84.0	18.4	20.7	85.6	89.0	19.2	21.7
2010	82.7	86.5	18.9	21.2	79.9	84.0	18.4	20.8	85.8	89.1	19.4	21.8
2011	82.8	86.6	19.0	21.3	79.9	84.1	18.5	20.8	85.9	89.2	19.5	21.9
2012	82.9	86.6	19.1	21.4	80.0	84.1	18.5	20.9	86.0	89.3	19.7	22.0
2013	83.0	86.7	19.1	21.5	80.0	84.2	18.6	20.9	86.1	89.4	19.8	22.1
2014	83.1	86.7	19.2	21.6	80.1	84.2	18.6	21.0	86.2	89.5	19.9	22.2
2015	83.1	86.8	19.3	21.6	80.1	84.2	18.7	21.0	86.4	89.6	20.1	22.4
2020	83.6	87.2	19.7	21.9	80.4	84.5	18.9	21.2	86.9	90.1	20.6	22.9
2025	84.0	87.5	20.0	22.2	80.7	84.7	19.0	21.3	87.5	90.5	21.2	23.3
2030	84.4	87.8	20.3	22.5	80.9	84.9	19.2	21.5	88.0	90.9	21.6	23.7
2035	84.8	88.1	20.6	22.8	81.2	85.1	19.4	21.6	88.5	91.3	22.1	24.1
2040	85.2	88.4	20.9	23.0	81.4	85.3	19.5	21.8	89.0	91.7	22.5	24.5
2045	85.5	88.7	21.2	23.3	81.6	85.4	19.7	21.9	89.5	92.1	22.9	24.9
2050	85.9	89.0	21.5	23.5	81.9	85.6	19.8	22.0	89.9	92.5	23.3	25.2
2055	86.2	89.3	21.7	23.8	82.1	85.8	20.0	22.2	90.3	92.8	23.7	25.6
2060	86.5	89.6	22.0	24.0	82.3	86.0	20.1	22.3	90.7	93.2	24.1	25.9
2065	86.8	89.8	22.2	24.2	82.5	86.2	20.3	22.4	91.1	93.5	24.4	26.2
2070	87.2	90.1	22.5	24.4	82.7	86.4	20.4	22.6	91.5	93.8	24.8	26.5
2075	87.5	90.3	22.7	24.7	83.0	86.5	20.6	22.7	91.9	94.1	25.1	26.8
2080	87.7	90.6	23.0	24.9	83.2	86.7	20.7	22.8	92.2	94.4	25.4	27.1
2085	88.0	90.8	23.2	25.1	83.4	86.9	20.9	23.0	92.6	94.7	25.7	27.4
2090	88.3	91.0	23.4	25.3	83.6	87.0	21.0	23.1	92.9	94.9	26.0	27.7

[a]The cohort life expectancy at a given age for a given year is the average remaining number of years expected prior to death for a person at that exact age, born on January 1, using the mortality rates for the series of years in which the individual will actually reach each succeeding age if he or she survives.
[b]Cohort life expectancy at birth for those born in the calendar year is based on a combination of actual and estimated death rates for birth years 1940 through 2011. For birth years after 2011, these values depend on estimated death rates.
[c]Age 65 cohort life expectancy for those attaining age 65 in calendar years 1940 though 2011 depends on actual death rates or on a combination of actual and estimated death rates. After 2011, these values depend on estimated death rates.

SOURCE: "Table V.A4. Cohort Life Expectancy," in *The 2015 Annual Report of the Board of Trustees of the Federal Old-Age and Survivors Insurance and Federal Disability Insurance Trust Funds*, U.S. Social Security Administration, Office of the Chief Actuary, July 2015, http://www.ssa.gov/oact/tr/2015/tr2015.pdf (accessed August 13, 2015)

CHAPTER 3
LIVING ARRANGEMENTS OF THE OLDER POPULATION

The vast majority of older Americans live independently in the community. They are not institutionalized in facilities such as nursing homes or retirement homes. The Administration on Aging (AoA) notes in *A Profile of Older Americans: 2014* (May 2015, http://www.aoa.acl .gov/Aging_Statistics/Profile/2014/docs/2014-Profile.pdf) that although the overall number of older Americans living in nursing homes was small—nearly 1.5 million (3.4%) people who were 65 years and older in 2013—the percentage of older adults in nursing homes increased dramatically with advancing age, from 1% of 65- to 74-year-olds, to 3% of 75- to 84-year-olds, and to 10% of those aged 85 years and older.

The living arrangements of older adults are important because they are closely associated with their health, well-being, and economic status. For example, older adults who live alone are more likely to live in poverty than those who live with their spouse or other family members. Older adults living alone may also be socially isolated, and their health may suffer because there are no family members or others nearby to serve as caregivers.

LIVING WITH A SPOUSE, OTHER RELATIVES, OR ALONE

Table 3.1 shows that 28.8 million (23.4%) out of 123.2 million households were headed by a person aged 65 years or older in 2014. It also shows that the median age of householders has consistently increased over the past three decades. Figure 3.1 shows the sharp rise of households headed by householders aged 65 years and older from 1975 to 2014, compared with the relatively unchanged number of households headed by people under the age of 30 years.

According to the AoA, in *A Profile of Older Americans 2014*, more than half (57%) of community-dwelling, civilian (noninstitutionalized—people who are not in the U.S. military, school, jail, or mental health facilities) older

adults lived with their spouse in 2014. Significantly more older men than women—72% (14.2 million) of older men, compared with 45.6% (11.3 million) of older women— lived with their spouse. (See Figure 3.2.) This disparity occurs because women usually live longer than men, are generally younger than the men they marry, and are far less likely to remarry after the death of a spouse, largely because there are relatively few available older men.

In addition, the proportion of older adults living with their spouse decreased with age. U.S. Census Bureau data reveal that in 2014, 16.8 million adults aged 65 to 74 years lived with their spouse, compared with 7 million adults aged 75 to 84 years and 1.6 million age 85 and older. (See Table 3.2.)

The percentage of older adults who live alone rises with age, largely because of the death of spouses. Of widowed females between the ages of 65 and 74, 1.8 million lived alone in 2013, as did 2.4 million widowed females ages 75 to 84 and 1.6 million widowed females aged 85 years and older. (See Table 3.3.) Of widowed males ages 65 to 74, 535,000 lived alone in 2014, as did 607,000 widowed males ages 75 to 84 and 442,000 widowed males aged 85 years and older. Table 3.4 shows that the numbers of older adults living alone as a result of divorce or separation decreases with advancing age.

Multigenerational Households

The U.S. Census Bureau in its American Community Survey (ACS; https://www.census.gov/programs-surveys/ acs) finds that 7.2 million grandparents were living in the same household with their grandchildren under the age of 18 years in 2013 and that 2.7 million (37%) of these grandparents were responsible for their grandchildren. (See Table 3.5.) Of these grandparents, nearly 1.2 million had income below the poverty level. (See Table 3.6.) In 2013 the median family income for households in

TABLE 3.1

Households by age of householder, 1960–2014

Year	All households	Under 25	25–29	30–34	35–44	45–54	55–64	65–74	75 and older	Median age
2014	123,229	6,404	9,300	10,677	21,123	23,733	23,205	15,981	12,806	51.2
2013	122,459	6,314	9,251	10,767	21,334	24,068	22,802	15,349	12,575	50.9
2012	121,084	6,180	9,208	10,638	21,240	24,196	22,779	14,517	12,326	50.6
2011	119,927	6,231	9,283	10,204	21,458	24,768	22,246	13,587	12,151	50.2
2011	118,682	6,140	9,331	10,241	21,251	24,530	21,828	13,348	12,015	50.1
2010	117,538	6,233	9,446	9,811	21,519	24,872	20,387	13,164	12,106	49.7
2009	117,181	6,357	9,463	9,839	22,171	24,633	19,883	12,842	11,992	49.3
2008	116,783	6,553	9,400	9,825	22,448	24,536	19,909	12,284	11,829	49
2007	116,011	6,662	9,667	9,767	22,779	24,141	19,266	11,926	11,803	48.6
2006	114,384	6,795	9,223	9,896	23,016	23,732	18,264	11,687	11,772	48.3
2005	113,343	6,734	9,173	10,141	23,248	23,392	17,503	11,528	11,623	48
2004	112,000	6,609	8,738	10,421	23,221	23,138	16,824	11,499	11,550	47.8
2003	111,278	6,611	8,535	10,521	24,069	22,623	16,261	11,361	11,299	47.5
2002	109,297	6,391	8,412	10,576	24,031	22,208	15,203	11,472	11,004	47.2
2001	108,209	6,409	8,521	10,510	24,054	21,969	14,277	11,490	10,979	47
2000	104,705	5,860	8,520	10,107	23,955	20,927	13,592	11,325	10,419	46.8
1999	103,874	5,770	8,519	10,300	23,969	20,158	13,571	11,373	10,216	46.6
1998	102,528	5,435	8,463	10,570	23,943	19,547	13,072	11,272	10,225	46.3
1997	101,018	5,160	8,647	10,667	23,823	18,843	12,469	11,679	9,729	46.1
1996	99,627	5,282	8,354	10,871	23,227	18,007	12,401	11,908	9,578	46
1995	98,990	5,444	8,400	11,052	22,914	17,590	12,224	11,803	9,562	45.9
1994	97,107	5,265	8,472	11,245	22,293	16,837	12,188	11,639	9,168	45.7
1993	96,426	5,257	8,859	11,198	21,862	16,413	12,154	11,668	9,014	45.6
1993	96,391	5,022	8,614	11,127	21,718	16,576	12,438	11,834	9,061	45.9
1992	95,669	4,859	8,810	11,197	21,774	15,547	12,559	12,043	8,878	45.7
1991	94,312	4,882	9,246	11,077	21,304	14,751	12,524	12,001	8,526	45.4
1990	93,347	5,121	9,423	11,049	20,555	14,514	12,529	11,733	8,423	45.3
1989	92,830	5,415	9,624	11,300	19,952	14,018	12,805	11,590	8,127	45.1
1988	91,066	5,228	9,614	10,969	19,323	13,630	12,846	11,410	8,045	45.3
1987	89,479	5,197	9,652	10,850	18,703	13,211	12,868	11,250	7,748	45.3
1986	88,458	5,503	9,781	10,629	17,997	13,099	12,852	11,157	7,439	45.2
1985	86,789	5,438	9,637	10,377	17,481	12,628	13,073	10,851	7,305	45.4
1984	85,407	5,510	9,848	9,960	16,596	12,471	13,121	10,700	7,201	45.6
1983	83,918	5,695	9,465	9,639	16,020	12,354	13,074	10,603	7,067	45.9
1982	83,527	6,109	9,525	9,802	15,326	12,505	12,947	10,379	6,933	45.8
1981	82,368	6,443	9,514	9,639	14,463	12,694	12,704	10,226	6,685	45.9
1980	80,776	6,569	9,252	9,252	13,980	12,654	12,525	10,112	6,432	46.1
1979	77,330	6,342	8,679	8,317	13,328	12,585	12,284	9,753	6,042	46.6
1978	76,030	6,220	8,598	8,233	12,969	12,602	12,183	9,383	5,842	46.6
1977	74,142	5,991	8,385	7,782	12,482	12,905	11,780	9,210	5,606	46.9
1976	72,867	5,877	8,298	7,212	12,227	12,820	11,631	9,258	5,544	47.2
1975	71,120	5,834	7,810	7,137	11,861	12,916	11,301	8,910	5,350	47.3
1974	69,859	5,857	7,527	6,804	11,703	12,939	11,149	8,716	5,162	47.3
1973	68,251	5,476	7,116	6,447	11,721	12,805	11,212	8,369	5,104	47.6
1972	66,676	5,194	6,794	6,009	11,529	12,758	11,138	8,165	5,090	48
1971	64,778	4,737	6,239	5,682	11,813	12,588	11,021	7,793	4,909	48.1
1970	63,401	4,359	6,101	5,593	11,810	12,216	10,824	7,744	4,756	48.1
1969	62,214	4,094	5,910	5,447	11,817	12,230	10,622	7,540	4,554	48.1
1968	60,813	3,852	5,536	5,325	12,003	12,038	10,394	7,536	4,327	48.2
1967	59,236	3,587	5,288	5,099	11,998	11,892	9,909	7,321	4,143	48.1
1966	58,406	3,571	4,991	5,086	11,944	11,806	9,745	7,224	4,038	48.1
1965	57,436	3,413	4,808	5,119	12,009	11,523	9,600	7,173	3,790	47.9
1964	56,149	3,110	4,546	5,167	12,176	11,192	9,327	6,998	3,630	47.7
1963	55,270	2,889	4,386	5,314	12,005	11,072	9,103	6,909	3,592	47.7
1962	54,764	2,909	4,349	5,435	11,802	10,906	9,057	6,960	3,346	47.6
1961	53,557	2,628	4,341	5,387	11,596	11,047	9,026	6,355	3,179	47.6
1960	52,799	2,559	4,317	5,407	11,614	10,878	8,599	6,380	3,045	47.3

SOURCE: "Table HH-3. Households, by Age of Householder: 1960 to Present," in *Families and Living Arrangements*, U.S. Census Bureau, 2014, https://www.census.gov/hhes/families/data/households.html (accessed May 5, 2015)

which grandparents were responsible for grandchildren was $48,016. In homes headed by grandparents in which the parents were not present, the median household income was $35,685.

The ACS further finds that nearly 1.6 million grandparents who were raising their grandchildren were also in the labor force in 2013, and about 667,000 grandparents raising grandchildren were disabled. Nearly 500,000 grandparents caring for their own grandchildren were foreign born. About 252,000 grandparents raising their grandchildren spoke another primary language but spoke English very well, whereas about 384,000 spoke English "less than very well."

Until recently, multigenerational living often occurred when older adults exhausted their resources. However, the Great Recession (which lasted from late

FIGURE 3.1

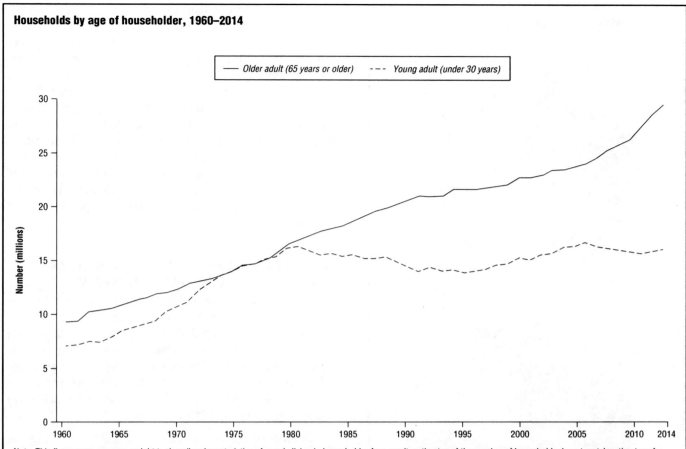

Households by age of householder, 1960–2014

Note: This figure uses a person weight to describe characteristics of people living in households. As a result, estimates of the number of households do not match estimates of housing units from the Housing Vacancy Survey (HVS). The HVS is weighted to housing units, rather than the population, in order to more accurately estimate the number of occupied and vacant housing units.

SOURCE: "Figure HH-3. Households by Selected Ages of the Householder," in *Families and Living Arrangements*, U.S. Census Bureau, 2014, https://www.census.gov/hhes/families/files/graphics/HH-3.pdf (accessed May 5, 2015)

2007 to mid-2009), job losses, and foreclosures have prompted younger adults to move in with parents and/or grandparents. In "Unique Considerations for Children Raised by Grandparents" (*Psychology Today*, October 21, 2014), Laura D. Pittman reports that multigenerational households often form in response to financial difficulties or working parents' need for help with child care. Other circumstances such as parents unable to care for their children because of incarceration, mental health issues, or substance abuse also may prompt grandparents to assume responsibility for their grandchildren.

HOMELESSNESS

The National Coalition on Homelessness notes in *Elder Homelessness* (2015, http://nationalhomeless.org/issues/elderly) that multiple studies reveal an increase in the proportion of older adults between the ages of 50 and 64 in the homeless population. The organization notes that older Americans may be less likely than younger Americans to be homeless because safety-net programs such as Social Security, Supplemental Security Income (SSI), Medicare (a medical insurance program for older adults and people with disabilities), and senior housing act to prevent homelessness.

There are reports of a growing population of homeless older adults. In the 2013 *Annual Homelessness Assessment Report (AHAR) to Congress, Part 2* (October 2014, https://www.hudexchange.info/onecpd/assets/File/2013-AHAR-Part-2.pdf), the U.S. Department of Housing and Urban Development (HUD) finds growing numbers and percentages of adults aged 62 years and older in shelters. In 2007, 4.1% of all people in shelters were older adults; in 2013 the older adult population rose to 5.4%. (See Figure 3.3.) The percentage of homeless adults between the ages of 51 and 61 in shelters also increased, from 18.9% in 2007 to 25% in 2013.

Among the concerns about homelessness are the inherent health-related issues. The relationship between homelessness, health, and illness is complex. Some health problems precede homelessness and contribute to

FIGURE 3.2

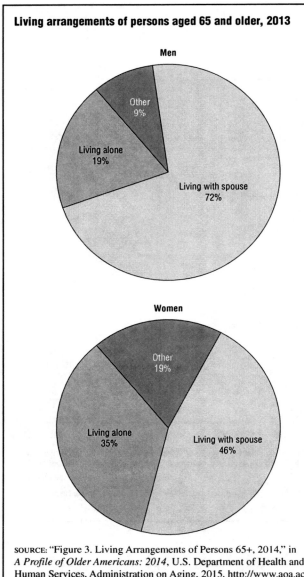

Living arrangements of persons aged 65 and older, 2013

Men

Other 9%

Living alone 19%

Living with spouse 72%

Women

Other 19%

Living alone 35%

Living with spouse 46%

SOURCE: "Figure 3. Living Arrangements of Persons 65+, 2014," in *A Profile of Older Americans: 2014*, U.S. Department of Health and Human Services, Administration on Aging, 2015, http://www.aoa.acl .gov/Aging_Statistics/Profile/2014/docs/2014-Profile.pdf (accessed May 7, 2015)

it, whereas others are consequences of homelessness. In addition, homelessness often complicates access and adherence to treatment. For example, mental illness or substance abuse (dependency on alcohol or drugs) may limit a person's ability to work, leading to poverty and homelessness. Without protection from the cold, rain, and snow, exposure to weather may result in illnesses such as bronchitis or pneumonia. Homelessness also increases exposure to crime and violence, which could lead to trauma and injuries.

There are many reasons that homeless people experience difficulties gaining access to health care services and receiving needed medical care. Lacking essentials such as transportation to medical facilities, money to pay for care, and knowledge about how to qualify for

health insurance and where to obtain health care services makes seeking treatment complicated and frustrating. Psychological distress or mental illness may prevent homeless people from attempting to obtain needed care, and finding food and shelter may take precedence over seeking treatment. Even when the homeless do gain access to medical care, following a treatment plan, filling prescriptions, and scheduling follow-up appointments often present insurmountable challenges to those who do not have a telephone number, address, or safe place to store medications. Furthermore, because chronic (long-term) homelessness can cause or worsen a variety of health problems, homeless people may not live to old age with the same frequency as their age peers who are not homeless.

LONG-TERM CARE, SUPPORTIVE HOUSING, AND OTHER RESIDENTIAL ALTERNATIVES

Spouses and other relatives are still the major caretakers of older, dependent members of American society. However, the number of people aged 65 years and older living in long-term care facilities such as nursing homes is rising because the older population is increasing rapidly. Although many older adults now live longer, healthier lives, the increase in overall length of life has amplified the need for long-term care facilities and supportive housing.

Growth of the home health care industry during the early 1990s only slightly slowed the increase in the numbers of Americans entering nursing homes. Supportive housing (assisted living, congregate housing, and continuing care retirement communities) offers alternatives to nursing home care. The overarching goal of supportive housing is to enable older adults to receive needed assistance while retaining as much independence as possible.

There are three broad classes of supportive housing for older adults. The smallest and most affordable options usually house 10 or fewer older adults and are often in homes in residential neighborhoods. Residents share bathrooms, bedrooms, and living areas. These largely unregulated facilities are alternately known as board-and-care facilities, domiciliary care, personal care homes, adult foster care, senior group homes, and sheltered housing.

Residential care facilities, assisted living residences, and adult congregate living facilities tend to be larger, more expensive, and offer more independence and privacy than board-and-care facilities. Most offer private rooms or apartments as well as large common areas for activities and meals.

Continuing care retirement communities and life care communities are usually large complexes that offer a comprehensive range of services from independent living to skilled nursing home care. These facilities are

TABLE 3.2

Older adults living with spouses, by age group and sex, 2014

[Numbers in thousands]

	Total 15 years and over	65–74 years	75–84 years	85+ years
All marital statuses				
Both sexes				
Total	252,224	25,787	13,427	5,246
Married spouse present				
Both sexes				
Total	123,700	16,842	7,043	1,625
Householder				
In family household	59,629	8,434	3,660	801
Not a householder				
In family household	63,858	8,392	3,378	824
Not in family household	213	17	4	—
Householder				
In family	59,629	8,434	3,660	801
Not a householder				
Child of householder with children under 18	428	—	—	—
Child of householder without children under 18	294	13	—	—
In family, other relative of householder[a]	63,136	8,378	3,378	824
Not in family	213	17	4	—
In primary family[b]				
Family householder	59,629	8,434	3,660	801
Spouse of householder	59,629	7,937	3,188	759
In related subfamily				
Child of householder	722	13	—	—
Other relative of householder	3,506	441	190	65
In unrelated subfamily				
Nonrelative of householder	213	17	4	—
Male				
Total	61,850	9,025	4,107	1,079
Householder				
In family household	36,160	5,684	2,621	604
Not a householder				
In family household	25,583	3,330	1,484	475
Not in family household	107	11	3	—
Householder				
In family	36,160	5,684	2,621	604
Not a householder				
Child of householder with children under 18	195	—	—	—
Child of householder without children under 18	139	5	—	—
In family, other relative of householder[a]	25,249	3,326	1,484	475
Not in family	107	11	3	—
In primary family[b]				
Family householder	36,160	5,684	2,621	604
Spouse of householder	23,469	3,076	1,367	435
In related subfamily				
Child of householder	334	5	—	—
Other relative of householder	1,780	250	117	40
In unrelated subfamily				
Nonrelative of householder	107	11	3	—
Female				
Total	61,850	7,817	2,935	547
Householder				
In family household	23,469	2,749	1,040	197
Not a householder				
In family household	38,275	5,062	1,894	349
Not in family household	107	6	1	—

specifically designed to provide nearly all needed care, except hospital care, within one community. Facilities in this group tend to be the most costly.

Nursing Homes

Nursing homes fall into three categories: residential care facilities, intermediate care facilities, and skilled nursing facilities. Each provides a different range and intensity of services:

- A residential care facility (RCF) provides meals and housekeeping for its residents, plus some basic medical monitoring, such as administering medications. This type of home is for people who are fairly independent and do not need constant medical attention

TABLE 3.2

Older adults living with spouses, by age group and sex, 2014 [CONTINUED]

[Numbers in thousands]

	Total 15 years and over	65–74 years	75–84 years	85+ years
Householder				
In family	23,469	2,749	1,040	197
Not a householder				
Child of householder with children under 18	232	—	—	—
Child of householder without children under 18	155	9	—	—
In family, other relative of householder[a]	37,887	5,053	1,894	349
Not in family	107	6	1	—
In primary family[b]				
Family householder	23,469	2,749	1,040	197
Spouse of householder	36,160	4,861	1,821	324
In related subfamily				
Child of householder	388	9	—	—
Other relative of householder	1,726	192	73	25
In unrelated subfamily				
Nonrelative of householder	107	6	1	—

[a]Includes spouses of householders.
[b]Excludes individuals who are also in related subfamilies.
Note: Prior to 2001, this table included people in group quarters.
Dash ("—") represents or rounds to zero.

SOURCE: Adapted from "Table A2. Family Status and Household Relationship of People 15 Years and over, by Marital Status, Age, and Sex: 2014," in *Families and Living Arrangements*, U.S. Census Bureau, 2014, http://www.census.gov/hhes/families/files/cps2014/tabA2-all.xls (accessed May 7, 2015)

but need help with tasks such as laundry and cleaning. Many RCFs also provide social activities and recreational programs for their residents.

- An intermediate care facility (ICF) offers room and board and nursing care as necessary for people who can no longer live independently. Much like RCFs, ICFs provide exercise and social programs, and some offer physical therapy and rehabilitation programs.

- A skilled nursing facility (SNF) provides around-the-clock nursing care, plus on-call physician coverage. SNFs are for patients who need intensive nursing care, as well as services such as occupational, physical, or respiratory therapies.

NURSING HOME RESIDENTS. The National Center for Health Statistics (NCHS) reports in *Health, United States, 2014* (May 2015, http://www.cdc.gov/nchs/data/hus/hus14.pdf) that there were 15,663 certified nursing homes in 2013. These facilities had an occupancy rate of 80.8% and housed nearly 1.4 million residents. The highest occupancy rates were in North Dakota (92.9%), the District of Columbia (92.9%), South Dakota (91.7%), Rhode Island (91.6%) and New Hampshire (90.7%) The lowest occupancy rates were in Texas (63.3%), Alaska (63.9%), and Indiana (65.8%). (See Table 3.7.)

In "Best Nursing Homes 2015" (USNews.com, March 5, 2015), data from Nursing Home Compare, a program run by the Centers for Medicare and Medicaid Services, the federal agency that sets and enforces standards for nursing homes, indicate that the state with the greatest number of five-star nursing homes is California, followed by Ohio, Florida, Illinois, and Texas.

DIVERSIFICATION OF NURSING HOMES. To remain competitive with home health care and the increasing array of alternative living arrangements for older adults, many nursing homes have begun offering specialized services. In *Long Term Care Services in the United States: 2013 Overview* (December 2013, http://www.cdc.gov/nchs/data/nsltcp/long_term_care_services_ 2013.pdf), the Centers for Disease Control and Prevention reports that in 2012 more than three-quarters (78.6%) of all nursing homes offered programs such as hospice (end-of-life) care. Many nursing homes also offer specialized pain management and wound treatment programs. According to the Alzheimer's Association, in *2015 Alzheimer's Disease Facts and Figures* (2015, http://www.alz.org/facts/downloads/facts_figures_2015.pdf), in 2014 about 4.4% of nursing home beds were reserved for people suffering from Alzheimer's disease or another dementia (loss of intellectual functioning accompanied by memory loss and personality changes). (Alzheimer's disease is a progressive form of dementia that is characterized by impairment of memory and intellectual functions.)

Tracey Drury observes in "Buffalo Nursing Home Operators Search for Bottom-Line Health" (BizJournals .com, April 10, 2015) that many nursing homes are expanding their service offerings to include pharmacy, assisted living, transportation services, diabetic care, stroke rehabilitation, or ventilator care to increase revenue.

Collaborating with other providers of health care services or on their own, many nursing homes also offer services such as adult day care and visiting nurse services for people who still live at home. Other programs include

TABLE 3.3

Widowed older adults living alone, by age group, 2014

[Numbers in thousands]

	Total 15 years and over	65–74 years	75–84 years	85+ years
All martial status				
Both sexes				
Total	252,224	25,787	13,427	5,246
Widowed				
Both sexes				
Total	14,274	3,489	4,442	3,038
Householder				
In family household	2,756	602	742	347
Not in family household	9,023	2,403	3,098	2,071
Not a householder				
In family household	2,034	406	542	579
Not in family household	460	78	60	41
Householder				
In family	2,756	602	742	347
Not in family, living alone	8,694	2,291	3,037	2,038
Not in family, living with nonrelatives	329	112	61	33
Not a householder				
Child of householder with children under 18	14	—	—	—
Child of householder without children under 18	112	11	1	—
In family, other relative of householder*	1,908	396	541	579
Not in family	460	78	60	41
In primary family				
Family householder	2,756	602	742	347
Child of householder	112	11	1	—
Other relative of householder	1,888	394	538	579
In related subfamily				
Child of householder	14	—	—	—
Other relative of householder	20	2	3	—
In unrelated subfamily				
Nonrelative of householder	22	—	—	—
Not in family groups				
Householder, living alone	8,694	2,291	3,037	2,038
Householder, living only with nonrelatives	329	112	61	33
Other nonrelative, living only with nonrelatives	438	78	60	41
Male				
Total	3,059	760	867	627
Householder				
In family household	495	92	118	69
Not in family household	2,057	581	643	455
Not a householder				
In family household	381	64	92	91
Not in family household	127	23	14	13
Householder				
In family	495	92	118	69
Not in family, living alone	1,926	535	607	442
Not in family, living with nonrelatives	130	46	36	13
Not a householder				
Child of householder with children under 18	3	—	—	—
Child of householder without children under 18	53	—	1	—
In family, other relative of householder*	325	64	90	91
Not in family	127	23	14	13
In primary family				
Family householder	495	92	118	69
Child of householder	53	—	1	—
Other relative of householder	320	64	90	91
In related subfamily				
Child of householder	3	—	—	—
Other relative of householder	5	—	—	—
In unrelated subfamily				
Nonrelative of householder	—	—	—	—
Not in family groups				
Householder, living alone	1,926	535	607	442
Householder, living only with nonrelatives	130	46	36	13
Other nonrelative, living only with nonrelatives	127	23	14	13

TABLE 3.3

Widowed older adults living alone, by age group, 2014 [CONTINUED]

[Numbers in thousands]

	Total 15 years and over	65–74 years	75–84 years	85+ years
Female				
Total	**11,214**	**2,729**	**3,575**	**2,411**
Householder				
In family household	2,261	510	623	279
Not in family household	6,967	1,823	2,455	1,616
Not a householder				
In family household	1,653	342	450	488
Not in family household	333	55	46	28
Householder				
In family	2,261	510	623	279
Not in family, living alone	6,768	1,756	2,430	1,596
Not in family, living with nonrelatives	199	66	26	21
Not a householder				
Child of householder with children under 18	11	—	—	—
Child of householder without children under 18	59	11	—	—
In family, other relative of householder*	1,584	332	450	488
Not in family	333	55	46	28
In primary family				
Family householder	2,261	510	623	279
Child of householder	59	11	—	—
Other relative of householder	1,568	330	447	488
In related subfamily				
Child of householder	11	—	—	—
Other relative of householder	15	2	3	—
In unrelated subfamily				
Nonrelative of householder	22	—	—	—
Not in family groups				
Householder, living alone	6,768	1,756	2,430	1,596
Householder, living only with nonrelatives	199	66	26	21
Other nonrelative, living only with nonrelatives	311	55	46	28

*Includes spouses of householders.

Note: Data are based on the Current Population Survey, Annual Social and Economic Supplement (CPS ASEC) sample of 980,000 addresses.

SOURCE: Adapted from "Table A2. Family Status and Household Relationship of People 15 Years and over, by Marital Status, Age, and Sex: 2014," in *Families and Living Arrangements*, U.S. Census Bureau, 2014, http://www.census.gov/hhes/families/files/cps2014/tabA2-all.xls (accessed May 7, 2015)

respite plans that allow caregivers who need to travel for business or vacation to leave an older relative in the nursing home temporarily.

THE PIONEER NETWORK. In response to concerns about quality of life and quality of care issues in nursing homes, leaders in nursing home reform efforts from throughout the United States established in 2000 the Pioneer Network as a forum for the culture change movement. The culture change in this instance was a focus on person-directed values that affirm and support each person's individuality and abilities and that apply to elders and to those who work with them. The Pioneer Network explains in "Mission, Vision and Values" (2015, http://www.pioneernetwork.net/AboutUs/Values) that it commits to the following values:

- Know each person
- Each person can and does make a difference
- Relationship is the fundamental building block of a transformed culture
- Respond to spirit, as well as mind and body
- Risk taking is a normal part of life
- Put person before task
- All elders are entitled to self-determination wherever they live
- Community is the antidote to institutionalization
- Do unto others as you would have them do unto you
- Promote the growth and development of all
- Shape and use the potential of the environment in all its aspects: physical, organizational, psycho/social/spiritual
- Practice self-examination, searching for new creativity and opportunities for doing better
- Recognize that culture change and transformation are not destinations but a journey, always a work in progress

INNOVATION AND CULTURE CHANGE IMPROVE THE QUALITY OF LIFE FOR RESIDENTS. Industry observers frequently decry the care that is provided in nursing homes. The media publicizes instances of elder abuse (neglect, exploitation, or mistreatment of older adults) and other quality of care issues. Several organizations, however, have actively sought to develop models of health service delivery that improve the clinical care and quality of life for nursing home residents.

TABLE 3.4

Divorced or separated older adults living alone, by age group, 2014

[Numbers in thousands]

	Total 15 years and over	65–74 years	75–84 years	85+ years
All marital statuses				
Both sexes				
Total	**252,224**	**25,787**	**13,427**	**5,246**
Divorced				
Both sexes				
Total	25,343	3,614	1,160	288
Householder				
In family household	6,733	501	146	21
Not in family household	12,254	2,603	855	220
Not a householder				
In family household	3,260	264	120	40
Not in family household	3,096	246	40	6
Householder				
In family	6,733	501	146	21
Not in family, living alone	10,425	2,380	810	211
Not in family, living with nonrelatives	1,830	223	45	9
Not a householder				
Child of householder with children under 18	300	—	—	—
Child of householder without children under 18	1,245	37	—	—
In family, other relative of householder[a]	1,715	227	120	40
Not in family	3,096	246	40	6
In primary family[b]				
Family householder	6,733	501	146	21
Child of householder	1,247	37	—	—
Other relative of householder	1,574	227	118	37
In related subfamily				
Child of householder	299	—	—	—
Other relative of householder	141	—	2	3
In unrelated subfamily				
Nonrelative of householder	191	—	—	—
Not in family groups				
Householder, living alone	10,425	2,380	810	211
Householder, living only with nonrelatives	1,830	223	45	9
Other nonrelative, living only with nonrelatives	2,905	246	40	6
Male				
Total	**10,729**	**1,421**	**417**	**96**
Householder				
In family household	1,807	136	36	12
Not in family household	5,855	1,105	325	72
Not a householder				
In family household	1,504	61	28	10
Not in family household	1,563	119	27	2
Householder				
In family	1,807	136	36	12
Not in family, living alone	4,845	976	305	66
Not in family, living with nonrelatives	1,011	130	21	6
Not a householder				
Child of householder with children under 18	73	—	—	—
Child of householder without children under 18	803	10	—	—
In family, other relative of householder[a]	628	51	28	10
Not in family	1,563	119	27	2
In primary family[b]				
Family householder	1,807	136	36	12
Child of householder	805	10	—	—
Other relative of householder	598	51	28	10
In related subfamily				
Child of householder	71	—	—	—
Other relative of householder	30	—	—	—
In unrelated subfamily				
Nonrelative of householder	29	—	—	—
Not in family groups				
Householder, living alone	4,845	976	305	66
Householder, living only with nonrelatives	1,011	130	21	6
Other nonrelative, living only with nonrelatives	1,534	119	27	2

TABLE 3.4

Divorced or separated older adults living alone, by age group, 2014 [CONTINUED]

[Numbers in thousands]

	Total 15 years and over	65–74 years	75–84 years	85+ years
Female				
Total	**14,614**	**2,193**	**743**	**192**
Householder				
In family household	4,926	365	109	9
Not in family household	6,399	1,498	530	148
Not a householder				
In family household	1,757	203	91	31
Not in family household	1,532	127	13	4
Householder				
In family	4,926	365	109	9
Not in family, living alone	5,580	1,404	506	145
Not in family, living with nonrelatives	819	94	24	3
Not a householder				
Child of householder with children under 18	228	—	—	—
Child of householder without children under 18	442	27	—	—
In family, other relative of householder[a]	1,087	176	91	31
Not in family	1,532	127	13	4
In primary family[b]				
Family householder	4,926	365	109	9
Child of householder	442	27	—	—
Other relative of householder	976	176	90	27
In related subfamily				
Child of householder	228	—	—	—
Other relative of householder	111	—	2	3
In unrelated subfamily				
Nonrelative of householder	161	—	—	—
Not in family groups				
Householder, living alone	5,580	1,404	506	145
Householder, living only with nonrelatives	819	94	24	3
Other nonrelative, living only with nonrelatives	1,371	127	13	4
Separated				
Both sexes				
Total	**5,391**	**331**	**89**	**23**
Householder				
In family household	1,951	73	5	—
Not in family household	1,729	192	58	13
Not a householder				
In family household	1,206	50	22	5
Not in family household	505	16	5	5
Householder				
In family	1,951	73	5	—
Not in family, living alone	1,492	174	54	11
Not in family, living with nonrelatives	238	19	4	2
Not a householder				
Child of householder with children under 18	163	—	—	—
Child of householder without children under 18	494	—	—	—
In family, other relative of householder[a]	549	50	22	5
Not in family	505	16	5	5
In primary family[b]				
Family householder	1,951	73	5	—
Child of householder	497	—	—	—
Other relative of householder	476	50	22	5
In related subfamily				
Child of householder	160	—	—	—
Other relative of householder	73	—	—	—
In unrelated subfamily				
Nonrelative of householder	35	—	—	—
Not in family groups				
Householder, living alone	1,492	174	54	11
Householder, living only with nonrelatives	238	19	4	2
Other nonrelative, living only with nonrelatives	470	16	5	5

The Innovations Exchange program (http://www.innovations.ahrq.gov) of the Agency for Healthcare Research and Quality (AHRQ) offers profiles of nursing home innovations and assessments of the effectiveness of these innovations in terms of improving residents' quality of life and satisfaction. The program also examines nursing homes' ability to attract and retain staff and their financial performance. By sharing and publicizing these innovations, the AHRQ aims to improve the quality of nursing home care.

TABLE 3.4

Divorced or separated older adults living alone, by age group, 2014 [CONTINUED]

[Numbers in thousands]

	Total 15 years and over	65–74 years	75–84 years	85+ years
Male				
Total	**2,226**	**136**	**52**	**9**
Householder				
In family household	423	20	—	—
Not in family household	945	90	36	4
Not a householder				
In family household	551	12	13	4
Not in family household	307	14	3	2
Householder				
In family	423	20	—	—
Not in family, living alone	817	77	32	2
Not in family, living with nonrelatives	129	13	4	2
Not a householder				
Child of householder with children under 18	34	—	—	—
Child of householder without children under 18	295	—	—	—
In family, other relative of householder[a]	222	12	13	4
Not in family	307	14	3	2
In primary family[b]				
Family householder	423	20	—	—
Child of householder	298	—	—	—
Other relative of householder	212	12	13	4
In related subfamily				
Child of householder	31	—	—	—
Other relative of householder	9	—	—	—
In unrelated subfamily				
Nonrelative of householder	2	—	—	—
Not in family groups				
Householder, living alone	817	77	32	2
Householder, living only with nonrelatives	129	13	4	2
Other nonrelative, living only with nonrelatives	305	14	3	2
Female				
Total	**3,165**	**195**	**37**	**14**
Householder				
In family household	1,528	53	5	—
Not in family household	784	103	22	9
Not a householder				
In family household	655	38	8	2
Not in family household	198	2	2	3
Householder				
In family	1,528	53	5	—
Not in family, living alone	675	97	22	9
Not in family, living with nonrelatives	109	6	—	—
Not a householder				
Child of householder with children under 18	128	—	—	—
Child of householder without children under 18	199	—	—	—
In family, other relative of householder[a]	327	38	8	2
Not in family	198	2	2	3
In primary family[b]				
Family householder	1,528	53	5	—
Child of householder	199	—	—	—
Other relative of householder	263	38	8	2
In related subfamily				
Child of householder	128	—	—	—
Other relative of householder	64	—	—	—
In unrelated subfamily				
Nonrelative of householder	33	—	—	—
Not in family groups				
Householder, living alone	675	97	22	9
Householder, living only with nonrelatives	109	6	—	—
Other nonrelative, living only with nonrelatives	165	2	2	3

For example, in "Messaging System Enables Nursing Home Residents to E-mail Loved Ones without a Computer, Leading to Enhanced Quality of Life" (August 27, 2014, https://innovations.ahrq.gov/profiles/messaging-system-enables-nursing-home-residents-e-mail-loved-ones-without-computer-leading), the AHRQ describes the use of a messaging system that enables residents to send and receive e-mail from family and friends without using a computer. Residents read incoming e-mail on printouts and respond by writing handwritten notes that are digitized and

	Total 15 years and over	65–74 years	75–84 years	85+ years
Never married				
Both sexes				
Total	**80,022**	**1,232**	**514**	**191**
Householder				
In family household	9,384	130	51	5
Not in family household	17,665	851	387	134
Not a householder				
In family household	42,302	174	49	40
Not in family household	10,672	77	26	11
Householder				
In family	9,384	130	51	5
Not in family, living alone	12,506	758	350	120
Not in family, living with nonrelatives	5,159	93	37	14
Not a householder				
Child of householder with children under 18	1,242	—	—	—
Child of householder without children under 18	34,145	24	—	—
In family, other relative of householder[a]	6,915	150	49	40
Not in family	10,672	77	26	11
In primary family[b]				
Family householder	9,384	130	51	5
Child of householder	34,215	24	—	—
Other relative of householder	5,955	146	49	40
In related subfamily				
Child of householder	1,172	—	—	—
Other relative of householder	960	4	—	—
In unrelated subfamily				
Nonrelative of householder	332	—	—	3
Not in family groups				
Householder, living alone	12,506	758	350	120
Householder, living only with nonrelatives	5,159	93	37	14
Other nonrelative, living only with nonrelatives	10,340	77	26	8
Male				
Total	**42,711**	**586**	**221**	**59**
Householder				
In family household	3,308	45	14	4
Not in family household	10,093	434	175	38
Not a householder				
In family household	23,467	61	19	15
Not in family household	5,843	46	14	3
Householder				
In family	3,308	45	14	4
Not in family, living alone	6,950	386	161	33
Not in family, living with nonrelatives	3,143	48	13	5
Not a householder				
Child of householder with children under 18	182	—	—	—
Child of householder without children under 18	19,295	14	—	—
In family, other relative of householder[a]	3,990	47	19	15
Not in family	5,843	46	14	3
In primary family[b]				
Family householder	3,308	45	14	4
Child of householder	19,356	14	—	—
Other relative of householder	3,642	47	19	15
In related subfamily				
Child of householder	121	—	—	—
Other relative of householder	348	—	—	—
In unrelated subfamily				
Nonrelative of householder	76	—	—	—
Not in family groups				
Householder, living alone	6,950	386	161	33
Householder, living only with nonrelatives	3,143	48	13	5
Other nonrelative, living only with nonrelatives	5,767	46	14	3

e-mailed. The AHRQ reports that improving residents' ability to communicate with others outside of the facility has "enhanced residents quality of life."

Besides physical modifications of the nursing homes to create more homelike dining rooms and bathrooms, the AHRQ reports in "Nursing Homes Create Home-Like,

[Numbers in thousands]

	Total 15 years and over	65–74 years	75–84 years	85+ years
Female				
Total	**37,311**	**646**	**292**	**132**
Householder				
In family household	6,076	85	37	2
Not in family household	7,572	417	213	97
Not a householder				
In family household	18,834	113	31	26
Not in family household	4,828	31	12	8
Householder				
In family	6,076	85	37	2
Not in family, living alone	5,556	372	189	87
Not in family, living with nonrelatives	2,016	45	24	9
Not a householder				
Child of householder with children under 18	1,059	—	—	—
Child of householder without children under 18	14,851	10	—	—
In family, other relative of householder[a]	2,924	103	31	26
Not in family	4,828	31	12	8
In primary family[b]				
Family householder	6,076	85	37	2
Child of householder	14,860	10	—	—
Other relative of householder	2,312	99	31	26
In related subfamily				
Child of householder	1,051	—	—	—
Other relative of householder	612	4	—	—
In unrelated subfamily				
Nonrelative of householder	255	—	—	3
Not in family groups				
Householder, living alone	5,556	372	189	87
Householder, living only with nonrelatives	2,016	45	24	9
Other nonrelative, living only with nonrelatives	4,573	31	12	4

[a]Includes spouses of householders.
[b]Excludes individuals who are also in related subfamilies.
Note: Prior to 2001, this table included people in group quarters.
Dash ("—") represents or rounds to zero.
The 2014 CPS ASEC included redesigned questions for income and health insurance coverage. All of the approximately 98,000 addresses were selected to receive the improved set of health insurance coverage items. The improved income questions were implemented using a split panel design. Approximately 68,000 addresses were selected to receive a set of income questions similar to those used in the 2013 CPS ASEC. The remaining 30,000 addresses were selected to receive the redesigned income questions. The source of data for this table is the CPS ASEC sample of 98,000 addresses.

SOURCE: Adapted from "Table A2. Family Status and Household Relationship of People 15 Years and over, by Marital Status, Age, and Sex: 2014," in *Families and Living Arrangements*, U.S. Census Bureau, 2014, http://www.census.gov/hhes/families/files/cps2014/tabA2-all.xls (accessed May 7, 2015)

Resident-Focused Environment and Culture, Leading to Better Quality and Financial Performance, Higher Resident Satisfaction, and Lower Staff Turnover" (January 21, 2010, http://www.leadingageiowa.org/files/public/homelike.pdf) on innovations that encourage communal "neighborhood" activities in nursing homes, such as decorating common areas or holding neighborhood celebrations of residents' birthdays. Instead of having the nursing home staff members rotate through the facility, they are permanently assigned to a specific neighborhood so they can get to know the residents and develop ongoing relationships. Staff members are given more scheduling flexibility, to better accommodate individual residents' preferences. At each nursing home a "quality of life specialist" visits with residents daily to assess and improve their comfort and quality of life.

The AHRQ reports that this initiative has resulted in improved quality of care as measured by key quality measures such as fewer reports of pain and fewer pressure ulcers (injuries to the skin and underlying tissue usually over a bony prominence that result from continuous pressure or friction in the area) as well as fewer formal complaints. Resident and family member satisfaction ratings rose from 59.5% in 2006 to 65% in 2007. Likewise, staff satisfaction increased between 2006 and 2007, from 58% to 75%. Staff retention also improved: the annual turnover rate of nursing assistants declined from 143% in 2005 to 96% in 2008.

The initiative has also improved the nursing homes' financial performance. Between 2005 and 2007 the nursing homes' census grew from 825 to 859, and this increase meant the facilities were operating very close to their capacity. Higher census counts and reduced staff turnover also significantly improved the nursing homes' net revenues, which tripled during this period.

THE EDEN ALTERNATIVE. Developed in 1991 by William Thomas, the Eden Alternative is a movement that, like the Pioneer Network, seeks to transform nursing homes. The Eden Alternative strives to create nursing homes that are rich and

TABLE 3.5

Grandparents living with grandchildren, 2013

	United States Estimate
Total	**189,483,359**
Living with own grandchildren under 18 years	7,188,581
Grandparent responsible for own grandchildren under 18 years	2,681,518
Grandparent responsible less than 6 months	276,990
Grandparent responsible 6 to 11 months	262,475
Grandparent responsible 1 or 2 years	617,232
Grandparent responsible 3 or 4 years	452,753
Grandparent responsible 5 years or more	1,072,068
Grandparent not responsible for own grandchildren under 18 years	4,507,063
Not living with own grandchildren under 18 years	182,294,778

SOURCE: "B10050. Grandparents Living with Own Grandchildren under 18 Years by Responsibility for Own Grandchildren by Length of Time Responsible for Own Grandchildren for the Population 30 Years and Over," in *American Community Survey*, U.S. Census Bureau, 2014, http://www2.census.gov/programs-surveys/acs/tech_docs/table_shells/2011/Detailed_Tables/B10050.xls (accessed May 7, 2015)

TABLE 3.6

Grandparents living with grandchildren, by poverty status, 2013

	United States Estimate
Total	**7,188,207**
Income in the past 12 months below poverty level	1,175,245
Grandparent responsible for own grandchildren under 18 years	569,251
30 to 59 years	389,217
60 years and over	180,034
Grandparent not responsible for own grandchildren under 18 years	605,994
Income in the past 12 months at or above poverty level	6,012,962
Grandparent responsible for own grandchildren under 18 years	2,112,147
30 to 59 years	1,295,828
60 years and over	816,319
Grandparent not responsible for own grandchildren under 18 years	3,900,815

SOURCE: "B10059. Poverty Status in the Past 12 Months of Grandparents Living with Own Grandchildren under 18 Years by Responsibility for Own Grandchildren and Age of Grandparent," in *American Community Survey*, U.S. Census Bureau, 2014, http://factfinder.census.gov/faces/tableservices/jsf/pages/productview.xhtml?src=bkmk (accessed May 7, 2015)

FIGURE 3.3

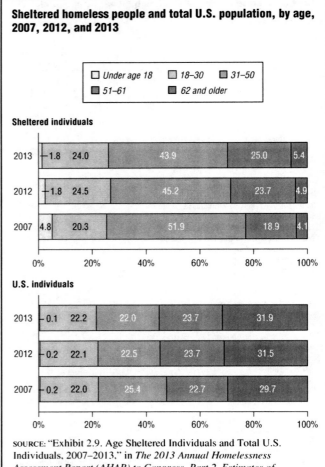

Sheltered homeless people and total U.S. population, by age, 2007, 2012, and 2013

SOURCE: "Exhibit 2.9. Age Sheltered Individuals and Total U.S. Individuals, 2007–2013," in *The 2013 Annual Homelessness Assessment Report (AHAR) to Congress. Part 2, Estimates of Homelessness in the United States*, U.S. Department of Housing and Urban Development, October 2014, https://www.hudexchange.info/onecpd/assets/File/2013-AHAR-Part-2.pdf (accessed May 8, 2015)

vibrant human habitats where plants, children, and animals bring life-enriching energy to residents. The philosophy of the Eden Alternative is that providing a stimulant-rich environment will help minimize the hopelessness that is often felt by nursing home residents. Nursing homes based on this model are being opened across the country.

By providing gardenlike settings filled with plants and encouraging relationships with children and pets, the Eden Alternative hopes to improve the human spirit and dispel loneliness. The 10 principles (2015, http://www.edenalt.org) of an Eden Alternative nursing home are:

1. The three plagues of loneliness, helplessness, and boredom account for the bulk of suffering among our Elders.

2. An Elder-centered community commits to creating a human habitat where life revolves around close and continuing contact with plants, animals, and children. It is these relationships that provide the young and old alike with a pathway to a life worth living.

3. Loving companionship is the antidote to loneliness. Elders deserve easy access to human and animal companionship.

4. An Elder-centered community creates opportunity to give as well as receive care. This is the antidote to helplessness.

5. An Elder-centered community imbues daily life with variety and spontaneity by creating an environment in which unexpected and unpredictable interactions and happenings can take place. This is the antidote to boredom.

6. Meaningless activity corrodes the human spirit. The opportunity to do things that we find meaningful is essential to human health.

TABLE 3.7

Nursing homes and occupancy rates, by state, selected years 1995–2013

[Data are based on a census of certified nursing facilities]

State	Residents				Occupancy rate*			
	1995	2000	2012	2013	1995	2000	2012	2013
				Number				
United States	1,479,550	1,480,076	1,383,488	1,371,926	84.5	82.4	81.2	80.8
Alabama	21,691	23,089	22,673	22,764	92.9	91.4	85.0	85.3
Alaska	634	595	591	498	77.9	72.5	87.0	63.9
Arizona	12,382	13,253	11,426	11,344	76.6	75.9	68.8	68.3
Arkansas	20,823	19,317	17,982	17,774	69.5	75.1	73.2	72.4
California	109,805	106,460	102,587	102,324	78.3	80.8	84.2	84.3
Colorado	17,055	17,045	16,136	15,957	85.7	84.2	79.2	78.3
Connecticut	29,948	29,657	24,948	24,610	91.2	91.4	89.5	88.4
Delaware	3,819	3,900	4,268	4,217	80.6	79.5	86.7	84.6
District of Columbia	2,576	2,858	2,604	2,569	80.3	92.9	94.1	92.9
Florida	61,845	69,050	72,286	72,679	85.1	82.8	87.1	87.4
Georgia	35,933	36,559	34,122	33,889	94.3	91.8	85.6	85.0
Hawaii	2,413	3,558	3,738	3,714	96.0	88.8	88.6	88.1
Idaho	4,697	4,640	4,074	3,909	81.7	75.1	68.7	65.9
Illinois	83,696	83,604	73,849	72,856	81.1	75.5	74.0	73.7
Indiana	44,328	42,328	39,310	38,649	74.5	74.6	66.3	65.8
Iowa	27,506	29,204	25,077	24,980	68.8	78.9	71.5	77.6
Kansas	25,140	22,230	18,596	18,400	83.8	82.1	73.1	71.7
Kentucky	20,696	22,730	23,051	22,818	89.1	89.7	88.7	87.2
Louisiana	32,493	30,735	25,906	25,600	86.0	77.9	72.7	72.8
Maine	8,587	7,298	6,395	6,342	92.9	88.5	90.6	90.3
Maryland	24,716	25,629	24,543	24,360	87.0	81.4	85.0	85.5
Massachusetts	49,765	49,805	42,204	41,595	91.3	88.9	86.7	85.5
Michigan	43,271	42,615	39,307	39,288	87.5	84.1	84.2	83.6
Minnesota	41,163	38,813	27,789	27,201	93.8	92.1	89.9	89.5
Mississippi	15,247	15,815	16,304	16,165	94.9	92.7	88.0	87.1
Missouri	39,891	38,586	37,998	37,828	75.7	70.4	68.9	68.7
Montana	6,415	5,973	4,657	4,689	89.0	77.9	68.7	69.9
Nebraska	16,166	14,989	12,235	12,070	89.0	83.8	76.6	76.1
Nevada	3,645	3,657	4,625	4,749	91.2	65.9	77.2	79.4
New Hampshire	6,877	7,158	6,938	6,813	92.8	91.3	91.7	90.7
New Jersey	40,397	45,837	45,499	45,450	91.9	87.8	87.3	86.7
New Mexico	6,051	6,503	5,669	5,531	86.8	89.2	82.2	82.4
New York	103,409	112,957	107,481	105,965	96.0	93.7	91.6	91.0
North Carolina	35,511	36,658	37,313	36,908	92.7	88.6	84.7	82.8
North Dakota	6,868	6,343	5,694	5,702	96.4	91.2	90.7	92.9
Ohio	79,026	81,946	78,075	77,129	73.9	78.0	84.7	84.2
Oklahoma	26,377	23,833	19,315	19,376	77.8	70.3	66.9	65.9
Oregon	11,673	9,990	7,334	7,373	84.1	74.0	60.0	60.1
Pennsylvania	84,843	83,880	80,055	79,554	91.6	88.2	90.4	90.1
Rhode Island	8,823	9,041	7,978	7,986	91.8	88.0	91.9	91.6
South Carolina	14,568	15,739	16,900	16,744	87.3	86.9	86.1	85.0
South Dakota	7,926	7,059	6,371	6,335	95.5	90.0	91.7	91.7
Tennessee	33,929	34,714	31,189	29,990	91.5	89.9	83.2	80.7
Texas	89,354	85,275	93,710	93,712	72.6	68.2	69.8	69.2
Utah	5,832	5,703	5,423	5,383	82.1	74.5	63.9	63.3
Vermont	1,792	3,349	2,761	2,726	96.2	89.5	86.3	85.2
Virginia	28,119	27,091	28,260	28,249	93.5	88.5	87.5	86.6
Washington	24,954	21,158	17,272	17,199	87.7	81.7	79.4	79.5
West Virginia	10,216	10,334	9,535	9,524	93.7	90.5	87.9	87.5
Wisconsin	43,998	38,911	29,000	28,062	90.2	83.9	82.5	80.8
Wyoming	2,661	2,605	2,435	2,377	87.7	83.5	81.6	79.7

—Data not available.

*Percentage of beds occupied (number of nursing home residents per 100 nursing home beds).

Notes: Annual numbers of nursing homes, beds, and residents are based on the Centers for Medicare & Medicaid Services' reporting cycle. Starting with 2013 data, a new editing rule was used for number of beds. For the U.S., the number of beds decreased by less than 1%. For most states, this caused little or no change in the data. For some states, the number of beds changed by up to 8%. The change in the number of beds also caused a change in some occupancy rates. Because of the methodology change, trends should be interpreted with caution. Data for additional years are available.

SOURCE: Adapted from "Table 101. Nursing Homes, Beds, Residents, and Occupancy Rates, by State: United States, Selected Years 1995–2013," in *Health, United States, 2014: With Special Feature on Adults Aged 55–64*, National Center for Health Statistics, May 2015, http://www.cdc.gov/nchs/data/hus/hus14.pdf (accessed May 8, 2015)

7. Medical treatment should be the servant of genuine human caring, never its master.

8. An Elder-centered community honors its Elders by de-emphasizing top-down bureaucratic authority, seeking instead to place the maximum possible decision-making authority into the hands of the Elders or into the hands of those closest to them.

9. Creating an Elder-centered community is a never-ending process. Human growth must never be separated from human life.

10. Wise leadership is the lifeblood of any struggle against the three plagues. For it, there can be no substitute.

Thomas's initiatives also include the Green House Project, the construction of small group homes for older adults, built to a residential scale that situates necessary clinical care within a social model in which primacy is given to the older adults' quality of life. The goal of this social model is to provide frail older adults with an environment that promotes autonomy, dignity, privacy, and choice. The Green House Project asserts that its model of care "delivers better outcomes than traditional nursing homes, reducing the cost of care, fostering stronger partnerships with referral sources and can be operated at costs comparable to traditional nursing care."

Green Houses are designed to feel more like homes than typical long-term care institutions and to blend easily into their community or surroundings. The first Green House in the nation opened in May 2003 in Tupelo, Mississippi, developed by United Methodist Senior Services of Mississippi. The Robert Wood Johnson Foundation (http://www.rwjf.org/en/grants/grantees/the-green-house-project.html) reports that in 2015 more than 260 Green Houses were operating or underway in 32 states.

Characteristics of People Receiving Long-Term Care

In "Long-Term Care Services in the United States, 2013 Overview" (*NCHS Statistics Report*, no. 1, 2013), Lauren Harris-Kojetin et al. present key findings from the NCHS National Study of Long-Term Care Providers. In 2012 there were 273,200 people in adult day services centers, 1,383,700 residents in nursing homes, and 713,300 people living in residential care communities. In 2011 about 4,742,500 patients received home health services, and 1,244,500 patients received hospice services. Together, these long-term care service providers served about 8.4 million people annually. Figure 3.4 shows the distribution of long-term care recipients by age and type of provider. Users of all types of long-term care services are overwhelmingly female and non-Hispanic white. (See Figure 3.5 and Figure 3.6.)

Many users of long-term care services received help with the activities of daily living. For example, 96.1% of

FIGURE 3.4

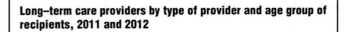

Long–term care providers by type of provider and age group of recipients, 2011 and 2012

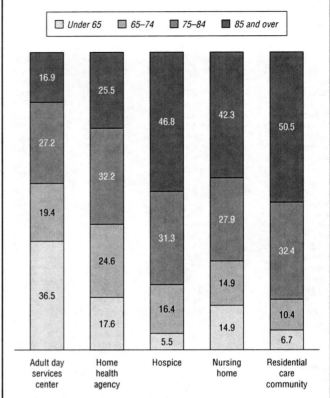

Notes: Denominators used to calculate percentages for adult day services centers, nursing homes, and residential care communities were the number of participants enrolled in adult day services centers, the number of residents in nursing homes, and the number of residents in residential care communities on a given day in 2012. Denominators used to calculate percentages for home health agencies and hospices were the number of patients whose episode of care in a home health agency ended at any time in 2011, and the number of patients who received care from Medicare-certified hospices at any time in 2011. Percentages may not add to 100 because of rounding. Percentages are based on the unrounded

SOURCE: Lauren Harris-Kojetin et al., "Figure 20. Percent Distribution of Long-Term Care Services Providers, by Provider Type and Age Group: United States, 2011 and 2012," in "Long-Term Care Services in the United States, 2013," *Vital Health Statistics*, series 3, no. 37, December 2013, http://www.cdc.gov/nchs/data/nsltcp/long_term_care_services_2013.pdf (accessed May 8, 2015)

nursing home residents needed help with bathing, 90.9% needed help dressing, 86.6% required assistance with toileting, and 56% needed help to eat. (See Figure 3.7.)

Assisted Living

Assisted living arose to bridge a gap in long-term care. It is a type of residential care intended to meet the needs of older adults who wish to live independently in the community but require some of the services (e.g., housekeeping, meals, transportation, and assistance with other activities of daily living) provided by a nursing home. Assisted living offers a flexible array of services that enable older adults to maintain as much independence as they can, for as long as possible.

FIGURE 3.5

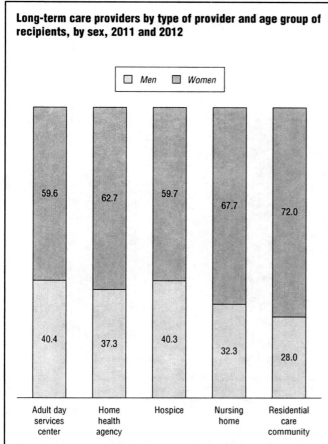

Long-term care providers by type of provider and age group of recipients, by sex, 2011 and 2012

Men Women

Adult day services center: Men 40.4, Women 59.6
Home health agency: Men 37.3, Women 62.7
Hospice: Men 40.3, Women 59.7
Nursing home: Men 32.3, Women 67.7
Residential care community: Men 28.0, Women 72.0

Notes: Denominators used to calculate percentages for adult day services centers, nursing homes, and residential care communities were the number of participants enrolled in adult day services centers, the number of residents in nursing homes, and the number of residents in residential care communities on a given day in 2012. Denominators used to calculate percentages for home health agencies and hospices were the number of patients whose episode of care in a home health agency ended at any time in 2011, and the number of patients who received care from Medicare-certified hospices at any time in 2011. Percentages may not add to 100 because of rounding. Percentages are based on the unrounded numbers.

SOURCE: Lauren Harris-Kojetin et al., Figure 21. Percent Distribution of Users of Long-Term Care Services Providers, by Provider Type and Sex: United States, 2011 and 2012," in "Long-Term Care Services in the United States, 2013," *Vital Health Statistics*, series 3, no. 37, December 2013, http://www.cdc.gov/nchs/data/nsltcp/long_term_care_services_2013.pdf (accessed May 8, 2015)

FIGURE 3.6

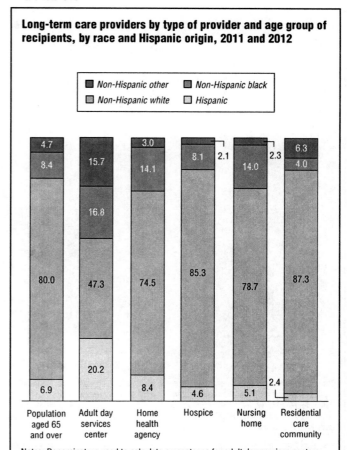

Long-term care providers by type of provider and age group of recipients, by race and Hispanic origin, 2011 and 2012

Non-Hispanic other Non-Hispanic black
Non-Hispanic white Hispanic

Population aged 65 and over: Non-Hispanic other 4.7, Non-Hispanic black 8.4, Non-Hispanic white 80.0, Hispanic 6.9
Adult day services center: Non-Hispanic black 15.7, Non-Hispanic other 16.8, Non-Hispanic white 47.3, Hispanic 20.2
Home health agency: 3.0, 14.1, 74.5, 8.4
Hospice: 8.1, 2.1, 85.3, 4.6
Nursing home: 14.0, 2.3, 78.7, 5.1
Residential care community: 6.3, 4.0, 87.3, 2.4

Notes: Denominators used to calculate percentages for adult day services centers, nursing homes, and residential care communities were the number of participants enrolled in adult day services centers, the number of residents in nursing homes, and the number of residents in residential care communities on a given day in 2012. Denominators used to calculate percentages for home health agencies and hospices were the number of patients whose episode of care in a home health agency ended at any time in 2011, and the number of patients who received care from Medicare-certified hospices at any time in 2011. Percentages may not add to 100 because of rounding. Percentages are based on the unrounded numbers.

SOURCE: Lauren Harris-Kojetin et al., "Figure 22. Percent Distribution of Users of Long-Term Care Services, by Provider Type and Race and Hispanic Origin: United States, 2011 and 2012," in "Long-Term Care Services in the United States, 2013," *Vital Health Statistics*, series 3, no. 37, December 2013, http://www.cdc.gov/nchs/data/nsltcp/long_term_care_services_2013.pdf (accessed May 8, 2015)

Because assisted living refers to a concept and philosophy as opposed to a regulated provider of health services such as a hospital or SNF, there is no uniform description of the services an assisted living residence must offer, and as a result there is considerable variation among assisted living facilities. These residences are regulated on a state level, and each state has its own definition of what constitutes an assisted living facility and its own set of rules that govern them. The AHRQ defines in "Assisted Living Defined" (2015, http://archive.ahrq.gov/professionals/systems/long-term-care/resources/facilities/ltcscan/ltc3.html) the term *assisted living* as "a type of residential long-term care setting known by nearly 30 different names" that includes "24-hour service and oversight, services that

meet scheduled and unscheduled needs, and care/services that promote independence, with an emphasis on dignity, autonomy, choice, privacy, and home-like environment."

In "Assisted Living" (2015, http://www.alfa.org/alfa/Assisted_Living_Information.asp), the Assisted Living Federation of America describes the goal of assisted living: "To provide personalized, resident-centered care in order to meet individual preferences and needs. Assisted living treats all residents with dignity, provides privacy and encourages independence and freedom of choice. Residents' family members and friends are encouraged to get involved in the assisted living community."

FIGURE 3.7

Percentages of long-term care users requiring assistance with the activities of daily living, 2011 and 2012

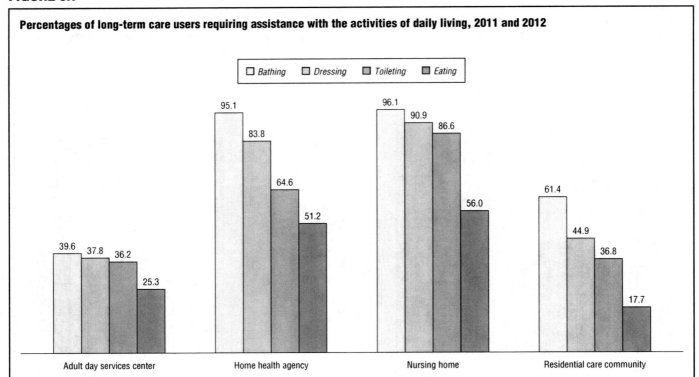

Notes: Denominators used to calculate percentages for adult day services centers, nursing homes, and residential care communities were the number of participants enrolled in adult day services centers, the number of residents in nursing homes, and the number of residents in residential care communities on a given day in 2012. Denominator used to calculate percentages for home health agencies was the number of patients whose episode of care in a home health agency ended at any time in 2011. Participants, patients, or residents were considered needing any assistance with a given activity if they needed help or supervision from another person, or they used special equipment to perform the activity. Percentages are based on the unrounded numbers.

SOURCE: Lauren Harris-Kojetin et al., "Figure 24. Percentage of Users of Long-Term Care Services Needing Any Assistance with Activities of Daily Living, by Provider Type and Activity: United States, 2011 and 2012," in "Long-Term Care Services in the United States, 2013," *Vital Health Statistics*, series 3, no. 37, December 2013, http://www.cdc.gov/nchs/data/nsltcp/long_term_care_services_2013.pdf (accessed May 8, 2015)

Assisted living residences may be located on the grounds of retirement communities or in nursing homes, or they may be freestanding residential facilities. They vary in size, location, and services. Some are high-rise apartment complexes, whereas others are converted private homes. Most contain between 25 and 120 units, which vary in size from one room to a full apartment.

Assisted living licensing regulations vary from state to state. Most states require staff certification and training, and all assisted living facilities must comply with local building codes and fire safety regulations.

BOARD-AND-CARE FACILITIES. Board-and-care facilities were the earliest form of assisted living. In *Licensed Board and Care Homes: Preliminary Findings from the 1991 National Health Provider Inventory* (April 11, 1994, http://aspe.hhs.gov/daltcp/reports/licbchom.htm), Robert F. Clark et al. define the term *board-and-care homes* as "non-medical community-based facilities that provide protective oversight and/or personal care in addition to meals and lodging to one or more residents with functional or cognitive limitations." Typically, board-and-care residents

have their own bedrooms and bathrooms or share them with one other person, whereas other living areas are shared.

Although many board-and-care facilities offer residents safe, homelike environments and attentive caregivers, there have been many well-publicized instances of fraud and abuse. Observers attribute the variability in quality of these facilities to the fact that they are unregulated in many states and as a result receive little oversight.

In an attempt to stem abuses, the federal government passed the Keys Amendment in 1978. Under the terms of this legislation, residents living in board-and-care facilities that fail to provide adequate care are subject to reduced SSI payments. This move was intended to penalize substandard board-and-care operators, but advocates for older adults contend that it actually penalizes the SSI recipients and that it has not reduced reports of abuse. With the 1992 reauthorization of the Older Americans Act of 1965, Congress provided for long-term care ombudsman programs that are designed to help prevent the abuse, exploitation, and neglect of residents in long-term care facilities such as board-and-care residences and nursing homes. Paid and volunteer ombudsmen monitor facilities and act as advocates for residents.

The AoA reports in "Data Highlight Extensive Services Provided to Persons Living in Long-Term Care Facilities" (December 31, 2014, http://www.aoa.acl.gov/AoA_Programs/Elder_Rights/Ombudsman/index.aspx) that in fiscal year (FY) 2013, 1,233 full-time long-term care ombudsmen and 8,290 trained volunteers investigated and resolved nearly three-quarters (73%) of a total of 190,592 complaints. The most frequent complaints leveled against nursing facilities in 2013 related to:

- Inadequate discharge/planning
- Unanswered requests for help
- Disrespectful treatment of residents, poor staff attitudes
- Resident/roommate conflict
- Administration of medications

The most frequent concerns at board-and-care facilities were:

- Quality, variety, and choice of food
- Administration and organization of medications
- Inadequate discharge/planning
- Disrespectful treatment of residents, poor staff attitudes
- Hazardous conditions or equipment in disrepair

Total program expenditures from all sources for the Long-Term Care Ombudsman Program including the Older Americans Act Title III, Title VII, and other federal, state, and local sources rose from $84.9 million in FY 2009 to $92.5 million in FY 2013. Interestingly, researchers investigating national trends in reporting abuse and neglect in nursing facilities find that complaints reported to long-term care ombudsmen decreased from 7.5 per 100 beds in 2006 to 5.6 per 100 beds in 2013. In "Trends in Reporting of Abuse and Neglect to Long-Term Care Ombudsmen: Data from the National Ombudsman Reporting System from 2006 to 2013" (*Geriatric Nursing*, April 30, 2015), Elizabeth M. Bloemen et al. find that the most frequent complaints, accounting for more than one-quarter of complaints (28%), involved physical abuse.

COSTS OF ASSISTED LIVING. The cost of assisted living varies based on geography, unit size, and the services needed. The *Genworth 2015 Cost of Care Survey* (2015, https://www.genworth.com/dam/Americas/US/PDFs/Consumer/corporate/130568_040115_gnw.pdf) reports that the national average assisted-living base rates increased by 2.9% in 2014. The national median monthly rate was $3,600. Most assisted living facilities charge monthly rates and some require long-term leases.

Residents or their families generally pay for assisted living using their own financial resources. Some health insurance programs or long-term care insurance policies reimburse for specific health-related care that is provided, and some state and local governments offer subsidies for rent or services for low-income older adults. Others may provide subsidies in the form of an additional payment for those who receive SSI or Medicaid.

Continuing Care Retirement Communities

Continuing care retirement communities (CCRCs), also known as life care communities, offer a continuum of care (independent living, assisted living, and nursing home care) in a single facility or on common grounds. The goal of CCRCs is to enable residents to age in place (remaining in their own home rather than relocating to assisted living facilities or other supportive housing). When residents become ill or disabled, for example, they do not have to relocate to a nursing home, because medical care is available on the CCRC campus.

Like assisted living facilities, CCRCs vary in location, design, and amenities. They range from urban high rises to semirural campuses and from 100 to more than 1,000 residents. Most include common dining rooms, activity and exercise areas, indoor and outdoor recreation areas, and swimming pools.

Typically, residents are required to pay an entrance fee and a fixed monthly fee in return for housing, meals, personal care, recreation, and nursing services. Many CCRCs offer other payment options, including both entrance fee and fee-for-service (paid for each visit, procedure, or treatment delivered) arrangements. In the past entrance fees were nonrefundable; by 2015, however, many CCRCs offered refundable or partially refundable entrance fees.

CCRCs may be operated by private, nonprofit, or religious organizations. According to Lori Johnston, in "The Big Boom in Continuing Care" (GulfshoreBusiness.com, February 2015), developers are investing heavily into new and existing communities and are emphasizing luxurious independent and assisted living accommodations. In existing communities in Florida, occupancy rates are 90% or higher. With few exceptions, government or private insurance does not cover the costs of CCRCs. The AARP reports in "About Continuing Care Communities" (September 2010, http://www.aarp.org/relationships/caregiving-resource-center/info-09-2010/ho_continuing_care_retirement_communities.html) that entrance fees range from $100,000 to $1 million and monthly fees range from $3,000 to $5,000.

Shared Housing and Cohousing

Older adults may share living quarters to reduce expenses, share household and home maintenance responsibilities, and gain companionship. Many choose to share the same homes in which they raised their families because these houses are often large enough to accommodate more than one or two people. Shared housing is often called cohousing, but the terms are not exactly the same.

Most shared housing consists of a single homeowner taking a roommate to share living space and expenses. Shared housing can also include households with three or more roommates and family-like cooperatives in which large groups of people live together. In contrast, cohousing usually refers to planned or intentional communities of private dwellings with shared common areas that include dining rooms, meeting rooms, and recreation facilities. Shared housing and cohousing are cost-effective alternatives for those who wish to remain in their own home and for older adults who cannot afford assisted living or CCRCs.

The cohousing concept originated in Denmark during the 1960s and spread to the United States during the 1980s. According to the Cohousing Association of the United States (http://www.cohousing.org/directory), in 2015 there were more than 200 cohousing communities in various stages of development in 37 states and the District of Columbia. Cohousing participants are involved in planning the community and maintaining it, and most cohousing groups make their decisions by consensus.

Shared housing or intergenerational cohousing may also meet the needs of younger as well as older people. Along with the benefits of cost-sharing and companionship, home sharers and cohousing residents may exchange services (for example, help with household maintenance in exchange for babysitting).

Elder Cottage Housing Opportunity Units

Elder cottage housing opportunity (ECHO) units, or "granny flats," are small, freestanding, removable housing units that are located on the same lot as a single-family house. Another name used by local zoning authorities is accessory apartments or units. Accessory dwellings are self-contained second living units built into or attached to an existing single-family dwelling. They are generally smaller than the primary unit, and usually contain one or two bedrooms, a bathroom, a sitting room, and a kitchen.

Generally, families construct ECHO units and accessory apartments for parents or grandparents so that the older adults can be nearby while maintaining their independence. Existing zoning laws and concerns about property values are obstacles to the construction of ECHO units, but as this alternative becomes more popular, local jurisdictions may be pressured to allow multifamily housing in neighborhoods that traditionally have had only single-family homes.

Although there are no available data about the number of new and existing ECHO units, in "The Hottest Home Amenity: In-Law Apartments" (WSJ.com, November 6, 2014), Katy McLaughlin reports that homes with accessory dwelling units typically sell for 60% more than similar single-family homes and have become "the hottest amenity in real estate these days." She reports that a building industry survey of homebuyers in 2012 indicated that nearly one-third (32%) of those with living parents "expected to have an aging relative live with them in the future," and the Miami, Florida–based builder Lenmar, which introduced multigenerational home plans in 2011, reported a 27% increase in sales of such units in one year. McLaughlin notes, "While the adult children get the peace of mind of having mom and dad nearby, real-estate agents say the in-law accommodations are adding value to their homes."

Retirement Communities

Developers such as the industry leader Del Webb (a division of PulteGroup) have constructed communities and even entire small "cities" exclusively for older adults. Examples include the Sun City communities in Arizona, Florida, and Texas. The Arizona and Florida communities opened during the 1960s and the Texas community in 1996.

In 2015 Del Webb (http://www.delwebb.com/index .aspx) boasted more than 50 communities in 22 states. Homes in most of these properties were available only to those families in which at least one member was 55 years or older, and no one under the age of 19 years was allowed to reside permanently. Sun City communities offer clubs, golf courses, social organizations, fitness clubs, organized travel, and recreational complexes. Medical facilities are located nearby.

Housing Slump Imperils Older Adults and Limits Their Mobility

Many older adults and baby boomers aspire to relocate to CCRCs or purchase new homes in active retirement communities, but it is likely that only those with considerable financial resources will be able to do so. The decline in residential real estate prices, which began in 2006 and persisted in many parts of the country throughout 2015, made it difficult for older adults to sell their homes. Besides losing equity in their homes as prices declined, many older adults also saw their retirement assets erode. Although retirement accounts had generally rebounded by 2015, the aftereffects of the Great Recession worried older adults, prompting many to forgo or postpone plans to relocate.

In "Housing America's Older Adults: Meeting the Needs of an Aging Population" (2014, http://www.aarp .org/content/dam/aarp/livable-communities/documents-2014/Harvard-Housing-Americas-Older-Adults-2014.pdf), the Joint Center for Housing Studies of Harvard University reports that "in the aftermath of the Great Recession, households in the 50–64-year-old age range are less prepared for their retirement years than previous generations. Indeed, these younger baby boomers have lower homeownership rates, more housing and non-housing debt, and fewer children to care for them in old age. It is critical that this population in particular consider now how they will meet their changing financial and housing needs."

OWNING AND RENTING A HOME

In the press release "Residential Vacancies and Homeownership in the First Quarter 2015" (April 28, 2015, http://www.census.gov/housing/hvs/files/qtr115/currenthvspress.pdf), the Census Bureau notes that the overall homeownership rate during the first quarter of 2015 was 63.7%, down from the highest rate of 69.2% during the fourth quarter of 2004. (See Figure 3.8.) During the first quarter of 2015, 75.8% of adults aged 55 to 64 years and 79% of adults aged 65 years and older owned their own homes. (See Table 3.8.)

The AoA reports in *A Profile of Older Americans: 2014* that in 2013 nearly half of older adults devoted more than a quarter of their income to housing costs (39% of homeowners and 69% of renters). In 2013 the median value (the middle value; half of all homes are lower and half are higher) of homes owned by older adults was $150,000, but because the median purchase price of these homes was just $63,900, 65% of older homeowners had no mortgage debt; they owned their homes free and clear.

Renters generally pay a higher percentage of their income for housing than do homeowners. Unlike most homeowners, who pay fixed monthly mortgage payments, renters often face annual rent increases. Many older adult renters living on fixed incomes are unprepared to pay these increases. Homeowners also benefit from their home equity and can borrow against it in times of financial need. In contrast, renters do not build equity and do not get a return on their investment. Also, mortgage payments are tax deductible, whereas rent payments are not.

Reverse Mortgages

To supplement their retirement income or to pay for health care, many older Americans turn to reverse mortgages. Reverse mortgages allow homeowners to convert some of their home equity into cash, making it possible for them to avoid selling their home.

In a traditional mortgage homeowners make monthly payments to the lender. In a reverse mortgage the lender pays the homeowner in monthly installments and in most cases no repayment is due until the homeowner dies, sells the house, or moves. Reverse mortgages help homeowners who have considerable equity in their home to stay in their home and still meet their financial obligations.

A key disadvantage of a reverse mortgage is that when the home is no longer used as the primary residence of the borrower, the cash, interest, and finance charges must be repaid. This is generally accomplished by selling the home, and the spouse or heirs only receive any funds in excess of this obligation.

FIGURE 3.8

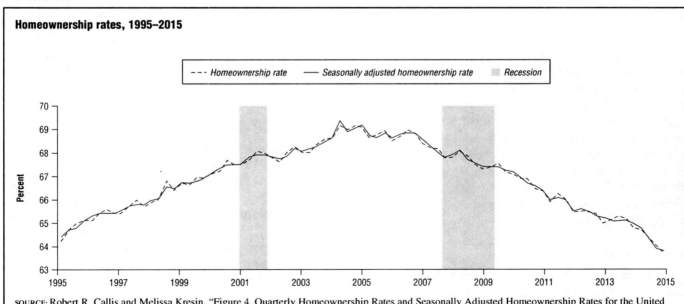

Homeownership rates, 1995–2015

SOURCE: Robert R. Callis and Melissa Kresin, "Figure 4. Quarterly Homeownership Rates and Seasonally Adjusted Homeownership Rates for the United States, 1995 to 2015," in *Residential Vacancies and Homeownership in the First Quarter 2015*, U.S. Census Bureau, April 28, 2015, http://www.census .gov/housing/hvs/files/qtr115/currenthvspress.pdf (accessed May 8, 2015)

TABLE 3.8

Homeownership rates, by age of householder, 2009–15

Year/quarter	Homeownership rates					
	United States	Under 35 years	35 to 44 years	45 to 54 years	55 to 64 years	65 years and over
2015						
First quarter	63.7	34.6	58.4	70.1	75.8	79.0
2014						
Fourth quarter	64.0	35.3	58.8	70.5	75.8	79.5
Third quarter	64.4	36.0	59.1	70.1	76.6	80.0
Second quarter	64.7	35.9	60.2	70.7	76.4	80.1
First quarter	64.8	36.2	60.7	71.4	76.4	79.9
2013						
Fourth quarter	65.2	36.8	60.9	71.4	76.5	80.7
Third quarter	65.3	36.8	61.1	71.3	76.2	81.2
Second quarter	65.0	36.7	60.3	70.9	76.7	80.9
First quarter	65.0	36.8	60.1	71.3	77.0	80.4
2012						
Fourth quarter	65.4	37.1	60.4	72.1	77.6	80.7
Third quarter	65.5	36.3	61.8	72.0	76.9	81.4
Second quarter	65.5	36.5	62.2	71.4	77.1	81.6
First quarter	65.4	36.8	61.4	71.3	77.8	80.9
2011						
Fourth quarter	66.0	37.6	62.3	72.7	79.0	80.9
Third quarter	66.3	38.0	63.4	72.7	78.6	81.1
Second quarter	65.9	37.5	63.8	72.3	77.8	80.8
First quarter	66.4	37.9	64.4	73.1	78.6	81.0
2010						
Fourth quarter	66.5	39.2	63.9	72.7	79.0	80.5
Third quarter	66.9	39.2	65.2	73.0	79.2	80.6
Second quarter	66.9	39.0	65.6	73.6	78.7	80.4
First quarter	67.1	38.9	65.3	74.8	79.1	80.6
2009						
Fourth quarter	67.2	40.4	65.7	74.0	78.9	80.2
Third quarter	67.6	39.8	66.5	74.5	79.4	80.9
Second quarter	67.4	39.0	66.8	74.5	79.9	80.4
First quarter	67.3	39.8	65.7	74.6	79.8	80.4

SOURCE: Robert R. Callis and Melissa Kresin, "Table 6. Homeownership Rates by Age of Householder: 2009 to 2015 (in Percent)," in *Residential Vacancies and Homeownership in the First Quarter 2015*, U.S. Census Bureau, April 28, 2015, http://www.census.gov/housing/hvs/files/qtr115/currenthvspress.pdf (accessed May 8, 2015)

In an effort to prevent loan defaults, in March 2015 the requirements for obtaining a reverse mortgage became more stringent. The new rules, which apply to reverse mortgage loans under the Home Equity Conversion Mortgage program, require borrowers to pass a financial assessment. Borrowers must show that they can pay property taxes and insurance premiums on the property. Historically, reverse mortgages were based on the borrower's age, the value of the home, and prevailing interest rates. Under the new rules, lenders consider borrowers' income and credit histories to ensure their ability to meet their financial obligations.

Sale/Leaseback with Life Tenancy

Another option for older homeowners is a sale/leaseback in which the homeowner gives up ownership of the home and becomes a renter. The former homeowner frequently requests life tenancy, retaining the right to live in the house as a renter for the rest of his or her life. The buyer pays the former homeowner in monthly installments and is responsible for property taxes, insurance, maintenance, and repairs.

Renting Is Often Unaffordable

In *Out of Reach 2013* (2014, http://nlihc.org/sites/default/files/oor/2014OOR.pdf), Althea Arnold et al. of the National Low Income Housing Coalition document income and rental housing cost data for the 50 states, the District of Columbia, and Puerto Rico. For each area, the researchers calculate the income that is needed to be able to afford the fair market rent of the housing. They also calculate the number of full-time minimum-wage jobs that are necessary to afford the fair market rent, which highlights the hardships that are faced by many families with varying numbers of wage earners.

Arnold et al. indicate that in 2014, 35% of all households were renters and that same year the number of renter households increased by 1.1 million, the single largest annual increase since the early 1980s. In 2014 rents rose 3.2% from 2013. The rental vacancy rate fell from 8% in 2009 to 4.1% at the end of 2013. In 2014 the average hourly wage was $14.64. The researchers observe, however, that renters must earn $18.92 per hour to afford an apartment while spending no more than 30% of their income on housing. Older adults relying solely on SSI payments could not afford rental housing. Arnold et al. state, "There is not a single county in the U.S. where even a modest efficiency apartment is affordable for an individual receiving the maximum federal SSI benefit."

HOUSING CHALLENGES FOR OLDER ADULTS
Physical Hazards and Accommodations

Home characteristics that are considered desirable by younger householders may present challenges to older adults. For example, the staircase in a two-story house may become a formidable obstacle to an older adult suffering from arthritis, heart disease, or other disabling conditions. Narrow halls and doorways cannot accommodate walkers and wheelchairs. High cabinets and shelves may be beyond the reach of an arthritis sufferer. Although houses can be modified to meet the physical needs of older or disabled people, some older houses cannot be remodeled as easily, and retrofitting them may be quite costly. Owners of condominiums in Florida, whose young-old (aged 65 to 74 years) residents once prized second- and third-floor units for their breezes and golf course views, are now considering installing elevators for residents in their 80s and 90s who find climbing stairs more difficult.

Older adults, as well as advocates on their behalf, express a strong preference for aging in place. Much research confirms that most people over the age of 55 years want to remain in familiar surroundings rather than move to alternative housing. To live more comfortably, those older adults who have the means can redesign and reequip their home to accommodate the physical changes that are associated with aging.

Simple adaptations include replacing doorknobs with levers that can be pushed downward with a fist or elbow, requiring no gripping or twisting; replacing light switches with flat "touch" switches; placing closet rods at adjustable heights; installing stoves with front- or side-mounted controls; and marking steps with bright colors. More complex renovations include replacing a bathroom with a wet room (a tiled space that is large enough to accommodate a wheelchair and equipped with a showerhead, waterproof chair, and sloping floor for a drain), placing electrical outlets higher than usual, and widening passageways and doorways for walkers, wheelchairs, or scooters.

Anticipating the increase in the older population, some real estate developers are manufacturing houses that are designed to meet the needs of older adults and prolong their ability to live independently. These houses feature accommodations such as nonskid flooring, walls strong enough to support grab bars, outlets at convenient heights, levers instead of knobs on doors and plumbing fixtures, and doorways and hallways wide enough for wheelchair access.

More technologically advanced homes, called smart homes, feature an array of adaptive technologies, such as embedded computers, sensors that detect motion and falls, and automated blood pressure monitoring, that aim to help older adults remain in their homes and age in place. For example, the article "'Magic Carpet' Could Help Prevent Falls" (September 4, 2012, http://www.manchester.ac.uk/aboutus/news/display/?id=8648) reports that researchers at the University of Manchester developed a carpet with optical fibers that sense and map walking patterns. By analyzing the movements of a person walking on it, the carpet can identify if the person's gait is unsteady or if the person has tripped or fallen. According to the Juniper Research report "Smart Home Ecosystems & the Internet of Things" (December 2, 2014, http://www.juniperresearch.com/researchstore/key-vertical-markets/smart-home-ecosystems-internet-of-things/market-trends-competitive-landscape), the global smart home market will grow from $33 billion in 2014 to $71 billion by 2018.

PUBLIC HOUSING

Congress passed the U.S. Housing Act of 1937 to create low-income public housing, but according to the Milbank Memorial Fund and the Council of Large Public Housing Authorities, in *Public Housing and Supportive Services for the Frail Elderly: A Guide for Housing Authorities and Their Collaborators* (September 2006, http://www.milbank.org/reports/0609publichousing/0609publichousing.pdf), by 1952 only a small percentage of available housing was occupied by older adults. After 1956, when Congress authorized the development of dedicated public housing for the elderly and specifically made low-income older adults eligible for such housing, the situation improved. During the 1960s and 1970s many developments for low-income older adults were constructed. These apartments were sufficient for most residents, but they were not designed to enable residents to age in place. They lacked the flexibility and the range of housing options necessary to meet the needs of frail older adults. Residents who entered public housing as young-old aged in place and are now the older-old (aged 75 years and older) and are in need of more supportive and health services than they were two decades ago.

Public housing itself has also aged. Most of it is more than 40 years old. Many developments are badly rundown and in need of renovation. Most are unequipped to offer the range of supportive services that are required by increasingly frail and dependent residents. Absent supportive services, the bleak alternative may be moving older people into costly, isolated institutions. Older adults may suffer unnecessary institutionalization, and nursing home care is far more costly than community-based services.

The Section 202 Supportive Housing for the Elderly Act was passed in 2010. The act supports the development and maintenance of housing options for older adults with very low incomes. It encourages the enhancement of existing units and expanding access to assisted living facilities and programs that enable older adults to remain in the community. It also supports HUD's creation of an information clearinghouse of affordable housing projects for older adults.

In "HUD's Public Housing Program" (2015, http:// portal.hud.gov/hudportal/HUD?src=/topics/rental_assistance/ phprog), HUD reports that in 2015 there were approximately 1.2 million households living in public housing units and 3,300 housing authorities that managed the housing for low-income residents. Eligibility for public housing is based on income (income limits vary by location), age, disability, family status, and U.S citizenship or eligible immigration status.

In "The Challenge of Affordable Senior Housing" (March 31, 2015, http://consecra.org/blog/view/131-the-challenge-of-affordable-senior-housing), Tim Rhodes describes the challenges of meeting the needs of an aging population with sharply limited budgets. He observes that even though many older adults want to remain in their homes, increasing health care costs as well as home maintenance costs and real estate taxes may make it impossible for some older adults to age in place. Rhodes also notes that there is not enough senior housing to meet the growing demand. In 2014 new housing units for older adults grew a scant 1.7%, which is less than half of the forecasted need.

CHAPTER 4
WORKING AND RETIREMENT: NEW OPTIONS FOR OLDER ADULTS

Americans head off to their jobs each day as much for daily meaning as for daily bread.

—Studs Terkel, *Working: People Talk about What They Do All Day and How They Feel about What They Do* (1974)

Historically, Americans aged 65 years and older have made substantial contributions to society. Examples of accomplished older adults include:

- Benjamin Franklin (1706–1790)—writer, scientist, inventor, and statesman—helped draft the Declaration of Independence at age 70.

- Thomas Alva Edison (1847–1931) worked on inventions, including the light bulb, the microphone, and the phonograph, until his death at the age of 84.

- Rear Admiral Grace Murray Hopper (1906–1992), one of the early computer scientists and a coauthor of the computer language COBOL, maintained an active speaking and consulting schedule until her death at age 85.

- Margaret Mead (1901–1978), the noted anthropologist, returned to New Guinea when she was 72 and exhausted a much younger television film crew as they tried to keep up with her.

- Albert Einstein (1879–1955), who formulated the theory of relativity, was working on a unifying theory of the universe when he died at age 76.

- Georgia O'Keeffe (1887–1986) created masterful paintings when she was more than 80 years of age.

Older adults continue to play vital roles in industry, government, and the arts. Notable examples include:

- Former senator John Glenn (1921–), who piloted the first manned U.S. spacecraft to orbit the earth, returned to space at age 77 as a payload specialist.

- Betty White (1922–), a popular actress, author, producer, radio host, singer, and philanthropist, won a primetime Emmy Award at age 88 in 2010 and a Grammy Award at age 90 in 2012.

- Warren Buffett (1930–) is the most successful investor of the 20th century and was the wealthiest person in the world in 2008 at age 78. With a fortune estimated at $67 billion in 2015, he has pledged to give nearly all of his fortune to charity after his death.

- U.S. Senator John McCain (1936–; R-AZ) was 76 years old when he was elected in 2012 to a 14th term as senator. He was the Republican presidential candidate in the 2008 election.

- Madeleine Albright (1937–), the U.S. secretary of state from 1997 to 2001, is the president of the Harry S. Truman Scholarship Foundation and chair of the National Democratic Institute for International Affairs. She also serves as cochair of the Commission on Legal Empowerment of the Poor and of the Pew Global Attitudes Project.

- Nancy Pelosi (1940–; D-CA) served as the Speaker of the U.S. House of Representatives from January 2007 to January 2011. She was the first woman to hold that position.

- James E. Hansen (1941–), the former head of the National Aeronautics and Space Administration's Goddard Institute for Space Studies and adjunct professor in the Department of Earth and Environmental Sciences at Columbia University, is known for increasing public awareness of global warming and its effects on climate change.

- Hillary Rodham Clinton (1947–) was the 67th U.S. secretary of state from 2009 to 2013 and is seeking the Democratic nomination in the 2016 presidential election. She was also the First Lady of the United States from 1993 to 2001 and a U.S. senator for New York from 2001 to 2009.

DEFINING AND REDEFINING RETIREMENT

Retirement in the United States is usually defined by withdrawal from the paid labor force and receipt of income from pension plans, Social Security, or other retirement plans. There are, however, many people who may be viewed as being retired, although they do not fulfill the criteria of the generally accepted definition of retirement. For example, workers who retire from the military or other federal employment, which provide pension benefits after 20 years of service, may choose to continue to work and remain in the labor force for years, collecting both a salary and a pension. Other workers retire from full-time employment but continue to work part time to supplement their pension, Social Security, or retirement benefits. As a result, not all workers collecting pensions are retired, and some workers collecting salaries are retired.

Besides expanding the definition of the term *retirement*, an increasing number of older Americans are not subscribing to the traditional timing and lifestyle of retirement. Retirement is no longer an event, it is a process, and work and retirement are no longer mutually exclusive. Although many older adults still choose to retire from full-time employment at age 65, they remain active by exploring new careers, working part time, volunteering, and engaging in a variety of leisure activities. An increasing proportion of older adults work well beyond age 65, and some choose not to retire at all.

In 2015 prospective retirees included the baby boom generation (people born between 1946 and 1964). This generation faces unique difficulties when contemplating retirement, including declining home values, high unemployment, low interest rates, and a post-recession economy. In *Only a Third of the Oldest Baby Boomers in U.S. Still Working* (January 27, 2015, http://www.gallup.com/poll/181292/third-oldest-baby-boomers-working.aspx), Frank Newport of the Gallup Organization reports that although some boomers say they plan to postpone retirement, the older boomers appear to be following conventional retirement schedules. According to Newport, "Boomers aged 65 to 68 are retiring at about the same rate as those who were in that age range a few years ago. By age 68, only about a third of boomers are still in the workforce, including just 16% who are working full time."

RECASTING WORK AND RETIREMENT

Throughout much of human history the average length of life was relatively short. According to the Centers for Disease Control and Prevention (CDC), in *Health United States 2014* (May 6, 2015, http://www.cdc.gov/nchs/data/hus/hus14.pdf), in 1900 life expectancy in the United States was just 47.3 years. In a world where most people did not expect to live beyond age 50, it was essential that personal, educational, and professional milestones be attained by certain ages. Obtaining an education, job training, marriage, parenthood, and retirement not only were designated to particular periods of life but also were expected generally to occur only once in a lifetime.

This regimented pattern of life was maintained by tradition and reinforced by laws and regulations. In the United States, government regulations and institutional rules prescribed the ages at which education began, work life ended, and pension and Social Security benefits commenced. This timetable was based on the assumptions that these activities were to be performed "on time" and in sequence and that most growth and development occurred during the first half of life, whereas the second half was, in general, characterized by decline and disinvestment.

Social and demographic trends (including increased longevity and improved health), technological advances, and economic realities have transformed the size and composition of the labor force as well as the nature of family and work. Examples of these changes include:

- Marriage and childbearing are often postponed in favor of pursuing education and careers. Advances in reproductive technology have enabled women to delay having children by 20 years. Table 4.1 shows that the rate of women aged 40 to 44 years giving birth rose from 5.5 births per 1,000 women in 1990 to 10.4 births per 1,000 women in 2013.

- Formal learning was once the exclusive province of the young. However, middle-aged and older adults are increasingly returning to school. According to the U.S. Census Bureau, in "Back to School: 2014–2015" (July 24, 2014, http://www.census.gov/newsroom/facts-for-features/2014/cb14-ff20.html), 14% of all college students were aged 35 years and older in 2012, and 32% of part-time students were age 35 and older. Distance learning programs and classes offered online have created opportunities for older adults who wish to continue their education.

- Career changes and retraining have become the norm rather than the exception. Americans once pursued a single career during their lifetime. Many workers now change jobs and even careers several times. According to the American Council on Education (2015, http://www.acenet.edu), an increasing number of adults, from military veterans to people aged 50 years and older, are returning to work in second, third, or even fourth careers.

- Age-based mandatory retirement no longer exists in most private-sector industries. Historically, mandatory retirement ages were justified by the argument that some occupations were either too dangerous for older workers or required high levels of physical and

TABLE 4.1

Birthrates by age of mother, 1970–2013

[Total fertility rates are sums of birth rates for 5-year age groups multiplied by 5. Birth rates are births per 1,000 women in specified group. Population based on counts enumerated as of April 1 for census years and estimated as of July 1 for all other years.]

Year and race	Total fertility rate	10–14	Age of mother (years) 15–19 Total	15–17	18–19	20–24	25–29	30–34	35–39	40–44	45–49[a]
All races[b]											
2013	1,857.5	0.3	26.5	12.3	47.1	80.7	105.5	98.0	49.3	10.4	0.8
2012	1,880.5	0.4	29.4	14.1	51.4	83.1	106.5	97.3	48.3	10.4	0.7
2011	1,894.5	0.4	31.3	15.4	54.1	85.3	107.2	96.5	47.2	10.3	0.7
2010	1,931.0	0.4	34.2	17.3	58.2	90.0	108.3	96.5	45.9	10.2	0.7
2009	2,002.0	0.5	37.9	19.6	64.0	96.2	111.5	97.5	46.1	10.0	0.7
2008	2,072.0	0.6	40.2	21.1	68.2	101.8	115.0	99.4	46.8	9.9	0.7
2007	2,120.0	0.6	41.5	21.7	71.7	105.4	118.1	100.6	47.6	9.6	0.6
2006	2,108.0	0.6	41.1	21.6	71.2	105.5	118.0	98.9	47.5	9.4	0.6
2005	2,057.0	0.6	39.7	21.1	68.4	101.8	116.5	96.7	46.4	9.1	0.6
2004	2,051.5	0.6	40.5	21.8	68.7	101.5	116.5	96.2	45.5	9.0	0.5
2003	2,047.5	0.6	41.1	22.2	69.6	102.3	116.7	95.7	43.9	8.7	0.5
2002	2,020.5	0.7	42.6	23.1	72.2	103.1	114.7	92.6	41.6	8.3	0.5
2001	2,030.5	0.8	45.0	24.5	75.5	105.6	113.8	91.8	40.5	8.1	0.5
2000	2,056.0	0.9	47.7	26.9	78.1	109.7	113.5	91.2	39.7	8.0	0.5
1999	2,007.5	0.9	48.8	28.2	79.1	107.9	111.2	87.1	37.8	7.4	0.4
1998	1,999.0	1.0	50.3	29.9	80.9	108.4	110.2	85.2	36.9	7.4	0.4
1997	1,971.0	1.1	51.3	31.4	82.1	107.3	108.3	83.0	35.7	7.1	0.4
1996	1,976.0	1.2	53.5	33.3	84.7	107.8	108.6	82.1	34.9	6.8	0.3
1995	1,978.0	1.3	56.0	35.5	87.7	107.5	108.8	81.1	34.0	6.6	0.3
1994	2,001.5	1.4	58.2	37.2	90.2	109.2	111.0	80.4	33.4	6.4	0.3
1993	2,019.5	1.4	59.0	37.5	91.1	111.3	113.2	79.9	32.7	6.1	0.3
1992	2,046.0	1.4	60.3	37.6	93.6	113.7	115.7	79.6	32.3	5.9	0.3
1991	2,062.5	1.4	61.8	38.6	94.0	115.3	117.2	79.2	31.9	5.5	0.2
1990	2,081.0	1.4	59.9	37.5	88.6	116.5	120.2	80.8	31.7	5.5	0.2
1989	2,014.0	1.4	57.3	36.4	84.2	113.8	117.6	77.4	29.9	5.2	0.2
1988	1,934.0	1.3	53.0	33.6	79.9	110.2	114.4	74.8	28.1	4.8	0.2
1987	1,872.0	1.3	50.6	31.7	78.5	107.9	111.6	72.1	26.3	4.4	0.2
1986	1,837.5	1.3	50.2	30.5	79.6	107.4	109.8	70.1	24.4	4.1	0.2
1985	1,844.0	1.2	51.0	31.0	79.6	108.3	111.0	69.1	24.0	4.0	0.2
1984[c]	1,806.5	1.2	50.6	31.0	77.4	106.8	108.7	67.0	22.9	3.9	0.2
1983[c]	1,799.0	1.1	51.4	31.8	77.4	107.8	108.5	64.9	22.0	3.9	0.2
1982[c]	1,827.5	1.1	52.4	32.3	79.4	111.6	111.0	64.1	21.2	3.9	0.2
1981[c]	1,812.0	1.1	52.2	32.0	80.0	112.2	111.5	61.4	20.0	3.8	0.2
1980[c]	1,839.5	1.1	53.0	32.5	82.1	115.1	112.9	61.9	19.8	3.9	0.2
1979[c]	1,808.0	1.2	52.3	32.3	81.3	112.8	111.4	60.3	19.5	3.9	0.2
1978[c]	1,760.0	1.2	51.5	32.2	79.8	109.9	108.5	57.8	19.0	3.9	0.2
1977[c]	1,789.5	1.2	52.8	33.9	80.9	112.9	111.0	56.4	19.2	4.2	0.2
1976[c]	1,738.0	1.2	52.8	34.1	80.5	110.3	106.2	53.6	19.0	4.3	0.2
1975[c]	1,774.0	1.3	55.6	36.1	85.0	113.0	108.2	52.3	19.5	4.6	0.3
1974[c]	1,835.0	1.2	57.5	37.3	88.7	117.7	111.5	53.8	20.2	4.8	0.3
1973[c]	1,879.0	1.2	59.3	38.5	91.2	119.7	112.2	55.6	22.1	5.4	0.3
1972[c]	2,010.0	1.2	61.7	39.0	96.9	130.2	117.7	59.8	24.8	6.2	0.4
1971[d]	2,266.5	1.1	64.5	38.2	105.3	150.1	134.1	67.3	28.7	7.1	0.4
1970[d]	2,480.0	1.2	68.3	38.8	114.7	167.8	145.1	73.3	31.7	8.1	0.5

[a]Beginning in 1997, birth rates are computed by relating births to women aged 45 and over to women aged 45–49.
[b]For 1970–1991, includes births to races not shown separately. For 1992 and later years, unknown race of mother is imputed.
[c]Based on 100% of births in selected states and on a 50% sample of births in all other states.
[d]Based on a 50% sample of births.

SOURCE: Joyce A. Martin et al., "Table 4. Birth Rates, by Age of Mother: United States, 1970–2013, and by Age and Race of Mother: United States, 1980–2013," in "Births: Final Data for 2013," *National Vital Statistics Reports*, vol. 64, no. 1, January 15, 2015, http://www.cdc.gov/nchs/data/nvsr/nvsr64/nvsr64_01.pdf (accessed May 9, 2015)

mental acuity. Mandatory retirement is still compulsory for federal law officers, correctional officers, firefighters, air traffic controllers, and commercial airline pilots. However, mandatory retirement ages have been faulted because they are arbitrary and are not based on actual physical evaluations of individual workers. As a result, some detractors view the practice of age-based mandatory retirement as a form of age discrimination.

Although a conventional American life generally included education, work, and retirement, in that order, the current cohort (a group of individuals that shares a common characteristic such as birth years and is studied over time) of workers and retirees has the opportunity to blend, reorder, and repeat these activities as desired. Many gerontologists (professionals who study the social, psychological, and biological aspects of aging) and other aging researchers posit that there is a "third age," a stage of working life when older workers can actively renegotiate their relationship with the labor force. Their choices, depending on life circumstances, may include remaining in the workforce, retiring, or returning to work for periods of part-time, full-time, or seasonal employment. Not all workers and retirees will choose to stray from the conventional course, but increasingly they have the option to do so.

A CHANGING ECONOMY AND CHANGING ROLES

The Agrarian Culture

When the U.S. economy was predominantly agricultural, children were put to work as soon as they were able to contribute to the family upkeep. Similarly, workers who lived beyond age 65 did not retire; they worked as long as they were physically able. When older adults were no longer able to work, younger family members cared for them. Older people were valued and respected for their accumulated knowledge and experience and were integral members of the interconnected family and labor systems.

Industrial Society

The Industrial Revolution shifted workers from the farm to manufacturing jobs. The work was physically demanding, the hours long, and the tasks rigidly structured. Women labored in factories and at home caring for the family. Older people found themselves displaced. Their skills and experience were not relevant to new technologies, and they could not physically compete with the large number of young workers eager to exploit new economic opportunities.

As industrial workers matured, some were promoted to positions as supervisors and managers. For older workers who had been with the same company for many years, labor unions provided a measure of job security through the seniority system ("first hired, last fired"). However, in an increasingly youth-oriented society older workers were often rejected in favor of younger laborers. Frequent reports of age discrimination prompted Congress to pass the Age Discrimination in Employment Act (ADEA). Enacted in 1967 to protect workers aged 40 to 65 years, ADEA made it illegal for employers or unions to discharge, refuse to hire, or otherwise discriminate on the basis of age. Victims are eligible for lost wages (the amount is doubled in the most blatant cases) and workers wrongfully terminated may also seek reinstatement. The ADEA Amendments of 1978 made 70 the upper age limit and prohibited mandatory retirement for most workers in the private sector and in the federal government. In 1986 Congress again amended the act to eliminate the upper age limit.

The Information Age

The U.S. economy continued its dramatic shift away from smokestack industries such as mining and manufacturing to an economy in which service occupations and the production and dissemination of information predominate. As a result, the demand for highly educated workers has grown, and the demand for workers who perform physical labor has slackened. Many information-age careers such as those in the fields of health, law, information technology, and communications are ideally suited for older workers because they do not require physical labor, and employers benefit from the cumulative experience of older workers.

THE AGING LABOR FORCE

As the baby boom generation approaches retirement age, the proportion of the U.S. population aged 65 years and older will increase significantly. However, the U.S. labor force is already undergoing a shift toward a greater number of older workers and a relative scarcity of new entrants.

According to the U.S. Bureau of Labor Statistics (BLS), the median age (the middle value; half are younger and half are older) of the U.S. labor force is increasing, from 37.1 years in 1992, to 41.9 years in 2012, to a projected 42.6 years in 2022. (See Table 4.2.)

Older Adults in the Labor Force

The BLS (2015, http://www.bls.gov/cps/cpsaat03.pdf) reports that in 2014 older workers accounted for 17.7% of the entire U.S. labor force. In *Older Workers* (July 2008, http://www.bls.gov/spotlight/2008/older_workers/pdf/older_workers_bls_spotlight.pdf), the BLS notes that between 1948 and 2007 the labor force participation of men aged

TABLE 4.2

Median age of the labor force, 1992, 2002, 2012 and projected 2022

Group	1992	2002	2012	2022
Total	37.1	39.8	41.9	42.6
Sex				
Men	37.2	39.8	41.8	42.2
Women	37.0	40.0	42.1	43.1
Race				
White	37.3	40.2	42.6	43.3
Black	35.5	38.1	39.7	40.3
Asian	36.2	38.8	40.9	42.9
Ethnicity				
Hispanic origin	32.5	34.0	36.9	38.9
White non-Hispanic	37.8	41.1	44.2	44.8

SOURCE: "Table 3.6. Median Age of the Labor Force, by Sex, Race and Ethnicity, 1992, 2002, 2012 and Projected 2022," in *Employment Projections*, U.S. Bureau of Labor Statistics, Office of Occupational Statistics and Employment Projections, December 19, 2013, http://www.bls.gov/emp/ep_table_306.htm (accessed May 11, 2015)

65 years and older generally declined until the late 1990s, when rates leveled off or even rose slightly. The observed decline in older adults' participation in the labor force during the 1970s and into the 1980s has been attributed to widespread mandatory retirement practices in many industries that forced workers to retire at age 65. In addition, the eligibility age for Social Security benefits was reduced from 65 to 62 years of age during the 1960s, enabling workers to retire earlier. The relatively stable proportion of older workers in the labor force since that time is in part because of the elimination of mandatory retirement and the liberalization of the Social Security earnings test (the earnings limits that prompt a reduction of Social Security benefits). The labor force participation rate for older workers was at record lows during the 1980s and early 1990s but has been increasing since the late 1990s as a larger share of older workers are remaining in or returning to the labor force.

The BLS indicates in *Older Workers* that between 1977 and 2007 the employment of workers aged 65 years and older increased by 101%. The number of employed men over the age of 65 years increased by 75% and the number of employed women rose by 147%. Although the overall percentage of workers aged 75 years and older was small, 0.8% in 2007, it increased a staggering 172% between 1977 and 2007. This increase in older workers may reflect several factors, including economic necessity, the fact that older adults are seeking to remain vital and active into their 70s, a desire for the challenge and social interactions that work offers, or some combination of these.

Unemployment among Older Adults

The BLS reports in "Record Unemployment among Older Workers Does Not Keep Them out of the Job Market" (March 2010, http://www.bls.gov/opub/ils/pdf/opbils81.pdf) that the unemployment rate for workers aged 55 years and older significantly increased from 2007 through 2010, when 7.1% of older adults in the labor force were unemployed. By April 2015 the unemployment rate among workers age 55 and older had decreased to 4%, the lowest of any age group except adults between the ages of 45 and 54 (3.8%). (See Table 4.3.)

Older Women Opt to Work Rather than Retire

Between 1992 and 2012 labor force participation rates generally rose among women aged 55 years and older, from 22.8% in 1992 to 28.5% in 2002 to 35.1% in 2012. (See Table 4.4.) The BLS projects that the participation rate of women aged 55 years and older will increase to 37.5% by 2022. Between 1992 and 2012 the participation rate for women aged 55 to 64 years rose from 46.5% to 59.4%, and among women aged 65 to 74 years the rate increased from 12.5% to 22.5%. Likewise, the labor force participation of women aged 70 to 74 years grew from 8.2% in 1992 to 15.4% in 2012, and among women aged 75 and older from 2.8% to 5%. These increases have narrowed the gap in labor force participation rates between men and women.

Most older women in the 21st century spent some time in the labor force when they were younger. However, the older the woman the less likely she is to have ever worked outside the home. In the United States the group of women in their late 50s and early 60s in 2015 was the first to work outside the home in large numbers and is approaching retirement. Women in this

TABLE 4.3

Unemployment by age groups, April 2014–April 2015

[Household data. Selected unemployment indicators, seasonally adjusted.]

Characteristic	Number of unemployed persons (in thousands)			Unemployment rates					
	Apr. 2014	Mar. 2015	Apr. 2015	Apr. 2014	Dec. 2014	Jan. 2015	Feb. 2015	Mar. 2015	Apr. 2015
Age and sex									
Total, 16 years and over	**9,696**	**8,575**	**8,549**	**6.2**	**5.6**	**5.7**	**5.5**	**5.5**	**5.4**
16 to 19 years	1,057	1,021	986	19.1	16.8	18.8	17.1	17.5	17.1
16 to 17 years	414	356	407	22.2	18.8	19.9	18.6	18.1	20.0
18 to 19 years	636	659	560	17.4	15.4	18.2	16.4	17.1	15.1
20 years and over	8,639	7,554	7,563	5.8	5.1	5.2	5.1	5.0	5.0
20 to 24 years	1,638	1,599	1,466	10.6	10.8	9.8	10.0	10.4	9.6
25 years and over	6,927	5,932	6,054	5.2	4.5	4.6	4.5	4.4	4.5
25 to 54 years	5,366	4,559	4,687	5.3	4.7	4.8	4.6	4.5	4.6
25 to 34 years	2,235	1,955	2,003	6.6	5.9	5.9	5.4	5.6	5.8
35 to 44 years	1,575	1,346	1,387	4.8	4.3	4.4	4.5	4.1	4.3
45 to 54 years	1,556	1,259	1,297	4.6	4.0	4.1	3.8	3.7	3.8
55 years and over	1,560	1,356	1,377	4.6	3.9	4.1	4.3	3.9	4.0

SOURCE: Adapted from "Table A-10. Selected Unemployment Indicators, Seasonally Adjusted," in *Employment Situation*, U.S. Bureau of Labor Statistics, Division of Labor Force Statistics, May 8, 2015, http://data.bls.gov/cgi-bin/print.pl/news.release/empsit.t10.htm (accessed May 11, 2015)

TABLE 4.4

Labor force participation rates, by age and gender, 1992, 2002, 2012, and projected 2022

Group	Participation rate				Percentage-point change			Annual growth rate		
	1992	2002	2012	2022	1992–2002	2002–2012	2012–2022	1992–2002	2002–2012	2012–2022
Total, 16 years and older	66.4	66.6	63.7	61.6	0.2	−2.9	2.1	0.0	0.4	0.3
16 to 24	66.1	63.3	54.9	49.6	−2.9	−8.4	−5.3	0.4	−1.4	−1.0
16 to 19	51.3	47.4	34.3	27.3	−3.8	13.1	−7.0	0.8	−3.2	−2.3
20 to 24	77.1	76.4	70.9	67.3	0.7	−5.5	−3.6	0.1	0.7	0.5
25 to 54	83.6	83.3	81.4	81.0	0.3	−1.9	0.4	0.0	0.2	0.1
25 to 34	83.7	83.7	81.7	81.1	0.0	−2.0	0.6	0.0	0.2	0.1
35 to 44	85.1	84.1	82.6	81.8	0.9	−1.5	0.8	0.1	0.2	0.1
45 to 54	81.5	82.1	80.2	79.9	0.6	−1.9	0.3	0.1	0.2	0.0
55 and older	29.7	34.5	40.5	41.5	4.9	6.0	1.0	1.5	1.6	0.3
55 to 64	56.2	61.9	64.5	67.5	5.7	2.6	3.0	1.0	0.4	0.5
55 to 59	67.4	70.7	72.5	75.5	3.2	1.8	3.0	0.5	0.3	0.4
60 to 64	45.0	50.5	55.2	59.8	5.5	4.7	4.6	1.2	0.9	0.8
60 to 61	56.0	59.7	63.8	68.4	3.7	4.1	4.6	0.6	0.7	0.7
62 to 64	37.7	43.7	49.1	53.8	5.9	5.4	4.7	1.5	1.2	0.9
65 and older	11.5	13.2	18.5	23.0	1.7	5.3	4.5	1.4	3.4	2.2
65 to 74	16.3	20.4	26.8	31.9	4.1	6.5	5.1	2.3	2.8	1.7
65 to 69	20.6	26.1	32.1	38.3	5.4	6.0	6.2	2.4	2.1	1.8
70 to 74	11.1	14.0	19.5	24.0	2.9	5.5	4.5	2.3	3.4	2.1
75 to 79	6.3	7.4	11.4	14.9	1.1	4.0	3.5	1.7	4.4	2.7
75 and older	4.5	5.1	7.6	10.5	0.6	2.5	2.9	1.3	4.1	3.3
Men, 16 years and older	75.8	74.1	70.2	67.6	−1.7	−3.9	−2.6	0.2	0.5	0.4
16 to 24	70.5	65.5	56.5	51.1	−5.0	−9.0	−5.4	0.7	−1.5	−1.0
16 to 19	53.4	47.5	34.0	27.8	−5.9	13.5	−6.2	−1.2	−3.3	−2.0
20 to 24	83.3	80.7	74.5	69.9	−2.6	−6.2	−4.6	0.3	0.8	0.6
25 to 54	93.0	91.0	88.7	88.2	−1.9	−2.3	0.5	0.2	0.3	0.1
25 to 34	93.8	92.4	89.5	88.8	−1.3	−2.9	0.7	0.1	0.3	0.1
35 to 44	93.7	92.1	90.7	90.4	−1.6	−1.4	0.3	0.2	0.2	0.0
45 to 54	90.7	88.5	86.1	85.1	−2.3	−2.4	−1.0	0.3	0.3	0.1
55 and older	38.4	42.0	46.8	46.2	3.6	4.8	0.6	0.9	1.1	0.1
55 to 64	67.0	69.2	69.9	71.0	2.2	0.7	1.1	0.3	0.1	0.2
55 to 59	79.0	78.0	78.0	77.8	−1.0	0.0	0.2	0.1	0.0	0.0
60 to 64	54.7	57.6	60.5	64.3	2.9	2.9	3.8	0.5	0.5	0.6
60 to 61	67.2	67.3	68.8	69.7	0.1	1.5	0.9	0.0	0.2	0.1
62 to 64	46.2	50.4	54.6	60.5	4.2	4.2	5.9	0.9	0.8	1.0
65 and older	16.1	17.9	23.6	27.2	1.8	5.7	3.6	1.1	2.8	1.4
65 to 74	21.1	25.5	31.8	35.9	4.4	6.3	4.1	1.9	2.2	1.2
65 to 69	26.0	32.2	37.1	41.6	6.3	4.9	4.5	2.2	1.4	1.2
70 to 74	15.0	17.6	24.2	28.8	2.6	6.6	4.6	1.6	3.2	1.8
75 to 79	9.0	10.2	15.9	19.0	1.2	5.7	3.1	1.2	4.6	1.8
75 and older	7.3	7.6	11.3	13.9	0.4	3.7	2.6	0.5	4.0	2.1
Women, 16 years and older	57.8	59.6	57.7	56.0	1.8	−1.9	−1.7	0.3	0.3	0.3
16 to 24	61.8	61.1	53.2	48.1	0.7	−7.9	−5.1	0.1	−1.4	−1.0
16 to 19	49.1	47.3	34.6	26.7	−1.7	−12.7	−7.9	0.4	−3.1	−2.6
20 to 24	70.9	72.1	67.4	64.7	1.2	−4.7	−2.7	0.2	0.7	0.4
25 to 54	74.6	75.9	74.5	73.8	1.3	−1.4	0.7	0.2	0.2	0.1
25 to 34	73.9	75.1	74.1	73.4	1.2	−1.0	0.7	0.2	0.1	0.1
35 to 44	76.7	76.4	74.8	73.3	0.3	−1.6	−1.5	0.0	0.2	0.2
45 to 54	72.6	76.0	74.7	74.9	3.4	−1.3	0.2	0.5	0.2	0.0
55 and older	22.8	28.5	35.1	37.5	5.7	6.6	2.4	2.3	2.1	0.7
55 to 64	46.5	55.2	59.4	64.3	8.7	4.2	4.9	1.7	0.7	0.8
55 to 59	56.8	63.8	67.3	73.3	7.0	3.5	6.0	1.2	0.5	0.9
60 to 64	36.4	44.1	50.4	55.6	7.7	6.3	5.2	1.9	1.4	1.0
60 to 61	45.7	52.8	59.2	67.2	7.1	6.4	8.0	1.5	1.1	1.3
62 to 64	30.5	37.6	44.1	47.7	7.2	6.5	3.6	2.1	1.6	0.8
65 and older	8.3	9.8	14.4	19.5	1.6	4.6	5.1	1.7	3.9	3.1
65 to 74	12.5	16.1	22.5	28.3	3.7	6.4	5.8	2.6	3.4	2.3
65 to 69	16.2	20.7	27.6	35.4	4.5	6.9	7.8	2.5	2.9	2.5
70 to 74	8.2	11.1	15.4	19.8	3.0	4.3	4.4	3.2	3.3	2.5
75 to 79	4.4	5.4	7.9	11.6	1.0	2.5	3.7	2.1	3.9	3.9
75 and older	2.8	3.5	5.0	8.0	0.7	1.5	3.0	2.3	3.7	4.8

SOURCE: Adapted from Mitra Toossi, "Table 3. Civilian Labor Force Participation Rate, by Age, Gender, Race and Ethnicity, 1992, 2002, 2012, and Projected 2022 (in Percent)," in "Labor Force Projections to 2022: the Labor Force Participation Rate Continues to Fall," *Monthly Labor Review*, December 2013, http://www.bls.gov/opub/mlr/2013/article/pdf/labor-force-projections-to-2022-the-labor-force-participation-rate-continues-to-fall.pdf (accessed May 11, 2015)

cohort who are single, widowed, or divorced often continue to work to support themselves because they do not have sufficient Social Security credits to retire.

Married older women are increasingly choosing to keep working after their husband retires, breaking with the practice of joining their husband in retirement. In

1977 about one-third of employed women aged 65 years and older were married, but the BLS reports in *Women in the Labor Force: A Databook* (December 2014, http://www.bls.gov/opub/reports/cps/women-in-the-labor-force-a-databook-2014.pdf) that in 2013 more than half (58.9%) of married women were employed. Historically, some of the reasons cited for the growing proportion of older married women in the workforce are:

- Older women have careers they find personally satisfying as well as financially rewarding.

- They need to secure their retirement to prevent the poverty that has historically afflicted widows.

- Their income helps maintain the family standard of living and may be vital when their husband has been pressured to retire by his employer or suffers failing health.

- They enjoy social interactions at the workplace. Women value relationships with coworkers more than men do, and as a result women often find retirement more isolating.

The Aging Labor Force

In "Labor Force Projections to 2022: The Labor Force Participation Rate Continues to Fall" (*Monthly Labor Review*, December 2013), Mitra Toossi of the BLS observes that older workers are the only group in which the labor participation rate has been rising substantially. The 55-and-older age group accounted for 11.8% of the labor force in 1992 and 20.9% in 2012, and is projected to reach 25.6% in 2022. (See Table 4.5.)

Part-Time versus Full-Time Work

Older workers may find increasing opportunities for flexible employment and alternative work arrangements, such as working as independent contractors or on-call workers rather than as employees or daily workers. For employers, hiring older part-time workers is often an

TABLE 4.5

Labor force participation rates, by age and gender, and ethnicity, 1992, 2002, 2012, and projected 2022

[Numbers in thousands]

Group	Level 1992	Level 2002	Level 2012	Level 2022	Change 1992–2002	Change 2002–2012	Change 2012–2022	Percent change 1992–2002	Percent change 2002–2012	Percent change 2012–2022	Percent distribution 1992	Percent distribution 2002	Percent distribution 2012	Percent distribution 2022	Annual growth rate 1992–2002
Total, 16 years and older	128,105	144,863	154,975	163,450	16,758	10,112	8,475	13.1	7.0	5.5	100.0	100.0	100.0	100.0	1.2
Age, years:															
16 to 24	21,617	22,366	21,285	18,462	749	−1,081	−2,823	3.5	−4.8	−13.3	16.9	15.4	13.7	11.3	
25 to 54	91,429	101,720	101,253	103,195	10,292	−467	1,942	11.3	−0.5	1.9	71.4	70.2	65.3	63.1	1.1
55 and older	15,060	20,777	32,437	41,793	5,717	11,660	9,356	38.0	56.1	28.8	11.8	14.3	20.9	25.6	3.3
Gender:															
Men	69,964	77,500	82,327	86,913	7,536	4,827	4,586	10.8	6.2	5.6	54.6	53.5	53.1	53.2	1.0
Women	58,141	67,364	72,648	76,537	9,223	5,284	3,889	15.9	7.8	5.4	45.4	46.5	46.9	46.8	1.5
Race:															
White	108,837	120,150	123,684	126,923	11,313	3,534	3,239	10.4	2.9	2.6	85.0	82.9	79.8	77.7	1.0
Black	14,162	16,565	18,400	20,247	2,403	1,835	1,847	17.0	11.1	10.0	11.1	11.4	11.9	12.4	1.6
Asian	5,106	6,604	8,188	10,135	1,498	1,584	1,947	29.3	24.0	23.8	4.0	4.6	5.3	6.2	2.6
All other groups[a]	—	1,544	4,703	6,145	—	3,159[b]	1,442	—	204.6[b]	30.7	—	1.1	3.0	3.8	
Ethnicity:															
Hispanic origin	11,338	17,943	24,391	31,179	6,605	6,448	6,788	58.3	35.9	27.8	8.9	12.4	15.7	19.1	4.7
Other than Hispanic origin	116,767	126,920	130,584	132,271	10,153	3,664	1,687	8.7	2.9	1.3	91.1	87.6	84.3	80.9	
White non-Hispanic	98,724	103,349	101,892	99,431	4,625	−1,457	−2,461	4.7	−1.4	−2.4	77.1	71.3	65.7	60.8	
Age of baby boomers	28 to 46	38 to 56	48 to 66	58 to 76	—	—	—	—	—	—	—	—	—	—	—

[a]The "all other groups" category includes (1) those classified as being of multiple racial origin and (2) the racial categories of (2a) American Indian and Alaska Native and (2b) Native Hawaiian and other Pacific Islanders.
[b]Number shown is based on calculated, rather than estimated, 2002 figure.
Note: Dash indicates no data collected for category. Details may not sum to totals because of rounding.

SOURCE: Mitra Toossi, "Table 1. Civilian Labor Force, by Age, Gender, and Ethnicity, 1992, 2002, 2012, and Projected 2022 (Numbers in Thousands)," in "Labor Force Projections to 2022: the Labor Force Participation Rate Continues to Fall," *Monthly Labor Review*, December 2013, http://www.bls.gov/opub/mlr/2013/article/pdf/labor-force-projections-to-2022-the-labor-force-participation-rate-continues-to-fall.pdf (accessed May 11, 2015)

attractive alternative to hiring younger full-time workers. Some employers value older workers' maturity, dependability, and experience. Others hire older workers to reduce payroll expenses. This reduction is achieved when part-time workers are hired as independent contractors and do not receive benefits.

Employers Favor Older Workers

In "The Suddenly Hot Job Market for Workers over 50" (Time.com/money, March 2, 2015), Dan Kadlec observes that in the mid-1990s, less than one-third of adults age 55 and older were employed or seeking employment compared with 40% in 2015. Kadlec reports that some companies are actively recruiting older workers with practical experience. He cites Barclays' apprenticeship program, which has been expanded to include candidates over age 50 for positions in the bank and the determination of organizations including the National Institutes of Health, Harvard Business School, and MetLife to recruit and retain older workers.

DISPELLING MYTHS AND STEREOTYPES ABOUT OLDER WORKERS

Older workers are often stereotyped by the mistaken belief that performance declines with age. Performance studies, however, reveal that older workers perform intellectually as well as or better than workers 30 years younger by maintaining their problem solving, communication, and creative skills. In "The Demands of Work in the 21st Century" (Lisa Finkelstein et al., editors, *Facing the Challenges of a Multiage Workforce: A Use-Inspired Approach*, 2015), Margaret E. Beier concludes, "there is no evidence to suggest that older workers will be at a disadvantage in the 21st-century workplace."

Myth: Older Workers Have Overly Increased Absenteeism

Because aging is associated with declining health, older workers are often assumed to have markedly higher rates of illnesses and absences from work. Somewhat surprisingly, the chronic (long-term) health conditions that older adults may suffer tend to be manageable and do not affect attendance records. In fact, absence rates for older full-time wage and salary workers are only slightly higher than those of younger workers. According to the BLS, in 2014 the absence rate for workers aged 55 years and older was 3.5%, compared with 3.3% for those aged 16 to 19 years. (See Table 4.6.)

Myth: It Costs More to Hire Older Workers

One widely accepted myth is that hiring and training older workers is not a sound investment because they will not remain on the job long. The BLS, however, indicates that in January 2014 workers aged 55 to 64 years had a median job tenure of 10.4 years, which was more than three times longer than the three years for workers aged 25 to 34 years. (See Table 4.7.) Research conducted by the AARP repeatedly demonstrates that workers between the ages of 50 and 60 work for an average of 15 years. Furthermore, the Mature Workers Employment Alliance, an organization that assists older workers to transition to new positions, asserts that the future work life of employees over the age of 50 generally exceeds the life of the technology for which they are trained.

The AARP indicates that although older workers' health, disability, and life insurance costs are higher than those of younger workers, they are offset by lower costs because of fewer dependents. Older workers have generally earned more vacation time and have higher pension costs, and they take fewer risks, which means they have lower accident rates. Workers over the age of 50 years file fewer workers' compensation claims than younger workers; the largest numbers of claims are filed by workers between the ages of 30 and 34 years. Fringe benefit costs for workers of all ages are about the same overall. Finally, retaining experienced older workers actually reduces employer costs that are associated with recruiting, hiring, and training new, younger workers.

Myth: Older Workers Are Technophobes

There is a pervasive myth that older adults are unable to learn or use new information technology. The AARP report "A Business Case for Workers Age 50+: A Look at the Value of Experience" (April 2015, http://www.aarp.org/content/dam/aarp/research/surveys_statistics/general/2015/A-Business-Case-Report-for-Workers%20Age%2050Plus-res-gen.pdf) dispels this myth, observing that a 2014 survey found that 91% of workers ages 50 and older have a computer, tablet, or smartphone and that older workers' interest in learning new skills and their willingness to use new technology are high.

Myth: Older Workers Are Not Innovators

The stereotype of older workers as slow to learn new skills, unwilling to take risks, and unable to adapt to change is fading as older entrepreneurs and innovators gain recognition. Vivek Wadhwa asserts in "There's No Age Requirement for Innovation" (WSJ.com, October 28, 2015) that innovation not only requires a willingness to challenge authority and break rules but also "to collaborate with others, obtain financing, understand markets, price products, develop distribution channels and deal with rejection and failure. You have to be able to inspire, manage and motivate others. In other words, you need business and management skills and maturity. These come with education, experience and age." He observes that Alfredo Zolezzi, who developed a water sanitization technology to help prevent waterborne illness, is 54, and David Albert, who built a heart monitor that connects to iPhones, is 56.

TABLE 4.6

Absences from work, by age and sex, 2014

[Numbers in thousands]

Characteristic	Full-time wage and salary workers[a]	Absence rate[a] Total	Absence rate[a] Illness or injury	Absence rate[a] Other reasons	Lost worktime rate[b] Total	Lost worktime rate[b] Illness or injury	Lost worktime rate[b] Other reasons
Age and sex							
Total, 16 years and over	106,418	2.9	2.0	0.9	1.5	1.0	0.5
16 to 19 years	1,124	3.3	2.3	1.0	1.3	0.7	0.5
20 to 24 years	8,447	3.0	2.0	1.0	1.3	0.8	0.5
25 years and over	96,848	2.9	2.0	0.9	1.5	1.1	0.5
25 to 54 years	75,630	2.8	1.8	1.0	1.4	0.9	0.5
55 years and over	21,218	3.5	2.8	0.7	1.9	1.6	0.3
Men, 16 years and over	**59,423**	**2.3**	**1.7**	**0.6**	**1.1**	**0.9**	**0.2**
16 to 19 years	692	2.5	1.7	0.8	0.9	0.5	0.4
20 to 24 years	4,788	2.2	1.7	0.5	0.9	0.7	0.2
25 years and over	53,943	2.3	1.7	0.6	1.2	0.9	0.2
25 to 54 years	42,383	2.0	1.5	0.5	1.0	0.8	0.2
55 years and over	11,559	3.1	2.5	0.6	1.6	1.4	0.2
Women, 16 years and over	**46,995**	**3.8**	**2.5**	**1.4**	**2.0**	**1.2**	**0.8**
16 to 19 years	432	4.6	3.2	1.5	1.8	1.1	0.8
20 to 24 years	3,658	3.9	2.3	1.6	1.9	0.9	1.0
25 years and over	42,905	3.8	2.5	1.3	2.0	1.2	0.8
25 to 54 years	33,247	3.7	2.3	1.5	2.0	1.1	0.9
55 years and over	9,658	4.1	3.1	0.9	2.2	1.8	0.4
Race and Hispanic or Latino ethnicity							
White	84,045	2.9	2.0	0.9	1.5	1.0	0.5
Black or African American	12,916	3.3	2.2	1.1	1.7	1.2	0.5
Asian	6,267	2.1	1.4	0.7	1.0	0.6	0.4
Hispanic or Latino	17,477	2.9	2.0	0.9	1.4	0.9	0.5

[a]Absences are defined as instances when persons who usually work 35 or more hours per week (full time) worked less than 35 hours during the reference week for one of the following reasons: own illness, injury, or medical problems; child care problems; other family or personal obligations; civic or military duty; and maternity or paternity leave. Excluded are situations in which work was missed due to vacation or personal days, holiday, labor dispute, and other reasons. For multiple jobholders, absence data refer only to work missed at their main jobs. The absence rate is the ratio of workers with absences to total full-time wage and salary employment.

[b]Hours absent as a percent of hours usually worked.

Notes: Estimates for the above race groups (white, black or African American, and Asian) do not sum to totals because data are not presented for all races. Persons whose ethnicity is identified as Hispanic or Latino may be of any race. All self-employed workers are excluded, both those with incorporated businesses and those with unincorporated businesses. The estimates of full-time wage and salary employment shown in this table do not match those in other tables because the estimates in this table are based on the full CPS sample and those in the other tables are based on a quarter of the sample only. Updated population controls are introduced annually with the release of January data.

SOURCE: "46. Absences from Work of Employed Full-Time Wage and Salary Workers by Age, Sex, Race, and Hispanic or Latino Ethnicity," in *Labor Force Statistics from the Current Population Survey*, U.S. Bureau of Labor Statistics, 2015, http://www.bls.gov/cps/cpsaat46.pdf (accessed May 11, 2015)

AGE DISCRIMINATION

Although the 1967 ADEA and its amendments were enacted to ban discrimination against workers based on their age, the act was also intended to promote the employment of older workers based on their abilities. Besides making it illegal for employers to discriminate based on age in hiring, discharging, and compensating employees, the act also prohibited companies from coercing older workers into accepting incentives to early retirement. In 1990 ADEA was strengthened with the passing of the Older Workers Benefit Protection Act. Besides prohibiting discrimination in employee benefits based on age, it provides that an employee's waiver of the right to sue for age discrimination, a clause sometimes included in severance packages, is invalid unless it is "voluntary and knowing."

Nevertheless, age bias and discrimination persist, even though age discrimination in the workplace is against the law. More than 15,000 claims of age discrimination are filed with the Equal Employment Opportunity Commission (EEOC) every year. Most cases involve older workers who believe they were terminated unfairly, but a number of the cases involve workers who believe they have experienced age discrimination in hiring practices.

The number of claims received by the EEOC rose from 19,921 in fiscal year (FY) 2002 to 20,588 in FY 2014. (See Table 4.8.) Agency data reveal that most claimants do not win. Of the claims that were resolved in FY 2014, the EEOC found "reasonable cause" that age discrimination may have occurred in just 552 cases and found "no reasonable cause" in 13,159 cases.

Pressure to Retire

There are many forms of subtle discrimination against older workers as well as ways that employers can directly or indirectly exert pressure on older employees to resign or retire. This form of discrimination is

TABLE 4.7

Median years of tenure with current employer for employed workers, by age and sex, selected years 2004–14

Age and sex	January 2004	January 2006	January 2008	January 2010	January 2012	January 2014
Total						
16 years and over	4.0	4.0	4.1	4.4	4.6	4.6
16 to 17 years	0.7	0.6	0.7	0.7	0.7	0.7
18 to 19 years	0.8	0.7	0.8	1.0	0.8	0.8
20 to 24 years	1.3	1.3	1.3	1.5	1.3	1.3
25 years and over	4.9	4.9	5.1	5.2	5.4	5.5
25 to 34 years	2.9	2.9	2.7	3.1	3.2	3.0
35 to 44 years	4.9	4.9	4.9	5.1	5.3	5.2
45 to 54 years	7.7	7.3	7.6	7.8	7.8	7.9
55 to 64 years	9.6	9.3	9.9	10.0	10.3	10.4
65 years and over	9.0	8.8	10.2	9.9	10.3	10.3
Men						
16 years and over	4.1	4.1	4.2	4.6	4.7	4.7
16 to 17 years	0.7	0.7	0.7	0.7	0.6	0.7
18 to 19 years	0.8	0.7	0.8	1.0	0.8	0.9
20 to 24 years	1.3	1.4	1.4	1.6	1.4	1.4
25 years and over	5.1	5.0	5.2	5.3	5.5	5.5
25 to 34 years	3.0	2.9	2.8	3.2	3.2	3.1
35 to 44 years	5.2	5.1	5.2	5.3	5.4	5.4
45 to 54 years	9.6	8.1	8.2	8.5	8.5	8.2
55 to 64 years	9.8	9.5	10.1	10.4	10.7	10.7
65 years and over	8.2	8.3	10.4	9.7	10.2	10.0
Women						
16 years and over	3.8	3.9	3.9	4.2	4.6	4.5
16 to 17 years	0.6	0.6	0.6	0.7	0.7	0.7
18 to 19 years	0.8	0.7	0.8	1.0	0.8	0.8
20 to 24 years	1.3	1.2	1.3	1.5	1.3	1.3
25 years and over	4.7	4.8	4.9	5.1	5.4	5.4
25 to 34 years	2.8	2.8	2.6	3.0	3.1	2.9
35 to 44 years	4.5	4.6	4.7	4.9	5.2	5.1
45 to 54 years	6.4	6.7	7.0	7.1	7.3	7.6
55 to 64 years	9.2	9.2	9.8	9.7	10.0	10.2
65 years and over	9.6	9.5	9.9	10.1	10.5	10.5

Note: Updated population controls are introduced annually with the release of January data.

SOURCE: "Table 1. Median Years of Tenure with Current Employer for Employed Wage and Salary Workers by Age and Sex, Selected Years, 2004–2014," in *Employee Tenure in 2014*, U.S. Bureau of Labor Statistics, September 18, 2014, http://www.bls.gov/news.release/tenure.t01.htm (accessed May 11, 2015)

"under the radar" and in many instances violates the spirit, if not the letter, of ADEA.

From an employer's standpoint, age discrimination is simply the consequence of efforts to reduce payroll expenses. Employment decisions are not only based on how much an employee contributes to the company but also on the salary and benefits the company must provide the employee, relative to the cost of other employees. Because salary tends to increase with longevity on the job, older workers usually receive higher wages than younger workers. Thus, if two employees are equally productive and the older one has a higher salary, a company has an economic incentive to lay off the older worker or strongly encourage early retirement.

For many workers, early retirement is untenable. Early retirement benefits are usually less than regular retirement benefits and may be insufficient to allow a retiree to live comfortably without working. Finding a new job is more challenging for older workers, particularly during periods of high unemployment, and they are frequently unemployed for longer periods than are younger job seekers. Furthermore, workers who refuse to accept early retirement may find themselves without jobs at all, perhaps with no pension and no severance pay.

Some labor economists contend that early retirements, whether voluntary or coerced, deprive the nation of skilled workers needed for robust growth and divest the government of the revenue that these workers would have contributed in payroll taxes.

Filing ADEA Claims: Suing the Company

The costs involved in filing an age discrimination suit are high. Besides the financial outlay for legal representation, workers who sue their employers may be stigmatized and face further discrimination. Future employers may be reluctant to hire a worker who has filed a discrimination suit against a former employer. Workers caught in this scenario can suffer emotional and financial damage that may adversely affect them for the rest of their life. Nonetheless, many workers do choose to sue their employers.

TABLE 4.8

Age Discrimination in Employment Act (ADEA) charges, fiscal years 1997–2014

	Fiscal year 1997	Fiscal year 1998	Fiscal year 1999	Fiscal year 2000	Fiscal year 2001	Fiscal year 2002	Fiscal year 2003	Fiscal year 2004	Fiscal year 2005	Fiscal year 2006	Fiscal year 2007	Fiscal year 2008	Fiscal year 2009	Fiscal year 2010	Fiscal year 2011	Fiscal year 2012	Fiscal year 2013	Fiscal year 2014
Receipts	15,785	15,191	14,141	16,008	17,405	19,921	19,124	17,837	16,585	16,548	19,103	24,582	22,778	23,264	23,465	22,857	21,396	20,588
Resolutions	18,279	15,995	15,448	14,672	15,155	18,673	17,352	15,792	14,076	14,146	16,134	21,415	20,529	24,800	26,080	27,335	22,371	20,148
Resolutions by type																		
Settlements	642	755	816	1,156	1,006	1,222	1,285	1,377	1,326	1,417	1,795	1,974	1,935	2,250	2,231	2,001	1,781	1,567
	3.5%	4.7%	5.3%	7.9%	6.6%	6.5%	7.4%	8.7%	9.4%	10.0%	11.1%	9.2%	9.4%	9.1%	8.6%	7.3%	8.0%	7.8%
Withdrawals w/benefits	762	580	578	560	551	671	710	787	764	767	958	1,252	1,161	1,322	1,369	1,280	1,296	1,251
	4.2%	3.6%	3.7%	3.8%	3.6%	3.6%	4.1%	5.0%	5.4%	5.4%	5.9%	5.8%	5.7%	5.3%	5.2%	4.7%	5.8%	6.2%
Administrative closures	4,986	4,175	3,601	3,232	3,963	6,254	2,824	3,550	2,537	2,639	2,754	6,387	4,031	4,167	4,230	4,045	3,642	3,619
	27.3%	26.1%	23.3%	22.0%	26.1%	33.5%	16.3%	22.5%	18.0%	18.7%	17.1%	29.8%	19.6%	16.8%	16.2%	14.8%	16.3%	18.0%
No reasonable cause	11,163	9,863	9,172	8,517	8,388	9,725	11,976	9,563	8,866	8,746	10,002	11,124	12,788	16,308	17,454	19,239	15,113	13,159
	61.1%	61.7%	59.4%	58.0%	55.3%	52.1%	69.0%	60.6%	63.0%	61.8%	62.0%	51.9%	62.3%	65.8%	66.9%	70.4%	67.6%	65.3%
Reasonable cause	726	622	1,281	1,207	1,247	801	557	515	583	612	625	678	614	753	796	770	539	552
	4.0%	3.9%	8.3%	8.2%	8.2%	4.3%	3.2%	3.3%	4.1%	4.3%	3.9%	3.2%	3.0%	3.0%	3.1%	2.8%	2.4%	2.7%
Successful conciliations	74	119	184	241	409	208	166	139	169	177	186	220	202	252	273	343	221	232
	0.4%	0.7%	1.2%	1.6%	2.7%	1.1%	1.0%	0.9%	1.2%	1.3%	1.2%	1.0%	1.0%	1.0%	1.0%	1.3%	1.0%	1.2%
Unsuccessful conciliations	652	503	1,097	966	838	593	391	376	414	435	439	458	412	501	523	427	318	320
	3.6%	3.1%	7.1%	6.6%	5.5%	3.2%	2.3%	2.4%	2.9%	3.1%	2.7%	2.1%	2.0%	2.0%	2.0%	1.6%	1.4%	1.6%
Merit resolutions	2,130	1,957	2,675	2,923	2,804	2,694	2,552	2,679	2,673	2,796	3,378	3,904	3,710	4,325	4,396	4,051	3,616	3,370
	11.7%	12.2%	17.3%	19.9%	18.5%	14.4%	14.7%	17.0%	19.0%	19.8%	20.9%	18.2%	18.1%	17.4%	16.9%	14.8%	16.2%	16.7%
Monetary benefits (millions)*	$44.3	$34.7	$38.6	$45.2	$53.7	$55.7	$48.9	$69.0	$77.7	$51.5	$66.8	$82.8	$72.1	$93.6	$95.2	$91.6	$97.9	$77.7

*Does not include monetary benefits obtained through litigation.

Notes: The total of individual percentages may not always sum to 100% due to rounding. Equal Employment Opportunity Commission (EEOC) total workload includes charges carried over from previous fiscal years, new charge receipts and charges transferred to EEOC from Fair Employment Practice Agencies (FEPAs). Resolution of charges each year may therefore exceed receipts for that year because workload being resolved is drawn from a combination of pending, new receipts and FEPA transfer charges rather than from new charges only.

SOURCE: "Age Discrimination in Employment Act FY 1997—FY 2014," in *Enforcement and Litigation Statistics*, U.S. Equal Opportunity Commission, 2015, http://www.eeoc.gov/eeoc/statistics/enforcement/adea.cfm (accessed May 12, 2015)

U.S. Supreme Court Decisions Augment ADEA

In response to the Great Recession, which lasted from late 2007 to mid-2009, and the continuing economic uncertainty, in 2015 many companies instituted layoffs and reductions in force in an effort to reduce costs and remain viable. Because reductions in force aim to reduce payroll, some target higher-paid workers, who are often older adults with longer tenures. ADEA is violated if an employment policy that seems neutral, such as the criteria for workers to be laid off, actually exerts a statistically significant adverse or "disparate impact" when applied to workers aged 40 years and older versus younger workers.

Protections for older workers were strengthened in 2005 by the U.S. Supreme Court decision in *Smith v. City of Jackson* (544 U.S. 228) that workers aged 40 years and older may prove discrimination under ADEA using a disparate impact theory. The court stated that plaintiffs in age discrimination lawsuits do not have to prove that employers intended to discriminate, only that layoffs had a "disparate impact" on older workers. This ruling is significant because claimants are not required to show that an employer deliberately targeted a single employee or group of employees. Instead, claimants can prevail if they are able to demonstrate that an employer used a neutral business practice (with no intent to discriminate) that had an adverse impact on people aged 40 years and older.

In 2008 the Supreme Court ruled in *Meacham et al. v. Knolls Atomic Power Laboratory* (No. 06-1505) that an employer defending against a disparate impact age bias claim, and not the employee making the charge, bears the burden of proving that the adverse action (in this case a reduction in workforce plan) was based on a reasonable factor other than age. The disparate impact theory is based on the principle that a policy that appears neutral may still have an adverse impact on a protected class, in this case, older workers.

The Supreme Court ruling in *Gross v. FBL Financial Services, Inc.* (No. 08-441 [2009]) essentially reversed its earlier position, making it more difficult for older workers to prevail in age discrimination suits. The ruling eliminated the requirement that employers prove they had a legitimate reason other than age for laying off older workers. Instead, the burden of proof now falls to older workers, who must prove that age was the key factor. The ruling reversed a jury verdict in favor of an insurance adjuster in Iowa who filed a claim because his company demoted him and gave his job to a younger worker. According to David G. Savage, in "Supreme Court Makes Age Bias Suits Harder to Win" (LATimes.com, June 19, 2009), the high court determined that "the judge had erred by allowing the plaintiff to win without proving he had been demoted because of his age." In "Reductions in Force: The Supreme Court Escalates the Legal Risks" (July 2008, http://www.lorman.com/newsletters/article.php?article_id=1028&newsletter_id=223&category_id=8&topic=LIT), Frank C. Morris Jr. of Epstein Becker & Green P.C. states that "precisely at a time when the economy may force employers to make more [reductions in force] decisions, the Supreme Court has made defending such decisions decidedly harder for employers."

RECENT AGE DISCRIMINATION CASES AND COURT DECISIONS. Dan Fastenberg reports in "Worker Debra Moreno Wins $193,000 in Age Discrimination Lawsuit" (HuffingtonPost.com, July 25, 2012) that Debra Moreno, a 54-year-old office worker in Maui, Hawaii, won $193,236 in a lawsuit that accused her employer of "outlandish discrimination." Moreno explained that although her supervisor described her as an efficient worker, the owner of the company said she looked and sounded old. The EEOC filed the suit on Moreno's behalf, averring, "What makes this case especially appalling is the flagrant disregard for a worker's abilities, coupled with disparaging ageist remarks and thinking."

The article "3M Settles Age-Discrimination Suit for up to $12M" (Associated Press, March 19, 2011) reports that in March 2011, 3M Co. settled an age discrimination suit filed in 2004 that charged the company with downgrading older workers' performance reviews and favoring younger workers for training and advancement. Although a company spokesperson said the proposed settlement, which applied to about 7,000 current and former employees, was not "an admission of liability," 3M agreed in August 2011 to pay $3 million to the plaintiffs in this case.

BABY BOOMERS AND RETIREES WANT TO DO GOOD WORK

Baby Boomers Will Transform Retirement

Large numbers of boomers are crafting their encores and helping to create a movement for personal renewal and social good.

—Marci Alboher, in *The Encore Career Handbook: How to Make a Living and a Difference in the Second Half of Life* (2013)

In *Encore Careers: The Persistence of Purpose* (2014, http://www.encore.org/files/2014EncoreResearch-Overview.pdf), Encore.org, an organization aiming to use older adults' skills and expertise to improve communities worldwide, and Penn Schoen Berland, a market research firm, indicate that about 25 million Americans ages 50 to 70 are interested in launching so-called encore careers to address social needs. The following are the key findings of the survey:

- More than half of Americans (55%) feel that using their skills and expertise to help others is a crucial part of what they want to do after their primary careers.

- In 2014 there were fewer financial barriers to starting encore careers than there were in 2011. Just one in eight (12%) of those interested in encore careers expressed concern about earning enough income in a social-impact encore.

- About one-third (34%) of those in encores have worked for more than a decade in their encores; just half (50 percent) have less than five years' experience.

- The majority of those in encore careers (86%) consider their encores as or more enjoyable than their prior careers.

- Nearly three-fifths (57%) of those in encores have household incomes of less than $45,000. Only about one in seven (14%) reported household incomes greater than $90,000.

The survey concludes that the option of pursuing an encore career is considered desirable by a large number of older adults. The researchers assert, "More likely to involve new kinds of work, including entrepreneurships, as extensions of familiar roles, social-impact encore careers offer millions of midlife Americans the means to apply their life skills and knowledge to contribute to the greater good, no matter their academic credentials or economic status."

Volunteerism in Retirement

Volunteerism among older adults is a relatively new phenomenon. Historically, older adults were seen as the segment of society most in need of care and support. As medical technology enables people to live longer, healthier lives, and as stereotypes about aging shatter, the older population is being recognized as a valuable resource for volunteer organizations.

Every day millions of older Americans perform volunteer work in their communities. With free time as well as the wisdom and experience derived from years of living, they make ideal volunteers. Older adult volunteers are educated and skilled and can offer volunteer organizations many of the professional services they would otherwise have to purchase, such as legal, accounting, public relations, information systems support, and human resource management. Perhaps more important, they have empathy and compassion because they have encountered many of the same problems that are faced by those they seek to help.

According to the BLS, in *Volunteering in the United States—2014* (February 25, 2015, http://www.bls.gov/news.release/pdf/volun.pdf), volunteer rates in September 2014 were the lowest for young adults aged 20 to 24 years (18.7% of the population) and those aged 25 to 34 years (22%), followed by adults aged 65 years and older (23.6%). (See Table 4.9.) Volunteers aged 65 years and older did, however, devote the most time (a median of 96 hours during the year) to volunteer activities. (See Table 4.10.)

Older volunteers were more likely to work for religious organizations than younger volunteers. The BLS notes that 43% of volunteers aged 65 years and older volunteered primarily for religious organizations, compared with 23.9% of volunteers aged 20 to 24 years. (See Table 4.11.)

NATIONAL SERVICE ORGANIZATIONS. Efforts to establish a national senior service during the administration of President John F. Kennedy (1917–1963) are described by Peter Shapiro in *A History of National Service in America* (1994). In 1963 Kennedy proposed the National Service Corps (NSC) "to provide opportunities for service for those aged persons who can assume active roles in community volunteer efforts." When the NSC was proposed, a scant 11% of the older population was involved in any kind of volunteerism. The plan to engage older adults in full-time, intensive service, with a minimum one-year commitment, to combat urban and rural poverty was viewed as revolutionary. Although the NSC proposal was championed by the Kennedy administration and widely supported in the public and private sectors, it was defeated in Congress, where reactionary lawmakers linked it to efforts aimed at promoting racial integration in the South.

Despite the defeat of the NSC, the idea of harnessing the volunteer power of older adults caught on. The Economic Opportunity Act of 1964 gave rise to the Volunteers in Service to America (VISTA) and eventually led to the launch of service programs involving low-income older adults, such as the Foster Grandparent, Senior Companion, and Senior Community Service Employment programs. The Foster Grandparent program matched 1,000 adults aged 60 years and older with 2,500 children living in orphanages and other institutions. The older adults would spend four hours a day, five days a week, feeding, cuddling, rocking, and exercising disabled children.

The success of the Foster Grandparent program exceeded all expectations. In 1971 the program was incorporated into the newly created ACTION agency, along with the Peace Corps, VISTA, the Service Corps of Retired Executives (SCORE), and the Active Corps of Executives. The Foster Grandparent program has since become part of the Senior Corps, a network of programs that tap the experience, skills, and talents of older adults to meet community challenges. Through its three programs (Foster Grandparent, Senior Companion, and Retired and Senior Volunteer programs), more than 360,000 Americans aged 55 years and older assisted local nonprofits, public agencies, and faith-based organizations in 2014. The Corporation for National and Community Service notes in "National Service Agency Awards $17.2 Million in Grants to Support Senior Volunteers" (March 9, 2015, http://www.nationalservice.gov/newsroom/press-releases/2015/national-service-agency-awards-172-million-grants-support-senior) that in 2014

TABLE 4.9

Volunteers by age groups and other selected characteristics, September 2014

[Numbers in thousands]

Characteristics in September 2014	Total, both sexes Civilian noninstitutional population	Volunteers Number	Volunteers Percent of population	Men Civilian noninstitutional population	Volunteers Number	Volunteers Percent of population	Women Civilian noninstitutional population	Volunteers Number	Volunteers Percent of population
Age									
Total, 16 years and over	248,446	62,757	25.3	120,004	26,375	22.0	128,442	36,381	28.3
16 to 24 years	38,679	8,469	21.9	19,498	3,771	19.3	19,180	4,698	24.5
16 to 19 years	16,615	4,334	26.1	8,437	1,982	23.5	8,178	2,351	28.8
20 to 24 years	22,064	4,135	18.7	11,061	1,789	16.2	11,003	2,347	21.3
25 years and over	209,768	54,288	25.9	100,506	22,604	22.5	109,262	31,684	29.0
25 to 34 years	42,242	9,291	22.0	20,902	3,714	17.8	21,340	5,577	26.1
35 to 44 years	39,568	11,783	29.8	19,391	4,847	25.0	20,177	6,936	34.4
45 to 54 years	42,762	12,204	28.5	20,897	5,229	25.0	21,865	6,975	31.9
55 to 64 years	39,929	10,331	25.9	19,198	4,428	23.1	20,731	5,903	28.5
65 years and over	45,266	10,679	23.6	20,118	4,386	21.8	25,148	6,293	25.0
Race and Hispanic or Latino ethnicity									
White	195,777	52,201	26.7	95,662	22,113	23.1	100,115	30,088	30.1
Black or African American	30,932	6,094	19.7	14,042	2,427	17.3	16,890	3,667	21.7
Asian	13,806	2,513	18.2	6,373	1,022	16.0	7,433	1,491	20.1
Hispanic or Latino ethnicity	38,596	5,982	15.5	19,344	2,555	13.2	19,252	3,427	17.8
Educational attainment[a]									
Less than a high school diploma	23,977	2,100	8.8	11,943	925	7.7	12,034	1,174	9.8
High school graduates, no college[b]	61,456	10,075	16.4	30,077	4,193	13.9	31,379	5,882	18.7
Some college or associate degree	56,748	15,494	27.3	26,253	6,051	23.0	30,495	9,443	31.0
Bachelor's degree and higher[c]	67,586	26,619	39.4	32,233	11,435	35.5	35,353	15,184	42.9
Marital status									
Single, never married	75,158	15,183	20.2	39,731	6,774	17.0	35,427	8,409	23.7
Married, spouse present	123,855	37,160	30.0	62,206	16,572	26.6	61,649	20,588	33.4
Other marital status[d]	49,434	10,414	21.1	18,067	3,030	16.8	31,367	7,384	23.5
Presence of own children under 18 years[e]									
Without own children under 18	181,912	41,751	23.0	90,931	18,184	20.0	90,981	23,567	25.9
With own children under 18	66,534	21,005	31.6	29,073	8,191	28.2	37,461	12,814	34.2
Employment status									
Civilian labor force	156,975	42,780	27.3	83,550	19,738	23.6	73,426	23,041	31.4
Employed	147,474	40,497	27.5	78,691	18,841	23.9	68,782	21,656	31.5
Full time[f]	119,300	31,557	26.5	68,408	16,261	23.8	50,893	15,296	30.1
Part time[g]	28,173	8,940	31.7	10,284	2,580	25.1	17,890	6,360	35.6
Unemployed	9,501	2,283	24.0	4,858	898	18.5	4,643	1,385	29.8
Not in the labor force	91,471	19,977	21.8	36,455	6,637	18.2	55,017	13,340	24.2

[a]Data refer to persons 25 years and over.
[b]Includes persons with a high school diploma or equivalent.
[c]Includes persons with bachelor's, professional, and doctoral degrees.
[d]Includes divorced, separated, and widowed persons.
[e]Own children include sons, daughters, stepchildren, and adopted children. Not included are nieces, nephews, grandchildren, and other related and unrelated children.
[f]Usually work 35 hours or more a week at all jobs.
[g]Usually work less than 35 hours a week at all jobs.
Note: Data on volunteers relate to persons who performed unpaid volunteer activities for an organization at any point from September 1, 2013, through the survey period in September 2014. Estimates for the above race groups (white, black or African American, and Asian) do not sum to totals because data are not presented for all races. Persons whose ethnicity is identified as Hispanic or Latino may be of any race.

SOURCE: "Table 1. Volunteers by Selected Characteristics, September 2014," in *Volunteering in the United States—2014*, U.S. Bureau of Labor Statistics, February 25, 2015, http://www.bls.gov/news.release/pdf/volun.pdf (accessed May 13, 2015)

more than 232,000 volunteers delivered more than 40.4 million hours of service in their communities.

Another successful national volunteer program involving older adults is SCORE, which uses retired business executives as counselors and consultants to small businesses. Established by the Small Business Administration (SBA) in 1964, the program works with recipients of SBA loans and others, assisting them to draft business plans, evaluate profitability, and develop marketing strategies. One objective of the program is to reduce default rates on these loans. SCORE mentors business owners and provides one-on-one counseling, consultation via e-mail, and training sessions.

Points of Light (2015, http://www.pointsoflight.org/facts) is anther organization that offers people of all ages opportunities to volunteer in their communities. The organization is

TABLE 4.10

Volunteers by annual hours volunteered and other selected characteristics, September 2014

Characteristics in September 2014	Total volunteers (thousands)	Total	Percent distribution of total annual hours spent volunteering at all organizations						Median annual hours[a]
			1 to 14 hour(s)	15 to 49 hours	50 to 99 hours	100 to 499 hours	500 hours and over	Not reporting annual hours	
Sex									
Total, both sexes	62,757	100.0	21.7	24.3	14.8	27.5	6.1	5.5	50
Men	26,375	100.0	21.5	23.5	15.1	27.9	6.4	5.6	52
Women	36,381	100.0	21.8	24.9	14.6	27.3	5.9	5.5	50
Age									
Total, 16 years and over	62,757	100.0	21.7	24.3	14.8	27.5	6.1	5.5	50
16 to 24 years	8,469	100.0	23.8	27.0	15.1	23.0	4.4	6.6	40
16 to 19 years	4,334	100.0	22.1	28.7	16.4	23.7	3.2	6.0	40
20 to 24 years	4,135	100.0	25.5	25.1	13.9	22.4	5.8	7.3	40
25 years and over	54,288	100.0	21.4	23.9	14.8	28.2	6.4	5.4	52
25 to 34 years	9,291	100.0	30.6	25.4	11.7	22.3	4.5	5.4	32
35 to 44 years	11,783	100.0	24.1	26.3	15.0	24.8	5.1	4.6	42
45 to 54 years	12,204	100.0	20.1	25.3	16.0	27.7	5.7	5.2	52
55 to 64 years	10,331	100.0	18.9	23.3	15.9	30.2	6.1	5.6	54
65 years and over	10,679	100.0	14.2	18.9	14.7	35.9	10.3	6.1	96
Race and Hispanic or Latino ethnicity									
White	52,201	100.0	21.3	24.5	15.1	28.0	5.9	5.1	52
Black or African American	6,094	100.0	21.6	21.1	13.8	27.8	7.9	7.7	52
Asian	2,513	100.0	27.8	25.6	12.8	20.8	3.5	9.6	36
Hispanic or Latino ethnicity	5,982	100.0	23.6	21.7	14.7	26.3	7.6	6.1	51
Educational attainment[b]									
Less than a high school diploma	2,100	100.0	23.6	22.5	14.6	24.3	8.4	6.6	50
High school graduates, no college[c]	10,075	100.0	23.4	22.2	14.3	26.3	7.6	6.2	52
Some college or associate degree	15,494	100.0	22.1	24.0	14.3	27.9	6.5	5.2	50
Bachelor's degree and higher[d]	26,619	100.0	20.0	24.6	15.2	29.5	5.7	5.0	52
Marital status									
Single, never married	15,183	100.0	25.2	25.5	14.0	23.6	5.0	6.8	40
Married, spouse present	37,160	100.0	20.3	24.2	15.4	28.9	6.4	4.8	52
Other marital status[e]	10,414	100.0	21.5	22.9	14.0	28.5	6.7	6.4	52
Presence of own children under 18 years[f]									
Men:									
No own children under 18 years old	18,184	100.0	20.9	22.9	14.8	27.9	7.1	6.3	52
With own children under 18 years old	8,191	100.0	22.8	24.7	15.8	27.7	4.8	4.1	50
Women:									
No own children under 18 years old	23,567	100.0	20.1	24.0	14.6	28.4	6.7	6.2	52
With own childrenunder 18 years old	12,814	100.0	25.1	26.5	14.6	25.3	4.3	4.1	40
Employment status									
Civilian labor force	42,780	100.0	23.4	25.8	15.0	25.8	4.6	5.3	48
Employed	40,497	100.0	23.4	26.0	15.0	25.8	4.5	5.3	47
Full time[g]	31,557	100.0	24.1	26.3	15.0	24.9	4.2	5.5	42
Part time[h]	8,940	100.0	21.1	24.7	14.9	28.8	5.7	4.8	52
Unemployed	2,283	100.0	23.3	22.1	16.1	26.8	6.6	5.0	52
Not in the labor force	19,977	100.0	18.0	21.2	14.3	31.2	9.2	6.0	67

involved in 250,000 service projects per year in 30 countries, and the 30 million hours of service its volunteers contribute annually is valued at $635 million.

Other volunteer service organizations that offer opportunities for older adults to contribute their time, energy, and talents include the AARP-sponsored Create the Good (http://createthegood.org), which connects people to volunteer programs and projects, and the Experience Corps (http://www.aarp.org/experience-corps), in which volunteers tutor and mentor students, providing literacy coaching and homework help, while serving as consistent role models.

aFor those reporting annual hours.
bData refer to persons 25 years and over.
cIncludes persons with a high school diploma or equivalent.
dIncludes persons with bachelor's, professional, and doctoral degrees.
eIncludes divorced, separated, and widowed persons.
fOwn children include sons, daughters, stepchildren, and adopted children. Not included are nieces, nephews, grandchildren, and other related and unrelated children.
gUsually work 35 hours or more a week at all jobs.
hUsually work less than 35 hours a week at all jobs.
Note: Data on volunteers relate to persons who performed unpaid volunteer activities for an organization at any point from September 1, 2013, through the survey period in September 2014. Estimates for the above race groups (white, black or African American, and Asian) do not sum to totals because data are not presented for all races. Persons whose ethnicity is identified as Hispanic or Latino may be of any race.

SOURCE: "Table 2. Volunteers by Annual Hours of Volunteer Activities and Selected Characteristics, September 2014," in *Volunteering in the United States—2014*, U.S. Bureau of Labor Statistics, February 25, 2015, http://www.bls.gov/news.release/pdf/volun.pdf (accessed May 13, 2015)

TABLE 4.11

Volunteers by type of organization and other selected characteristics, September 2014

Characteristics in September 2014	Total volunteers (thousands)	Total	Civic, political, professional, or international	Educational or youth service	Environmental or animal care	Hospital or other health	Public safety	Religious	Social or community service	Sport, hobby, cultural, or arts	Other	Not determined
Sex												
Total, both sexes	62,757	100.0	5.2	25.1	2.6	7.4	1.1	33.3	14.4	3.9	4.3	2.6
Men	26,375	100.0	6.6	23.7	2.6	6.1	1.8	32.2	14.8	4.7	4.7	2.7
Women	36,381	100.0	4.2	26.2	2.6	8.4	0.5	34.1	14.2	3.3	4.0	2.6
Age												
Total, 16 years and over	62,757	100.0	5.2	25.1	2.6	7.4	1.1	33.3	14.4	3.9	4.3	2.6
16 to 24 years	8,469	100.0	3.9	28.7	3.9	9.9	1.3	26.1	15.0	3.7	3.9	3.7
16 to 19 years	4,334	100.0	3.7	33.2	3.0	7.0	1.0	28.3	13.7	3.3	3.3	3.5
20 to 24 years	4,135	100.0	4.0	24.0	4.8	12.9	1.5	23.9	16.4	4.1	4.6	3.9
25 years and over	54,288	100.0	5.4	24.6	2.4	7.0	1.0	34.4	14.4	3.9	4.4	2.5
25 to 34 years	9,291	100.0	4.5	29.7	2.5	8.6	1.8	27.6	14.1	3.1	5.1	3.0
35 to 44 years	11,783	100.0	3.8	39.3	2.1	5.7	0.9	27.9	11.0	3.6	3.2	2.3
45 to 54 years	12,204	100.0	5.0	29.1	2.3	6.1	0.8	33.7	13.1	3.8	3.8	2.3
55 to 64 years	10,331	100.0	6.5	14.8	3.4	7.6	1.1	39.9	15.7	5.0	3.7	2.3
65 years and over	10,679	100.0	7.4	8.1	2.0	7.6	0.7	43.0	18.3	4.3	6.3	2.5
Race and Hispanic or Latino ethnicity												
White	52,201	100.0	5.5	25.0	2.9	7.5	1.2	32.4	14.4	4.2	4.4	2.4
Black or African American	6,094	100.0	3.7	21.0	0.7	6.2	0.3	44.0	15.1	2.2	3.1	3.8
Asian	2,513	100.0	3.7	31.1	1.5	9.6	—	28.9	13.6	3.3	4.4	4.0
Hispanic or Latino ethnicity	5,982	100.0	3.4	30.6	0.9	5.9	1.1	39.2	10.8	1.9	3.7	2.5
Educational attainment[b]												
Less than a high school diploma	2,100	100.0	3.4	21.3	1.8	3.3	1.1	49.6	11.8	2.1	4.1	1.5
High school graduates, no college[c]	10,075	100.0	4.5	20.5	2.5	5.4	1.7	41.0	14.5	3.1	4.5	2.4
Some college or associate degree	15,494	100.0	5.1	23.7	2.4	7.6	1.3	35.7	14.1	3.7	4.2	2.2
Bachelor's degree and higher[d]	26,619	100.0	6.1	26.8	2.5	7.6	0.6	30.0	14.7	4.6	4.4	2.7
Marital status												
Single, never married	15,183	100.0	4.5	25.8	3.8	9.9	1.5	24.7	17.0	4.2	4.8	3.7
Married, spouse present	37,160	100.0	5.1	26.2	2.1	6.1	0.9	37.2	12.6	3.7	3.9	2.2
Other marital status[e]	10,414	100.0	6.5	20.1	2.8	8.5	0.9	31.9	17.2	4.2	5.1	2.7
Presence of own children under 18 years[f]												
Men:												
No own children under 18 years old	18,184	100.0	7.4	16.9	3.2	6.8	1.8	33.1	17.4	4.8	5.5	3.0
With own children under 18 years old	8,191	100.0	4.7	38.6	1.3	4.6	1.6	30.4	9.0	4.5	3.1	2.2
Women:												
No own children under 18 years old	23,567	100.0	5.2	15.4	3.3	10.2	0.7	36.7	17.1	3.8	4.7	2.9
With own children under 18 years old	12,814	100.0	2.2	46.0	1.4	5.0	0.3	29.3	8.9	2.3	2.7	1.9
Employment status												
Civilian labor force	42,780	100.0	5.3	26.9	2.9	7.7	1.3	31.0	14.1	4.2	4.1	2.6
Employed	40,497	100.0	5.3	26.7	2.9	7.8	1.3	31.1	14.0	4.2	4.1	2.6
Full time[g]	31,557	100.0	5.5	26.8	2.8	7.8	1.5	30.2	14.3	4.1	4.1	2.7
Part time[h]	8,940	100.0	4.6	26.3	3.0	7.6	0.8	34.0	13.0	4.4	3.9	2.5
Unemployed	2,283	100.0	3.9	30.4	3.0	5.8	0.9	29.8	14.9	5.4	4.1	2.0
Not in the labor force	19,977	100.0	5.1	21.3	2.2	6.9	0.5	38.2	15.3	3.2	4.8	2.7

[a]Main organization is defined as the organization for which the volunteer worked the most hours during the year.
[b]Data refer to persons 25 years and over.
[c]Includes persons with a high school diploma or equivalent.
[d]Includes persons with bachelor's, professional, and doctoral degrees.
[e]Includes divorced, separated, and widowed persons.
[f]Own children include sons, daughters, stepchildren, and adopted children. Not included are nieces, nephews, grandchildren, and other related and unrelated children.
[g]Usually work 35 hours or more a week at all jobs.
[h]Usually work less than 35 hours a week at all jobs.
Note: Data on volunteers relate to persons who performed unpaid volunteer activities for an organization at any point from September 1, 2013, through the survey period in September 2014. Estimates for the above race groups (white, black or African American, and Asian) do not sum to totals because data are not presented for all races. Persons whose ethnicity is identified as Hispanic or Latino may be of any race. Dash represents or rounds to zero.

SOURCE: "Table 4. Volunteers by Type of Main Organization for Which Volunteer Activities Were Performed and Selected Characteristics, September 2014," in *Volunteering in the United States—2014*, U.S. Bureau of Labor Statistics, February 25, 2015, http://www.bls.gov/news.release/pdf/volun.pdf (accessed May 13, 2015)

CHAPTER 5
EDUCATION, VOTING, AND POLITICAL BEHAVIOR

EDUCATIONAL ATTAINMENT OF OLDER AMERICANS

Educational attainment influences employment and socioeconomic status, which in turn affect the quality of life of older adults. Higher levels of education are often associated with greater earning capacity, higher standards of living, and better overall health status.

In 2014, 30.4% of adults aged 55 years and older had earned a high school diploma, and 11.3% had obtained an undergraduate college degree. (See Table 5.1.) Table 5.2 shows that among both women and men the number of those aged 55 years and older that had completed high school and college grew steadily between 1940 and 2014, yet even in 2014 slightly more men than women had completed four or more years of college.

In *A Profile of Older Americans: 2014* (2015, http://www.aoa.acl.gov/Aging_Statistics/Profile/2014/docs/2014-Profile.pdf), the Administration on Aging (AoA) reports that from 1970 to 2014, the percentage of adults aged 65 years and older that had completed high school grew from 28% to 84%. In 2014 about one-quarter (26%) had earned a bachelor's degree or higher. The percentage who had completed high school varied considerably by race and ethnic origin in 2014: 88% of non-Hispanic whites, 76% of Asian Americans, 74% of non-Hispanic African Americans, 76% of Native Americans/Alaskan Natives, and 54% of Hispanics.

Lifelong Learning

Live as if you were to die tomorrow. Learn as if you were to live forever.

—Mohandas Gandhi

Campuses are graying as a growing number of older people head back to school. Older adults are major participants in programs once called adult education (college courses that do not lead to a formal degree). They are also attending two- and four-year colleges to pursue undergraduate and graduate degrees, as well as taking personal enrichment classes and courses that are sponsored by community senior centers and parks and recreation facilities. For example, in "2015 Community College Fast Facts" (2015, http://www.aacc.nche.edu/AboutCC/Pages/fastfactsfactsheet.aspx), the American Association of Community Colleges indicates that as of 2013, 14% of community college students were aged 40 years and older. In 2016 an estimated 4 million (18%) students in degree-granting programs were aged 35 years and older. (See Table 5.3.) By 2021 this number is anticipated to increase to 4.5 million (19%).

The American Association of Community Colleges notes in *Plus 50 Programs in Practice: How AACC's Plus 50 Initiative Is Helping Community Colleges Transform Programs and Services for Adults Age 50 and Over* (January 2015, http://plus50.aacc.nche.edu/Documents/Plus50_Programs_in_Practice_2015.pdf) that the Plus 50 Initiative was established in 2008 to help a pilot group of 13 community colleges expand their offerings for students aged 50 years and older. By 2014 the number of students had increased by 37,494, and 12,192 older adults had completed a degree or certificate. Another ambitious initiative, the Plus 50 Encore Completion Program, helps older adults earn certificates in high-demand occupations that "give back" in such areas as education, health care, and social services.

Older adults' motivations for returning to school have changed over time. Although they once may have taken courses primarily for pleasure, older students in the 21st century are as likely to return to school for work-related education. They are learning new skills, retraining for new careers, or enhancing their existing skills to remain competitive. Homemakers displaced by divorce or widowhood are often seeking training to enable them to reenter the workforce.

ROAD SCHOLAR MEETS OLDER ADULTS' NEEDS FOR EDUCATION AND ADVENTURE. Founded in 1975, Road Scholar (formerly known as Elderhostel) is a nonprofit organization that offers learning adventures for people

TABLE 5.1

Educational attainment by sex and age group, 2014

[Numbers in thousands. Civilian noninstitutionalized population*.]

Detailed years of school	All races Number	All races Percent	Males Number	Males Percent	Females Number	Females Percent	25 to 34 years old Number	25 to 34 years old Percent	35 to 54 years old Number	35 to 54 years old Percent	55 years old and over Number	55 years old and over Percent
	209,287	100	100,592	100	108,695	100	42,466	100	82,687	100	84,134	100
Elementary or High school, no diploma												
Less than 1 year, no diploma	826	0.4	370	0.4	456	0.4	104	0.3	297	0.4	424	0.5
1st–4th grade, no diploma	1,699	0.8	814	0.8	885	0.8	182	0.4	577	0.7	941	1.1
5th–6th grade, no diploma	3,217	1.5	1,634	1.6	1,583	1.5	481	1.1	1,386	1.7	1,350	1.6
7th–8th grade, no diploma	4,171	2.0	2,128	2.1	2,043	1.9	466	1.1	1,226	1.5	2,479	3.0
9th grade, no diploma	3,460	1.7	1,688	1.7	1,772	1.6	718	1.7	1,362	1.7	1,381	1.6
10th grade, no diploma	4,112	2.0	2,061	2.1	2,051	1.9	740	1.7	1,410	1.7	1,962	2.3
11th grade, no diploma	4,306	2.1	2,256	2.2	2,050	1.9	953	2.2	1,558	1.9	1,795	2.1
12th grade, no diploma	2,667	1.3	1,398	1.4	1,270	1.2	608	1.4	1,102	1.3	956	1.1
Elementary or High school, GED												
Less than 1 year, GED	16	—	1	—	15	—	4	—	5	—	8	—
1st–4th grade, GED	72	—	47	0.1	25	—	11	—	42	0.1	20	—
5th–6th grade, GED	71	—	33	—	37	—	6	—	23	—	42	0.1
7th–8th grade, GED	325	0.2	175	0.2	150	0.1	71	0.2	70	0.1	183	0.2
9th grade, GED	739	0.4	376	0.4	362	0.3	136	0.3	289	0.4	314	0.4
10th grade, GED	1,561	0.8	802	0.8	758	0.7	329	0.8	615	0.7	617	0.7
11th grade, GED	2,274	1.1	1,317	1.3	956	0.9	526	1.2	1,019	1.2	729	0.9
12th grade, GED	1,338	0.6	747	0.7	592	0.5	373	0.9	511	0.6	455	0.5
High school diploma	55,845	26.7	27,220	27.1	28,625	26.3	9,586	22.6	20,665	25.0	25,595	30.4
College, no degree												
Less than 1 year college, no degree	5,503	2.6	2,477	2.5	3,026	2.8	1,108	2.6	2,149	2.6	2,246	2.7
One year of college, no degree	11,315	5.4	5,160	5.1	6,154	5.7	2,392	5.6	4,298	5.2	4,624	5.5
Two years of college, no degree	13,029	6.2	6,307	6.3	6,723	6.2	2,825	6.7	4,964	6.0	5,240	6.2
Three years of college, no degree	3,591	1.7	1,685	1.7	1,906	1.8	1,050	2.5	1,330	1.6	1,211	1.4
Four or more years of college, no degree	1,481	0.7	829	0.8	652	0.6	409	1.0	568	0.7	504	0.6
Associate's degree, vocational												
Less than 1 year college, vocational/associates	587	0.3	244	0.2	343	0.3	116	0.3	220	0.3	251	0.3
One year of college, vocational/associates	1,231	0.6	547	0.5	685	0.6	304	0.7	533	0.6	394	0.5
Two years of college, vocational/associates	5,575	2.7	2,598	2.6	2,977	2.7	1,060	2.5	2,476	3.0	2,039	2.4
Three years of college, vocational/associates	813	0.4	320	0.3	493	0.5	154	0.4	366	0.4	293	0.4
Four or more years of college, vocational/associates	926	0.4	480	0.5	445	0.4	231	0.5	405	0.5	289	0.3
Associate's degree, academic												
Less than 1 year college, academic/associates	216	0.1	108	0.1	108	0.1	34	0.1	105	0.1	76	0.1
One year of college, academic/associates	676	0.3	262	0.3	414	0.4	134	0.3	330	0.4	212	0.3
Two years of college, academic/associates	7,779	3.7	3,207	3.2	4,572	4.2	1,613	3.8	3,357	4.1	2,809	3.3
Three years of college, academic/associates	1,550	0.7	617	0.6	933	0.9	396	0.9	664	0.8	490	0.6
Four or more years of college, academic/associates	1,437	0.7	590	0.6	847	0.8	351	0.8	705	0.9	381	0.5
Bachelors degree only	31,123	14.9	15,216	15.1	15,907	14.6	8,013	18.9	13,605	16.5	9,505	11.3
Graduate school, no master's degree												
Less than 1 year of graduate school, no master's degree	3,202	1.5	1,378	1.4	1,824	1.7	762	1.8	1,395	1.7	1,045	1.2
One or more years of graduate school, no master's degree	7,931	3.8	3,506	3.5	4,426	4.1	1,781	4.2	2,884	3.5	3,266	3.9
Master's degree programs												
Master's degree 1 year program	1,360	0.7	609	0.6	751	0.7	327	0.8	440	0.5	593	0.7
Master's degree 2 years program	11,443	5.5	4,936	4.9	6,507	6.0	2,228	5.3	4,992	6.0	4,223	5.0
Master's degree 3 or more years program	4,969	2.4	2,301	2.3	2,668	2.5	843	2.0	2,017	2.4	2,109	2.5
Professional degree	3,148	1.5	1,821	1.8	1,327	1.2	535	1.3	1,268	1.5	1,345	1.6
Doctorate degree	3,703	1.8	2,329	2.3	1,374	1.3	508	1.2	1,456	1.8	1,739	2.1

GED = General Educational Development.
Dash (—) = represents zero or rounds to zero.
*Excluding members of the amed forces living in barracks.

SOURCE: Adapted from "Table 3. Detailed Years of School Completed by People 25 Years and over by Sex, Age Groups, Race and Hispanic Origin: 2014," in *Educational Attainment in the United States: 2014–Detailed Tables*, U.S. Census Bureau, May 1, 2015, http://www.census.gov/hhes/socdemo/education/data/cps/2014/tables.html (accessed May 18, 2015).

aged 55 years and older. In *2014 Annual Report* (2015, http://pdf.roadscholar.org/educational-travel/PDFs/rs_annualreport_oct14_nodonors.pdf), Road Scholar states that it provided educational opportunities to more than 97,000 older adults in 2014. Road Scholar programs are conducted in every state and 150 countries around the world. Programs include three- to five-day classes, field trips, and cultural excursions. They provide older adults

TABLE 5.2

Educational attainment of adults aged 55 and older, 1940–2014

[Numbers in thousands. Noninstitutionalized population except where otherwise specified.]

Age, sex, and years	Total	Years of school completed						Median
		Elementary		High school		College		
		0 to 4 years	5 to 8 years	1 to 3 years	4 years	1 to 3 years	4 years or more	
55 years and older								
Both sexes								
2014	84,134	1,365	3,829	6,094	27,962	21,059	23,825	NA
2013	81,778	1,306	3,931	6,043	27,046	20,387	23,066	NA
2012	79,478	1,348	3,974	6,344	26,531	19,343	21,937	NA
2011	76,163	1,372	4,073	5,983	25,622	18,408	20,705	NA
2010	74,008	1,440	4,118	6,051	25,125	17,354	19,920	NA
2009	72,077	1,555	4,101	6,338	24,154	16,877	19,051	NA
2008	70,092	1,411	4,294	6,338	23,779	16,378	17,892	NA
2007	68,226	1,576	4,458	6,680	23,408	15,505	16,599	NA
2006	66,485	1,628	4,610	6,508	22,961	14,824	15,956	NA
2005	64,745	1,614	4,803	6,784	22,392	14,083	15,069	NA
2004	63,034	1,465	4,907	6,821	21,918	13,434	14,488	NA
2003	61,633	1,589	5,372	6,876	21,554	12,884	13,358	NA
2002	59,644	1,528	5,639	7,258	20,728	12,117	12,374	NA
2001	58,238	1,544	5,589	7,178	20,622	11,864	11,440	NA
2000	56,008	1,524	5,780	6,921	20,059	11,126	10,598	NA
1999	55,303	1,589	5,978	7,096	19,742	10,722	10,174	NA
1998	54,337	1,624	6,126	7,385	19,526	10,022	9,654	NA
1997	53,352	1,628	6,622	7,543	18,823	9,565	9,169	NA
1996	52,742	1,642	6,716	7,520	18,549	9,642	8,677	NA
1995	52,022	1,755	7,048	7,232	18,320	9,662	8,005	NA
1994	51,516	1,802	7,382	7,454	18,228	8,890	7,761	NA
1993	52,117	2,058	8,038	7,637	18,626	8,106	7,652	NA
1992	51,740	2,118	8,133	7,756	18,397	8,005	7,332	NA
1991	51,439	2,341	8,668	7,675	18,954	6,540	7,258	12.6
1990	50,798	2,349	9,239	7,893	18,050	6,202	7,064	12.3
1989	50,421	2,412	9,395	7,907	18,102	5,914	6,693	12.3
1988	50,128	2,325	9,969	7,860	18,004	5,705	6,263	12.3
1987	49,858	2,408	10,544	7,766	17,310	5,799	6,033	12.2
1986	49,383	2,611	10,699	7,917	16,876	5,515	5,767	12.2
1985	48,969	2,612	11,052	7,872	16,516	5,208	5,708	12.2
1984	48,324	2,584	11,131	7,636	16,353	5,026	5,593	12.2
1983	47,723	2,769	11,348	7,703	15,470	4,915	5,514	12.1
1982	47,102	2,818	11,541	7,751	15,091	4,807	5,095	12.1
1981	46,391	2,983	11,909	7,600	14,464	4,721	4,711	12.0
1980	45,670	2,994	12,326	7,451	13,869	4,494	4,535	12.0
1979	43,806	2,924	12,230	6,999	13,088	4,321	4,245	12.0
1978	42,977	3,013	12,593	7,069	12,376	4,086	3,843	11.6
1977	42,176	3,047	12,740	6,823	11,977	3,835	3,754	11.3
1976	41,429	3,107	12,674	6,915	11,346	3,709	3,677	11.1
1975	40,613	3,303	13,045	6,730	10,798	3,442	3,295	10.8
1974	39,817	3,461	13,302	6,615	10,060	3,233	3,145	10.4
1973	39,163	3,424	13,467	6,504	9,604	3,060	3,105	10.2
1972	38,659	3,471	13,706	6,351	9,136	2,952	3,042	10.0
1971	38,787	3,808	14,430	6,225	8,463	2,878	2,982	9.6
1970	38,126	3,957	14,647	5,877	8,005	2,797	2,843	9.2
1969	37,424	4,012	14,576	5,801	7,768	2,615	2,653	9.1
1968	36,789	4,244	14,522	5,760	7,085	2,624	2,558	8.9
1967	36,155	4,310	14,849	5,495	6,622	2,443	2,434	8.7
1966	35,540	4,438	14,742	5,392	6,240	2,358	2,370	8.6
1965	34,969	4,612	14,814	5,293	5,844	2,194	2,215	8.5
1964	34,335	4,888	14,701	4,954	5,598	2,159	2,033	8.3
1962	33,247	5,048	14,707	4,442	4,994	2,166	1,890	8.1
1960	31,902	5,169	14,944	4,503	3,757	2,051	1,479	8.5
1959	30,567	4,752	13,485	4,060	3,996	1,775	1,545	8.1
1957	29,548	5,153	12,996	3,602	3,864	1,462	1,461	8.0
1952	26,206	4,554	12,638	2,982	3,080	1,346	1,264	7.7
1950	25,427	4,940	11,947	2,791	2,704	1,170	1,005	8.3
1947	23,234	4,393	11,601	2,179	2,581	1,003	825	7.5
1940	19,592	4,178	10,467	1,656	1,633	685	579	8.2

with opportunities to study diverse cultures, explore ancient histories, study literature and art, and learn about modern people and issues. Some participants attend programs that are held on local college or university campuses, whereas others embark on programs that involve transcontinental or international travel.

TABLE 5.2

Educational attainment of adults aged 55 and older, 1940–2014 [CONTINUED]

[Numbers in thousands. Noninstitutionalized population except where otherwise specified.]

		Years of school completed						
		Elementary		High school		College		
Age, sex, and years	Total	0 to 4 years	5 to 8 years	1 to 3 years	4 years	1 to 3 years	4 years or more	Median
Male								
2014	38,850	544	1,790	2,800	12,150	9,320	12,246	NA
2013	37,621	557	1,790	2,605	11,539	9,060	12,070	NA
2012	36,489	614	1,775	2,754	11,220	8,574	11,552	NA
2011	35,027	597	1,934	2,625	10,676	8,230	10,966	NA
2010	33,778	647	1,923	2,611	10,399	7,672	10,525	NA
2009	32,814	689	1,874	2,669	9,886	7,456	10,241	NA
2008	31,841	631	1,932	2,751	9,510	7,259	9,759	NA
2007	30,920	721	2,060	2,884	9,505	6,723	9,026	NA
2006	30,060	705	2,090	2,784	9,488	6,193	8,837	NA
2005	29,198	717	2,157	2,896	8,918	6,167	8,341	NA
2004	28,347	639	2,192	2,885	8,631	5,841	8,159	NA
2003	27,694	729	2,423	2,912	8,425	5,694	7,510	NA
2002	26,608	664	2,601	3,048	8,063	5,257	6,975	NA
2001	25,908	697	2,558	2,964	8,073	5,131	6,485	NA
2000	25,023	706	2,696	2,817	7,816	4,906	6,079	NA
1999	24,694	712	2,746	2,911	7,712	4,756	5,856	NA
1998	24,197	755	2,740	3,000	7,745	4,461	5,496	NA
1997	23,668	773	3,026	3,060	7,417	4,139	5,255	NA
1996	23,352	795	3,058	2,998	7,198	4,254	5,055	NA
1995	22,881	839	3,153	2,980	6,980	4,254	4,675	NA
1994	22,669	894	3,327	3,037	6,987	3,962	4,462	NA
1993	23,038	992	3,595	3,174	7,178	3,587	4,508	NA
1992	22,836	1,033	3,676	3,277	6,991	3,549	4,312	NA
1991	22,708	1,217	3,980	3,183	7,287	2,850	4,193	12.4
1990	22,337	1,182	4,141	3,274	6,986	2,707	4,046	12.4
1989	22,167	1,202	4,198	3,317	7,003	2,616	3,829	12.3
1988	21,989	1,117	4,471	3,366	6,968	2,455	3,609	12.3
1987	21,855	1,160	4,762	3,261	6,673	2,504	3,496	12.3
1986	21,622	1,275	4,813	3,286	6,509	2,355	3,385	12.2
1985	21,391	1,252	5,001	3,234	6,387	2,229	3,289	12.2
1984	21,014	1,209	4,951	3,270	6,265	2,185	3,132	12.2
1983	20,769	1,343	4,986	3,282	5,906	2,141	3,117	12.1
1982	20,508	1,362	5,026	3,313	5,759	2,102	2,946	12.1
1981	20,237	1,394	5,165	3,292	5,597	2,032	2,758	12.0
1980	19,967	1,424	5,436	3,206	5,409	1,986	2,506	11.9
1979	19,292	1,446	5,479	2,964	5,167	1,935	2,301	11.8
1978	18,939	1,467	5,701	2,919	4,919	1,824	2,110	11.4
1977	18,608	1,502	5,770	2,787	4,835	1,700	2,011	11.2
1976	18,233	1,507	5,733	2,884	4,473	1,646	1,989	11.0
1975	17,903	1,628	5,845	2,871	4,308	1,480	1,768	10.5
1974	17,579	1,693	6,042	2,817	3,993	1,356	1,682	10.1
1973	17,263	1,678	6,111	2,774	3,811	1,245	1,645	9.9
1972	17,120	1,728	6,252	2,698	3,612	1,215	1,614	9.6
1971	17,288	1,913	6,629	2,668	3,285	1,214	1,579	9.1
1970	17,074	2,011	6,655	2,583	3,127	1,182	1,516	9.0
1969	16,822	2,003	6,701	2,536	3,099	1,086	1,397	8.8
1968	16,609	2,137	6,728	2,523	2,816	1,078	1,328	8.7
1967	16,398	2,247	6,827	2,379	2,685	989	1,271	8.5
1966	16,201	2,288	6,944	2,317	2,491	939	1,223	8.3
1965	16,015	2,368	6,992	2,265	2,331	893	1,164	8.2
1964	15,789	2,504	6,897	2,159	2,237	876	1,113	8.1
1962	15,440	2,644	6,813	2,032	2,030	864	1,057	8.0
1960	14,895	2,704	7,121	1,969	1,453	853	796	8.4
1959	14,304	2,491	6,436	1,759	1,584	718	857	7.9
1957	13,967	2,696	6,244	1,570	1,493	608	831	7.7
1952	12,544	2,428	6,162	1,318	1,262	528	636	7.5
1950	12,277	2,609	5,808	1,209	1,111	500	569	8.2
1947	11,424	2,393	5,656	939	1,109	464	482	7.3
1940	9,815	2,293	5,249	724	660	313	361	8.1
Female								
2014	45,284	821	2,039	3,295	15,812	11,739	11,578	NA
2013	44,158	749	2,141	3,438	15,507	11,327	10,996	NA
2012	42,989	734	2,199	3,590	15,311	10,769	10,384	NA
2011	41,136	775	2,140	3,358	14,946	10,178	9,739	NA
2010	40,230	793	2,195	3,440	14,725	9,682	9,395	NA
2009	39,263	867	2,228	3,669	14,268	9,421	8,810	NA

TABLE 5.2

Educational attainment of adults aged 55 and older, 1940–2014 [CONTINUED]

[Numbers in thousands. Noninstitutionalized population except where otherwise specified.]

| Age, sex, and years | Total | Elementary | | High school | | College | | Median |
		0 to 4 years	5 to 8 years	1 to 3 years	4 years	1 to 3 years	4 years or more	
2008	38,251	780	2,362	3,588	14,269	9,119	8,133	NA
2007	37,306	855	2,398	3,796	13,902	8,781	7,573	NA
2006	36,425	922	2,521	3,761	13,472	8,630	7,119	NA
2005	35,547	897	2,645	3,887	13,474	7,916	6,728	NA
2004	34,687	826	2,715	3,936	13,287	7,593	6,329	NA
2003	33,939	860	2,949	3,964	13,129	7,190	5,848	NA
2002	33,035	864	3,038	4,210	12,664	6,860	5,399	NA
2001	32,329	847	3,032	4,213	12,549	6,733	4,956	NA
2000	30,985	817	3,085	4,105	12,243	6,218	4,517	NA
1999	30,609	879	3,232	4,186	12,031	5,965	4,319	NA
1998	30,140	868	3,386	4,386	11,780	5,560	4,160	NA
1997	29,684	855	3,596	4,483	11,407	5,427	3,916	NA
1996	29,390	848	3,659	4,523	11,350	5,387	3,623	NA
1995	29,142	915	3,894	4,255	11,340	5,410	3,330	NA
1994	28,848	909	4,054	4,419	11,242	4,926	3,298	NA
1993	29,080	1,066	4,442	4,462	11,447	4,519	3,149	NA
1992	28,904	1,084	4,456	4,478	11,409	4,455	3,021	NA
1991	28,729	1,125	4,687	4,495	11,667	3,690	3,066	12.3
1990	28,461	1,167	5,098	4,619	11,063	3,495	3,019	12.3
1989	28,255	1,211	5,195	4,587	11,099	3,300	2,863	12.3
1988	28,139	1,208	5,498	4,495	11,034	3,250	2,655	12.3
1987	28,004	1,248	5,782	4,504	10,637	3,294	2,539	12.2
1986	27,762	1,336	5,886	4,630	10,367	3,160	2,382	12.2
1985	27,578	1,360	6,052	4,638	10,129	2,979	2,420	12.2
1984	27,309	1,377	6,183	4,363	10,086	2,843	2,459	12.2
1983	26,954	1,428	6,364	4,423	9,567	2,774	2,398	12.1
1982	26,593	1,458	6,511	4,435	9,330	2,705	2,150	12.1
1981	26,152	1,589	6,742	4,308	8,868	2,690	1,954	12.0
1980	25,703	1,571	6,889	4,245	8,460	2,509	2,030	12.0
1979	24,514	1,474	6,750	4,034	7,920	2,389	1,944	12.0
1978	24,038	1,545	6,889	4,149	7,457	2,263	1,733	11.6
1977	23,568	1,546	6,972	4,034	7,141	2,135	1,742	11.0
1976	23,196	1,602	6,942	4,029	6,871	2,063	1,690	11.0
1975	22,710	1,675	7,198	3,858	6,490	1,962	1,527	10.9
1974	22,238	1,762	7,261	3,799	6,068	1,880	1,463	10.7
1973	21,900	1,746	7,359	3,729	5,790	1,814	1,461	10.5
1972	21,539	1,743	7,455	3,654	5,526	1,737	1,425	10.3
1971	21,500	1,896	7,805	3,556	5,179	1,665	1,402	9.9
1970	21,052	1,946	7,993	3,292	4,879	1,615	1,327	9.5
1969	20,601	2,009	7,878	3,264	4,669	1,526	1,255	9.4
1968	20,180	2,106	7,795	3,237	4,269	1,544	1,229	9.2
1967	19,756	2,063	8,021	3,117	3,937	1,454	1,164	8.9
1966	19,339	2,152	7,797	3,074	3,749	1,419	1,147	8.9
1965	18,955	2,243	7,821	3,026	3,514	1,300	1,048	8.7
1964	18,546	2,383	7,805	2,794	3,360	1,282	920	8.5
1962	17,807	2,404	7,894	2,410	2,964	1,302	833	8.3
1960	17,007	2,465	7,823	2,534	2,304	1,198	683	8.6
1959	16,263	2,261	7,049	2,301	2,412	1,057	688	8.3
1957	15,581	2,457	6,752	2,032	2,371	854	630	8.2
1952	13,662	2,126	6,476	1,664	1,818	818	628	7.9
1950	13,150	2,331	6,139	1,582	1,593	670	436	8.4
1947	11,810	2,000	5,945	1,240	1,472	539	343	7.6
1940	9,777	1,886	5,217	932	973	372	219	8.3

Notes: Starting in 2012, data were created using population controls based on Census 2010 data.
Starting in 2001, data were created using population controls based on Census 2000 data.
Starting in 2001, data are from the expanded Current Population Survey (CPS) sample.
Begining with data for 1992, a new question results in different categories than for earlier years.
Data shown as "high school, 4 years" is now collected by the category "high school graduate."
Data shown as "college 1 to 3 year," is now collected by "some college"; and two "associate degree" categories. Data shown as "college 4 years or more," is now collected by the categories, "bachelor's degree; master's degree"; "doctorate degree"; and "professional degree." Due to the change in question format, median years of schooling cannot be derived.
Total includes persons who did not report on years of school completed.
NA = not available.

SOURCE: Adapted from, "Table A-1. Years of School Completed by People 25 Years and over, by Age and Sex: Selected Years 1940 to 2014," in "CPS Historical Time Series Tables," in *Educational Attainment*, U.S. Census Bureau, January 20, 2015, http://www.census.gov/hhes/socdemo/education/data/cps/historical/ (accessed May 18, 2015)

TABLE 5.3

Enrollment in degree-granting institutions, by sex and age, selected years 1970–2021

[In thousands]

Attendance status, sex, and age	1970	1980	1990	2000	2003	2004	2005	2006	2007	2008	2009	Projected 2010	2011	2012	2013	2016	2021
1	2	3	4	5	6	7	8	9	10	11	12	13	14	15	16	17	18
All students	8,581	12,097	13,819	15,312	16,911	17,272	17,487	17,759	18,248	19,103	20,428	21,016	20,994	21,253	21,485	22,194	23,755
14 to 17 years old	263	257	153	131	169	166	187	184	200	195	217	202	202	207	208	219	244
18 and 19 years old	2,579	2,852	2,777	3,258	3,355	3,367	3,444	3,561	3,690	3,813	4,041	4,056	4,025	4,343	4,331	4,358	4,765
20 and 21 years old	1,885	2,395	2,593	3,005	3,391	3,516	3,563	3,573	3,570	3,649	3,945	4,101	4,174	4,386	4,368	4,361	4,603
22 to 24 years old	1,469	1,947	2,202	2,600	3,086	3,166	3,114	3,185	3,280	3,443	3,594	3,758	3,708	3,823	3,922	3,996	4,037
25 to 29 years old	1,091	1,843	2,083	2,044	2,311	2,418	2,469	2,506	2,651	2,840	3,096	3,253	3,319	3,057	3,116	3,389	3,545
30 to 34 years old	527	1,227	1,384	1,333	1,418	1,440	1,438	1,472	1,519	1,609	1,741	1,805	1,807	1,678	1,726	1,833	2,037
35 years old and over	767	1,577	2,627	2,942	3,181	3,199	3,272	3,277	3,339	3,554	3,794	3,840	3,758	3,759	3,812	4,038	4,524
Males	5,044	5,874	6,284	6,722	7,260	7,387	7,456	7,575	7,816	8,189	8,770	9,045	9,026	9,107	9,160	9,261	9,741
14 to 17 years old	125	106	66	58	67	62	68	69	88	93	103	94	95	90	90	92	101
18 and 19 years old	1,355	1,368	1,298	1,464	1,474	1,475	1,523	1,604	1,669	1,704	1,806	1,820	1,819	1,896	1,886	1,876	2,040
20 and 21 years old	1,064	1,219	1,259	1,411	1,541	1,608	1,658	1,628	1,634	1,695	1,876	1,948	1,973	2,102	2,088	2,060	2,154
22 to 24 years old	1,004	1,075	1,129	1,222	1,411	1,437	1,410	1,445	1,480	1,555	1,606	1,723	1,682	1,760	1,798	1,799	1,792
25 to 29 years old	796	983	1,024	908	1,007	1,039	1,057	1,040	1,148	1,222	1,382	1,410	1,442	1,354	1,370	1,452	1,491
30 to 34 years old	333	564	605	581	602	619	591	628	638	691	709	731	715	691	707	729	792
35 years old and over	366	559	902	1,077	1,158	1,147	1,149	1,160	1,159	1,228	1,287	1,320	1,300	1,215	1,223	1,252	1,372
Females	3,537	6,223	7,535	8,591	9,651	9,885	10,032	10,184	10,432	10,914	11,658	11,971	11,968	12,146	12,325	12,933	14,014
14 to 17 years old	137	151	87	73	102	104	119	115	112	102	114	108	108	118	119	127	143
18 and 19 years old	1,224	1,484	1,479	1,794	1,880	1,892	1,920	1,956	2,021	2,109	2,236	2,236	2,206	2,447	2,446	2,482	2,725
20 and 21 years old	821	1,177	1,334	1,593	1,851	1,908	1,905	1,945	1,936	1,954	2,069	2,154	2,201	2,284	2,280	2,301	2,449
22 to 24 years old	464	871	1,073	1,378	1,675	1,729	1,704	1,740	1,800	1,888	1,987	2,036	2,027	2,063	2,125	2,197	2,245
25 to 29 years old	296	859	1,059	1,136	1,304	1,379	1,413	1,466	1,502	1,618	1,713	1,844	1,877	1,703	1,746	1,937	2,055
30 to 34 years old	194	663	779	752	816	821	847	844	881	918	1,032	1,074	1,092	987	1,020	1,103	1,246
35 years old and over	401	1,018	1,725	1,865	2,023	2,052	2,123	2,117	2,180	2,326	2,507	2,520	2,458	2,544	2,590	2,786	3,152
Full-time	5,816	7,098	7,821	9,010	10,326	10,610	10,797	10,957	11,270	11,748	12,723	13,082	13,001	13,146	13,262	13,586	14,497
14 to 17 years old	246	231	134	121	146	138	152	148	169	168	181	170	171	163	164	174	194
18 and 19 years old	2,374	2,544	2,471	2,823	2,934	2,960	3,026	3,120	3,244	3,359	3,513	3,495	3,413	3,644	3,637	3,665	4,014
20 and 21 years old	1,649	2,007	2,137	2,452	2,841	2,926	2,976	2,972	2,985	3,043	3,271	3,363	3,392	3,438	3,427	3,426	3,623
22 to 24 years old	904	1,181	1,405	1,714	2,083	2,143	2,122	2,127	2,205	2,347	2,535	2,584	2,504	2,689	2,758	2,808	2,846
25 to 29 years old	426	641	791	886	1,086	1,132	1,174	1,225	1,299	1,369	1,520	1,605	1,628	1,477	1,507	1,641	1,723
30 to 34 years old	113	272	383	418	489	517	547	571	556	571	663	744	759	646	665	705	785
35 years old and over	104	221	500	596	747	795	800	794	812	890	1,041	1,121	1,135	1,088	1,104	1,168	1,312
Males	3,504	3,689	3,808	4,111	4,638	4,739	4,803	4,879	5,029	5,234	5,671	5,837	5,793	5,843	5,873	5,931	6,263
14 to 17 years old	121	95	55	51	58	49	53	52	74	73	78	71	75	58	58	60	67
18 and 19 years old	1,261	1,219	1,171	1,252	1,291	1,297	1,339	1,404	1,465	1,516	1,580	1,574	1,532	1,588	1,581	1,578	1,722
20 and 21 years old	955	1,046	1,035	1,156	1,305	1,360	1,398	1,372	1,366	1,407	1,547	1,586	1,591	1,642	1,632	1,617	1,698
22 to 24 years old	686	717	768	834	995	1,001	982	992	1,043	1,105	1,177	1,214	1,171	1,269	1,296	1,301	1,305
25 to 29 years old	346	391	433	410	503	498	506	533	578	597	665	714	736	640	649	693	719
30 to 34 years old	77	142	171	186	209	231	225	235	231	249	281	301	296	291	298	310	341
35 years old and over	58	80	174	222	277	302	300	291	273	287	343	376	392	355	359	371	412

TABLE 5.3

Enrollment in degree-granting institutions, by sex and age, selected years 1970–2021 [CONTINUED]

[In thousands]

Attendance status, sex, and age	1970	1980	1990	2000	2003	2004	2005	2006	2007	2008	2009	2010	2011	2012	2013	Projected 2016	2021
1	2	3	4	5	6	7	8	9	10	11	12	13	14	15	16	17	18
Females	**2,312**	**3,409**	**4,013**	**4,899**	**5,668**	**5,871**	**5,994**	**6,078**	**6,240**	**6,513**	**7,052**	**7,245**	**7,208**	**7,303**	**7,388**	**7,655**	**8,234**
14 to 17 years old	125	136	78	70	88	89	98	95	95	95	103	99	96	104	105	113	127
18 and 19 years old	1,113	1,325	1,300	1,571	1,643	1,662	1,687	1,716	1,779	1,843	1,933	1,921	1,801	2,057	2,056	2,087	2,292
20 and 21 years old	693	961	1,101	1,296	1,536	1,566	1,578	1,601	1,619	1,636	1,724	1,777	1,801	1,797	1,794	1,808	1,925
22 to 24 years old	218	464	638	880	1,088	1,142	1,140	1,135	1,163	1,242	1,358	1,370	1,333	1,421	1,462	1,507	1,540
25 to 29 years old	80	250	358	476	583	634	668	692	721	772	855	890	892	837	858	948	1,004
30 to 34 years old	37	130	212	232	280	286	322	336	324	322	382	444	463	355	367	395	445
35 years old and over	46	141	326	374	471	493	500	503	539	603	697	745	743	733	745	797	900
Part-time	**2,765**	**4,999**	**5,998**	**6,303**	**6,585**	**6,662**	**6,690**	**6,802**	**6,978**	**7,355**	**7,705**	**7,934**	**7,993**	**8,107**	**8,224**	**8,608**	**9,258**
14 to 17 years old	16	26	19	10	23	28	36	36	31	27	36	32	31	45	44	46	50
18 and 19 years old	205	308	306	435	421	407	417	440	446	453	528	561	612	699	694	693	751
20 and 21 years old	236	388	456	553	551	590	586	601	585	606	674	739	782	947	942	936	980
22 to 24 years old	564	765	796	886	1,003	1,023	992	1,058	1,074	1,096	1,059	1,174	1,204	1,134	1,164	1,188	1,192
25 to 29 years old	665	1,202	1,291	1,158	1,224	1,286	1,296	1,282	1,352	1,471	1,576	1,649	1,692	1,580	1,609	1,748	1,823
30 to 34 years old	414	954	1,001	915	929	923	891	901	963	1,037	1,078	1,060	1,047	1,032	1,061	1,128	1,252
35 years old and over	663	1,356	2,127	2,345	2,434	2,404	2,472	2,483	2,527	2,664	2,753	2,719	2,624	2,671	2,708	2,870	3,212
Males	**1,540**	**2,185**	**2,476**	**2,611**	**2,622**	**2,648**	**2,653**	**2,696**	**2,786**	**2,955**	**3,099**	**3,208**	**3,233**	**3,264**	**3,287**	**3,329**	**3,478**
14 to 17 years old	4	12	11	7	9	13	15	17	14	20	25	23	20	31	31	32	34
18 and 19 years old	94	149	127	212	183	178	184	200	204	188	226	245	287	308	305	298	318
20 and 21 years old	108	172	224	255	236	248	260	257	269	289	329	362	382	460	456	443	456
22 to 24 years old	318	359	361	388	416	436	428	452	438	450	430	508	510	491	502	498	487
25 to 29 years old	450	592	591	498	504	540	551	507	570	625	717	695	706	714	721	759	772
30 to 34 years old	257	422	435	395	392	388	365	393	406	442	428	430	419	400	408	419	451
35 years old and over	309	479	728	855	882	845	850	869	886	941	944	944	908	859	864	881	960
Females	**1,225**	**2,814**	**3,521**	**3,692**	**3,963**	**4,014**	**4,038**	**4,106**	**4,192**	**4,401**	**4,606**	**4,726**	**4,760**	**4,843**	**4,936**	**5,279**	**5,780**
14 to 17 years old	12	14	9	3	14	15	21	20	17	7	11	9	12	13	13	14	15
18 and 19 years old	112	159	179	223	238	230	233	240	242	265	303	316	325	390	389	395	433
20 and 21 years old	128	216	233	298	315	342	327	344	317	318	345	377	400	487	486	492	524
22 to 24 years old	246	407	435	497	587	588	564	605	637	646	629	666	694	643	663	690	705
25 to 29 years old	216	609	700	660	721	746	745	774	781	846	858	953	985	866	888	989	1,050
30 to 34 years old	158	532	567	520	537	535	526	508	557	595	651	630	629	632	653	709	801
35 years old and over	354	876	1,399	1,491	1,552	1,560	1,623	1,614	1,640	1,723	1,810	1,775	1,716	1,812	1,844	1,989	2,252

Note: Distributions by age are estimates based on samples of the civilian noninstitutional population from the U.S. Census Bureau's Current Population Survey. Data through 1995 are for institutions of higher education, while later data are for degree-granting institutions. Degree-granting institutions grant associate's or higher degrees and participate in Title IV federal financial aid programs. The degree-granting classification is very similar to the earlier higher education classification, but it includes more 2-year colleges and excludes a few higher education institutions that did not grant degrees. Detail may not sum to totals because of rounding.

SOURCE: "Table 224. Total Fall Enrollment in Degree-Granting Institutions, by Attendance Status, Sex, and Age: Selected Years, 1970 through 2021," in *Advance Release of Selected 2012 Digest Tables,* National Center for Education Statistics, 2012, http://nces.ed.gov/programs/digest/d12/tables/dt12_224.asp (accessed May 18, 2015)

Adventure programs combine learning with outdoor sports such as walking, hiking, camping, kayaking, and biking. For example, a bicycle tour of the Netherlands also includes instruction about the country's history, art, and people. Shipboard programs explore history, art, ecology, and culture aboard a floating classroom.

Service-learning programs involve both education and hands-on work to serve the needs of a community. Older adults conduct wildlife or marine research, tutor children, or build affordable housing. The organization also offers a series of intergenerational programs in which older adults and their grandchildren explore subjects that appeal to both young and old, including dinosaurs, hot-air ballooning, and space travel.

OLDER ADULTS ARE TECH-SAVVY AND ONLINE. Rapid technological change has intensified the need for information management skills and ongoing technology training. The growing importance of knowledge- and information-based jobs has created a workforce that is rapidly becoming accustomed to continuous education, training, and retraining throughout one's work life.

Computer technology, especially use of the Internet, has also gained importance in Americans' lives outside of work, facilitating communication via e-mail and enabling interactions and transactions that once required travel to now occur in their home. Examples include online banking and shopping, e-mail communication with physicians and other health care providers, and participation in online support groups.

In *Older Adults and Technology Use* (April 3, 2014, http://www.pewinternet.org/files/2014/04/PIP_Seniors-and-Tech-Use_040314.pdf), Aaron Smith of the Pew Research Center reports high Internet use by older adults. In 2013, 59% of adults aged 65 years and older were using the Internet, and nearly half (47%) had a high-speed broadband connection at home. Although the proportion of older adults who go online increased by six percentage points from 2012 to 2013, more than one-third of older adults (41%) did not use the Internet at all in 2013, and more than half (53%) did not have broadband access at home.

Smith further notes that the percentage of adults who used the Internet and had broadband service decreased with advancing age in 2013: 68% of adults in their early 70s went online, and 55% had broadband in their home. Less than half (47%) of adults aged 75 to 79 years used the Internet, and just 35% had broadband in their home at that time.

Younger (aged 65 to 69 years), higher-income (annual household income of $75,000 or more), and more educated older adults used the Internet and broadband at rates comparable to younger adults in 2013. Smith reports that about three-quarters of adults aged 65 to 69 years

used the Internet, and 65% in that age group had broadband access. Ninety percent of older adults with incomes in excess of $75,000 per year were online, and 82% had broadband access in their home. Similarly, 87% of older adult college graduates went online, and about three-quarters (76%) had broadband access.

More than three-quarters (77%) of adults aged 65 years and older owned a cell phone in 2013, up from 69% in 2012. Smith reports that just 18% of adults aged 65 years and older owned a smartphone (a mobile phone with advanced capabilities including Internet access), and the same percentage own an e-book reader or tablet.

OLDER ADULTS JOIN SOCIAL NETWORKS. Smith finds that although young people are still much more likely than older Internet users to participate in social networking sites, in 2013 nearly one-half (46%) of older adults used social networking sites such as Facebook. More than half (52%) of adults aged 65 years and older accessed social networking sites, but this use was largely by those between the ages of 65 and 79; just 27% of those aged 80 years and older used social networking sites.

Online communities and social networks can help older adults stay in touch with family and friends, preventing social isolation. There is also evidence that using social media can help support the health of older adults. Anja K. Leist of the University of Luxembourg explains in "Social Media Use of Older Adults: A Mini-Review" (*Gerontology*, vol. 59, no. 4, 2013) that social media provides the opportunity for older adults to engage in meaningful social contact, exchange health information, share experiences managing illnesses, and provide and receive social support.

THEY ALSO TEXT, BLOG, AND TWEET. There are few reliable statistics about the numbers of older adults who create and maintain blogs or send text messages. Smith reports in *Older Adults and Technology Use* that in 2013 the percentage of all Internet users on Twitter, a blogging service that limits entries to 140 characters, rose to 19% but just 6% of older adults who are online (or 3% of all older Americans) post or enter a status update on that site.

OLDER ADULTS PLAY VIDEO GAMES. Video games are popular among older adults. For some, console game versions of their once-favorite sports help them to stay "in the game," even when an injury, disability, or illness prevents them from actually participating in tennis, bowling, or golf. Others feel that playing video games helps them to exercise their brains, eye-hand coordination, and reflexes. Still others simply find video games as diverting and entertaining as do younger players.

Age Breakdown of Video Game Players in the United States in 2015, a survey conducted by Ipsos for the

Entertainment Software Association (http://www.statista.com/statistics/189582/age-of-us-video-game-players-since-2010), finds that in 2015, 27% of video game players were aged 50 years and older. This proportion is comparable to video gaming in younger age groups; 26% of gamers were under the age of 18 years, and 30% were between 18 and 35 years.

Jason C. Allaire et al. find in "Successful Aging through Digital Games: Socioemotional Differences between Older Adult Gamers and Non-gamers" (*Computers in Human Behavior*, vol. 29, no. 4, July 2013) that adults aged 63 years and older who played video games, even those who played only occasionally, reported higher levels of emotional and social well-being and less depression than did nongamers.

Playing video games improves a number of cognitive functions. In "Video Game Training Enhances Cognition of Older Adults: A Meta-analytic Study" (*Psychology and Aging*, vol. 29, no. 3, September 2014), Pilar Toril, José M. Reales, and Soledad Ballesteros reviewed 20 studies published between 1986 and 2013, to determine video game training enhances cognitive functions. The investigators find that video game training in older adults produces positive effects on several cognitive functions that decline with aging, including reaction time, attention, and memory.

THE POLITICS OF OLDER ADULTS

Older adults are vitally interested in politics and government, and they are especially interested in the issues that directly influence their lives, including eligibility for and reform to Social Security as well as benefits and coverage by Medicare (a medical insurance program for older adults and people with disabilities). Historically, they are more likely to vote than adults in other age groups, and because many have retired from the workforce they have time to advocate for the policies and candidates they favor.

The Pew Research Center reports in "Deep Dive into Party Affiliation" (April 7, 2015, http://www.people-press.org/files/2015/04/4-7-2015-Party-ID-release.pdf) that the Silent Generation (people born between 1929 and 1946) who were aged 69 to 86 years in 2014, lean Republican. The Silent Generation is the most Republican of all age cohorts.

In *Party Identification Varies Widely across the Age Spectrum* (July 10, 2014, http://www.gallup.com/poll/172439/party-identification-varies-widely-across-age-spectrum.aspx), Frank Newport of the Gallup Organization reports that polls conducted in 2014 find that baby boomers between the ages of 60 and 63 tend to lean Democratic, and Republican identification increases among Americans aged 70 years and older.

Financial Outlook Divides Older and Younger Americans

Lydia Saad of the Gallup Organization notes in *Americans' Money Worries Unchanged from 2014* (April 20, 2015, http://www.gallup.com/poll/182768/americans-money-worries-unchanged-2014.aspx) that "half of Americans have substantial financial anxiety," with "lacking money for retirement" the top worry for most. An April 2015 Gallup poll found that in 2015, one-quarter (24%) of adults between the ages of 50 and 64 and 15% of those aged 65 years and older said they were "very worried" about their personal finances. More than one-third (41%) of adults aged 65 years and older had "no worries about their personal finances." By contrast, just one in five adults aged 30 to 49 years (20%) and those aged 50 to 64 years (19%) said they had no financial worries. (See Table 5.4.)

Older Adults' Views on Major Social Issues

Joy Wilke and Lydia Saad of the Gallup Organization observe in *Older Americans' Moral Attitudes Changing* (June 3, 2013, http://www.gallup.com/poll/162881/older-americans-moral-attitudes-changing.aspx) that younger and older Americans differ in terms of their views about the moral acceptability of a wide range of social and political issues. For example, the proportion of adults aged 18 to 34 years who consider pornography, sex between teenagers, polygamy, and

TABLE 5.4

Percentage of Americans worried about their personal finances by sex, income, marital status, age and Hispanic origin, 2015

	No worry (0 issues)	Low worry (1 to 2 issues)	Moderate worry (3 to 5 issues)	High worry (6 to 7 issues)
	%	%	%	%
Total	25	25	27	23
Less than $30,000	13	15	28	44
$30,000 to $74,999	23	27	29	21
$75,000 or more	38	33	23	6
Men	27	26	28	19
Women	22	24	27	27
Married men	29	25	28	19
Unmarried men	27	26	28	19
Married women	25	28	28	19
Unmarried women	20	21	25	33
Non-Hispanic whites	26	26	29	19
Nonwhites	20	24	23	33
18 to 29	23	24	25	28
30 to 49	20	30	26	23
50 to 64	19	23	34	24
65+	41	21	24	15

SOURCE: Lydia Saad, "Summary of Americans' Anxiety about Personal Financial Matters," in *Americans' Money Worries Unchanged from 2014*, The Gallup Organization, April 20, 2015, http://www.gallup.com/poll/182768/americans-money-worries-unchanged-2014.aspx?utm_source=financial%20outlook%20by%20age&utm_medium=search&utm_campaign=tiles (accessed May 20, 2015). Copyright © 2015 Gallup, Inc. All rights reserved. The content is used with permission; however, Gallup retains all rights of republication.

TABLE 5.5

Support for legal same-sex marriage by age group, 1996, 2013, and 2014

	% should be legal, 1996	% should be legal, 2013	% should be legal, 2014	Change, 1996–2014 (pct. pts.)
18 to 29 years	41	70	78	+37
30 to 49 years	30	53	54	+24
50 to 64 years	15	46	48	+33
65+ years	14	41	42	+28

SOURCE: Justin McCarthy, "Support for Legal Same-Sex Marriage by Age, 1996, 2013, and 2014," in *Same-Sex Marriage Support Reaches New High at 55%*, The Gallup Organization, May 21, 2014, http://www.gallup.com/poll/169640/sex-marriage-support-reaches-new-high.aspx (accessed May 20, 2015). Copyright © 2015 Gallup, Inc. All rights reserved. The content is used with permission; however, Gallup retains all rights of republication.

cloning humans to be morally acceptable is more than twice that of adults aged 55 years and older.

Justin McCarthy reports in "Record-High 60% of Americans Support Same-Sex Marriage" (CNN.com, May 19, 2015) that although support for same-sex marriage rose to a record high of 60% in 2015, up from 55% in 2014, people aged 65 years and older are still more likely to oppose it. Table 5.5 shows that although support for legal same-sex marriage has increased among people of all ages, it is lowest among those aged 65 years and older.

U.S. Politicians Are Growing Older

In "The Grayest Congress" (NBCNews.com, 2013), Jennifer Colby reports that in 2013 Congress was the oldest it has ever been. The average age of a U.S. senator was 60, and the average age of a member of the U.S. House of Representatives was 55. By 2015 the median age of currently serving senators was nearly 62. There were 32 U.S. senators in their 60s, 18 in their 70s, and five in their 80s: Dianne Feinstein (1933–; D-CA), Chuck Grassley (1933–; R-IA), Orrin G. Hatch (1934–; R-UT), Jim Inhofe (1934–; R-OK), and Richard Shelby (1934–; R-AL).

In 2015, 137 members of the House of Representatives were in their 60s, 41 members were in their 70s, and six were in their 80s: John Conyers (1929–; D-MI), Sam Johnson (1930–; R-TX), Sander Levin (1931–; D-MI), Charles Rangel (1930–; D-NY), Louise Slaughter (1929–; D-NY), and Donald Young (1933–; R-AK).

"GRAY POWER": A POLITICAL BLOC

AARP believes strongly in the principles of collective purpose, collective voice and the collective power of the 50 and over population to change the market based on their needs. These principles guide our efforts.

—AARP, "What We Do" (2015)

A higher proportion of adults aged 55 to 74 years vote than than any other age group, and it is inevitable that the increasing number of Americans in this cohort (a group of individuals that shares a common characteristic such as birth years and is studied over time) will wield an enormous political impact. With more than 37 million members, the AARP (2015, http://www.aarp.org/about-aarp) exercises considerable influence when lobbying political leaders about the issues that concern older Americans.

As part of its mission, the AARP advocates on behalf of older adults. It is known as a powerful advocate on a range of legislative, consumer, and legal issues. To this end, the organization monitors issues that are pertinent to the lives of older Americans, assesses public opinion on such issues, and keeps policy makers apprised of these opinions. Advocacy efforts include becoming involved in litigation when the decision could have a significant effect on the lives of older Americans. In cases regarding age discrimination, pensions, health care, economic security, and consumer issues, AARP lawyers file amicus briefs (legal documents filed by individuals or groups that are not actual parties to a lawsuit but that are interested in influencing the outcome of the lawsuit) and support third-party lawsuits to promote the interests of older people.

The AARP responds to political and policy issues of concern to its constituency. For example, it asserts in the press release "AARP Statement on GOP Budget Plan" (May 6, 2015, http://www.aarp.org/about-aarp/press-center/info-05-2015/statement-on-gop-budget.html) that it disagreed with the proposed GOP budget agreement because it asks older adults to shoulder more out-of-pocket health care costs without improving health care for Medicare beneficiaries. It also opposes repeal of the Patient Protection and Affordable Care Act, asserting "Medical costs are rising at the lowest rates in years, insurance premiums have stabilized, families have the security of keeping their children on their insurance plans until they are age 26, and those between the ages of 50 and 64 have the peace of mind that insurance coverage is affordable and they won't be denied health insurance because of a preexisting condition."

CHAPTER 6
ON THE ROAD: OLDER ADULT DRIVERS

Readily available transportation is a vital factor in the quality of life of older adults. Transportation is essential for accessing health care, establishing and maintaining social and family relationships, obtaining food and other necessities, and preserving independence and self-esteem.

The ability to drive often determines whether an older adult is able to live independently. Driving is the primary mode of transportation in the United States, and personal vehicles remain the transportation mode of choice for almost all Americans, including older people. Surveys conducted by the AARP repeatedly confirm that people over the age of 65 years make nearly all their trips in private vehicles, either as drivers or passengers. Even in urban areas where public transit is readily available, private vehicles are still used by most older people, and nondrivers rely on family members or friends for transport. The National Highway Traffic Safety Administration (NHTSA) confirms in "Alternative Transportation—It Could Work for You" (2015, http://www.nhtsa.gov/people/injury/olddrive/Driving%20Safely%20Aging%20Web/page6.html) that older adult nondrivers rely on alternative forms of transportation, such as rides from family or friends, public transportation, walking, or senior vans or taxicabs.

The NHTSA states in *Older Driver Program: Five-Year Strategic Plan 2012–2017* (December 2010, http://www.nhtsa.gov/staticfiles/nti/pdf/811432.pdf) that older adults are a significant and growing segment of the driving population. The Insurance Institute for Highway Safety (IIHS) reports that in 2013 there were 23.6 million licensed drivers aged 70 years and older, which is more than three-quarters (78%) of the population age 70 and older and about 11% of drivers of all ages.

Federal Highway Administration data reveal that in 2013 the percentage of older drivers was comparable for men and women. (See Table 6.1.) Donald H. Camph

notes in *A New Vision of America's Highways: Long-Distance Travel, Recreation, Tourism, and Rural Travel* (March 2007) that as the baby boomers (people born between 1946 and 1964) join the ranks of older adults, the number of drivers aged 65 years and older will continue to grow, exceeding 40 million by 2020.

Camph observes, however, that although many older adults drive and many more are expected to in the future, driving is not a viable alternative for a significant number of older people. Many older adults choose to stop or limit their driving for health or safety reasons. Others do not have access to a vehicle. Camph also asserts that "more than 50 percent of non-drivers age 65 and older—or 3.6 million Americans—stay home on any given day at least partially because they lack transportation options."

Limited income also restricts many older adults' use of automobiles. According to the U.S. Bureau of Labor Statistics, car ownership costs are the second-largest household expense in the United States, and the average household spends nearly as much to own and operate a car as it does on food and health care combined. Table 6.2 shows that the percent of total annual expenditures for transportation rose to 17.6% in 2013 from 16% in 2010. In 2013 adults between the ages of 65 and 74 spent $7,972 per year on transportation, and those age 75 and older spent $5,149 annually. (See Table 6.3.)

For the first time since 2009, gas prices decreased in 2013. Nonetheless, the cost of owning and operating an automobile, especially during periods of rising fuel prices, may be prohibitive for older adults living on fixed incomes. (See Figure 6.1.) As a result, an ever-increasing proportion of the older population depends on alternative forms of transport in those areas where such transport is available. Some older adults, however, remain isolated and immobilized by the absence of accessible, affordable transportation in their communities.

TABLE 6.1

Licensed drivers, by sex and percentage in each age group and relation to population, 2013

Age	Male drivers Number	Percent of total drivers	Drivers as percent of age group*	Female drivers Number	Percent of total drivers	Drivers as percent of age group*	Total drivers Number	Percent of total drivers	Drivers as percent of age group*
Under 16	31,490	0.0	1.5	30,863	0.0	1.5	62,353	0.0	1.5
16	584,266	0.6	27.5	584,291	0.5	28.8	1,168,557	0.6	28.1
17	1,023,516	1.0	47.6	986,599	0.9	48.3	2,010,115	0.9	48.0
18	1,381,031	1.3	62.8	1,298,719	1.2	62.3	2,679,750	1.3	62.5
19	1,577,900	1.5	70.1	1,483,512	1.4	69.7	3,061,412	1.4	69.9
(19 and under)	4,598,203	4.4	42.4	4,383,984	4.1	42.5	8,982,187	4.2	42.5
20	1,689,607	1.6	73.8	1,604,807	1.5	74.4	3,294,414	1.6	74.1
21	1,747,064	1.7	74.4	1,687,494	1.6	76.0	3,434,558	1.6	75.2
22	1,806,956	1.7	75.9	1,768,611	1.7	77.8	3,575,567	1.7	76.8
23	1,858,427	1.8	78.2	1,830,556	1.7	80.4	3,688,983	1.7	79.3
24	1,842,863	1.8	80.7	1,831,867	1.7	83.7	3,674,730	1.7	82.2
(20–24)	8,944,917	8.5	76.6	8,723,335	8.1	78.5	17,668,252	8.3	77.5
25–29	9,128,669	8.7	83.3	9,212,559	8.6	86.7	18,341,228	8.6	85.0
30–34	9,083,416	8.7	85.0	9,273,260	8.7	87.6	18,356,676	8.7	86.3
35–39	8,566,880	8.2	87.5	8,707,025	8.1	88.7	17,273,905	8.1	88.1
40–44	9,333,347	8.9	90.1	9,411,540	8.8	89.7	18,744,887	8.8	89.9
45–49	9,620,974	9.2	91.6	9,678,345	9.0	90.4	19,299,319	9.1	91.0
50–54	10,206,701	9.7	92.2	10,401,105	9.7	90.5	20,607,806	9.7	91.3
55–59	9,563,697	9.1	93.0	9,834,818	9.2	90.1	19,398,515	9.1	91.5
60–64	8,179,029	7.8	94.3	8,477,708	7.9	89.7	16,656,737	7.9	91.9
65–69	6,494,023	6.2	93.9	6,733,139	6.3	87.5	13,227,162	6.2	90.5
70–74	4,532,716	4.3	92.8	4,774,599	4.5	83.4	9,307,315	4.4	87.7
75–79	3,091,299	2.9	91.2	3,328,898	3.1	77.6	6,420,197	3.0	83.6
80–84	2,075,522	2.0	87.6	2,323,360	2.2	68.4	4,398,882	2.1	76.3
85 and over	1,588,277	1.5	77.8	1,888,383	1.8	47.2	3,476,660	1.6	57.6
Total	**105,007,670**	**100.0**	**86.1**	**107,152,058**	**100.0**	**82.0**	**212,159,728**	**100.0**	**83.2**

*These percentages are computed using population estimates of the Bureau of the Census. Under-16 age group is compared to 14 and 15-year-old population estimates; the other age brackets coincide with those from the Bureau of the Census.

SOURCE: "Distribution of Licensed Drivers—2013 by Sex and Percentage in Each Age Group and Relation to Population," in *Highway Statistics 2013*, U.S. Department of Transportation, Federal Highway Administration, January 2015, http://www.fhwa.dot.gov/policyinformation/statistics/2013/pdf/dl20.pdf (accessed May 22, 2015)

According to the U.S. Government Accountability Office (GAO), in *Transportation for Older Adults: Measuring Results Could Help Determine If Coordination Efforts Improve Mobility* (December 10, 2014, http://www.gao.gov/assets/670/667375.pdf), state and local transportation agencies and aging organizations use a variety of approaches to coordinate transportation services for older adults. For example, travel-training programs help older adults identify and gain access to transportation resources. Other programs offer transportation services directly. For example, Ride Connection in Oregon (http://www.rideconnection.org/ride/default.aspx), which relies on volunteers, provides more than 400,000 rides a year to older adults and others.

TRANSPORTATION INITIATIVES ADDRESS NEEDS OF OLDER ADULTS

Because ensuring access to transportation is key to older adults' independence and quality of life, several federal agencies and initiatives aim to address this need. The Administration on Aging (AoA) funds state and local agencies that provide transportation services for older adults. Within the Department of Transportation (DOT),

the Federal Transit Administration Enhanced Mobility of Seniors and Individuals with Disabilities program also serves older adults. Other federal agency programs, including some within the Department of Veterans Affairs, fund access to transportation services for older adult beneficiaries. The Interagency Coordinating Council on Access and Mobility (Coordinating Council) leads federal efforts to improve the efficiency and effectiveness of transportation services.

The Coordinating Council sponsors United We Ride, a national interagency initiative that supports states and their localities to develop coordinated human service delivery systems. The National Center on Senior Transportation (NCST) aims to assist older adults to remain active, vital members of their communities by offering a range of transportation options and alternatives. The NCST-sponsored Senior Transportation program is a collaborative effort that coordinates research and services intended to develop new transportation solutions, especially for rural areas. The program also champions the creative use of technology to connect volunteers, older drivers, and older adults in need of transportation services. The NCST is overseen by Easter

TABLE 6.2

Percentage distribution of total annual expenditures by major category, 2010–13

Spending category	2010	2011	2012	2013
Average annual expenditures	100.0	100.0	100.0	100.0
Food	12.7	13.0	12.8	12.9
Food at home	7.5	7.7	7.6	7.8
Food away from home	5.2	5.3	5.2	5.1
Alcoholic beverages	0.9	0.9	0.9	0.9
Housing	34.4	33.8	32.8	33.6
Shelter	20.4	19.8	19.2	19.7
Utilities, fuels, and public services	7.6	7.5	7.1	7.3
Household operations	2.1	2.3	2.3	2.2
Housekeeping supplies	1.3	1.2	1.2	1.3
Household furnishings and equipment	3.0	3.0	3.1	3.0
Apparel and services	3.5	3.5	3.4	3.1
Transportation	16.0	16.7	17.5	17.6
Vehicle purchases (net outlay)	5.4	5.4	6.2	6.4
Gasoline and motor oil	4.4	5.3	5.4	5.1
Other vehicle expenses	5.1	4.9	4.8	5.1
Public and other transportation	1.0	1.0	1.1	1.1
Healthcare	6.6	6.7	6.9	7.1
Entertainment	5.2	5.2	5.1	4.9
Personal care products and services	1.2	1.3	1.2	1.2
Reading	0.2	0.2	0.2	0.2
Education	2.2	2.1	2.3	2.2
Tobacco products and smoking supplies	0.8	0.7	0.6	0.6
Miscellaneous	1.8	1.6	1.6	1.3
Cash contributions	3.4	3.5	3.7	3.6
Personal insurance and pensions	11.2	10.9	10.9	10.8
Life and other personal insurance	0.7	0.6	0.7	0.6
Pensions and Social Security	10.5	10.3	10.2	10.2

SOURCE: "Table B. Percent Distribution of Total Annual Expenditures by Major Category for All Consumer Units, Consumer Expenditure Survey, 2010–2013," in "Consumer Expenditures in 2013," *BLS Reports*, U.S. Bureau of Labor Statistics, February 2015, http://www.bls.gov/cex/csxann13 .pdf (accessed May 22, 2015)

Seals Inc. and receives funding via the DOT's Federal Transit Administration.

MOTOR VEHICLE ACCIDENTS

The IIHS, a nonprofit organization dedicated to reducing losses from motor vehicle accidents, reports that apart from the youngest drivers, older drivers have the highest rates of fatal crashes per mile driven. Although older drivers tend to limit their number of miles driven as they age and they drive at the safest times (in daylight and avoiding rush-hour traffic), their rate of accidents per mile is high. In "Older Drivers: 2013" (2015, http://www.iihs.org/iihs/topics/t/older-drivers/fatalityfacts/older-people), the IIHS observes that in 2012, motor vehicle crashes accounted for less than 1% of fatalities among people aged 70 years and older and that fatal crash rates increase markedly at ages 70 to 74 years and are highest among drivers 85 years and older.

The oldest and youngest drivers have the highest fatality rates on a per-mile-driven basis, but a key difference between the two age groups is that older drivers involved in crashes are less likely than younger drivers to hurt others; older drivers pose more of a danger to themselves. Drivers under the age of 35 years are also more

likely to be speeding and are responsible for far more of the speeding-related fatal crashes than are older adult drivers. (See Figure 6.2.).

Table 6.4 shows that in 2013 the death rate (the number of deaths per 100,000 people) for motor vehicle–related injuries for adults aged 65 years and older was 15.1%, compared with 12.1% for adults aged 45 to 64 years. The higher fatality rates of adults aged 75 to 84 years (17.8%) and 85 years and older (21%) who were involved in crashes are attributable to older adults' fragility as opposed to the likelihood of being involved in an accident. Older people are more susceptible to injury, especially chest injuries, and are more likely to die as a result of those injuries.

The IIHS reports in "Older Drivers: 2013" that in 2013, 75% of motor vehicle crash fatalities among people aged 70 years and older involved occupants in passenger vehicles, and 16% were pedestrians. Since 1997, deaths of older adult passengers have declined 35%, and deaths of older pedestrians declined 30%.

In 2013, 40% of fatalities involving drivers aged 80 years and older were multiple-vehicle crashes that occurred at intersections. The IIHS in "Older Drivers: 2013" observes that older drivers are more likely than younger drivers to have accidents when making left turns and attributes this to the fact that older drivers take longer to make turns, increasing the risk of a crash.

Older adults also suffer nonfatal injuries as drivers or passengers in motor vehicle crashes. In 2013 the National Center for Injury Prevention and Control recorded 265,668 nonfatal motor vehicle injuries in adults aged 65 to 85 years. (See Table 6.5; this figure shows the 197,646 injuries to occupants of vehicles and the 68,022 injuries attributable to other transport.) Motor vehicle accidents (called unintentional MV-occupant) were the fourth-leading cause of nonfatal injuries among adults aged 65 to 85 years in the United States in 2013.

The data about older drivers are not all bad. According to the Centers for Disease Control and Prevention (CDC), in "New Data on Older Adult Drivers" (April 29, 2015, http://www.cdc.gov/features/dsolderdrivers/index.html), older drivers take fewer risks than younger drivers by limiting their driving on high-speed roads, during bad weather and at night, and in heavy traffic. Figure 6.3 shows the percentages of older adult drivers who tend to avoid driving under certain conditions.

AGE-RELATED CHANGES MAY IMPAIR OLDER DRIVERS' SKILLS

Most older adults retain their driving skills, but some age-related changes in vision, hearing, cognitive functions (attention, memory, and reaction times), reflexes, and flexibility of the head and neck may impair the skills

TABLE 6.3

Average annual expenditures, by age, 2013

Item	All consumer units	Under 25 years	25–34 years	35–44 years	45–54 years	55–64 years	65 years and older	65–74 years	75 years and older
Number of consumer units (in thousands)	125,670	8,275	20,707	21,257	24,501	22,887	28,042	16,024	12,018
Consumer unit characteristics:									
Income before taxes	$63,784	$27,914	$59,002	$78,385	$78,879	$74,182	$45,157	$53,451	$34,097
Age of reference person	50.1	21.6	29.8	39.7	49.7	59.2	74.3	68.8	81.6
Average number in consumer unit:									
People	2.5	2.0	2.8	3.4	2.7	2.1	1.8	1.9	1.6
Children under 18	0.6	0.4	1.1	1.4	0.6	0.2	0.1	0.1	*
Adults 65 and older	0.3	*	*	*	0.1	0.1	1.4	1.4	1.3
Earners	1.3	1.3	1.5	1.6	1.6	1.3	0.5	0.7	0.2
Vehicles	1.9	1.1	1.6	2.0	2.2	2.2	1.6	1.9	1.3
Percent homeowner	64	14	40	62	69	79	81	82	79
Average annual expenditures	$51,100	$30,373	$48,087	$58,784	$60,524	$55,892	$41,403	$46,757	$34,382
Food	6,602	4,698	6,197	7,920	7,907	6,711	5,191	6,020	4,144
Food at home	3,977	2,602	3,559	4,641	4,701	4,232	3,327	3,728	2,825
Cereals and bakery products	544	363	467	646	650	573	457	488	418
Meats, poultry, fish, and eggs	856	580	775	993	1,048	898	689	809	538
Dairy products	414	274	383	495	475	426	351	380	314
Fruits and vegetables	751	448	689	866	857	797	663	730	580
Other food at home	1,412	936	1,245	1,641	1,672	1,538	1,168	1,320	975
Food away from home	2,625	2,096	2,639	3,280	3,206	2,479	1,864	2,292	1,319
Alcoholic beverages	445	379	489	443	545	465	326	400	232
Housing	17,148	10,379	17,207	20,619	19,001	17,937	14,204	15,639	12,314
Shelter	10,080	6,944	10,712	12,271	11,208	10,251	7,755	8,410	6,882
Owned dwellings	6,108	1,003	4,560	7,981	7,378	7,265	5,284	6,072	4,234
Rented dwellings	3,324	5,728	5,881	3,834	2,938	1,937	1,808	1,444	2,292
Other lodging	649	213	271	455	892	1,049	663	894	356
Utilities, fuels, and public services	3,737	1,842	3,186	4,299	4,277	4,135	3,480	3,824	3,022
Household operations	1,144	428	1,404	1,612	1,020	1,034	1,007	984	1,037
Housekeeping supplies	645	323	497	674	751	706	682	803	532
Household furnishings and equipment	1,542	842	1,408	1,763	1,745	1,811	1,280	1,618	841
Apparel and services	1,604	1,513	1,832	1,960	1,826	1,563	1,022	1,222	768
Transportation	9,004	5,672	9,183	10,519	10,782	9,482	6,760	7,972	5,149
Vehicle purchases (net outlay)	3,271	2,262	3,641	4,010	3,958	3,275	2,133	2,396	1,783
Gasoline and motor oil	2,611	1,717	2,676	3,218	3,093	2,792	1,799	2,233	1,220
Other vehicle expenses	2,584	1,444	2,416	2,740	3,074	2,824	2,302	2,677	1,805
Public and other transportation	537	249	450	552	657	591	527	665	341
Healthcare	3,631	943	2,189	3,188	3,801	4,378	5,069	5,188	4,910
Entertainment	2,482	1,243	2,214	2,958	3,070	2,651	2,027	2,488	1,422
Personal care products and services	608	342	538	672	723	638	563	619	491
Reading	102	46	60	105	88	132	138	146	127
Education	1,138	2,055	1,019	903	1,970	1,241	319	349	280
Tobacco products and smoking supplies	330	219	309	331	447	438	185	258	89
Miscellaneous	645	207	577	643	686	841	628	672	571
Cash contributions	1,834	473	970	1,440	2,007	2,382	2,574	2,391	2,817
Personal insurance and pensions	5,528	2,203	5,304	7,081	7,672	7,033	2,396	3,392	1,068
Life and other personal insurance	319	50	125	290	367	440	421	559	237
Pensions and Social Security	5,209	2,153	5,178	6,791	7,305	6,593	1,975	2,833	832

*Value is too small to display.

SOURCE: "Table 4. Age of Reference Person: Average Annual Expenditures and Characteristics, Consumer Expenditure Survey, 2013," in "Consumer Expenditures in 2013." *BLS Reports*, U.S. Bureau of Labor Statistics, February 2015, http://www.bls.gov/cex/csxann13.pdf (accessed May 22, 2015)

that are critical for safe driving. For example, reaction time becomes slower and more variable with advancing age, and arthritis (inflammation that causes pain and loss of movement of the joints) in the neck or shoulder may limit sufferers' ability to turn their necks well enough to merge into traffic, see when backing up, and navigate intersections where the angle of intersecting roads is less than perpendicular.

Changes such as reduced muscle mass and the resultant reduction in strength, as well as decreases in the efficiency of the circulatory, cardiac, and respiratory systems, are strictly related to aging. Others are attributable to the fact that certain diseases, such as arthritis and glaucoma (a disease in which fluid pressure inside the eyes slowly rises, leading to vision loss or blindness), tend to strike at later ages. The functional losses that are associated with these conditions are usually gradual, and many afflicted older drivers are able to adapt to them. Most older adults do not experience declines until very old age, and most learn to adjust to the limitations imposed by age-related changes. Still, a substantial proportion of older adults do stop driving in response to age-related changes.

FIGURE 6.1

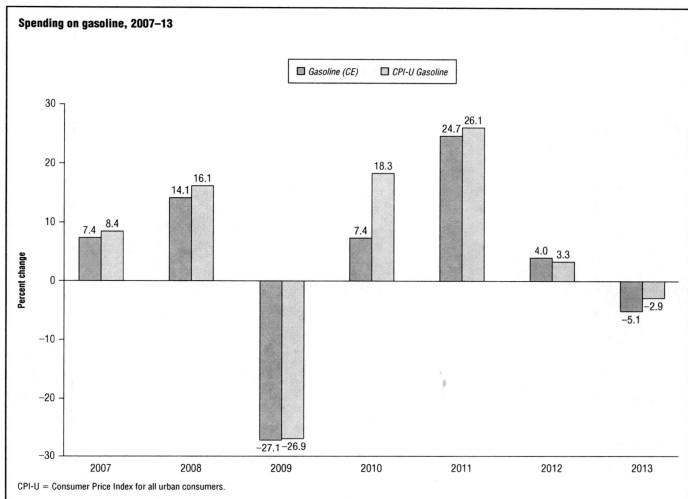

Spending on gasoline, 2007–13

Legend: Gasoline (CE) | CPI-U Gasoline

Y-axis: Percent change

Year	Gasoline (CE)	CPI-U Gasoline
2007	7.4	8.4
2008	14.1	16.1
2009	−27.1	−26.9
2010	7.4	18.3
2011	24.7	26.1
2012	4.0	3.3
2013	−5.1	−2.9

CPI-U = Consumer Price Index for all urban consumers.

SOURCE: "Chart 2. Spending and Price Index Percent Changes on Gasoline, Consumer Expenditure Survey (CE), Consumer Price Index (CPI), 2007–2013 in "Consumer Expenditures in 2013", *BLS Reports*, February 2015, Bureau of Labor Statistics, http://www.bls.gov/cex/csxann13.pdf (accessed May 22, 2015)

In "New Data on Older Drivers," the CDC reports that of older adults who reduced their driving, 40% said they did so because of vision problems.

The *Physician's Guide to Assessing and Counseling Older Drivers* (2010, http://geriatricscareonline.org/Product Abstract/physicians-guide-to-assessing-and-counseling-older-drivers/B013), published by the American Medical Association (AMA) and the NHTSA, details medical conditions and their potential effect on driving and highlights treatment methods and counseling measures that can minimize these effects. The AMA and the NHTSA identify motor vehicle injuries as the leading cause of injury-related deaths among 65- to 75-year-olds and the second-leading cause of deaths among 75- to 84-year-olds. They posit that significant growth in the older population and an increase in miles driven by older adults could triple the number of traffic fatalities in the coming years. Believing that the medical community can help stem this increase, the AMA and the NHTSA

call on physicians to help their patients maintain or even improve their driving skills by periodically assessing them for disease- and medication-related conditions that might impair their capacity to function as safe drivers.

Acute and Chronic Medical Problems

According to the AMA and the NHTSA, in *Physician's Guide to Assessing and Counseling Older Drivers*, patients discharged from the hospital following treatment for serious illnesses may be temporarily, or even permanently, unable to drive safely. Examples of acute (short-term) medical problems that can impair driving performance include:

• Acute myocardial infarction (heart attack)

• Stroke (sudden death of a portion of the brain cells due to a lack of blood flow and oxygen) and other traumatic brain injury

• Syncope (fainting) and vertigo (dizziness)

FIGURE 6.2

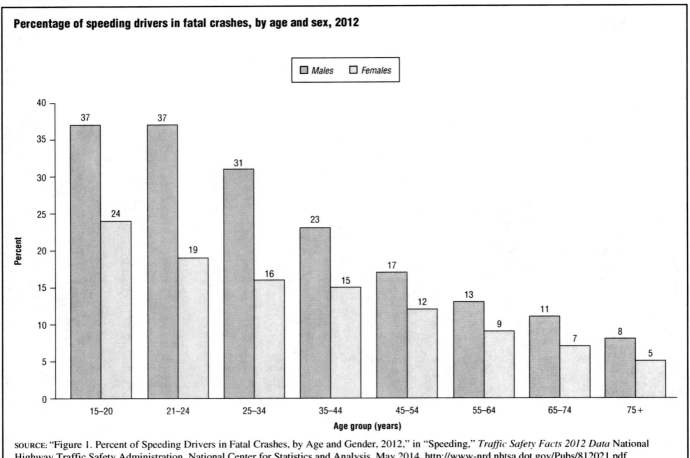

Percentage of speeding drivers in fatal crashes, by age and sex, 2012

SOURCE: "Figure 1. Percent of Speeding Drivers in Fatal Crashes, by Age and Gender, 2012," in "Speeding," *Traffic Safety Facts 2012 Data* National Highway Traffic Safety Administration, National Center for Statistics and Analysis, May 2014, http://www-nrd.nhtsa.dot.gov/Pubs/812021.pdf (accessed May 22, 2015)

• Seizures (sudden attacks or convulsions characterized by generalized muscle spasms and loss of consciousness)

• Surgery

• Delirium (altered mental state characterized by wild, irregular, and incoherent thoughts and actions) from any cause

The AMA and the NHTSA note that a variety of chronic (long-term) medical conditions can also compromise driving function, including:

• Visual disorders such as cataracts, diabetic retinopathy (damage to the blood vessels that supply the retina that can result in blindness), macular degeneration (a degenerative condition that can cause blurred vision), glaucoma, retinitis pigmentosa (an inherited condition that causes night blindness and tunnel vision), and low visual acuity (the inability to distinguish fine details) even after correction with lenses. Along with visual acuity, other visual functions decline with advancing age. For example, sensitivity to glare increases and may be exacerbated by cataracts. Because driving is largely a visual task, impaired vision can significantly compromise the ability to read signs, see lane lines, and identify pedestrians in the dark or during inclement weather.

• Cardiovascular disorders such as angina (chest pain from a blockage in a coronary artery that prevents oxygen-rich blood from reaching part of the heart) or syncope pose dangers to drivers because acute pain or even transient loss of consciousness increases the risk of accidents.

• Neurologic diseases such as seizures, dementia (loss of intellectual functioning accompanied by memory loss and personality changes), multiple sclerosis (a progressive nerve disease that can result in the loss of the ability to walk or speak), Parkinson's disease (a degenerative disease that causes tremors and slowed movement and speech), peripheral neuropathy (numbness or tingling in the hands and/or feet), and residual deficits (losses or disability) resulting from stroke all may impair the driver's ability to operate a vehicle and/or exercise sufficient caution when driving.

• Psychiatric diseases, especially those mental disorders in which patients suffer hallucinations, severe anxiety,

TABLE 6.4

Death rates for motor vehicle-related injuries, by selected characteristics, selected years 1950–2013

[Data are based on death certificates]

Sex, race, Hispanic origin, and age	1950[a, b]	1960[a, b]	1970[b]	1980[b]	1990[b]	2000[c]	2010[c]	2012[c]	2013[c]
All persons				Deaths per 100,000 resident population					
All ages, age-adjusted[d]	24.6	23.1	27.6	22.3	18.5	15.4	11.3	11.4	10.9
All ages, crude	23.1	21.3	26.9	23.5	18.8	15.4	11.4	11.6	11.2
Under 1 year	8.4	8.1	9.8	7.0	4.9	4.4	2.0	1.8	1.7
1–14 years	9.8	8.6	10.5	8.2	6.0	4.3	2.3	2.2	2.2
1–4 years	11.5	10.0	11.5	9.2	6.3	4.2	2.8	2.9	2.7
5–14 years	8.8	7.9	10.2	7.9	5.9	4.3	2.2	2.0	2.1
15–24 years	34.4	38.0	47.2	44.8	34.1	26.9	16.6	16.1	15.2
15–19 years	29.6	33.9	43.6	43.0	33.1	26.0	13.6	12.6	11.4
20–24 years	38.8	42.9	51.3	46.6	35.0	28.0	19.7	19.3	18.8
25–34 years	24.6	24.3	30.9	29.1	23.6	17.3	14.0	14.5	13.9
35–44 years	20.3	19.3	24.9	20.9	16.9	15.3	11.6	11.8	11.4
45–64 years	25.2	23.0	26.5	18.0	15.7	14.3	11.9	12.4	12.1
45–54 years	22.2	21.4	25.5	18.6	15.6	14.2	12.0	12.6	12.2
55–64 years	29.0	25.1	27.9	17.4	15.9	14.4	11.9	12.2	11.9
65 years and over	43.1	34.7	36.2	22.5	23.1	21.4	16.0	15.7	15.1
65–74 years	39.1	31.4	32.8	19.2	18.6	16.5	12.3	13.0	12.2
75–84 years	52.7	41.8	43.5	28.1	29.1	25.7	18.8	17.9	17.8
85 years and over	45.1	37.9	34.2	27.6	31.2	30.4	23.8	22.1	21.0
Male									
All ages, age-adjusted[d]	38.5	35.4	41.5	33.6	26.5	21.7	16.2	16.5	15.9
All ages, crude	35.4	31.8	39.7	35.3	26.7	21.3	16.3	16.6	16.1
Under 1 year	9.1	8.6	9.3	7.3	5.0	4.6	2.2	1.9	1.7
1–14 years	12.3	10.7	13.0	10.0	7.0	4.9	2.7	2.5	2.5
1–4 years	13.0	11.5	12.9	10.2	6.9	4.7	3.0	3.1	3.0
5–14 years	11.9	10.4	13.1	9.9	7.0	5.0	2.5	2.3	2.4
15–24 years	56.7	61.2	73.2	68.4	49.5	37.4	23.1	22.5	21.2
15–19 years	46.3	51.7	64.1	62.6	45.5	33.9	17.8	16.2	14.7
20–24 years	66.7	73.2	84.4	74.3	53.3	41.2	28.5	28.4	27.3
25–34 years	40.8	40.1	49.4	46.3	35.7	25.5	21.0	21.5	20.8
35–44 years	32.5	29.9	37.7	31.7	24.7	22.0	16.9	17.6	16.9
45–64 years	37.7	33.3	38.9	26.5	21.9	20.2	17.9	18.6	18.2
45–54 years	33.6	31.6	37.2	27.6	22.0	20.4	17.9	18.8	18.3
55–64 years	43.1	35.6	40.9	25.4	21.7	19.8	17.8	18.5	18.1
65 years and over	66.6	52.1	54.4	33.9	32.1	29.5	22.2	22.1	21.5
65–74 years	59.1	45.8	47.3	27.3	24.2	21.7	17.1	18.5	17.5
75–84 years	85.0	66.0	68.2	44.3	41.2	35.6	25.9	24.8	24.9
85 years and over	78.1	62.7	63.1	56.1	64.5	57.5	40.2	35.3	35.3
Female									
All ages, age-adjusted[d]	11.5	11.7	14.9	11.8	11.0	9.5	6.5	6.5	6.2
All ages, crude	10.9	11.0	14.7	12.3	11.3	9.7	6.8	6.7	6.4
Under 1 year	7.6	7.5	10.4	6.7	4.9	4.2	1.8	1.8	1.8
1–14 years	7.2	6.3	7.9	6.3	4.9	3.7	2.0	1.9	1.9
1–4 years	10.0	8.4	10.0	8.1	5.6	3.8	2.5	2.6	2.3
5–14 years	5.7	5.4	7.2	5.7	4.7	3.6	1.8	1.7	1.8
15–24 years	12.6	15.1	21.6	20.8	17.9	15.9	9.9	9.3	8.9
15–19 years	12.9	16.0	22.7	22.8	20.0	17.5	9.2	8.9	7.9
20–24 years	12.2	14.0	20.4	18.9	16.0	14.2	10.5	9.8	9.9
25–34 years	9.3	9.2	13.0	12.2	11.5	8.8	6.9	7.4	6.9
35–44 years	8.5	9.1	12.9	10.4	9.2	8.8	6.2	6.2	5.9
45–64 years	12.6	13.1	15.3	10.3	10.1	8.7	6.3	6.4	6.3
45–54 years	10.9	11.6	14.5	10.2	9.6	8.2	6.3	6.5	6.3
55–64 years	14.9	15.2	16.2	10.5	10.8	9.5	6.3	6.4	6.2
65 years and over	21.9	20.3	23.1	15.0	17.2	15.8	11.3	10.8	10.0
65–74 years	20.6	19.0	21.6	13.0	14.1	12.3	8.2	8.2	7.5
75–84 years	25.2	23.0	27.2	18.5	21.9	19.2	13.7	12.9	12.5
85 years and over	22.1	22.0	18.0	15.2	18.3	19.3	15.9	15.5	13.7
White male[e]									
All ages, age-adjusted[d]	37.9	34.8	40.4	33.8	26.3	21.8	16.7	17.0	16.3
All ages, crude	35.1	31.5	39.1	35.9	26.7	21.6	17.0	17.3	16.7
Under 1 year	9.1	8.8	9.1	7.0	4.8	4.2	2.0	1.9	1.7
1–14 years	12.4	10.6	12.5	9.8	6.6	4.8	2.7	2.4	2.4
15–24 years	58.3	62.7	75.2	73.8	52.5	39.6	24.6	24.5	22.9
25–34 years	39.1	38.6	47.0	46.6	35.4	25.1	21.4	22.0	21.1
35–44 years	30.9	28.4	35.2	30.7	23.7	21.8	17.4	18.0	17.3
45–64 years	36.2	31.7	36.5	25.2	20.6	19.7	18.3	19.0	18.5
65 years and over	67.1	52.1	54.2	32.7	31.4	29.4	22.7	22.6	22.1

TABLE 6.4

Death rates for motor vehicle-related injuries, by selected characteristics, selected years 1950–2013 [CONTINUED]

[Data are based on death certificates]

^aIncludes deaths of persons who were not residents of the 50 states and the District of Columbia (D.C.).
^bUnderlying cause of death was coded according to the 6th Revision of the *International Classification of Diseases* (ICD) in 1950, 7th Revision in 1960, 8th Revision in 1970, and 9th Revision in 1980–1998.
^cStarting with 1999 data, cause of death is coded according to ICD–10.
^dAge-adjusted rates are calculated using the year 2000 standard population. Prior to 2001, age-adjusted rates were calculated using standard million proportions based on rounded population numbers. Starting with 2001 data, unrounded population numbers are used to calculate age-adjusted rates.
^eThe race groups, white, black, Asian or Pacific Islander, and American Indian or Alaska Native, include persons of Hispanic and non-Hispanic origin. Persons of Hispanic origin may be of any race. Death rates for Hispanic, American Indian or Alaska Native, and Asian or Pacific Islander persons should be interpreted with caution because of inconsistencies in reporting Hispanic origin or race on the death certificate (death rate numerators) compared with population figures (death rate denominators). The net effect of misclassification is an underestimation of deaths and death rates for races other than white and black.
Notes: Starting with *Health, United States, 2003*, rates for 1991–1999 were revised using intercensal population estimates based on the 1990 and 2000 censuses. For 2000, population estimates are bridged-race April 1 census counts. Starting with *Health, United States, 2012*, rates for 2001–2009 were revised using intercensal population estimates based on the 2000 and 2010 censuses. For 2010, population estimates are bridged-race April 1 census counts. Rates for 2011 and beyond were computed using 2010-based postcensal estimates. Age groups were selected to minimize the presentation of unstable age-specific death rates based on small numbers of deaths and for consistency among comparison groups. Starting with 2003 data, some states allowed the reporting of more than one race on the death certificate. The multiple-race data for these states were bridged to the single-race categories of the 1977 Office of Management and Budget standards, for comparability with other states. Rates based on fewer than 20 deaths are considered unreliable and are not shown.

SOURCE: Adapted from "Table 31. Death Rates for Motor Vehicle-Related Injuries, by Sex, Race, Hispanic Origin, and Age: United States, Selected Years 1950–2013," in *Health, United States, 2014: With Special Feature on Adults Aged 55–64*, National Center for Health Statistics, May 2015, http://www.cdc.gov/nchs/data/hus/hus14.pdf (accessed May 22, 2015)

TABLE 6.5

Ten leading causes of nonfatal injuries, ages 65–85, 2013

Rank	Age groups 65–85	
1	Unintentional fall	2,495,397
2	Unintentional struck by/against	281,279
3	Unintentional overexertion	212,293
4	Unintentional MV-occupant	197,646
5	Unintentional cut/pierce	156,693
6	Unintentional poisoning	100,988
7	Unintentional other bite/sting	90,850
8	Unintentional other specified	86,729
9	Unintentional unknown/unspecified	74,864
10	Unintentional other transport	68,022

SOURCE: "10 Leading Causes of Nonfatal Injury, United States 2013, All Races, Both Sexes, Disposition: All Cases," National Center for Injury Prevention and Control, 2015, http://webapp.cdc.gov/cgi-bin/broker.exe?_PROGRAM=wisqnf.nfilead.sas&_SERVICE=v8prod&log=0&rept=nfil&year1=2013&year2=2013&Racethn=0&Sex=0&disp=0&ranking=10&PRTFMT=FRIENDLY&lcnifmt=custom&intent=0&c_age1=65&c_age2=85&_debug=0 (accessed May 22, 2015)

and irrational thoughts and are unable to distinguish between reality and imagination, can affect judgment and impair the driver's ability to operate a vehicle.

• Metabolic diseases, such as diabetes mellitus (a condition in which there is increased sugar in the blood and urine because the body is unable to use sugar to produce energy) and hypothyroidism (decreased production of the thyroid hormone by the thyroid gland), can act to impair judgment and response time.

• Musculoskeletal disabilities, such as arthritis and injuries, can impair response time.

Driving requires a range of sophisticated cognitive skills, which is why some cognitive changes can compromise

driving ability. It is not unusual for memory, attention, processing speed, and executive skills (the capacity for logical analysis) to decline with advancing age. Weakening memory may make it difficult for some older drivers to process information from traffic signs and to navigate correctly. As multiple demands are made on older drivers' attention, the AMA and the NHTSA state that "drivers must possess selective attention—the ability to prioritize stimuli and focus on only the most important—in order to attend to urgent stimuli (such as traffic signs) while not being distracted by irrelevant ones (such as roadside ads)." Selective attention problems challenge older drivers to distinguish the most critical information when they are faced with many signs and signals. Drivers have to divide their attention to concentrate "on the multiple stimuli required by most driving tasks." Processing speed affects perception-reaction time and is critical in situations where drivers must immediately choose between actions such as accelerating, braking, or steering. Executive skills enable drivers to make correct decisions after evaluating the stimuli that are related to driving, such as to stop at a red light or stop at a crosswalk when a pedestrian is crossing the street.

Medications

The AMA and the NHTSA indicate in *Physician's Guide to Assessing and Counseling Older Drivers* that many commonly used prescription and over-the-counter (nonprescription) medications can impair driving performance. In general, drugs with strong central nervous system effects, such as antidepressants, antihistamines, muscle relaxants, narcotic analgesics (painkillers), anticonvulsants (used to prevent seizures), and stimulants, have the potential to adversely affect the ability to operate a motor vehicle. The extent to which driving skills are compromised varies from person to person and between different medications that are used for the same purpose. The effects of prescription and over-the-counter medications may be intensified in combination with other drugs or alcohol.

Driving performance may also be affected by medication side effects, such as "drowsiness, dizziness, blurred vision, unsteadiness, fainting, [and] slowed reaction time." Generally, these side effects are dose-dependent and lessen over time, but older adults are often more sensitive to the effects of medications and may take longer to metabolize them, prolonging their effects. Medications such as prescription sleep aids "that cause drowsiness, euphoria, and/ or anterograde amnesia may also diminish insight, and the patient may experience impairment without being aware of it."

Some Fears about Older Drivers Are Unwarranted

As the ranks of older adults swell, many states and organizations—the AMA and the NHTSA are chief among these groups—are taking action to ensure driver safety. Concern about older driver safety has intensified in recent years in response to a spate of media reports describing serious crashes involving older drivers. However, some of this concern may be unwarranted. In "Older Drivers" the IIHS observes that drivers age 60 and older kill fewer pedestrians, bicyclists, motorcyclists and occupants of other vehicles than do drivers ages 30 to 59.

These findings contradict earlier research, which predicted that older drivers would make up a substantially larger proportion of drivers in fatal crashes. The IIHS explains in "Q&A: Older Drivers" (April 2015, http://www.iihs.org/iihs/topics/t/older-drivers/qanda) that older drivers largely threaten their own safety and their passengers' safety. In 2013 three-quarters of people killed in crashes involving drivers age 70 or older were either the older drivers themselves (61%) or their older passengers (15%).

Ensuring the Safety of Older Drivers

In *Physician's Guide to Assessing and Counseling Older Drivers*, the AMA and the NHTSA advocate coordinated efforts among the medical and research communities, policy makers, community planners, the automobile industry, and government agencies to achieve the common goal of safe transportation for the older population. The AMA and the NHTSA call for refined diagnostic tools to assist physicians in assessing patients' crash risk, improved access to driver assessment and rehabilitation, safer roads and vehicles, and better alternatives to driving for older adults.

Some auto insurance companies reduce payments for older adults who successfully complete driving classes such as the AARP Driver Safety program. The AARP notes in "AARP Driver Safety: History and Facts" (January 1,

2010, http://www.aarp.org/home-garden/transportation/info-05-2010/dsp_article_program_history_and_facts.html) that since 2006 it has offered an online refresher course that provides guidance in assessing physical abilities and making adjustments accordingly. By 2010, 36 states and the District of Columbia granted insurance discounts to drivers who have taken the course. The American Automobile Association offers a similar program called Safe Driving for Mature Operators that aims to improve the skills of older drivers. These courses address the aging process and help drivers adjust to age-related changes that can affect driving. Both organizations provide resources that help older drivers and their families determine whether they can safely continue driving.

As of June 2015 there were no upper age limits for driving. The National Institute on Aging observes that because people age at different rates, it is not possible to choose a specific age at which to suspend driving. Setting an age limit would leave some drivers on the road too long, whereas others would be forced to stop driving prematurely. Heredity, general health, lifestyle, and surroundings all influence how people age.

Many states are acting to reduce risks for older drivers by improving roadways to make driving less hazardous. In *Older Driver Safety: Knowledge Sharing Should Help States Prepare for Increase in Older Driver Population* (April 2007, http://www.gao.gov/new.items/d07413.pdf), the GAO reports that several states have adopted Federal Highway Administration practices to help older drivers, including:

- Wider highway lanes
- Intersections that give drivers a longer view of oncoming traffic and allow more time for left turns
- Road signs with larger, more visible letters and numbers
- Advance street name signs before intersections

Another program to improve older drivers' safety is CarFit (2015, http://www.car-fit.org), an educational program that offers older adults an opportunity to find out how well their personal vehicles "fit" them. Developed by the AAA, AARP, and the American Occupational Therapy Association, it encourages conversations between older drivers and their families about driving safety, helps older drivers maintain safe driving independence, and helps older adults feel more comfortable and safely fit behind the wheel. An April 25, 2015, media release, "Older Drivers in Florida Get 'Fit' and Push Safety Program to Milestone" (http://www.prnewswire.com/news-releases/older-drivers-in-florida-get-fit-and-push-safety-program-to-milestone-300063030.html) describes the key "fit" challenges for older drivers—ensuring adequate distance from

FIGURE 6.3

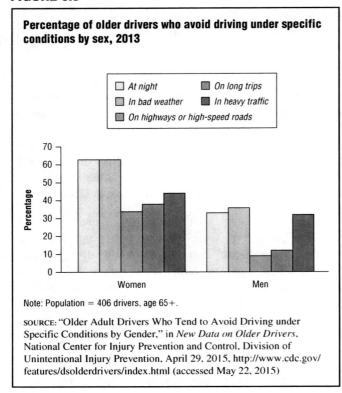

Percentage of older drivers who avoid driving under specific conditions by sex, 2013

Note: Population = 406 drivers, age 65+.

SOURCE: "Older Adult Drivers Who Tend to Avoid Driving under Specific Conditions by Gender," in *New Data on Older Drivers*, National Center for Injury Prevention and Control, Division of Unintentional Injury Prevention, April 29, 2015, http://www.cdc.gov/features/dsolderdrivers/index.html (accessed May 22, 2015)

steering wheel, adequate and safe views from side mirrors, and proper seat and head restraint height.

Technology Aids Older Drivers

Along with "fit" assessments and modifications, smarter cars equipped with technology such as global positioning system navigation devices that provide turn-by-turn directions can help older adults drive more safely and comfortably. In "'Smart' Car Features Can Help Older Drivers Stay Safe" (Edmunds.com, January 9, 2014), Kathleen Doheny reports that adjustable and heated seats can make older drivers more comfortable.

High-contrast instrument panels are easier to read, and high-intensity high beams and auto-dimming rear- and side-view mirrors help minimize glare, enabling older adults with vision problems to see the road. Parking aids can help people with limited mobility, and some crash prevention systems not only alert drivers to dangers but also automatically apply the brakes if sensors detect a person or object in the vehicle's pathway.

In "10 Best Cars for Older Drivers" (Consumer Reports.org, August 2014), Consumer Reports assessed cars for "access, visibility, front-seat comfort, driving position, and controls" as well as reliability and most electronic stability control. Consumer Reports observes, "for drivers who find it difficult to turn their heads, features such as rear-backup cameras, blind-spot-detection systems, small convex mirrors added to a car's regular side mirrors, and cross-traffic alerts that detect passing cars in the rear when backing up help increase visibility and awareness of surrounding cars."

PROVIDING ALTERNATIVE MEANS OF TRANSPORTATION

In *Transportation-Disadvantaged Populations* (November 6, 2013, http://www.gao.gov/assets/660/658766.pdf), the GAO considers issues and services for "transportation-disadvantaged" older adults—those who cannot drive or have limited their driving, or those who have an income restraint, disability, or medical condition that limits their ability to travel. The GAO identifies the federal programs that address this population's mobility issues, the extent to which these programs meet their mobility needs, the cost-effectiveness of service delivery, obstacles to addressing mobility needs, and strategies for overcoming these obstacles. According to the GAO, there are 80 federal programs designed to meet the transportation needs of older adults. For example, the U.S. Department of Health and Human Services funds Community Services Block Grant programs, which provide taxicab vouchers and bus tokens that enable low-income older adults to take general trips, and Social Services Block Grants, which provide assistance for transport to and from medical or social service appointments.

The GAO reports that demand for Americans with Disabilities Act (ADA) specialized, door-to-door transport service (which is more costly to operate than traditional fixed-route transit and that is often used by transportation-disadvantaged populations including older adults) has increased because of the growing older population.

The IIHS observes in "Q&A: Older Drivers" that public transportation is not available in many parts of the country and that although volunteer drivers and van programs meet some older adults' needs, rural communities often lack viable alternatives to driving for older adults.

Types of Transportation for Nondrivers

Transportation for older adults can include door-to-door services such as taxis or van services, public buses that travel along fixed routes, or ride sharing in carpools. According to the AoA, in *Because We Care: A Guide for People Who Care* (2009, https://www.dshs.wa.gov/sites/default/files/ALTSA/hcs/documents/BecauseWeCare.pdf), there are three general classes of alternative transportation for older adults:

- Demand-response services generally require advance reservations and provide door-to-door service from one specific location to another. Such systems offer older adults comfortable and relatively flexible transport, with the potential for adapting to the needs of individual riders. Payment of fares for demand-response transport is usually required on a per-ride basis.

- Fixed route and scheduled services follow a predetermined route, stopping at established locations at specific times to allow passengers to board and disembark. This type of service typically requires payment of fares on a per-ride basis. Older adults are often eligible for discounted rates.

- Ride-sharing programs connect people who need rides with drivers who have room in their cars and are willing to take passengers. This system generally offers scheduled transportation to a particular destination, such as a place of employment, a senior center, or a medical center.

Meeting the Transportation Needs of Older Adults

In *Transportation-Disadvantaged Seniors: Efforts to Enhance Senior Mobility Could Benefit from Additional Guidance and Information* (August 2004, http://www.gao.gov/new.items/d04971.pdf), the GAO cites research by the Beverly Foundation that identifies five attributes that are necessary for alternative transportation services for older adults:

- Availability—older adults can travel to desired locations at the times they want to go.

- Accessibility—vehicles can be accessed by those with disabilities, services can be door-to-door or door-through-door as necessary, and stops are pedestrian-friendly. Door-through-door transport offers personal, hands-on assistance for older adults who may have difficulties exiting their homes, disembarking from vehicles, and/or opening doors. It is also called assisted transportation, supported (or supportive) transportation, and escorted transportation.

- Acceptability—transport is safe, clean, and easy to use.

- Affordability—financial assistance is available if necessary.

- Adaptability—multiple trips and special equipment can be accommodated.

The GAO highlights specific unmet needs: "Seniors who rely on alternative transportation have difficulty making trips for which the automobile is better suited, such as trips that involve carrying packages; … life-enhancing needs are less likely to be met than life-sustaining needs; and … mobility needs are less likely to be met in nonurban communities (especially rural communities) than in urban communities." It also identifies obstacles to addressing transportation-disadvantaged older adults' mobility needs, potential strategies that federal and other government entities might take to better meet these needs, and trade-offs that are associated with implementing each strategy. For example, the GAO finds that older drivers are not encouraged to investigate or plan for a time when they will be unable to drive. One way to address this obstacle might be to institute educational programs that would ease older adults' transition from driver to nondriver. This strategy does, however, have the potential to increase demand for alternative transportation services and the costs that are associated with their provision.

To increase and improve alternative transportation services, the GAO suggests enlisting the aid of volunteer drivers, sponsoring demonstration programs, identifying best practices, increasing cooperation among federal programs, and establishing a central clearinghouse of information that could be accessed by stakeholders in the various programs. It recommends that the AoA improve the value and consistency of information pertaining to older adults' transportation needs that is received from area agencies on aging, including providing guidance for those agencies on assessing mobility needs. The AoA is also called on to keep older adults and their caregivers better informed of alternative transportation programs and to ensure that the best methods and practices are shared among transportation and social service providers to enhance the older population's mobility.

Lift Hero Offers Ride Sharing for Older Adults

Lift Hero (2015, https://www.lifthero.com) connects older adults to drivers using their own vehicles, in the same way the ride-sharing service Uber does in many U.S. cities. The difference is that Lift Hero focuses exclusively on providing non-emergency transportation for older adults, much like the service a family member would provide. Lift Hero debuted in late 2014 and recruits health professionals and students as drivers and trains them to meet the needs of older adults. Users can book rides online, by phone or using a web app. In "The Evolution of Uber Leads to Lift Hero, Ridesharing for the Elderly" (VentureBeat.com, October 8, 2014), Lift Hero founder Jay Connolly explains, "Uber, Lyft, and Sidecar have made Lift Hero possible by normalizing ridesharing in consumers' minds, blazing the regulatory trail, and helping to define a new category of insurance that was needed. We're adapting many of the same innovations for people who wouldn't otherwise benefit from them."

CHAPTER 7

THE HEALTH AND MEDICAL PROBLEMS OF OLDER ADULTS

Among the fears many people have about aging is coping with losses—not only declining mental and physical abilities but also the prospect of failing health, chronic (long-term) illness, and disability. Although aging is associated with physiological changes, the rate and extent of these changes varies widely. One person may be limited by arthritis at age 65, whereas another is vigorous and active at age 90.

Despite the increasing proportion of active healthy older adults, it is true that the incidence (the rate of new cases of a disorder over a specified period) and prevalence (the total number of cases of a disorder in a given population at a specific time) of selected diseases as well as the utilization of health care services increase with advancing age. For example, the incidence of some diseases, such as diabetes, heart disease, breast cancer, Parkinson's disease, and Alzheimer's disease (a progressive disease that is characterized by memory loss, impaired thinking, and declining ability to function), increases with age. In contrast, the incidence of other diseases, such as human immunodeficiency virus (HIV) infection, multiple sclerosis, and schizophrenia, decreases with age.

This chapter considers the epidemiology of aging (the distribution and determinants of health and illness in the population of older adults). It describes trends in aging and the health of aging Americans; distinctions among healthy aging, disease, and disability; health promotion and prevention as applied to older people; and selected diseases and conditions that are common in old age.

GENERAL HEALTH OF OLDER AMERICANS

The proportion of adults rating their health as fair or poor increases with advancing age. In 2013, 19.2% of adults aged 55 to 64 years, 19.7% of adults aged 65 to 74 years, and 27.6% of adults aged 75 years and older considered themselves to be in fair or poor health, compared with just 6.2% of adults aged 18 to 44 years. (See Table 7.1.)

The Administration on Aging (AoA) indicates in *A Profile of Older Americans: 2014* (May 2015, http://www.aoa.acl.gov/Aging_Statistics/Profile/2014/docs/2014-Profile.pdf) that during the period 2011 to 2013, 47% of non-Hispanic whites aged 65 years and older said their health was good or better than good, compared with just 27% of African Americans, 28% of Native Americans/Alaskan Natives, 33% of Asian Americans, and 30% of Hispanics.

Most older people have at least one chronic condition, and many have several. In "Multiple Chronic Conditions among U.S. Adults: A 2012 Update" (*Preventing Chronic Disease*, vol. 11, April 17, 2014), Brian W. Ward et al. report that 86% of older adults (those aged 65 years and older) in the United States had at least one chronic condition in 2012, and the majority (61%) had two or more chronic conditions. Among the most frequently occurring conditions of older adult Medicare beneficiaries in 2012 were high blood pressure (55%), high cholesterol (45%), arthritis (29%), ischemic (decreased blood flow) heart disease (29%), and diabetes (27%). (See Figure 7.1.)

The National Center for Health Statistics (NCHS) reports in *Health, United States, 2014* (May 2015, http://www.cdc.gov/nchs/data/hus/hus14.pdf) that the percentage of people with difficulties performing basic actions, such as limitations in movement or in emotional, sensory, or cognitive functioning (thinking and reasoning) associated with a health problem and complex activities such as working, maintaining a household, and living independently, increase with advancing age. In 2013 the prevalence of basic actions difficulty was higher among those aged 65 years and older (58.9%) compared with those between the ages of 18 and 64 (24.7%). The prevalence of complex activity limitation also was higher among those aged 65 years and older (32%) compared with those ages 18 to 64. (See Figure 7.2.)

TABLE 7.1

Percentage of adults who reported their health as fair or poor, by selected characteristics, selected years 1991–2013

[Data are based on household interviews of a sample of the civilian noninstitutionalized population]

Characteristic	1991[a]	1995[a]	1997	2000	2005	2010	2012	2013
	\multicolumn{8}{c}{Percent of persons with fair or poor health}							
All ages, age-adjusted[b, c]	10.4	10.6	9.2	9.0	9.2	9.6	9.5	9.4
All ages, crude[c]	10.0	10.1	8.9	8.9	9.3	10.1	10.3	10.2
Age								
Under 18 years	2.6	2.6	2.1	1.7	1.8	2.0	2.1	1.7
Under 6 years	2.7	2.7	1.9	1.5	1.6	1.8	1.5	1.6
6–17 years	2.6	2.5	2.1	1.8	1.9	2.2	2.4	1.8
18–44 years	6.1	6.6	5.3	5.1	5.5	6.3	6.4	6.2
18–24 years	4.8	4.5	3.4	3.3	3.3	3.9	3.8	3.6
25–44 years	6.4	7.2	5.9	5.7	6.3	7.2	7.4	7.2
45–54 years	13.4	13.4	11.7	11.9	11.6	13.3	14.2	14.1
55–64 years	20.7	21.4	18.2	17.9	18.3	19.4	19.3	19.2
65 years and over	29.0	28.3	26.7	26.9	26.6	24.4	22.7	23.1
65–74 years	26.0	25.6	23.1	22.5	23.4	21.2	19.6	19.7
75 years and over	33.6	32.2	31.5	32.1	30.2	28.3	26.6	27.6
Sex[b]								
Male	10.0	10.1	8.8	8.8	8.8	9.2	9.2	9.0
Female	10.8	11.1	9.7	9.3	9.5	10.0	9.9	9.8
Race[b, d]								
White only	9.6	9.7	8.3	8.2	8.6	8.8	8.8	8.7
Black or African American only	16.8	17.2	15.8	14.6	14.3	14.9	14.9	14.3
American Indian or Alaska Native only	18.3	18.7	17.3	17.2	13.2	17.8	16.5	15.3
Asian only	7.8	9.3	7.8	7.4	6.8	8.1	7.9	7.7
Native Hawaiian or other Pacific Islander only	—	—	—	*	*	*	*	*
2 or more races	—	—	—	16.2	14.5	15.6	13.0	13.9
Black or African American; white	—	—	—	*14.5	8.3	*16.7	16.3	*19.0
American Indian or Alaska Native; white	—	—	—	18.7	17.2	19.0	14.4	16.2
Hispanic origin and race[b, d]								
Hispanic or Latino	15.6	15.1	13.0	12.8	13.3	13.1	13.3	12.7
Mexican	17.0	16.7	13.1	12.8	14.3	13.7	13.6	13.3
Not Hispanic or Latino	10.0	10.1	8.9	8.7	8.7	9.2	9.1	9.0
White only	9.1	9.1	8.0	7.9	8.0	8.2	8.1	8.2
Black or African American only	16.8	17.3	15.8	14.6	14.4	14.9	15.0	14.2
Percent of poverty level[b, e]								
Below 100%	22.8	23.7	20.8	19.6	20.4	20.9	21.6	21.8
100%–199%	14.7	15.5	13.9	14.1	14.4	15.2	14.9	14.4
200%–399%	7.9	7.9	8.2	8.4	8.3	8.3	8.4	8.2
400% or more	4.9	4.7	4.1	4.5	4.7	4.3	3.9	4.0
Hispanic origin and race and **percent of poverty level[b, d, e]**								
Hispanic or Latino:								
Below 100%	23.6	22.7	19.9	18.7	20.2	19.2	20.9	20.3
100%–199%	18.0	16.9	13.5	15.3	15.3	15.6	14.5	14.3
200%–399%	10.3	10.1	10.0	10.3	10.3	10.3	10.0	10.3
400% or more	6.6	4.0	5.7	5.5	7.6	6.4	6.7	5.3
Not Hispanic or Latino:								
White only:								
Below 100%	21.9	22.8	19.7	18.8	20.1	20.9	21.1	22.2
100%–199%	14.0	14.8	13.3	13.4	13.8	14.8	15.3	14.4
200%–399%	7.5	7.3	7.7	7.9	7.9	7.7	7.7	7.7
400% or more	4.7	4.6	3.9	4.2	4.3	4.0	3.5	3.8
Black or African American only:								
Below 100%	25.8	27.7	25.3	23.8	23.3	23.9	25.0	24.8
100%–199%	17.0	19.3	19.2	18.2	17.6	18.3	16.9	17.5
200%–399%	12.0	11.4	12.2	11.7	11.2	11.2	11.9	9.8
400% or more	5.9	6.5	6.1	7.3	7.1	6.8	6.6	5.0

Data from the U.S. Census Bureau American Community Survey reveal that 36% of adults aged 65 years and older had some sort of difficulty in hearing, vision, cognition, ambulation, self-care, or independent living in 2013. Nearly one-quarter (23%) had difficulty ambulating (walking or moving from place to place). (See Figure 7.3.)

Hospital Utilization and Physician Visits

Adults aged 65 years and older have the highest rates of inpatient hospitalization and the longest average lengths of stay. In 2013 adults age 65 and older were most likely to have had one or more hospital stays in the preceding year. (See Table 7.2.)

TABLE 7.1

Percentage of adults who reported their health as fair or poor, by selected characteristics, selected years 1991–2013 [CONTINUED]

[Data are based on household interviews of a sample of the civilian noninstitutionalized population]

Characteristic	1991[a]	1995[a]	1997	2000	2005	2010	2012	2013
Disability measure among adults 18 years and over[b, f]				Percent of persons with fair or poor health				
Any basic actions difficulty or complex activity limitation	—	—	27.0	27.6	28.5	28.7	30.2	30.5
Any basic actions difficulty	—	—	27.3	27.7	29.1	28.9	30.6	30.7
Any complex activity limitation	—	—	42.9	45.6	46.3	46.0	46.6	47.8
No disability	—	—	3.4	3.8	3.6	3.5	3.6	3.8
Geographic region[b]								
Northeast	8.3	9.1	8.0	7.6	7.5	7.9	8.0	8.2
Midwest	9.1	9.7	8.1	8.0	8.3	9.0	9.1	8.8
South	13.1	12.3	10.8	10.7	11.0	11.1	10.8	10.6
West	9.7	10.1	8.8	8.8	8.6	9.2	9.1	9.1
Location of residence [b, g]								
Within MSA	9.9	10.1	8.7	8.5	8.7	9.2	9.0	9.1
Outside MSA	11.9	12.6	11.1	11.1	11.2	11.9	12.3	11.4

Notes: — means data not available. An asterisk means estimates are considered unreliable and have a relative standard error (RSE) of 20% to 30%. Data not show have an RSE greater than 30%.
[a]Data prior to 1997 are not strictly comparable with data for later years due to the 1997 questionnaire redesign.
[b]Estimates are age-adjusted to the year 2000 standard population using six age groups: under 18 years, 18–44 years, 45–54 years, 55–64 years, 65–74 years, and 75 years and over. The disability measure is age-adjusted using the five adult age groups.
[c]Includes all other races not shown separately and unknown disability status.
[d]The race groups, white, black, American Indian or Alaska Native, Asian, Native Hawaiian or other Pacific Islander, and 2 or more races, include persons of Hispanic and non-Hispanic origin. Persons of Hispanic origin may be of any race. Starting with 1999 data, race-specific estimates are tabulated according to the 1997 *Revisions to the Standards for the Classification of Federal Data on Race and Ethnicity* and are not strictly comparable with estimates for earlier years. The five single-race categories plus multiple-race categories shown in the table conform to the 1997 Standards. Starting with 1999 data, race-specific estimates are for persons who reported only one racial group; the category 2 or more races includes persons who reported more than one racial group. Prior to 1999, data were tabulated according to the 1977 Standards with four racial groups, and the Asian only category included Native Hawaiian or other Pacific Islander. Estimates for single-race categories prior to 1999 included persons who reported one race or, if they reported more than one race, identified one race as best representing their race. Starting with 2003 data, race responses of other race and unspecified multiple race were treated as missing, and then race was imputed if these were the only race responses. Almost all persons with a race response of other race were of Hispanic origin.
[e]Percent of poverty level is based on family income and family size and composition using U.S. Census Bureau poverty thresholds. Missing family income data were imputed for 1991 and beyond.
[f]Any basic actions difficulty or complex activity limitation is defined as having one or more of the following limitations or difficulties: movement difficulty, emotional difficulty, sensory (seeing or hearing) difficulty, cognitive difficulty, self-care (activities of daily living or instrumental activities of daily living) limitation, social limitation, or work limitation. Starting with 2007 data, the hearing question, a component of the basic actions difficulty measure, was revised. Consequently, data prior to 2007 are not comparable with data for 2007 and beyond.
[g]MSA is metropolitan statistical area. Starting with 2006 data, MSA status is determined using 2000 census data and the 2000 standards for defining MSAs.

SOURCE: "Table 50. Respondent-Assessed Fair-Poor Health Status, by Selected Characteristics: United States, Selected Years 1991–2013," in *Health, United States, 2014: With Special Feature on Adults Aged 55–64*, National Center for Health Statistics, May 2015, http://www.cdc.gov/nchs/data/hus/hus14.pdf (accessed May 22, 2015).

The growing older population also uses more physician services. Visit rates increase with age among adults aged 65 years and older and were two and a half times as high as visit rates for children under the age of 18 years in 2010, the most recent year for which data were available. (See Table 7.3.) Although women generally make more physician visits than men, the difference practically disappears among older adults. (See Table 7.4.)

CHRONIC DISEASES AND CONDITIONS

Chronic diseases are prolonged illnesses such as arthritis, asthma, heart disease, diabetes, and cancer that do not resolve spontaneously and are rarely cured. According to the Centers for Disease Control and Prevention (CDC), in "Chronic Diseases and Health Promotion" (May 18, 2015, http://www.cdc.gov/chronicdisease/overview/index.htm), chronic illnesses account for 70% of all deaths in the United States annually. In 2013 five of the 10 leading causes of death among adults aged 65 years and older were chronic diseases: heart disease, malignant neoplasms (cancer), chronic lower respiratory diseases, cerebrovascular diseases (stroke), and diabetes mellitus (a condition in which there is increased sugar in the blood and urine because the body is unable to use sugar to produce energy). (See Table 7.5.) Among adults aged 55 to 65 years, the death rates for several chronic diseases (cancer, heart disease, chronic lower respiratory diseases, and diabetes) decreased from 2003 to 2013. (See Figure 7.4.)

The prevalence of some chronic conditions such as hypertension (high blood pressure) and diabetes is increasing in the general population and among older adults. In 2009–12 more than half (51.4%) of people aged 55 to 64 years had hypertension, 40.6% were obese, about half (50.1%) had elevated cholesterol levels (associated with increased risk for cardiovascular disease), and 18.9% suffered from diabetes. (See Figure 7.5.) Between 1988–94 and 2009–12 the rate of diabetes among adults aged 65 years and older increased from 19.4% to 26.8%. (See Table 7.6.) The rate of hypertension also increased

FIGURE 7.1

Prevalence of chronic conditions among Medicare beneficiaries, 2012

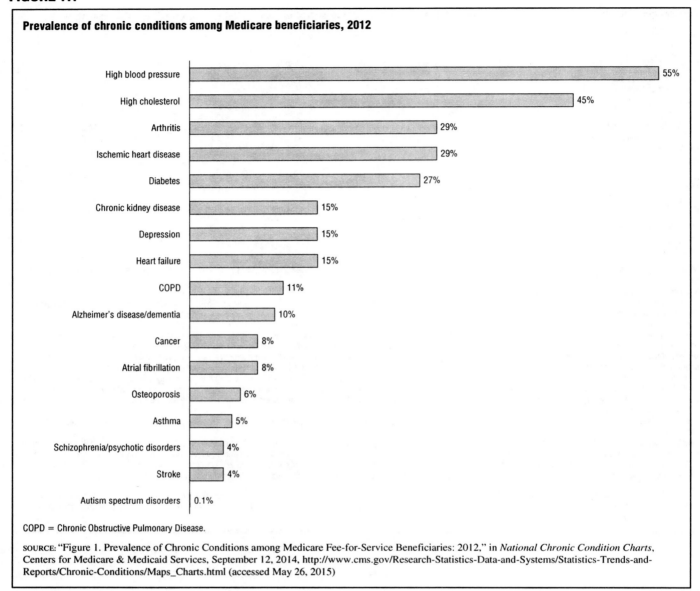

COPD = Chronic Obstructive Pulmonary Disease.

SOURCE: "Figure 1. Prevalence of Chronic Conditions among Medicare Fee-for-Service Beneficiaries: 2012," in *National Chronic Condition Charts*, Centers for Medicare & Medicaid Services, September 12, 2014, http://www.cms.gov/Research-Statistics-Data-and-Systems/Statistics-Trends-and-Reports/Chronic-Conditions/Maps_Charts.html (accessed May 26, 2015)

during this same period. (See Table 7.7.) The increase is largely attributable to increasing rates of obesity, which is implicated in the development of diabetes, hypertension, and many other chronic conditions.

Arthritis

The word *arthritis* literally means "joint inflammation," and it is applied to dozens of related diseases known as rheumatic diseases. When a joint (the point where two bones meet) becomes inflamed, swelling, redness, pain, and loss of motion occur. In the most serious forms of the disease, the loss of motion can be physically disabling.

More than 100 types of arthritis have been identified, but four major types affect large numbers of older Americans:

- Osteoarthritis—the most common type, generally affects people as they grow older. Sometimes called degenerative arthritis, it causes the breakdown of bones and cartilage (connective tissue that attaches to bones) and pain and stiffness in the fingers, knees, feet, hips, and back. In "Osteoarthritis" (March 27, 2015, http://emedicine.medscape.com/article/330487-overview), Carlos J. Lozada of the University of Miami reports that more than 20 million Americans are affected by osteoarthritis, and more than half of adults age 65 and older are affected.

- Fibromyalgia—affects the muscles and connective tissues and causes widespread pain, as well as fatigue, sleep problems, and stiffness. Fibromyalgia also causes "tender points" that are more sensitive to pain than other areas of the body. The National Fibromyalgia Association estimates in "Prevalence"

FIGURE 7.2

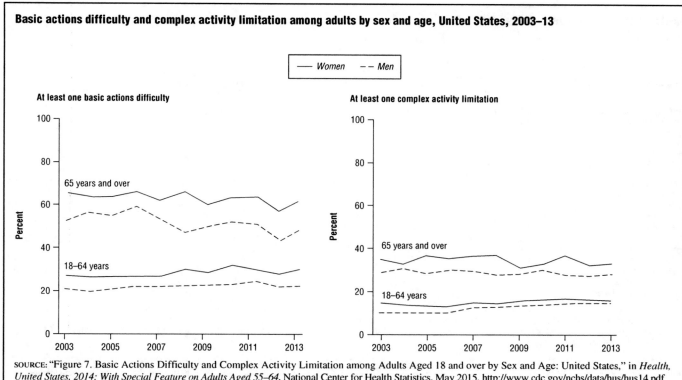

Basic actions difficulty and complex activity limitation among adults by sex and age, United States, 2003–13

SOURCE: "Figure 7. Basic Actions Difficulty and Complex Activity Limitation among Adults Aged 18 and over by Sex and Age: United States," in *Health, United States, 2014: With Special Feature on Adults Aged 55–64*, National Center for Health Statistics, May 2015, http://www.cdc.gov/nchs/data/hus/hus14.pdf (accessed May 22, 2015)

FIGURE 7.3

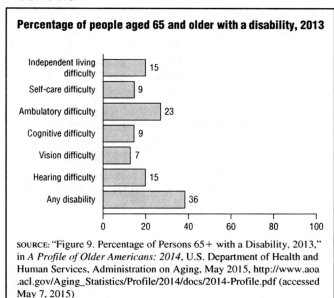

Percentage of people aged 65 and older with a disability, 2013

SOURCE: "Figure 9. Percentage of Persons 65+ with a Disability, 2013," in *A Profile of Older Americans: 2014*, U.S. Department of Health and Human Services, Administration on Aging, May 2015, http://www.aoa.acl.gov/Aging_Statistics/Profile/2014/docs/2014-Profile.pdf (accessed May 7, 2015)

(2015, http://www.fmaware.org/about-fibromyalgia/prevalence) that 10 million Americans suffer from this condition.

• Rheumatoid arthritis—an inflammatory form of arthritis caused by a flaw in the body's immune system. The result is inflammation and swelling in the joint lining, followed by damage to bone and cartilage in the hands, wrists, feet, knees, ankles, shoulders, or elbows. The Arthritis Foundation indicates in "What Is Rheumatoid Arthritis?" (2015, http://www.arthritistoday.org/conditions/rheumatoid-arthritis/all-about-ra/what-is-ra.php) that rheumatoid arthritis affects approximately 1.5 million Americans.

• Gout—inflammation of a joint caused by an accumulation of a natural substance, uric acid, in the joint, usually the big toe, knee, or wrist. The uric acid forms crystals in the affected joint, causing severe pain and swelling. This form affects more men than women, claiming about a million sufferers.

PREVALENCE. Arthritis is a common problem and is the leading cause of disability in the United States. In "Arthritis: National Statistics" (February 4, 2015, http://www.cdc.gov/arthritis/data_statistics/national-statistics.html), the CDC reports that 52.5 million Americans (22.7% of adults) have been diagnosed with arthritis, and 22.7 million adults have activity limitations that are attributable to the disease. The CDC projects that the total number of people with arthritis will increase to 67 million by 2030. (See Figure 7.6.) At that time, about 25 million people with arthritis are projected to have activity limitations attributable to the disease.

Osteoporosis

Osteoporosis is a skeletal disorder characterized by compromised bone strength, which predisposes affected

TABLE 7.2

Hospital stays in the past year, by age, 1997–2013

[Data are based on household interviews of a sample of the civilian noninstitutionalized population]

Characteristic	One or more hospital stays[a]					Two or more hospital stays[a]				
	1997	2000	2010	2012	2013	1997	2000	2010	2012	2013
	Percent									
1 year and over, age-adjusted[b, c]	7.8	7.6	7.0	6.8	6.7	1.8	1.8	1.8	1.8	1.7
1 year and over, crude[b]	7.7	7.5	7.2	7.0	6.9	1.7	1.8	1.9	1.9	1.8
Age										
1–17 years	2.8	2.5	2.4	2.0	2.1	0.5	0.4	0.5	0.4	0.4
1–5 years	3.9	3.8	3.4	2.9	3.4	0.7	0.7	0.6	0.6	0.6
6–17 years	2.3	1.9	1.9	1.7	1.6	0.4	0.3	0.5	0.3	0.3
18–44 years	7.4	7.0	6.3	6.1	6.1	1.2	1.1	1.3	1.3	1.1
18–24 years	7.9	7.0	5.7	5.6	5.3	1.3	1.1	1.1	1.0	1.0
25–44 years	7.3	7.0	6.6	6.3	6.4	1.2	1.2	1.3	1.4	1.2
45–64 years	8.2	8.4	8.3	8.0	7.8	2.2	2.2	2.5	2.3	2.2
45–54 years	6.9	7.3	7.3	6.8	6.2	1.7	1.8	2.1	2.0	1.8
55–64 years	10.2	10.0	9.5	9.3	9.7	2.9	2.8	2.9	2.7	2.6
65 years and over	18.0	18.2	16.1	15.9	15.3	5.4	5.8	4.9	5.3	4.7
65–74 years	16.1	16.1	13.6	13.6	12.6	4.8	4.9	3.8	4.7	3.4
75 years and over	20.4	20.7	19.0	19.0	19.0	6.2	6.8	6.2	6.2	6.5
75–84 years	19.8	20.1	18.3	17.6	17.6	6.1	6.2	6.1	5.6	6.0
85 years and over	22.8	23.4	20.8	23.1	22.4	6.2	9.0	6.6	8.0	7.9

[a]These estimates exclude hospitalizations for institutionalized persons and those who died while hospitalized, because they are outside the scope of this survey.
[b]Includes all other races not shown separately, unknown health insurance status, and unknown disability status.
[c]Estimates are for persons 1 year of age and over and are age-adjusted to the year 2000 standard population using six age groups: 1–17 years, 18–44 years, 45–54 years, 55–64 years, 65–74 years, and 75 years and over.

SOURCE: Adapted from "Table 87. Persons with Hospital Stays in the Past Year, by Selected Characteristics: United States, Selected Years 1997–2013," in *Health, United States, 2014: With Special Feature on Adults Aged 55–64*, National Center for Health Statistics, May 2015, http://www.cdc.gov/nchs/data/hus/hus14.pdf (accessed May 22, 2015)

individuals to increased risk of fracture, especially of the hip, spine, and wrist, although any bone can be affected. The National Osteoporosis Foundation observes in "Learn about Osteoporosis" (2015, http://nof.org/learn) that although some bone loss occurs naturally with advancing age, the stooped posture (kyphosis) and loss of height (greater than 1 to 2 inches [2.5 to 5.1 cm]) that are experienced by many older adults result from vertebral fractures caused by osteoporosis.

According to the National Osteoporosis Foundation, in "What Is Osteoporosis?" (2015, http://nof.org/articles/7), about 54 million Americans have osteoporosis and have low bone mass, which means they are considered to be at risk of developing the condition. The National Osteoporosis Foundation reports that one out of two women and one out of four men over the age of 50 will have an osteoporosis-related fracture in their remaining lifetime. The aging of the population and the historic lack of focus on bone health may together cause the number of fractures due to osteoporosis in the United States to exceed 3 million by 2025.

One of the goals of the treatment of osteoporosis is to maintain bone health by preventing bone loss and by building new bone. Another goal is to minimize the risk and impact of falls because they can cause fractures. Figure 7.7 shows the pyramid of prevention and treatment of osteoporosis. At its base is nutrition (with adequate intake of calcium, vitamin D, and other minerals), physical exercise, and preventive measures to reduce the risk of falls. The second layer of the pyramid involves identifying and treating diseases that can cause osteoporosis, such as thyroid disease. The peak of the pyramid involves drug therapy for osteoporosis. There are two primary types of drugs used to treat osteoporosis. Antiresorptive agents act to reduce bone loss, and anabolic agents are drugs that build bone. Antiresorptive therapies include use of bisphosphonates, estrogen, selective estrogen receptor modulators, and calcitonin. They reduce bone loss, stabilize the architecture of the bone, and decrease bone turnover (the continuous process of remodeling in which bone is lost through resorption and new bone is formed).

Diabetes

Diabetes is a disease that affects the body's use of food, causing blood glucose (sugar levels in the blood) to become too high. People with diabetes can convert food to glucose, but there is a problem with insulin. In one type of diabetes (insulin-dependent diabetes, or type 1), the pancreas does not manufacture enough insulin, and in another type (noninsulin-dependent, or type 2), the body has insulin but cannot use the insulin effectively (this latter condition is called insulin resistance). When insulin is either absent or ineffective, glucose cannot get into the cells to be used for energy. Instead, the unused glucose builds up in the bloodstream and circulates through the

TABLE 7.3

Visits to physician offices, hospital outpatient departments, and emergency departments, by age, 1995–2011

[Data are based on reporting by a sample of office-based physicians, hospital outpatient departments, and hospital emergency departments]

Age, sex, and race	All places[a]				Physician offices			
	1995	2000	2010	2011	1995	2000	2010	2011
Age			Number of visits, in thousands					
Total	860,859	1,014,848	1,239,387	—	697,082	823,542	1,008,802	—
Under 18 years	194,644	212,165	246,228	—	150,351	163,459	191,500	—
18–44 years	285,184	315,774	342,797	—	219,065	243,011	261,941	—
45–64 years	188,320	255,894	352,001	—	159,531	216,783	296,385	—
45–54 years	104,891	142,233	171,039	—	88,266	119,474	140,819	—
55–64 years	83,429	113,661	180,962	—	71,264	97,309	155,566	—
65 years and over	192,712	231,014	298,362	—	168,135	200,289	258,976	—
65–74 years	102,605	116,505	151,075	—	90,544	102,447	132,201	—
75 years and over	90,106	114,510	147,287	—	77,591	97,842	126,775	—
			Number of visits per 100 persons					
Total, age-adjusted[b]	334	374	401	—	271	304	325	—
Total, crude	329	370	408	—	266	300	332	—
Under 18 years	275	293	331	—	213	226	257	—
18–44 years	264	291	310	—	203	224	237	—
45–64 years	364	422	441	—	309	358	371	—
45–54 years	339	385	388	—	286	323	320	—
55–64 years	401	481	505	—	343	412	434	—
65 years and over	612	706	767	—	534	612	666	—
65–74 years	560	656	713	—	494	577	624	—
75 years and over	683	766	831	—	588	654	715	—
Sex and age								
Male, age-adjusted[b]	290	325	350	—	232	261	283	—
Male, crude	277	314	350	—	220	251	283	—
Under 18 years	273	302	340	—	209	231	262	—
18–44 years	190	203	205	—	139	148	151	—
45–54 years	275	316	324	—	229	260	265	—
55–64 years	351	428	460	—	300	367	396	—
65–74 years	508	614	680	—	445	539	597	—
75 years and over	711	771	871	—	616	670	760	—
Female, age-adjusted[b]	377	420	452	—	309	345	367	—
Female, crude	378	424	464	—	310	348	379	—
Under 18 years	277	285	322	—	217	221	252	—
18–44 years	336	377	415	—	265	298	323	—
45–54 years	400	451	450	—	339	384	372	—
55–64 years	446	529	546	—	382	453	469	—
65–74 years	603	692	741	—	534	609	647	—
75 years and over	666	763	804	—	571	645	685	—

—Data not available.
[a]Based on the 1997–2013 National Health Interview Surveys, about 21%–30% of persons aged 65 and over were edentulous (having lost all their natural teeth). In 1997–2013, about 69%–73% of older dentate persons, compared with 17%–23% of older edentate persons, had a dental visit in the past year.
[b]Respondents were asked, "About how long has it been since you last saw or talked to a dentist?"

SOURCE: Adapted from "Table 82. Visits to Physician Offices, Hospital Outpatient Departments, and Hospital Emergency Departments, by Age, Sex, and Race: United States, Selected Years 1995–2011," in *Health, United States, 2014: With Special Feature on Adults Aged 55–64*, National Center for Health Statistics, May 2015, http://www.cdc.gov/nchs/data/hus/hus14.pdf (accessed May 22, 2015)

kidneys. If the blood-glucose level rises high enough, the excess glucose "spills" over into the urine, causing frequent urination. This leads to an increased feeling of thirst as the body tries to compensate for the fluid that is lost through urination.

Type 2 diabetes is most often seen in adults. In type 2 diabetes the pancreas produces insulin, but it is not used effectively, and the body resists responding to it. Heredity is a predisposing factor in the genesis of diabetes, but because the pancreas continues to produce insulin in people suffering from type 2 diabetes, the disease is considered to be more of a problem of insulin resistance, in which the body is not using the hormone efficiently.

Complications can threaten the lives of diabetics. The healing process of the body is slowed and there is an increased risk of infection. Diabetics are at greater risk of heart disease; circulatory problems, especially in the legs, which are sometimes severe enough to require surgery or even amputation; diabetic retinopathy, a condition that can cause blindness; kidney disease that may require dialysis; and dental problems. Close attention to preventive health care, such as regular eye, dental, and

TABLE 7.4

Visits to primary care physicians, by age, sex, and race, selected years 1980–2010

[Data are based on reporting by a sample of office-based physicians]

	Type of primary care generalist physician[a]											
Age, sex, and race	All primary care generalists				General and family practice				Internal medicine			
	1980	1990	2000	2010	1980	1990	2000	2010	1980	1990	2000	2010
Age					Percent distribution							
Total	**66.2**	**63.6**	**58.9**	**55.2**	**33.5**	**29.9**	**24.1**	**21.1**	**12.1**	**13.8**	**15.3**	**13.9**
Under 18 years	77.8	79.5	79.7	80.9	26.1	26.5	19.9	15.3	2.0	2.9	*	*
18–44 years	65.3	65.2	62.1	62.7	34.3	31.9	28.2	27.8	8.6	11.8	12.7	11.6
45–64 years	60.2	55.5	51.2	46.7	36.3	32.1	26.4	23.1	19.5	18.6	20.1	18.5
45–54 years	60.2	55.6	52.3	48.7	37.4	32.0	27.8	26.2	17.1	17.1	18.7	15.7
55–64 years	60.2	55.5	49.9	44.8	35.4	32.1	24.7	20.4	21.8	20.0	21.7	21.0
65 years and over	61.6	52.6	46.5	38.3	37.5	28.1	20.2	16.4	22.7	23.3	24.5	20.5
65–74 years	61.2	52.7	46.6	37.3	37.4	28.1	19.7	17.5	22.1	23.0	24.5	18.2
75 years and over	62.3	52.4	46.4	39.2	37.6	28.0	20.8	15.4	23.5	23.7	24.5	22.8
Sex and age												
Male:												
Under 18 years	77.3	78.1	77.7	80.1	25.6	24.1	18.3	15.7	2.0	3.0	*	*
18–44 years	50.8	51.8	51.5	51.7	38.0	35.9	34.2	33.7	11.5	15.0	14.4	16.4
45–64 years	55.6	50.6	49.4	43.7	34.4	31.0	28.7	24.4	20.5	19.2	19.8	19.1
65 years and over	58.2	51.2	43.1	36.6	35.6	27.7	19.3	16.2	22.3	23.3	23.8	20.3
Female:												
Under 18 years	78.5	81.1	82.0	81.7	26.6	29.1	21.7	14.9	2.0	2.8	*	*
18–44 years	72.1	71.3	67.2	67.9	32.5	30.0	25.3	25.0	7.3	10.3	11.9	9.4
45–64 years	63.4	58.8	52.5	48.9	37.7	32.8	24.9	22.2	18.9	18.2	20.2	18.1
65 years and over	63.9	53.5	48.9	39.6	38.7	28.3	20.9	16.7	22.9	23.3	25.0	20.5
Race and age[b]												
White:												
Under 18 years	77.6	79.2	78.5	79.6	26.4	27.1	21.2	15.6	2.0	2.3*		*
18–44 years	64.8	64.4	61.4	61.2	34.5	31.9	29.2	27.9	8.6	10.6	11.0	11.1
45–64 years	59.6	54.2	49.3	45.2	36.0	31.5	27.3	22.8	19.2	17.6	17.1	17.5
65 years and over	61.4	51.9	45.1	37.6	36.6	27.5	20.3	16.6	23.3	23.1	23.0	19.7
Black or African American:												
Under 18 years	79.9	85.5	87.3	88.0	23.7	20.2	*	16.5*	2.2*	9.8	*	*
18–44 years	68.5	68.3	65.0	72.6	31.7	31.9	22.0	29.4	9.0	18.1	20.9	14.0*
45–64 years	66.1	61.6	61.7	57.0	38.6	31.2	23.3	26.7	22.6	26.9	35.9	24.5
65 years and over	64.6	58.6	52.8	45.2	49.0	28.9	18.5*	18.6*	14.2	28.7	33.4	25.4*

*Estimates are considered unreliable.

[a]Type of physician is based on physician's self-designated primary area of practice. Primary care generalist physicians are defined as practitioners in the fields of general and family practice, general internal medicine, general obstetrics and gynecology, and general pediatrics and exclude primary care specialists. Primary care generalists in general and family practice exclude primary care specialties, such as sports medicine and geriatrics. Primary care internal medicine physicians exclude internal medicine specialists, such as allergists, cardiologists, and endocrinologists. Primary care obstetrics and gynecology physicians exclude obstetrics and gynecology specialties, such as gynecological oncology, maternal and fetal medicine, obstetrics and gynecology critical care medicine, and reproductive endocrinology. Primary care pediatricians exclude pediatric specialists, such as adolescent medicine specialists, neonatologists, pediatric allergists, and pediatric cardiologists.

[b]Estimates by racial group should be used with caution because information on race was collected from medical records. In 2010, race data were missing and imputed for 23% of visits. Information on the race imputation process used in each data year is available in the public-use file documentation. Starting with 1999 data, the instruction for the race item on the patient record form was changed so that more than one race could be recorded. In previous years only one racial category could be checked. Estimates for racial groups presented in this table are for visits where only one race was recorded. Because of the small number of responses with more than one racial group checked, estimates for visits with multiple races checked are unreliable and are not presented.

Notes: This table presents data on visits to physician offices and excludes visits to other sites, such as hospital outpatient and emergency departments. In 1980, the survey excluded Alaska and Hawaii. Data for all other years include all 50 states and the District of Columbia. Visits with specialty of physician unknown are excluded. Starting with *Health, United States, 2005*, data for 2001 and later years for physician offices use a revised weighting scheme.

SOURCE: Adapted from "Table 83. Visits to Primary Care Generalist and Specialty Care Physicians, by Selected Characteristics and Type of Physician: United States, Selected Years 1980–2010," in *Health, United States, 2014: With Special Feature on Adults Aged 55–64*, National Center for Health Statistics, May 2015, http://www.cdc.gov/nchs/data/hus/hus14.pdf (accessed May 22, 2015)

foot examinations and control of blood sugar levels, can prevent or delay some of the consequences of diabetes.

The relatively recent rise in type 2 diabetes is in part attributed to rising obesity among adults. Between 1988–94 and 2009–12 the percentage of adults aged 20 years and older diagnosed with diabetes increased from 8.8% to 11.7%. (See Table 7.6.) The NCHS indicates in *Early Release of Selected Estimates Based on Data from the January–March 2014 National Health Interview Survey* (March 2015, http://www.cdc.gov/nchs/data/nhis/earlyrelease/earlyrelease201503_14.pdf) that of all the adult age groups in 2014, the highest rate of diagnosed diabetes was among adults aged 65 years and older (21%). (See Figure 7.8.) Nearly one-quarter (23.5%) of men and 19% of women over age 65 had been diagnosed with diabetes as of 2014.

TABLE 7.5

Leading causes of death and numbers of deaths, by age, 1980 and 2013

[Data are based on death certificates]

Age and rank order	1980		2013*	
	Cause of death	Deaths	Cause of death	Deaths
65 years and over				
Rank	All causes	1,341,848	All causes	1,904,640
1	Diseases of heart	595,406	Diseases of heart	488,156
2	Malignant neoplasms	258,389	Malignant neoplasms	407,558
3	Cerebrovascular diseases	146,417	Chronic lower respiratory diseases	127,194
4	Pneumonia and influenza	45,512	Cerebrovascular diseases	109,602
5	Chronic obstructive pulmonary diseases	43,587	Alzheimer's disease	83,786
6	Atherosclerosis	28,081	Diabetes mellitus*	53,751
7	Diabetes mellitus	25,216	Influenza and pneumonia	48,031
8	Unintentional injuries	24,844	Unintentional injuries	45,942
9	Nephritis, nephrotic syndrome, and nephrosis	12,968	Nephritis, nephrotic syndrome and nephrosis*	39,080
10	Chronic liver disease and cirrhosis	9,519	Septicemia	28,815

*Starting with 2011 data, the rules for selecting renal failure as the underlying cause of death were changed, affecting the number of deaths in the nephritis, nephrotic syndrome and nephrosis and diabetes categories. These changes directly affect deaths with mention of Renal failure and other associated conditions, such as diabetes mellitus with renal complications. The result is a decrease in the number of deaths for nephritis, nephrotic syndrome and nephrosis and an increase in the number of deaths for diabetes mellitus. Therefore, trend data for these two causes of death should be interpreted with caution.

SOURCE: Adapted from "Table 21. Leading Causes of Death and Numbers of Deaths, by Age: United States, 1980 and 2013," in *Health, United States, 2014: With Special Feature on Adults Aged 55–64*, National Center for Health Statistics, May 2015, http://www.cdc.gov/nchs/data/hus/hus14.pdf (accessed May 22, 2015)

Prostate Problems

Prostate problems typically occur after age 50. There are three common prostate disorders: prostatitis (inflammation of the prostate gland), benign prostatic hyperplasia (BPH; noncancerous enlargement of the prostate), and prostate cancer. Prostatitis causes painful or difficult urination and frequently occurs in younger men. According to the National Kidney and Urologic Diseases Information Clearinghouse, in "Prostate Enlargement: Benign Prostatic Hyperplasia" (September 24, 2014, http://kidney.niddk.nih.gov/kudiseases/pubs/prostateenlargement), about 50% of men between the ages of 51 and 60 and up to 90% of men age 80 and older have BPH.

Prostate cancer is the second-most common cause of cancer death after lung cancer in American men, and the risk of developing the disease increases with age. Table 7.8 shows the percentage of men that will develop prostate cancer over different periods, based on the man's current age. For example, 6.3% of men who were 60 years old in 2009–11 will develop prostate cancer sometime during the next decade.

The American Cancer Society reports in *Cancer Facts and Figures, 2015* (2015, http://www.cancer.org/acs/groups/content/@editorial/documents/document/acspc-044552.pdf) that an estimated 220,800 men were diagnosed with prostate cancer in 2015, and 27,540 men died from it. When diagnosed and treated early, prostate cancer is generally not life threatening because it progresses slowly and remains localized for a long time. As a result, many men who are diagnosed late in life do not die from this disease.

Incontinence

Urinary incontinence is the uncontrollable loss of urine that is so severe that it has social or hygienic consequences. Bowel incontinence refers to accidental leakage of mucus, liquid stool, or solid stool. In *Prevalence of Incontinence among Older Americans* (June 2014, http://www.cdc.gov/nchs/data/series/sr_03/sr03_036.pdf), Yelena Gorina and her colleagues at the CDC report that about 50% of adults aged 65 and older suffer from urinary and/or bowel incontinence. The problem is more common in women than in men, although it affects men of all ages. Incontinence can lead to many complications. For example, if untreated it increases the risk of developing serious bladder and kidney infections, skin rashes, and pressure sores.

Age-related changes affect the ability to control urination. The maximum capacity of urine that the bladder can hold diminishes, as does the ability to postpone urination when a person feels the urge to urinate. As a person ages, the rate of urine flow out of the bladder and through the urethra slows, and the volume of urine remaining in the bladder after urination is finished increases. In women the urethra shortens and its lining becomes thinner as the level of estrogen declines during menopause, decreasing the ability of the urinary sphincter to close tightly. Among older men, the prostate gland enlarges, sometimes blocking the flow of urine through the urethra.

Along with age, the risk factors for bowel incontinence include chronic diarrhea, inadequate fiber and water intake, and chronic constipation, diabetes, stroke,

FIGURE 7.4

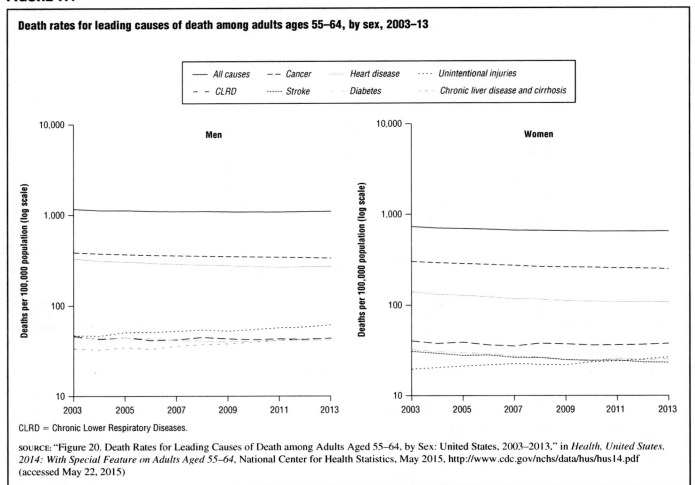

Death rates for leading causes of death among adults ages 55–64, by sex, 2003–13

Legend:
— All causes — – Cancer ···· Heart disease ···· Unintentional injuries
– – CLRD ······ Stroke — Diabetes – – – Chronic liver disease and cirrhosis

Men — Deaths per 100,000 population (log scale)

Women — Deaths per 100,000 population (log scale)

CLRD = Chronic Lower Respiratory Diseases.

SOURCE: "Figure 20. Death Rates for Leading Causes of Death among Adults Aged 55–64, by Sex: United States, 2003–2013," in *Health, United States, 2014: With Special Feature on Adults Aged 55–64*, National Center for Health Statistics, May 2015, http://www.cdc.gov/nchs/data/hus/hus14.pdf (accessed May 22, 2015)

neurologic and psychiatric conditions, cognitive impairment, and mobility impairment as well as certain medications. Figure 7.9 shows the percentage of noninstitutionalized men and women age 65 and older that suffer from urinary and bowel incontinence.

Although incontinence is common, highly treatable, and frequently curable, it is underdiagnosed and often untreated because sufferers do not seek treatment. Many older adults are fearful, embarrassed, or incorrectly assume that incontinence is a normal consequence of growing old. The disorder exacts a serious emotional toll; sufferers are often homebound, isolated, or depressed and are more likely to report their health as fair to poor than their peers. Incontinence may lead to institutionalization because many of those afflicted have some activity limitations and because incontinence is difficult for caregivers to manage.

Malnutrition

The older population is vulnerable to nutrition-related health problems. As people age, their energy needs decline, and it is vital for them to consume nutrient-dense foods in a lower calorie diet. According to the National

Resource Center on Nutrition, Physical Activity, and Aging, in "Malnutrition and Older Americans" (2015, http://nutritionandaging.fiu.edu/aging_network/malfact2.asp), 35% to 50% of older adults in long-term care facilities and up to 65% of older adults in hospitals are at risk for malnutrition. Concerning homebound older adults, an estimated 1 million are also at risk for malnutrition.

Older adults' nutrition may be affected by many factors, including loneliness, depression, a cognitive disorder, poor appetite, or a lack of transportation. An older adult may forgo meal preparation when there is no longer someone else to cook for or eat with, and a bereaved or frail older adult may not have the stamina or motivation to shop or cook. Malnutrition may also be the result of poverty. When faced with fixed incomes and competing needs, older adults may be forced to choose between buying food or the prescription medications they need.

Hearing Loss

There are many causes of hearing loss, the most common being age-related changes in the ear's mechanism. Hearing loss is a common problem among older adults

FIGURE 7.5

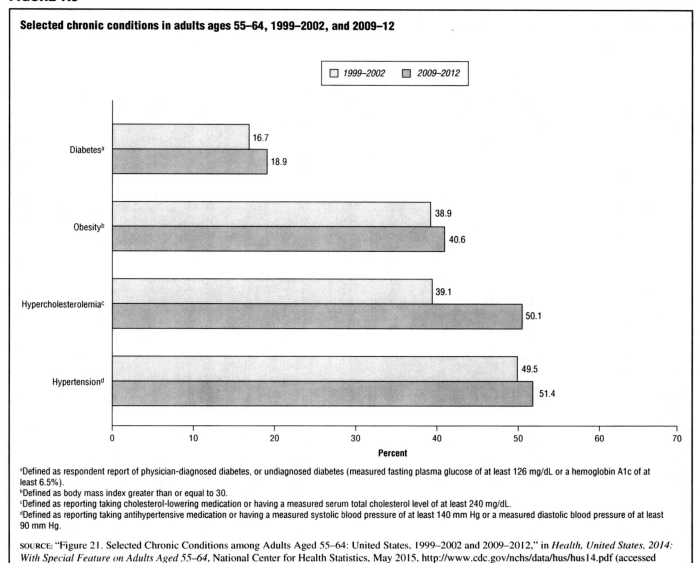

Selected chronic conditions in adults ages 55–64, 1999–2002, and 2009–12

☐ 1999–2002   ▨ 2009–2012

[a]Defined as respondent report of physician-diagnosed diabetes, or undiagnosed diabetes (measured fasting plasma glucose of at least 126 mg/dL or a hemoglobin A1c of at least 6.5%).
[b]Defined as body mass index greater than or equal to 30.
[c]Defined as reporting taking cholesterol-lowering medication or having a measured serum total cholesterol level of at least 240 mg/dL.
[d]Defined as reporting taking antihypertensive medication or having a measured systolic blood pressure of at least 140 mm Hg or a measured diastolic blood pressure of at least 90 mm Hg.

SOURCE: "Figure 21. Selected Chronic Conditions among Adults Aged 55–64: United States, 1999–2002 and 2009–2012," in *Health, United States, 2014: With Special Feature on Adults Aged 55–64*, National Center for Health Statistics, May 2015, http://www.cdc.gov/nchs/data/hus/hus14.pdf (accessed May 22, 2015)

and can seriously compromise quality of life. People suffering from hearing loss may withdraw from social contact and are sometimes misdiagnosed as cognitively impaired or mentally ill. The National Institute on Deafness and Other Communication Disorders (NIDCD; it is one of the National Institutes of Health) reports in "Quick Statistics" (April 20, 2015, http://www.nidcd.nih.gov/health/statistics/pages/quick.aspx) that the prevalence of disabling hearing loss increases with age, from 8.5% of adults ages 55 to 64 to 25% of those ages 65 to 74, and 50% of those age 75 and older.

Dane J. Genther et al. find in "Association of Hearing Loss with Hospitalization and Burden of Disease in Older Adults" (*Journal of the American Medical Association*, vol. 309, no. 22, June 12, 2013) that compared with older adults with normal hearing, older adults with hearing loss were more likely to have risk factors for heart disease and stroke. Those with hearing loss (23.8%) were more likely than those with normal hearing (18.7%) to have been hospitalized during the prior year and had more hospitalizations (1.52 on average, compared with 1.27).

There is an expanding array of devices and services to mitigate the effects of hearing loss. Hearing-impaired people may benefit from high-tech hearing aids, amplifiers for doorbells and telephones, infrared amplifiers, and even companion dogs that are trained to respond to sounds on behalf of their owner.

Medicare does not cover routine hearing examinations, hearing aids, or exams for fitting hearing aids for older adults but does cover diagnostic hearing exams ordered by a physician or other health care provider. The NIH explains that a wide range of hearing aid technologies is available. Digital hearing aids, which require

TABLE 7.6

Diabetes rates by sex, age, and race, selected years 1988–94 and 2009–12

[Data are based on interviews and physical examinations of a sample of the civilian noninstitutionalized population]

Sex, age, and race and Hispanic origin[c]	Physician-diagnosed and undiagnosed diabetes[a,b]				Physician-diagnosed diabetes[a]				Undiagnosed diabetes[b]			
	1988–1994	1999–2002	2003–2006	2009–2012	1988–1994	1999–2002	2003–2006	2009–2012	1988–1994	1999–2002	2003–2006	2009–2012
20 years and over, age-adjusted[d]					Percent of population							
All persons[e]	8.8	9.9	10.6	11.7	5.2	6.6	7.7	8.4	3.6	3.2	3.0	3.3
Male	9.6	11.2	11.1	13.2	5.5	7.3	7.0	9.0	4.1	3.9	4.1	4.2
Female	8.2	8.6	10.2	10.3	5.1	5.9	8.2	7.8	3.2	2.7	2.0	2.5
Not Hispanic or Latino:												
White only	7.7	8.5	8.9	9.1	4.8	5.5	6.2	6.6	2.9	3.0	2.7	2.5
Black or African American only	16.3	14.0	16.7	17.9	9.1	9.2	13.0	13.3	7.2	4.8	3.8	4.7
Mexican origin	15.6	13.9	17.1	20.5	10.7	10.8	12.9	13.9	5.0	3.1	4.2	6.6
Percent of poverty level:[f]												
Below 100%	14.2	14.6	14.8	17.1	8.8	9.0	12.4	12.1	5.4*	5.6	*	5.0
100% or more	8.1	9.3	10.1	10.8	4.8	6.4	7.1	7.8	3.3	2.9	3.0	3.0
100%–199%	9.7	13.1	13.9	14.8	5.2	9.4	9.5	11.4	4.4	3.6*	4.4	3.4
200% or more	7.8	8.2	8.9	9.4	4.7	5.5	6.3	6.5	3.1	2.7	2.6	2.9
200%–399%	7.8	10.5	10.5	11.5	4.3	7.3	7.5	8.4	3.6	3.2	3.1*	3.1
400% or more	7.8	6.7	7.0	7.7	5.3	4.3	5.2	5.2*	2.5	2.3	*	2.5
20 years and over, crude												
All persons[e]	8.3	9.8	10.9	12.3	4.9	6.6	7.9	8.9	3.4	3.2	3.0	3.5
Male	8.6	10.8	11.0	13.5	4.9	7.1	6.9	9.1	3.7	3.7	4.0	4.4
Female	8.0	8.9	10.8	11.2	5.0	6.1	8.7	8.7	3.1	2.8	2.1	2.6
Not Hispanic or Latino:												
White only	7.6	8.9	9.6	10.5	4.7	5.6	6.7	7.6	2.9	3.2	3.0	2.8
Black or African American only	13.3	12.5	15.8	17.1	7.2	8.3	12.3	12.5	6.1	4.2	3.5	4.6
Mexican origin	10.4	9.3	12.6	15.8	6.3	7.2	8.8	10.1	4.1	2.0	3.8*	5.7
Percent of poverty level:[f]												
Below 100%	11.6	13.4	12.7	14.3	7.2	8.4	10.6	9.8	4.4	5.1	*	4.5
100% or more	7.6	9.2	10.5	11.8	4.5	6.3	7.3	8.6	3.1	2.9	3.1	3.3
100%–199%	9.1	12.9	14.9	15.8	5.2	9.3	10.2	12.3	3.9	3.6*	4.7	3.5
200% or more	7.1	8.0	9.1	10.4	4.3	5.4	6.5	7.3	2.8	2.6	2.7	3.2
200%–399%	6.8	10.2	11.0	12.3	3.7	7.0	7.7	9.0	3.1	3.1*	3.2*	3.3
400% or more	7.6	6.4	7.4	8.9	5.2	4.1	5.3	5.8*	2.5*	2.3	2.2*	3.1*
Age												
20–44 years	2.1*	4.4	3.9	3.7	*	3.2	2.8	2.1	1.1	*	1.1*	1.6
45–64 years	14.0	12.8	13.7	16.2	7.9	8.3	10.1	11.4	6.0	4.5	3.5	4.8
65 years and over	19.4	20.4	24.9	26.8	12.7	13.7	17.5	21.2	6.7	6.7	7.4	5.5

*Estimates are considered unreliable.

[a]Physician-diagnosed diabetes was obtained by self-report and excludes women who are pregnant.

[b]Undiagnosed diabetes is defined as a fasting plasma glucose (FPG) of at least 126 mg/dL or a hemoglobin A1c of at least 6.5% and no reported physician diagnosis. Respondents had fasted for at least 8 hours and less than 24 hours. Pregnant females are excluded. Starting in 2005–2006, testing was performed at a different laboratory and using different instruments than testing in earlier years. The National Health and Nutrition Examination Survey (NHANES) conducted crossover studies to evaluate the impact of these changes on FPG and A1c measurements and recommended adjustments to the FPG data. The adjustments recommended by NHANES were incorporated into the data presented here. The revised definition of undiagnosed diabetes was based on recommendations from the American Diabetes Association. To ensure data comparability, the revised definition of undiagnosed diabetes was applied to all data in this table.

[c]Persons of Mexican origin may be of any race. Starting with 1999 data, race-specific estimates are tabulated according to the 1997 Revisions to the Standards for the Classification of Federal Data on Race and Ethnicity and are not strictly comparable with estimates for earlier years. The two non-Hispanic race categories shown in the table conform to the 1997 Standards. Starting with 1999 data, race-specific estimates are for persons who reported only one racial group. Prior to data year 1999, estimates were tabulated according to the 1977 Standards. Estimates for single-race categories prior to 1999 included persons who reported one race or, if they reported more than one race, identified one race as best representing their race.

[d]Estimates are age-adjusted to the year 2000 standard population using three age groups: 20–44 years, 45–64 years, and 65 years and over. Age-adjusted estimates in this table may differ from other age-adjusted estimates based on the same data and presented elsewhere if different age groups are used in the adjustment procedure.

[e]Includes all other races and Hispanic origins not shown separately.

[f]Percent of poverty level was calculated by dividing family income by the U.S. Department of Health and Human Services' poverty guideline specific to family size, as well as the appropriate year, and state. Persons with unknown percent of poverty level are excluded (7% in 2009–2012).

Notes: Pregnant women are excluded. Fasting weights were used to obtain estimates of total, physician-diagnosed, and undiagnosed diabetes prevalence. Examination weights were used to obtain the poor glycemic control estimates. Estimates in this table may differ from other estimates based on the same data and presented elsewhere if different weights, age adjustment groups, definitions, or trend adjustments are used.

SOURCE: Adapted from "Table 44. Diabetes Prevalence and Glycemic Control among Adults Aged 20 and over, by Sex, Age, and Race and Hispanic Origin: United States, Selected Years 1988–1994 through 2009–2012," in *Health, United States, 2014: With Special Feature on Adults Aged 55–64*, National Center for Health Statistics, May 2015, http://www.cdc.gov/nchs/data/hus/hus14.pdf (accessed May 22, 2015)

TABLE 7.7

Hypertension, by selected characteristics, selected years, 1988–94 and 2009–12

[Data are based on interviews and physical examinations of a sample of the civilian noninstitutionalized population]

Sex, age, race and Hispanic origin[a], and percent of poverty level	Hypertension[b, c] (measured high blood pressure and/or taking antihypertensive medication)				Uncontrolled high blood pressure among persons with hypertension[d]			
	1988–1994	1999–2002	2003–2006	2009–2012	1988–1994	1999–2002	2003–2006	2009–2012
20 years and over, age-adjusted[e]				Percent of population				
Both sexes[f]	25.5	30.0	31.3	30.0	77.2	70.6	63.3	55.1
Male	26.4	28.8	31.8	30.6	83.2	73.3	65.0	62.0
Female	24.4	30.6	30.3	29.3	68.5	61.8	53.6	44.7
Not Hispanic or Latino:								
White only, male	25.6	27.6	31.2	29.6	82.6	70.3	63.3	58.7
White only, female	23.0	28.5	28.3	27.5	67.0	63.6	47.5	42.8
Black or African American only, male	37.5	40.6	42.2	42.5	84.0	74.3	70.2	68.9
Black or African American only, female	38.3	43.5	44.1	44.2	71.1	67.2	59.0	46.8
Mexican origin male	26.9	26.8	24.8	27.3	87.9	89.5	70.7	76.4
Mexican origin female	25.0	27.9	28.6	29.3	77.6	71.5	66.1	47.1
Percent of poverty level:[g]								
Below 100%	31.7	33.9	35.0	33.4	75.0	71.2	69.8	56.3
100%–199%	26.6	33.5	34.1	33.1	76.0	73.4	68.2	57.6
200%–399%	24.7	30.2	31.9	30.6	76.2	67.8	63.9	51.5
400% or more	22.6	26.4	28.9	27.3	81.5	70.3	56.8	60.2
20 years and over, crude								
Both sexes[f]	24.1	30.2	32.1	32.2	73.9	67.3	58.6	47.4
Male	23.8	27.6	31.3	31.6	79.3	67.1	58.4	50.7
Female	24.4	32.7	32.9	32.8	68.8	67.4	58.8	44.2
Not Hispanic or Latino:								
White only, male	24.3	28.3	32.4	33.1	78.0	64.0	56.2	47.2
White only, female	24.6	32.8	33.4	33.7	67.8	66.9	58.2	42.6
Black or African American only, male	31.1	35.9	38.8	39.9	83.3	71.3	65.9	60.5
Black or African American only, female	32.5	41.9	42.8	44.5	70.0	67.5	55.5	45.8
Mexican origin male	16.4	16.5	16.6	19.1	86.5	86.9	66.9	69.8
Mexican origin female	15.9	18.8	20.0	22.0	80.6	74.5	68.6	52.8
Percent of poverty level:[g]								
Below 100%	25.7	30.3	28.8	27.3	74.0	71.3	67.3	54.8
100%–199%	26.7	34.8	36.8	35.3	75.1	70.7	63.2	49.8
200%–399%	22.4	29.9	33.1	33.4	73.4	64.4	58.0	45.7
400% or more	22.0	26.8	29.2	31.5	74.3	63.8	53.4	43.1
Male								
20–44 years	10.9	12.1	14.2	11.2	90.5	79.7	71.1	70.3
20–34 years	7.1	8.1*	9.2	5.8	92.6	89.9	83.1	88.4
35–44 years	17.1	17.1	21.1	19.1	89.0	73.3	63.6	62.0
45–64 years	34.2	36.4	41.2	42.2	73.1	61.4	57.0	50.2
45–54 years	29.2	31.0	36.2	33.6	76.2	66.4	59.3	47.7
55–64 years	40.6	45.0	50.2	51.9	70.3	55.9	53.9	52.0
65–74 years	54.4	59.6	64.1	61.7	74.3	59.1	45.9	36.9
75 years and over	60.4	69.0	65.0	75.1	82.5	74.3	59.7	48.9
Female								
20–44 years	6.5	8.3	6.9	8.7	63.4	58.3	49.1	46.5
20–34 years	2.9	2.7*	2.2*	3.9	82.2	56.9	47.9*	49.0
35–44 years	11.2	15.1	12.6	15.5	56.8	58.6	49.4	45.5
45–64 years	32.8	40.0	43.4	39.5	62.1	60.5	55.5	36.5
45–54 years	23.9	31.8	36.2	29.5	58.5	61.1	57.4	36.2
55–64 years	42.6	53.9	54.4	51.0	64.3	60.0	53.6	36.8
65–74 years	56.2	72.7	70.8	66.7	68.7	73.5	58.5	45.4
75 years and over	73.6	83.1	80.2	79.3	81.9	78.1	70.3	57.8

sophisticated fittings, cost from $1,500 to $5,000 each. The NIDCD observes that although most health insurance plans do not cover hearing aids, some nonprofit organizations provide financial assistance for hearing aids.

Vision Changes

Almost no one escapes age-related changes in vision. Over time it becomes increasingly difficult to read small print or thread a needle at the usual distance. For many older adults, night vision declines. This is often caused by a condition called presbyopia (tired eyes) and is a common occurrence. People who were previously nearsighted may actually realize some improvement in eyesight as they become slightly farsighted. In 2013, 11.5% of adults aged 65 to 74 years and 18% of those aged 75 years and older had vision limitations. (See Table 7.9.)

TABLE 7.7

Hypertension, by selected characteristics, selected years, 1988–94 and 2009–12 [CONTINUED]

*Estimates are considered unreliable.

[a]Persons of Mexican origin may be of any race. Starting with 1999 data, race-specific estimates are tabulated according to the 1997 Revisions to the Standards for the Classification of Federal Data on Race and Ethnicity and are not strictly comparable with estimates for earlier years. The two non-Hispanic race categories shown in the table conform to the 1997 Standards. Starting with 1999 data, race-specific estimates are for persons who reported only one racial group. Prior to data year 1999, estimates were tabulated according to the 1977 Standards. Estimates for single-race categories prior to 1999 included persons who reported one race or, if they reported more than one race, identified one race as best representing their race.

[b]Hypertension is defined as having measured high blood pressure and/or taking antihypertensive medication. High blood pressure is defined as having measured systolic pressure of at least 140 mm Hg or diastolic pressure of at least 90 mm Hg. Those with high blood pressure also may be taking prescribed medicine for high blood pressure. Those taking antihypertensive medication may not have measured high blood pressure but are still classified as having hypertension.

[c]Respondents were asked, "Are you now taking prescribed medicine for your high blood pressure?"

[d]Uncontrolled high blood pressure among persons with hypertension is defined as measured systolic pressure of at least 140 mm Hg or diastolic pressure of at least 90 mm Hg, among those with measured high blood pressure or reporting taking antihypertensive medication.

[e]Estimates are age-adjusted to the year 2000 standard population using five age groups: 20–34 years, 35–44 years, 45–54 years, 55–64 years, and 65 years and over. Age-adjusted estimates in this table may differ from other age-adjusted estimates based on the same data and presented elsewhere if different age groups are used in the adjustment procedure.

[f]Includes persons of all races and Hispanic origins, not just those shown separately

[g]Percent of poverty level was calculated by dividing family income by the U.S. Department of Health and Human Services' poverty guideline specific to family size, as well as the appropriate year, and state. Persons with unknown percent of poverty level are excluded (7% in 2009–2012).

Notes: Percentages are based on the average of blood pressure measurements taken. In 2009–2012, 84% of participants had three systolic or diastolic blood pressure readings. Excludes pregnant women.

SOURCE: Adapted from "Table 60. Hypertension among Adults Aged 20 and over, by Selected Characteristics: United States, Selected Years 1988–1994 through 2009–2012," in *Health, United States, 2014: With Special Feature on Adults Aged 55–64*, National Center for Health Statistics, May 2015, http://www.cdc.gov/nchs/data/hus/hus14.pdf (accessed May 22, 2015)

FIGURE 7.6

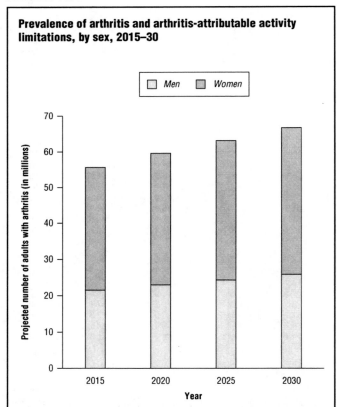

Prevalence of arthritis and arthritis-attributable activity limitations, by sex, 2015–30

SOURCE: Adapted from "Figure 1. Projected Prevalence of Doctor-Diagnosed Arthritis among U.S. Adults Aged 18 Years and Older, 2005–2030," in *Arthritis: National Statistics*, National Center for Chronic Disease Prevention and Health Promotion, Division of Population Health, Centers for Disease Control and Prevention, February 25, 2015, http://www.cdc.gov/arthritis/data_statistics/national-statistics.html (accessed May 30, 2015)

Major Eye Diseases

Cataracts, glaucoma, age-related macular degeneration, and diabetic retinopathy are the leading causes of vision impairment and blindness in older adults. Cataracts are the leading cause of blindness in the world. Glaucoma is a chronic disease that often requires lifelong treatment to control. Age-related macular degeneration is the most common cause of blindness and vision impairment in Americans aged 60 years and older. Diabetic retinopathy is a common complication of diabetes and is considered to be a leading cause of blindness in the industrialized world.

CATARACTS. A cataract is an opacity, or clouding, of the naturally clear lens of the eye. The prevalence of cataracts increases dramatically with age and most develop slowly over time as they progressively compromise vision. Once a clouded lens develops, surgery to remove the affected lens and replace it with an artificial lens is the recommended treatment. The AARP reports in "Eye Diseases of the Aging—Symptoms, Causes and Treatments" (2013, http://www.aarp.org/health/conditions-treatments/info-05-2013/eye-diseases-of-aging.html) that cataracts affect nearly 25 million Americans over the age of 40 years and more than half of Americans aged 65 years and older.

GLAUCOMA. Glaucoma is a disease that causes gradual damage to the optic nerve, which carries visual information from the eye to the brain. The loss of vision is not experienced until a significant amount of nerve damage has occurred. Because the onset is gradual, as many as half of all people with glaucoma are unaware that they have the disease. In "Vision Problems in the U.S." (2012, http://www.visionproblemsus.org), Prevent Blindness America indicates that in 2010 glaucoma affected approximately 2.7 million Americans over the age of 40 years.

FIGURE 7.7

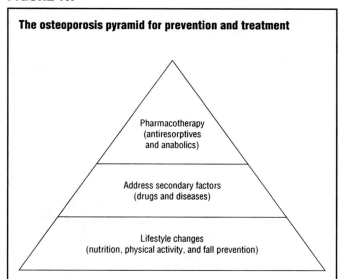

The osteoporosis pyramid for prevention and treatment

Pharmacotherapy
(antiresorptives
and anabolics)

Address secondary factors
(drugs and diseases)

Lifestyle changes
(nutrition, physical activity, and fall prevention)

Note:

The base of the pyramid: The first step in the prevention and treatment of osteoporosis and the prevention of fractures is to build a foundation of nutrition and lifestyle measures that maximize bone health. The diet should not only be adequate in calcium and vitamin D, but should have a healthy balance of other nutrients. A weight-bearing exercise program should be developed. Cigarette smoking and excessive alcohol use must be avoided. In the older individual, at high risk for fractures, the changes in lifestyle would include a plan not only to maximize physical activity, but also to minimize the risk of falls. The use of hip protectors can be considered in some high-risk patients. Diseases that increase the risk of falls by causing visual impairment, postural hypotension (a drop in blood pressure on standing, which leads to dizziness), or poor balance should be treated. Drugs that cause bone loss or increase the risk of falls should be avoided or given at the lowest effective dose.

The second level of the pyramid: The next step is to identify and treat diseases that produce secondary osteoporosis or aggravate primary osteoporosis. These measures are the foundation upon which specific pharmacotherapy is built and should never be forgotten.

The third level of the pyramid: If there is sufficiently high risk of fracture to warrant pharmacotherapy, the patient is usually started on antiresorptives. Anabolic agents are used in individuals in whom antiresorptive therapy is not adequate to prevent bone loss or fractures.

SOURCE: "Figure 9-1. The Osteoporosis Pyramid for Prevention and Treatment," in *Bone Health and Osteoporosis: A Report of the Surgeon General*, U.S. Department of Health and Human Services, Public Health Service, Office of the Surgeon General, October 14, 2004, http://www.ncbi.nlm.nih.gov/books/NBK45501/ (accessed May 29, 2015)

Routine glaucoma testing is especially important for older people. There is no cure for glaucoma and no way to restore lost vision; however, medication can generally manage the condition. At later stages, laser therapy and surgery are effective in preventing further damage.

AGE-RELATED MACULAR DEGENERATION. Age-related macular degeneration is a condition in which the macula, a specialized part of the retina that is responsible for sharp central and reading vision, is damaged. Symptoms include blurred vision, a dark spot in the center of the vision field, and vertical line distortion. Prevent Blindness America notes in "Vision Problems in the U.S." that in 2010 nearly 2.1 million adults aged 50 years and older had the advanced form of the condition.

In "Forecasting Age-Related Macular Degeneration through the Year 2050: The Potential Impact of New Treatments" (*Archives of Ophthalmology*, vol. 127, no. 4, April 2009), David B. Rein et al. predict that the prevalence of early age-related macular degeneration will increase substantially, from 9.1 million in 2010 to 17.8 million in 2050.

DIABETIC RETINOPATHY. Diabetic retinopathy occurs when the small blood vessels in the retina become blocked, break down, leak fluid that distorts vision, and sometimes release blood into the center of the eye, causing blindness. Photocoagulation (laser treatment) can help reduce the risk of loss of vision in advanced cases. According to Prevent Blindness America, in "Vision Problems in the U.S.," in 2010 diabetic retinopathy affected 7.7 million Americans aged 40 years and older. The prevalence of diabetic retinopathy increases with age, reflecting the higher rates of diabetes in older people.

Oral Health Problems

According to the CDC, in "Oral Health for Older Americans" (July 10, 2013, http://www.cdc.gov/oralhealth/publications/factsheets/adult_oral_health/adult_older.htm), one-fourth of adults aged 60 years and older have lost all their teeth, and nearly one-quarter (23%) of adults ages 65 to 74 have periodontal (gum) disease. Older adults with the worst oral health are those who are poor and members of racial and ethnic minorities as well as those who are disabled, homebound, or institutionalized.

Parkinson's Disease

According to the Parkinson's Disease Foundation, in "Statistics on Parkinson's" (2015, www.pdf.org/en/parkinson_statistics), Parkinson's disease (PD) affects about 1 million people in the United States. An estimated 60,000 people in the United States are diagnosed with PD each year and thousands of others have the disease but are not diagnosed. The incidence of PD increases with advancing age (just 4% of cases are diagnosed in people under the age of 50 years). In "Movement Disorders" (*Medical Clinics of North America*, vol. 93, no. 2, March 2009), Meghan K. Harris et al. observe that the prevalence of PD is 1% to 2% in the population aged 65 years and older and up to 4% in individuals older than age 85. PD usually begins during the 70s, but up to 10% of those affected are aged 50 years and younger.

PD is caused by the death of about half a million brain cells in the basal ganglia. These cells secrete dopamine, a neurotransmitter (chemical messenger), whose function is to allow nerve impulses to move smoothly from one nerve cell to another. These nerve cells, in turn, transmit messages to the muscles of the body to begin movement. When the normal supply of dopamine is reduced, the messages are not sent correctly, and the

FIGURE 7.8

Prevalence of diagnosed diabetes by age group and sex, January–September, 2014

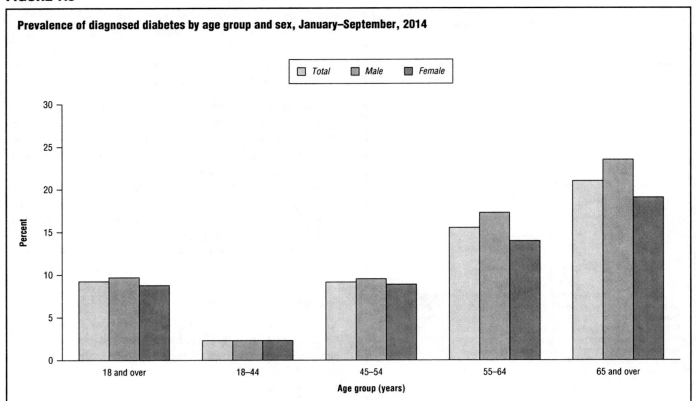

Notes: Data are based on household interviews of a sample of the civilian noninstitutionalized population. Prevalence of diagnosed diabetes is based on self-report of ever having been diagnosed with diabetes by a doctor or other health professional. Persons reporting "borderline" diabetes status and women reporting diabetes only during pregnancy were not coded as having diabetes in the analyses. The analyses excluded the <0.1% of persons with unknown diabetes status.

SOURCE: "Figure 14.2. Prevalence of Diagnosed Diabetes among Adults Aged 18 and over, by Age Group and Sex: United States, January–September 2014," in *Early Release of Selected Estimates Based on Data from the National Health Interview Survey, January–September 2014*, Centers for Disease Control and Prevention, National Center for Health Statistics, March 2015, http://www.cdc.gov/nchs/data/nhis/earlyrelease/earlyrelease201503_14.pdf (accessed March 30, 2015)

TABLE 7.8

Percentage of men who develop prostate cancer over 10-, 20-, and 30-year intervals by their current age, 2009–11

Current age	10 years	20 years	30 years
30	0.01	0.34	2.49
40	0.33	2.52	8.04
50	2.26	7.98	13.47
60	6.29	12.34	14.57
70	7.52	10.30	N/A

SOURCE: "Percent of U.S. Men Who Develop Prostate Cancer over 10-, 20-, and 30-Year Intervals According to Their Current Age, 2009–2011," in *Prostate Cancer Risk by Age*, Centers for Disease Control and Prevention, Division of Cancer Prevention and Control, September 16, 2014, http://www.cdc.gov/cancer/prostate/statistics/age.htm (accessed May 30, 2015)

symptoms—mild tremor (shaking), change in walking, or a decreased arm swing—of PD begin to appear.

The four early warning signs of PD are tremors, muscle stiffness, unusual slowness (bradykinesia), and a stooped posture. Medications can control initial symptoms, but over time they become less effective. As the disease worsens, patients develop more severe tremors, causing them to fall or jerk uncontrollably. (The jerky body movements PD patients experience are called dyskinesias.) At other times, rigidity sets in, rendering them unable to move. About one-third of patients also develop dementia (loss of intellectual functioning accompanied by memory loss and personality changes).

TREATMENT OF PARKINSON'S DISEASE. Management of PD is individualized and includes drug therapy and daily exercise. Exercise can often lessen the rigidity of muscles, prevent weakness, and improve the ability to walk.

The main goal of drug treatment is to restore the chemical balance between dopamine and another neurotransmitter, acetylcholine. Most patients are given levodopa (L-dopa), a compound that the body converts into dopamine. Treatment with L-dopa does not, however, slow the progressive course of the disease or even delay the changes in the brain PD produces, and it may produce some unpleasant side effects such as dyskinesias.

FIGURE 7.9

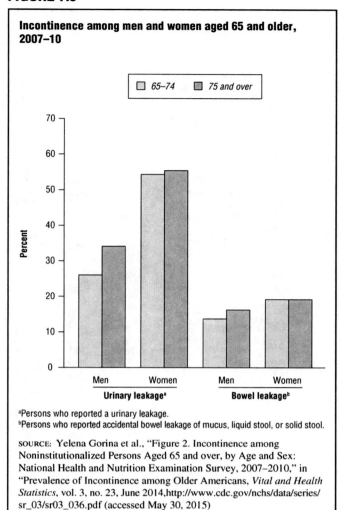

Incontinence among men and women aged 65 and older, 2007–10

Legend: 65–74 | 75 and over

Urinary leakage[a] — Men, Women
Bowel leakage[b] — Men, Women

[a]Persons who reported a urinary leakage.
[b]Persons who reported accidental bowel leakage of mucus, liquid stool, or solid stool.

SOURCE: Yelena Gorina et al., "Figure 2. Incontinence among Noninstitutionalized Persons Aged 65 and over, by Age and Sex: National Health and Nutrition Examination Survey, 2007–2010," in "Prevalence of Incontinence among Older Americans, *Vital and Health Statistics*, vol. 3, no. 23, June 2014,http://www.cdc.gov/nchs/data/series/sr_03/sr03_036.pdf (accessed May 30, 2015)

INFECTIOUS DISEASES

Infectious (contagious) diseases are caused by microorganisms (viruses, bacteria, parasites, or fungi) that are transmitted from one person to another through casual contact, such as with the transmittal of influenza; through bodily fluids, such as with the transmittal of HIV; or from contaminated food, air, or water supplies. The CDC reports that in 2013 influenza and pneumonia ranked seventh among the top-10 causes of death for older adults, responsible for 48,031 deaths of people aged 65 years and older. (See Table 7.5.) Influenza-related deaths can result from pneumonia as well as from exacerbation of chronic diseases.

Influenza

Influenza (flu) is a contagious respiratory disease caused by a virus. The virus is expelled by an infected individual in droplets into the air and may be inhaled by anyone nearby. It can also be transmitted by direct hand contact. The flu primarily affects the lungs, but the whole body experiences symptoms. Influenza is an acute (short-term) illness characterized by fever, chills, weakness, loss of appetite,

and aching muscles in the head, back, arms, and legs. The accompanying fever rises quickly—sometimes reaching 104 degrees Fahrenheit (40 degrees Celsius)—but usually subsides after two or three days. Influenza leaves the patient exhausted.

For healthy individuals, the flu is typically a moderately severe illness, but for older people who are not in good general health, the flu can be severe and even fatal. Complications such as secondary bacterial infections may develop, taking advantage of the body's weakened condition and lowered resistance. The most common bacterial complication is pneumonia, affecting the lungs, but sinuses, bronchi (larger air passages of the lungs), and inner ears can also become secondarily infected. Less common but serious complications include viral pneumonia, encephalitis (inflammation of the brain), acute renal (kidney) failure, and nervous system disorders. These complications can be fatal.

Influenza can be prevented by inoculation with a current influenza vaccine, which is formulated annually to contain the influenza viruses expected to cause the flu the upcoming year. Immunization produces antibodies to the influenza viruses, which become most effective after one or two months. The CDC advises that older adults get flu shots early in the fall because peak flu activity usually occurs around the beginning of the new calendar year. From 2003 to 2013, the percentage of adults between the ages of 50 and 74 that had received a flu shot increased but was stable among those aged 75 years and older. (See Figure 7.10.) In "People at High Risk of Developing Flu-Related Complications" (January 8, 2015, http://www.cdc.gov/flu/about/disease/high_risk.htm), the CDC asserts that adults aged 65 years and older are at high risk of developing serious complications such as pneumonia should they contract the flu.

Pneumonia

Pneumonia is a serious lung infection. Symptoms of pneumonia are fever, chills, cough, shortness of breath, chest pain, and increased sputum production. Pneumonia may be caused by viruses, bacteria, or fungi; the pneumococcus bacterium, however, is the most important cause of serious pneumonia.

Older adults are two to three times more likely than other adults to develop pneumococcal infections. A single vaccination can prevent most cases of pneumococcal pneumonia. The CDC recommends that all people aged 65 years and older receive the pneumonia vaccine, and since 2003 increasing percentages of adults ages 65 to 74 and age 75 and older report having been vaccinated. (See Figure 7.11.)

MANDATORY IMMUNIZATION FOR NURSING HOME RESIDENTS. Nursing home residents are required to be immunized against influenza and pneumonia; nursing homes that fail to enforce this requirement risk losing

TABLE 7.9

Vision limitations by age and sex, selected years 1997–2013

[Data are based on household interviews of a sample of the civilian noninstitutionalized population]

Characteristic	Any trouble seeing, even with glasses or contacts[a]									
	1997	2000	2005	2007	2008	2009	2010	2011	2012	2013
	Percent of adults									
18 years and over, age-adjusted[b, c]	10.0	9.0	9.2	9.9	10.9	8.3	9.1	8.8	8.4	8.7
18 years and over, crude[c]	9.8	8.9	9.3	10.0	11.2	8.6	9.4	9.2	8.8	9.1
Age										
18–44 years	6.2	5.3	5.5	6.9	7.2	5.3	6.2	5.5	5.4	5.5
18–24 years	5.4	4.2	5.0	6.9	7.8	4.8	5.8	5.2	5.1	5.5
25–44 years	6.5	5.7	5.7	6.8	7.0	5.6	6.3	5.6	5.5	5.5
45–64 years	12.0	10.7	11.2	12.2	13.8	10.8	11.6	12.0	11.3	11.1
45–54 years	12.2	10.9	11.0	12.3	13.3	10.5	10.7	11.7	11.2	10.6
55–64 years	11.6	10.5	11.5	12.1	14.4	11.2	12.7	12.4	11.5	11.7
65 years and over	18.1	17.4	17.4	15.3	17.5	13.1	13.9	13.6	12.7	14.3
65–74 years	14.2	13.6	13.2	12.9	14.3	10.3	12.2	12.2	11.0	11.5
75 years and over	23.1	21.9	22.0	17.9	21.1	16.5	16.1	15.2	14.9	18.0
Sex[b]										
Male	8.8	7.9	7.9	8.5	9.3	7.2	7.9	7.6	7.1	7.5
Female	11.1	10.1	10.5	11.2	12.5	9.3	10.3	10.1	9.7	9.8
Sex and age										
Male:										
18–44 years	5.3	4.4	4.5	5.6	6.1	4.5	5.2	4.2	4.4	4.5
45–54 years	10.1	8.8	8.8	10.6	11.3	9.1	9.1	10.4	9.3	9.4
55–64 years	10.5	9.5	10.5	10.0	11.9	9.7	10.7	11.8	9.8	10.4
65–74 years	13.2	12.8	11.4	11.4	11.3	9.3	10.5	9.7	9.9	10.9
75 years and over	21.4	20.7	20.4	17.2	19.8	15.1	15.7	14.9	12.8	14.7
Female:										
18–44 years	7.1	6.2	6.5	8.1	8.4	6.2	7.1	6.9	6.4	6.5
45–54 years	14.2	12.8	13.2	13.9	15.2	11.9	12.3	13.0	12.9	11.8
55–64 years	12.6	11.5	12.4	14.2	16.7	12.6	14.6	13.0	13.1	12.9
65–74 years	15.0	14.4	14.8	14.2	16.9	11.2	13.6	14.5	11.9	12.1
75 years and over	24.2	22.7	23.0	18.4	22.0	17.4	16.4	15.4	16.4	20.3
Race[b, d]										
White only	9.7	8.8	9.1	9.9	10.9	8.1	8.8	8.6	8.4	8.7
Black or African American only	12.8	10.6	10.9	10.5	11.7	10.4	12.1	10.8	9.2	10.0
American Indian or Alaska Native only	19.2	16.6	14.9*	18.0	14.2	12.3*	15.0	15.0	13.0	13.7
Asian only	6.2	6.3	5.5	5.7	8.9	5.5	5.3	6.3	5.7	4.9
Native Hawaiian or other Pacific Islander only	—	*	*	*	*	*	*	*	*	*
2 or more races	—	16.2	16.4	16.9	16.1	14.8	13.1	12.4	15.6	11.8
Hispanic origin and race[b, d]										
Hispanic or Latino	10.0	9.7	9.6	9.9	10.4	8.7	9.2	9.4	9.4	9.7
Mexican	10.2	8.3	9.9	10.1	10.4	8.7	9.0	10.4	9.3	10.9
Not Hispanic or Latino	10.0	9.1	9.2	10.0	11.0	8.3	9.2	8.8	8.4	8.6
White only	9.8	8.9	9.1	10.1	11.1	8.1	8.9	8.6	8.4	8.6
Black or African American only	12.8	10.6	10.9	10.6	11.7	10.5	12.2	10.7	9.3	10.1
Education[e, f]										
25 years of age and over:										
No high school diploma or GED	15.0	12.2	13.5	13.4	15.9	12.6	14.1	13.9	12.9	12.8
High school diploma or GED	10.6	9.5	10.3	10.9	11.2	9.2	10.5	10.4	9.3	10.0
Some college or more	8.9	8.9	8.6	9.2	10.4	7.6	8.0	7.9	7.9	8.0
Percent of poverty level[b, g]										
Below 100%	17.0	12.9	15.3	15.0	16.7	14.3	14.8	14.2	13.7	15.6
100%–199%	12.9	11.6	11.5	13.0	14.2	11.1	12.2	11.5	10.9	11.2
200%–399%	9.1	8.8	8.9	9.4	11.3	8.0	9.0	8.7	7.9	7.6
400% or more	7.3	7.1	6.9	7.8	7.8	5.7	6.4	6.0	6.1	6.4
Hispanic origin and race and percent of poverty level[b, d, g]										
Hispanic or Latino:										
Below 100%	12.8	11.0	13.6	13.4	12.9	12.2	10.8	13.9	13.1	13.1
100%–199%	11.2	9.4	8.8	11.1	11.3	8.1	10.8	9.6	10.0	10.6
200%–399%	8.1	9.2	8.2	7.2	10.2	9.0	8.9	8.3	6.8	7.4
400% or more	8.1*	10.5	8.0	10.6	7.5	4.6*	5.3	5.1	7.8	9.0

reimbursement from Medicare (a medical insurance program for older adults and people with disabilities) and Medicaid (a federal and state health care program for people below the poverty level). The regulation, which was issued by the Centers for Medicare and Medicaid Services in August 2005, intends to ensure that the most

TABLE 7.9

Vision limitations by age and sex, selected years 1997–2013 [CONTINUED]

[Data are based on household interviews of a sample of the civilian noninstitutionalized population.]

	Any trouble seeing, even with glasses or contacts[a]									
Characteristic	1997	2000	2005	2007	2008	2009	2010	2011	2012	2013
Not Hispanic or Latino:										
White only:										
Below 100%	17.9	13.1	16.2	16.3	19.5	13.4	16.8	14.4	14.5	17.7
100%–199%	13.1	12.0	12.7	14.2	15.6	12.1	12.6	12.3	11.7	11.8
200%–399%	9.2	9.2	9.0	10.3	11.5	8.3	8.8	9.0	8.5	7.8
400% or more	7.3	7.0	6.9	7.7	7.9	5.8	6.7	5.9	6.0	6.4
Black or African American only:										
Below 100%	17.9	13.6	16.0	15.1	16.9	17.8	15.8	15.5	13.7	15.3
100%–199%	16.0	12.9	11.3	14.0	14.5	11.7	14.9	12.3	11.3	11.4
200%–399%	9.3	7.7	9.7	7.3	9.8	8.1	12.0	8.5	6.8	8.0
400% or more	7.7	8.3	6.4	6.9	7.4	5.6	6.6	8.6	6.4	6.7
Geographic region[b]										
Northeast	8.6	7.4	8.1	8.1	9.3	7.3	7.8	7.6	6.4	7.4
Midwest	9.5	9.6	9.7	10.3	10.7	8.2	9.1	8.7	8.7	9.0
South	11.4	9.2	9.8	10.1	12.4	8.7	10.6	9.4	9.1	8.9
West	9.7	9.9	8.6	10.5	10.2	8.6	8.0	9.1	8.9	9.1
Location of residence[b, h]										
Within MSA	9.5	8.5	8.6	9.6	10.6	8.2	8.6	8.6	8.2	8.4
Outside MSA	12.0	11.1	11.7	11.4	12.5	9.0	11.6	10.3	9.8	10.6

*Estimates are considered unreliable.
—Data not available.
[a]Respondents were asked, "Do you have any trouble seeing, even when wearing glasses or contact lenses?" Respondents were also asked, "Are you blind or unable to see at all?" In this analysis, any trouble seeing and blind are combined into one category.
[b]Estimates are age-adjusted to the year 2000 standard population using five age groups: 18–44 years, 45–54 years, 55–64 years, 65–74 years, and 75 years and over. Age-adjusted estimates in this table may differ from other age-adjusted estimates based on the same data and presented elsewhere if different age groups are used in the adjustment procedure.
[c]Includes all other races not shown separately and unknown education level.
[d]The race groups, white, black, American Indian or Alaska Native, Asian, Native Hawaiian or other Pacific Islander, and 2 or more races, include persons of Hispanic and non-Hispanic origin. Persons of Hispanic origin may be of any race. Starting with 1999 data, race-specific estimates are tabulated according to the 1997 Revisions to the Standards for the Classification of Federal Data on Race and Ethnicity and are not strictly comparable with estimates for earlier years. The five single-race categories plus multiple-race categories shown in the table conform to the 1997 Standards. Starting with 1999 data, race-specific estimates are for persons who reported only one racial group; the category 2 or more races includes persons who reported more than one racial group. Prior to 1999, data were tabulated according to the 1977 Standards with four racial groups, and the Asian only category included Native Hawaiian or other Pacific Islander. Estimates for single-race categories prior to 1999 included persons who reported one race or, if they reported more than one race, identified one race as best representing their race. Starting with 2003 data, race responses of other race and unspecified multiple race were treated as missing, and then race was imputed if these were the only race responses. Almost all persons with a race response of other race were of Hispanic origin.
[e]Estimates are for persons aged 25 and over and are age-adjusted to the year 2000 standard population using five age groups: 25–44 years, 45–54 years, 55–64 years, 65–74 years, and 75 years and over.
[f]GED is General Educational Development high school equivalency diploma.
[g]Percent of poverty level is based on family income and family size and composition using U.S. Census Bureau poverty thresholds. Missing family income data were imputed for 1997 and beyond.
[h]MSA is metropolitan statistical area. Starting with 2006 data, MSA status is determined using 2000 census data and the 2000 standards for defining MSAs.

SOURCE: Adapted from "Table 48. Vision Limitations among Adults Aged 18 and over, by Selected Characteristics: United States, Selected Years 1997–2013," in *Health, United States, 2014: With Special Feature on Adults Aged 55–64*, National Center for Health Statistics, May 2015, http://www.cdc.gov/nchs/data/hus/hus14.pdf (accessed May 22, 2015)

vulnerable older adults receive their flu and pneumococcal vaccinations. People aged 65 years and older are among the most vulnerable, especially those in the close quarters of nursing homes, where infection can spread more easily.

DISABILITY IN THE OLDER POPULATION

Americans are not only living longer but also are developing fewer chronic diseases and disabilities. The current cohort (a group of individuals that shares a common characteristic such as birth years and is studied over time) of older Americans are defying the stereotype that aging is synonymous with increasing disability and dependence.

In "Trends in Disability and Related Chronic Conditions among the Forty-and-Over Population: 1997–2010 " (*Disability Health Journal*, vol. 7, no. 10, January 2014), Linda G. Martin and Robert F. Schoeni analyzed National Health Interview Survey data and find that from 1997 to 2010 the downward trend in activity limitations leveled off in adults aged 65 years and older, but during this period there were increases in activity limitations among people between the ages of 40 and 64. Figure 7.2 shows comparative activity limitations among adults aged 18 to 64 and those age 65 and older from 2003 to 2013. Table 7.10 shows that the percentage of adults ages 55 to 64 that was not employed due to disability increased from 11.5% in 2002–03 to 12.7% in 2012–13.

FIGURE 7.10

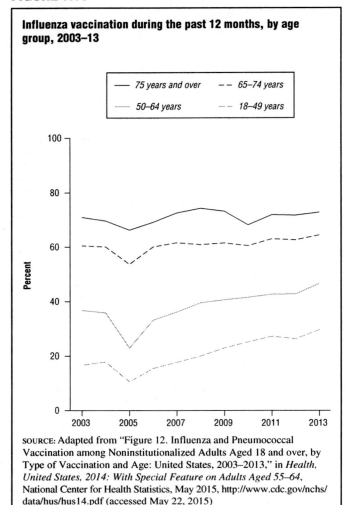

Influenza vaccination during the past 12 months, by age group, 2003–13

SOURCE: Adapted from "Figure 12. Influenza and Pneumococcal Vaccination among Noninstitutionalized Adults Aged 18 and over, by Type of Vaccination and Age: United States, 2003–2013," in *Health, United States, 2014: With Special Feature on Adults Aged 55–64*, National Center for Health Statistics, May 2015, http://www.cdc.gov/nchs/data/hus/hus14.pdf (accessed May 22, 2015)

FIGURE 7.11

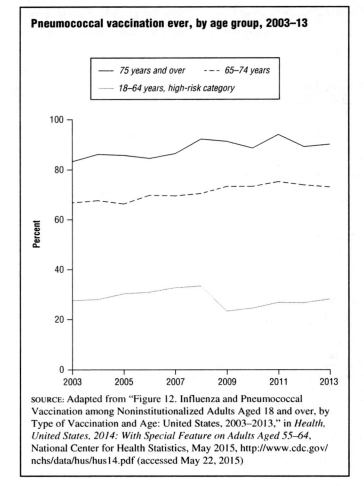

Pneumococcal vaccination ever, by age group, 2003–13

SOURCE: Adapted from "Figure 12. Influenza and Pneumococcal Vaccination among Noninstitutionalized Adults Aged 18 and over, by Type of Vaccination and Age: United States, 2003–2013," in *Health, United States, 2014: With Special Feature on Adults Aged 55–64*, National Center for Health Statistics, May 2015, http://www.cdc.gov/nchs/data/hus/hus14.pdf (accessed May 22, 2015)

Martin and Schoeni observe that adults between the ages of 40 and 64 not only report difficulty with physical functions but also the need for help performing the activities of daily living. They also note that declines in chronic disability observed at the end of the 20th century have not continued in the 21st century. In the first years of the 21st century there was a significant increase in difficulty with physical functions for the 65-and-older population. They attribute much of the need for assistance with activities of daily living to increased obesity.

Although the increase in limitations among adults ages 40 to 64 through 2010 is worrisome, whether these limitations will become disabilities when this cohort ages remains to be seen. Nevertheless, the news is not all bad. Unlike previous analyses, Martin and Schoeni find a significant decrease in hearing impairments in both cohorts and some improvement in vision for those aged 65 years and older.

DRUG USE AMONG OLDER ADULTS

According to the National Institute on Drug Abuse, in *Prescription Drug Abuse: Older Adults* (November 2014, http://www.drugabuse.gov/publications/research-reports/prescription-drugs/trends-in-prescription-drug-abuse/older-adults), although adults aged 65 years and older make up 13% of the population, they account for more than one-third of all medications that are prescribed in the United States.

Prescription drug use increased from 1988–94 to 2009–12. The percent of adults aged 65 years and older that took at least one prescription drug in the past 30 days rose from 73.6% in 1988–94 to 89.8% in 2009–12, and the percentage that took three or more prescription drugs grew from 35.3% to 64.8%. (See Table 7.11.)

Older Adults Respond Differently to Drugs

Many factors influence the efficacy (the ability of an intervention to produce the intended diagnostic or therapeutic effect in optimal circumstances), safety, and success of drug therapy with older patients. These factors include the effects of aging on pharmacokinetics (the absorption, distribution, metabolism, and excretion of drugs). Of the four, absorption is the least affected by

TABLE 7.10

Adults ages 55–64 not employed due to disability, 2002–03 and 2012–13

Characteristic	2002–2003 Percent distribution	2012–2013 Percent distribution
Sex		
Men	48.0	48.0
Women	52.0	52.0
Race/ethnicity[a]		
Hispanic	7.5	9.6
Not Hispanic:		
White only	78.9	73.6
Black only	9.5	10.9
Education[b]		
Less than high school diploma	16.1	11.7
High school diploma or GED	31.8	27.4
Some college	25.0	29.6
Bachelor's degree or higher	27.1	31.3
Percent of poverty level[c]		
Below 100%	9.3	10.0
100%–199%	13.7	14.7
200%–399%	27.9	28.1
400% or more	49.1	47.2
Employment status in past week[d]		
Employed	60.0	61.4
Not employed due to retirement	17.0	14.6
Not employed due to disability	11.5	12.7
Other	11.5	11.3
Marital status		
Married	71.7	67.6
Divorced or separated	14.6	16.5
Widowed	6.8	4.7
Never married	4.4	7.3
Cohabitating	2.5	3.9

[a]Does not sum to 100% because all racial and ethnic groups are not presented.
[b]GED is General Educational Development high school equivalency diploma.
[c]Percent of poverty level is based on family income and family size and composition, using U.S. Census Bureau poverty thresholds. Missing family income data were imputed.
[d]Employment status was assessed by asking respondents what they were doing last week. If they responded they had a job but were not working or not working and not looking for work, a followup question was asked that probed the main reason they were not working last week. Other includes adults who were looking for work, or those who were not working and not looking for work (excluding those who responded they were not looking for work because they were retired or disabled).

SOURCE: Adapted from "*Health, United States, 2014*: Profile of the 55–64 Age Group," in *Health, United States, 2014: With Special Feature on Adults Aged 55–64*, National Center for Health Statistics, May 2015, http://www.cdc.gov/nchs/data/hus/hus14.pdf (accessed May 22, 2015)

aging. In older people, absorption is generally complete, just slower. The distribution of most medications is related to body weight and composition changes that occur with aging, such as decreased lean muscle mass, increased fat mass, and decreased total body water.

Health professionals who care for older adults know that drug dosages must often be modified based on changing organ function and estimates of lean body mass. They coined the adage "start low and go slow" to guide prescribing drugs for older adults. For example, some initial doses of drugs should be lower because older adults have decreased total body water, which might increase the concentration of the drug. Fat-soluble drugs may also have to be administered in lower doses because they may accumulate in fatty tissues, resulting in longer durations of action. The mechanism used to clear a drug via metabolism in the liver or clearance (excretion) through the kidneys changes with aging and is affected by interactions with other medications. Pharmacodynamics (tissue sensitivity to drugs) also changes with advancing age. Among older adults, the complete elimination of a drug from body tissues, including the brain, can take weeks longer than it might in younger people.

Adherence, Drug-Drug Interactions, and Polypharmacy

Adherence (taking prescription medications regularly and correctly) is a challenge for older people who may suffer from memory loss, impaired vision, or arthritis. Abigail Flinders et al. note in "Prescribing for Older People" (*Nursing Older People*, vol. 21, no. 2, March 2009) that about half of older adults fail to take their medications at the right times and in the right amounts. Strategies to improve adherence include weekly pill boxes, calendars, and easy-to-open bottles with large-print labels.

Drug-drug interactions are more frequent among older adults because they are more likely than people of other ages to be taking multiple medications. Dangerous drug-drug interactions may occur when two or more drugs act together to either intensify or diminish one another's potency and effectiveness or when in combination they produce adverse side effects. For example, a person who takes heparin, a blood-thinning medication, should not take aspirin, which also acts to thin the blood. Similarly, antacids can interfere with the absorption of certain drugs that are used to treat Parkinson's disease, hypertension, and heart disease.

Polypharmacy is the use of many medications at the same time. It also refers to prescribing more medication than is needed or a medication regimen that includes at least one unnecessary medication. The major risk associated with polypharmacy is the potential for adverse drug reactions and interactions. Drug-induced adverse events may masquerade as other illnesses or precipitate confusion, falls, and incontinence, potentially prompting the physician to prescribe yet another drug. This "prescribing cascade" is easily prevented. It requires that physicians ensure that all medications prescribed are appropriate, safe, effective, and taken correctly.

In "Polypharmacy in Older Adults at Home: What It Is and What to Do about It—Implications for Home Healthcare and Hospice" (*Home Healthcare Nurse*, vol. 30, no. 8, September 2012), Gretchen I. Riker and Stephen M. Setter find that increasing prescription drug use increases the likelihood of polypharmacy. Because polypharmacy is potentially dangerous, Riker and Setter suggest that "periodic medication reviews and effective and constant communication between healthcare providers and patients can help to identify potentially inappropriate medications."

TABLE 7.11

Prescription drug use in past 30 days, by age group, selected years, 1988–94 to 2009–12

[Data are based on a sample of the civilian noninstitutionalized population]

	All persons[a]			Not Hispanic or Latino White only[b]			Not Hispanic or Latino Black or African American only[b]			Mexican origin[b, c]		
Sex and age	1988–1994	1999–2002	2009–2012	1988–1994	1999–2002	2009–2012	1988–1994	1999–2002	2009–2012	1988–1994	1999–2002	2009–2012
	Percent of population with at least one prescription drug in past 30 days											
Both sexes, age-adjusted[d]	39.1	45.2	47.3	41.1	48.7	52.4	36.9	40.1	43.7	31.7	31.7	34.0
Male	32.7	39.8	42.7	34.2	43.0	47.2	31.1	35.4	37.5	27.5	25.8	30.7
Female	45.0	50.3	51.8	47.6	54.3	57.6	41.4	43.8	48.8	36.0	37.8	37.6
Both sexes, crude	37.8	45.0	48.7	41.4	50.7	56.5	31.2	36.0	42.0	24.0	23.6	26.4
Male	30.6	38.6	43.4	33.5	43.8	50.7	25.5	30.7	35.1	20.1	18.8	23.5
Female	44.6	51.1	53.9	48.9	57.5	62.1	36.2	40.6	48.0	28.1	28.9	29.5
Under 18 years	20.5	23.8	23.5	22.9	27.0	26.7	14.8	18.5	22.8	16.1	15.8	16.1
18–44 years	31.3	35.9	38.1	34.3	41.3	46.7	27.8	28.5	30.7	21.1	19.1	21.2
45–64 years	54.8	64.1	67.2	55.5	66.1	70.9	57.5	62.3	64.6	48.1	49.3	49.0
65 years and over	73.6	84.7	89.8	74.0	85.4	90.3	74.5	81.1	90.3	67.7	72.0	83.9
Male:												
Under 18 years	20.4	25.7	23.1	22.3	29.9	24.8	15.5	19.6	23.6	16.3	16.2	16.6
18–44 years	21.5	27.1	29.6	23.5	31.2	37.3	21.1	21.5	20.2	14.9	13.0	17.1
45–64 years	47.2	55.6	63.1	48.1	57.4	67.3	48.2	54.0	55.6	43.8	36.4	43.0
65 years and over	67.2	80.1	87.7	67.4	81.0	88.7	64.4	78.1	88.0	61.3	66.8	80.0
Female:												
Under 18 years	20.6	21.7	23.8	23.6	24.0	28.7	14.2	17.3	21.9	16.0	15.4	15.6
18–44 years	40.7	44.6	46.4	44.7	51.7	56.3	33.4	34.2	39.3	28.1	26.2	25.9
45–64 years	62.0	72.0	71.1	62.6	74.7	74.2	64.4	69.0	72.2	52.2	62.4	55.5
65 years and over	78.3	88.1	91.4	78.8	88.8	91.7	81.3	83.1	91.8	73.0	76.3	87.5
	Percent of population with three or more prescription drugs in past 30 days											
Both sexes, age-adjusted[d]	11.8	17.8	20.6	12.4	18.9	22.0	12.6	16.5	21.9	9.0	11.2	15.4
Male	9.4	14.8	19.1	9.9	15.9	20.2	10.2	14.5	19.2	7.0	9.5	14.0
Female	13.9	20.4	22.0	14.6	21.8	23.8	14.3	18.1	24.0	11.0	12.8	16.8
Both sexes, crude	11.0	17.6	21.8	12.5	20.6	25.9	9.2	13.5	20.2	4.8	6.1	9.2
Male	8.3	13.9	19.4	9.5	16.5	23.1	7.0	10.9	16.9	3.4	4.8	8.3
Female	13.6	21.1	24.1	15.4	24.5	28.5	11.1	15.7	23.1	6.4	7.5	10.2
Under 18 years	2.4	4.1	3.6	3.2	4.9	3.3	1.5	2.5	5.2	1.2*	2.0	3.1
18–44 years	5.7	8.4	9.6	6.3	10.1	12.2	5.4	6.6	8.8	3.0	2.7	3.5
45–64 years	20.0	30.8	34.7	20.9	31.6	36.9	21.9	31.1	38.2	16.0	20.7	24.4
65 years and over	35.3	51.8	64.8	35.0	52.6	64.5	41.2	50.3	67.9	31.3	39.5	61.7
Male:												
Under 18 years	2.6	4.3	4.1	3.3	5.2	3.2	1.7	3.0	6.4	0.9*	1.9	3.7*
18–44 years	3.6	6.7	7.5	4.1	8.4	9.4	4.2	4.4	6.6	1.8*	1.7*	3.1*
45–64 years	15.1	23.6	31.4	15.8	24.0	34.0	18.7	26.3	31.1	11.6	18.2	20.7
65 years and over	31.3	46.3	64.6	30.9	47.2	64.5	31.7	48.7	64.0	27.6	34.2	57.3
Female:												
Under 18 years	2.3	3.9	3.1	3.0	4.7	3.4	1.2*	2.0*	3.9	1.5*	2.2	2.4*
18–44 years	7.6	10.2	11.8	8.5	11.9	15.1	6.4	8.5	10.7	4.3	4.0	4.1*
45–64 years	24.7	37.5	37.8	25.8	39.1	39.6	24.3	35.0	44.3	20.3	23.3	28.3
65 years and over	38.2	55.9	64.9	38.0	56.7	64.5	47.7	51.3	70.5	34.5	44.0	65.7

*Estimates are considered unreliable.
[a]Includes persons of all races and Hispanic origins, not just those shown separately.
[b]Starting with 1999 data, race-specific estimates are tabulated according to the 1997 Revisions to the Standards for the Classification of Federal Data on Race and Ethnicity and are not strictly comparable with estimates for earlier years. The two non-Hispanic race categories shown in the table conform to the 1997 Standards. Starting with 1999 data, race-specific estimates are for persons who reported only one racial group. Prior to data year 1999, estimates were tabulated according to the 1977 Standards. Estimates for single-race categories prior to 1999 included persons who reported one race or, if they reported more than one race, identified one race as best representing their race.
[c]Persons of Mexican origin may be of any race.
[d]Estimates are age-adjusted to the year 2000 standard population using four age groups: Under 18 years, 18–44 years, 45–64 years, and 65 years and over. Age-adjusted estimates in this table may differ from other age-adjusted estimates based on the same data and presented elsewhere if different age groups are used in the adjustment procedure.

SOURCE: "Table 85. Prescription Drug Use in the Past 30 Days, by Sex, Age, Race and Hispanic Origin: United States, Selected Years 1988–1994 through 2009–2012," in *Health, United States, 2014: With Special Feature on Adults Aged 55–64*, National Center for Health Statistics, May 2015, http://www.cdc.gov/nchs/data/hus/hus14.pdf (accessed May 22, 2015)

LEADING CAUSES OF DEATH

The number of deaths among people aged 65 years and older attributable to heart disease and cerebrovascular diseases decreased from 1980 to 2013, whereas deaths attributable to malignant neoplasms increased. (See Table 7.5.) The two leading causes of death among adults aged 55 to 64 years (heart disease and malignant neoplasms) decreased between 2003 and 2013. (See Figure 7.4.)

Heart Disease

Although deaths from heart disease have declined, it still kills more Americans than any other single disease.

According to the American Heart Association, in "Older Americans and Cardiovascular Diseases" (2015, http://www.heart.org/idc/groups/heart-public/@wcm/@sop/@smd/documents/downloadable/ucm_472923.pdf), 80% of people who die of heart disease are aged 65 years and older. Among adults aged 60 to 79 years, 19.9% of men and 9.7% of women have heart disease. Among those aged 80 years and older the percentages increase to 32.2% of men and 17.3% of women. The average age of a first heart attack is 65 for men and 71.8 for women. Because women are generally older when they suffer heart attacks, they are more likely to die within weeks of the attack.

Table 7.5 shows the decrease in the numbers of deaths from heart disease and cerebrovascular diseases between 1980 and 2013. Several factors account for the decreasing numbers of deaths from heart disease, including better control of hypertension and cholesterol levels and changes in exercise and diet. The increasing ranks of trained paramedics and the widespread use of cardiopulmonary resuscitation and immediate treatment have also increased the likelihood of surviving an initial heart attack.

The growing use of statin drugs (drugs that reduce blood cholesterol levels) to reduce the risk of heart disease as well as procedures such as cardiac catheterization, coronary bypass surgery, pacemakers, angioplasty (a procedure to open narrowed or blocked blood vessels of the heart), and stenting (using wire scaffolds that hold arteries open) have improved the quality, and in some instances extended the lives, of people with heart disease.

Nonetheless, the Mayo Clinic explains in "Statins: Are These Cholesterol-Lowering Drugs Right for You?" (April 8, 2015, http://www.mayoclinic.com/health/statins/CL00010) that statin use may produce side effects such as joint and muscle pain, nausea, diarrhea, and constipation. Although these common side effects often subside with continued use of the drugs, less frequent but serious side effects such as liver and kidney damage, severe muscle pain, and elevated blood sugar may occur with statin treatment.

Cancer

Cancer is the second-leading cause of death among older adults. (See Table 7.5.) The American Cancer Society indicates in *Cancer Facts and Figures, 2015* that about 78% of all cancers are diagnosed after age 55. The likelihood of dying of cancer increases every decade after the age of 30. In 2013, among adults aged 65 to 74 years, there were 616.9 cancer deaths per 100,000 people; for adults aged 75 to 84 years, this rate was 1,139.4 deaths per 100,000 people; and for adults aged 85 years and older, it was 1,635.4 deaths per 100,000 people. (See Table 7.12.)

Cancer risk increases with advancing age because some age-related changes such as diminished immunity, decreased ability of the hormone insulin to regulate blood sugar, and chronic inflammation may spur the growth of cancer. Older adults may also be more susceptible to cancer-causing agents in the environment such as second-hand smoke and chemical pollutants (e.g., asbestos and radiation).

Success in treating certain cancers, such as Hodgkin's disease and some forms of leukemia, has been offset by the rise in rates of other cancers, such as breast and lung cancers. Table 7.5 shows that the number of cancer deaths among adults aged 65 years and older rose sharply from 258,389 in 1980 to 407,558 in 2013. Progress in treating cancer has largely been related to screenings, early diagnoses, and new drug therapies.

Stroke

Stroke (cerebrovascular disease or "brain attack") is the fourth-leading cause of death and is the principal cause of disability among older adults. (See Table 7.5.) In "Older Americans and Cardiovascular Diseases," the American Heart Association reports that among adults aged 60 to 79 years the risk of stroke is 6.1% for men and 5.2% for women. Among those aged 80 years and older, the risk rises to 15.8% for men and 14% for women.

According to the NCHS, in *Health, United States, 2014*, strokes killed 146,417 people aged 65 years and older in 1980. In 2013, among people aged 65 years and older, 109,602 deaths were attributable to stroke. (See Table 7.5.) The death rate for people aged 65 to 74 years declined as well, from 128.6 per 100,000 population in 2000 to 74.2 per 100,000 population in 2013. There was a comparable decline for people aged 75 to 84 years. There were 268.9 deaths from stroke per 100,000 population for this age group in 2013, down from 461.3 deaths per 100,000 population in 2000. The improvement was even greater for people aged 85 years and older. There were 906 deaths from stroke per 100,000 population for this age group in 2013, less than half the rate of 2,283.7 per 100,000 population in 1980. (See Table 7.13.)

In "Stroke Recovery: Regaining Arm Use" (April 2, 2015, http://www.webmd.com/stroke/regaining-arm-use-after-stroke-10/slideshow-stroke), WebMD observes that about 80% of stroke victims suffer some weakness or paralysis on the opposite side of the body from where the stroke occurred in the brain. Although stroke rehabilitation improves the chances of recovery, some stroke survivors must learn to live with disability.

HEALTHY AGING

According to the CDC, ample research demonstrates that healthy lifestyles have a greater effect than genetic

TABLE 7.12

Death rates for malignant neoplasms, selected characteristics, selected years 1950–2013

[Data are based on death certificates]

Sex, race, Hispanic origin, and age	1950[a]	1960[a]	1970	1980	1990	2000	2012	2013
All persons				Deaths per 100,000 resident population				
All ages, age-adjusted[b]	193.9	193.9	198.6	207.9	216.0	199.6	166.5	163.2
All ages, crude	139.8	149.2	162.8	183.9	203.2	196.5	185.6	185.0
Under 1 year	8.7	7.2	4.7	3.2	2.3	2.4	1.6	1.6
1–4 years	11.7	10.9	7.5	4.5	3.5	2.7	2.4	2.1
5–14 years	6.7	6.8	6.0	4.3	3.1	2.5	2.2	2.2
15–24 years	8.6	8.3	8.3	6.3	4.9	4.4	3.6	3.4
25–34 years	20.0	19.5	16.5	13.7	12.6	9.8	8.7	8.6
35–44 years	62.7	59.7	59.5	48.6	43.3	36.6	28.0	28.1
45–54 years	175.1	177.0	182.5	180.0	158.9	127.5	108.5	105.5
55–64 years	390.7	396.8	423.0	436.1	449.6	366.7	293.2	288.2
65–74 years	698.8	713.9	754.2	817.9	872.3	816.3	632.2	616.9
75–84 years	1,153.3	1,127.4	1,169.2	1,232.3	1,348.5	1,335.6	1,161.7	1,139.4
85 years and over	1,451.0	1,450.0	1,320.7	1,594.6	1,752.9	1,819.4	1,658.9	1,635.4
Male								
All ages, age-adjusted[b]	208.1	225.1	247.6	271.2	280.4	248.9	200.3	196.0
All ages, crude	142.9	162.5	182.1	205.3	221.3	207.2	197.9	197.6
Under 1 year	9.7	7.7	4.4	3.7	2.4	2.6	1.7	1.5
1–4 years	12.5	12.4	8.3	5.2	3.7	3.0	2.7	2.2
5–14 years	7.4	7.6	6.7	4.9	3.5	2.7	2.4	2.2
15–24 years	9.7	10.2	10.4	7.8	5.7	5.1	4.1	3.8
25–34 years	17.7	18.8	16.3	13.4	12.6	9.2	8.4	8.6
35–44 years	45.6	48.9	53.0	44.0	38.5	32.7	24.0	24.0
45–54 years	156.2	170.8	183.5	188.7	162.5	130.9	110.1	106.5
55–64 years	413.1	459.9	511.8	520.8	532.9	415.8	336.9	331.3
65–74 years	791.5	890.5	1,006.8	1,093.2	1,122.2	1,001.9	746.7	726.2
75–84 years	1,332.6	1,389.4	1,588.3	1,790.5	1,914.4	1,760.6	1,447.6	1,414.5
85 years and over	1,668.3	1,741.2	1,720.8	2,369.5	2,739.9	2,710.7	2,303.1	2,272.6
Female								
All ages, age-adjusted[b]	182.3	168.7	163.2	166.7	175.7	167.6	142.1	139.5
All ages, crude	136.8	136.4	144.4	163.6	186.0	186.2	173.7	172.8
Under 1 year	7.6	6.8	5.0	2.7	2.2	2.3	1.5	1.8
1–4 years	10.8	9.3	6.7	3.7	3.2	2.5	2.2	1.9
5–14 years	6.0	6.0	5.2	3.6	2.8	2.2	2.0	2.1
15–24 years	7.6	6.5	6.2	4.8	4.1	3.6	3.0	3.0
25–34 years	22.2	20.1	16.7	14.0	12.6	10.4	8.9	8.6
35–44 years	79.3	70.0	65.6	53.1	48.1	40.4	31.9	32.1
45–54 years	194.0	183.0	181.5	171.8	155.5	124.2	107.0	104.6
55–64 years	368.2	337.7	343.2	361.7	375.2	321.3	252.5	248.1
65–74 years	612.3	560.2	557.9	607.1	677.4	663.6	531.9	520.8
75–84 years	1,000.7	924.1	891.9	903.1	1,010.3	1,058.5	950.0	933.3
85 years and over	1,299.7	1,263.9	1,096.7	1,255.7	1,372.1	1,456.4	1,336.4	1,310.1

[a]Includes deaths of persons who were not residents of the 50 states and the District of Columbia (D.C.).

[b]Age-adjusted rates are calculated using the year 2000 standard population. Prior to 2001, age-adjusted rates were calculated using standard million proportions based on rounded population numbers. Starting with 2001 data, unrounded population numbers are used to calculate age-adjusted rates.

Notes: Starting with *Health, United States, 2003*, rates for 1991–1999 were revised using intercensal population estimates based on the 1990 and 2000 censuses. For 2000, population estimates are bridged-race April 1 census counts. Starting with *Health, United States, 2012*, rates for 2001–2009 were revised using intercensal population estimates based on the 2000 and 2010 censuses. For 2010, population estimates are bridged-race April 1 census counts. Rates for 2011 and beyond were computed using 2010-based postcensal estimates. Age groups were selected to minimize the presentation of unstable age-specific death rates based on small numbers of deaths and for consistency among comparison groups. Starting with 2003 data, some states allowed the reporting of more than one race on the death certificate. The multiple-race data for these states were bridged to the single-race categories of the 1977 Office of Management and Budget standards, for comparability with other states.

SOURCE: Adapted from "Table 26. Death Rates for Malignant Neoplasms, by Sex, Race, Hispanic Origin, and Age: United States, Selected Years 1950–2013," in *Health, United States, 2014: With Special Feature on Adults Aged 55–64*, National Center for Health Statistics, May 2015, http://www.cdc.gov/nchs/data/hus/hus14.pdf (accessed May 22, 2015)

factors in helping to prevent the deterioration that is traditionally associated with aging. People who are physically active, eat a healthy diet, and do not smoke reduce their risk for chronic diseases, have half the rate of disability of those who do not, and can delay disability by as many as 10 years.

Among the recommended health practices for older adults is participating in early detection practices such as screenings for hypertension, cancer, diabetes, and depression. Screening detects diseases early in their course, when they are most treatable; however, many older adults do not obtain the recommended screenings.

Because falls are the most common cause of injuries in older adults, injury prevention is a vitally important way to prevent disability. The CDC reports in "Older Adult Falls: Get the Facts" (July 1, 2015, http://www.cdc.gov/HomeandRecreationalSafety/Falls/adultfalls.html) that

TABLE 7.13

Death rates for cerebrovascular disease, by age group, selected years 1950–2013

[Data are based on death certificates]

Sex, race, Hispanic origin, and age	1950[a]	1960[a]	1970	1980	1990	2000	2012	2013
All persons				Deaths per 100,000 resident population				
All ages, age-adjusted[b]	180.7	177.9	147.7	96.2	65.3	60.9	36.9	36.2
All ages, crude	104.0	108.0	101.9	75.0	57.8	59.6	40.9	40.8
Under 1 year	5.1	4.1	5.0	4.4	3.8	3.3	2.6	2.7
1–4 years	0.9	0.8	1.0	0.5	0.3	0.3	0.3	0.2
5–14 years	0.5	0.7	0.7	0.3	0.2	0.2	0.2	0.2
15–24 years	1.6	1.8	1.6	1.0	0.6	0.5	0.4	0.3
25–34 years	4.2	4.7	4.5	2.6	2.2	1.5	1.3	1.2
35–44 years	18.7	14.7	15.6	8.5	6.4	5.8	4.3	4.2
45–54 years	70.4	49.2	41.6	25.2	18.7	16.0	12.8	12.4
55–64 years	194.2	147.3	115.8	65.1	47.9	41.0	28.7	28.9
65–74 years	554.7	469.2	384.1	219.0	144.2	128.6	75.7	74.2
75–84 years	1,499.6	1,491.3	1,254.2	786.9	498.0	461.3	272.2	268.9
85 years and over	2,990.1	3,680.5	3,014.3	2,283.7	1,628.9	1,589.2	931.2	906.0
Male								
All ages, age-adjusted[b]	186.4	186.1	157.4	102.2	68.5	62.4	37.1	36.7
All ages, crude	102.5	104.5	94.5	63.4	46.7	46.9	34.1	34.5
Under 1 year	6.4	5.0	5.8	5.0	4.4	3.8	2.6	3.0
1–4 years	1.1	0.9	1.2	0.4	0.3	*	0.4	0.3
5–14 years	0.5	0.7	0.8	0.3	0.2	0.2	0.2	0.2
15–24 years	1.8	1.9	1.8	1.1	0.7	0.5	0.5	0.4
25–34 years	4.2	4.5	4.4	2.6	2.1	1.5	1.4	1.3
35–44 years	17.5	14.6	15.7	8.7	6.8	5.8	4.8	4.7
45–54 years	67.9	52.2	44.4	27.2	20.5	17.5	14.2	14.2
55–64 years	205.2	163.8	138.7	74.6	54.3	47.2	34.5	35.1
65–74 years	589.6	530.7	449.5	258.6	166.6	145.0	85.7	85.0
75–84 years	1,543.6	1,555.9	1,361.6	866.3	551.1	490.8	277.7	277.9
85 years and over	3,048.6	3,643.1	2,895.2	2,193.6	1,528.5	1,484.3	832.1	808.4
Female								
All ages, age-adjusted[b]	175.8	170.7	140.0	91.7	62.6	59.1	36.1	35.2
All ages, crude	105.6	111.4	109.0	85.9	68.4	71.8	47.6	46.9
Under 1 year	3.7	3.2	4.0	3.8	3.1	2.7	2.6	2.5
1–4 years	0.7	0.7	0.7	0.5	0.3	0.4	0.3	*
5–14 years	0.4	0.6	0.6	0.3	0.2	0.2	0.2	0.2
15–24 years	1.5	1.6	1.4	0.8	0.6	0.5	0.3	0.3
25–34 years	4.3	4.9	4.7	2.6	2.2	1.5	1.1	1.1
35–44 years	19.9	14.8	15.6	8.4	6.1	5.7	3.8	3.7
45–54 years	72.9	46.3	39.0	23.3	17.0	14.5	11.4	10.6
55–64 years	183.1	131.8	95.3	56.8	42.2	35.3	23.3	23.1
65–74 years	522.1	415.7	333.3	188.7	126.7	115.1	67.0	64.8
75–84 years	1,462.2	1,441.1	1,183.1	740.1	466.2	442.1	268.2	262.1
85 years and over	2,949.4	3,704.4	3,081.0	2,323.1	1,667.6	1,632.0	980.9	955.8

*Rates based on fewer than 20 deaths are considered unreliable and are not shown.

[a]Includes deaths of persons who were not residents of the 50 states and the District of Columbia (D.C.).

[b]Age-adjusted rates are calculated using the year 2000 standard population. Prior to 2001, age-adjusted rates were calculated using standard million proportions based on rounded population numbers. Starting with 2001 data, unrounded population numbers are used to calculate age-adjusted rates.

Notes: Starting with *Health, United States, 2003*, rates for 1991–1999 were revised using intercensal population estimates based on the 1990 and 2000 censuses. For 2000, population estimates are bridged-race April 1 census counts. Starting with *Health, United States, 2012*, rates for 2001–2009 were revised using intercensal population estimates based on the 2000 and 2010 censuses. For 2010, population estimates are bridged-race April 1 census counts. Rates for 2011 and beyond were computed using 2010-based postcensal estimates. Age groups were selected to minimize the presentation of unstable age-specific death rates based on small numbers of deaths and for consistency among comparison groups. Starting with 2003 data, some states allowed the reporting of more than one race on the death certificate. The multiple-race data for these states were bridged to the single-race categories of the 1977 Office of Management and Budget standards, for comparability with other states.

SOURCE: Adapted from "Table 25. Death Rates for Cerebrovascular Diseases, by Sex, Race, Hispanic Origin, and Age: United States, Selected Years 1950–2013," in *Health, United States, 2014: With Special Feature on Adults Aged 55–64*, National Center for Health Statistics, May 2015, http://www.cdc.gov/nchs/data/hus/hus14.pdf (accessed May 22, 2015)

over one-third of adults aged 65 years and older fall each year, and of those who fall, 20% to 30% suffer injuries that impair mobility and independence. Removing tripping hazards in the home, such as rugs, and installing grab bars in bathrooms are simple measures that can greatly reduce older Americans' risk for falls and fractures.

The current cohort of older adults is better equipped to prevent the illness, disability, and death associated with many chronic diseases than any previous generation. They are less likely to smoke, drink, or experience detrimental stress than younger people, and older adults have better eating habits than their younger counterparts. For example, the percentage of men aged 65 years and older who smoke cigarettes declined from 28.5% in 1965 to 10.6% in 2013. (See Table 7.14.) In contrast, the percentage of women the same age who smoke remained relatively constant during this period, decreasing slightly from 9.6% to 7.5%.

Maintaining a Healthy Weight

The United States is in the throes of an obesity epidemic. Obesity is defined as a body mass index (a number that shows body weight adjusted for height) greater than or equal to 30 kilograms per meters squared. In 2014, 29.2% of adults aged 60 years and older were obese, and the group of adults aged 40 to 59 years that will soon join the ranks of older Americans reported the highest rate of obesity, at 32.8%. (See Figure 7.12.)

Obesity increases the risk for multiple health problems, including hypertension, high cholesterol, type 2 diabetes, coronary heart disease, congestive heart failure, stroke, arthritis, obstructive sleep apnea, and other serious conditions.

Smoking

Data from the 2014 National Health Interview Survey reveal that adults aged 65 years and older were the

TABLE 7.14

Current cigarette smoking by age and sex, selected years 1965–2013

[Data are based on household interviews of a sample of the civilian noninstitutionalized population]

Sex, race, and age	1965[a]	1974[a]	1979[a]	1985[a]	1990[a]	2000	2005	2010	2011	2012	2013
18 years and over, age-adjusted[b]					Percent of adults who were current cigarette smokers[c]						
All persons	41.9	37.0	33.3	29.9	25.3	23.1	20.8	19.3	19.0	18.2	17.9
Male	51.2	42.8	37.0	32.2	28.0	25.2	23.4	21.2	21.2	20.6	20.5
Female	33.7	32.2	30.1	27.9	22.9	21.1	18.3	17.5	16.8	15.9	15.5
White male[d]	50.4	41.7	36.4	31.3	27.6	25.4	23.3	21.4	21.4	20.7	20.5
Black or African American male[d]	58.8	53.6	43.9	40.2	32.8	25.7	25.9	23.3	23.2	22.0	21.8
White female[d]	33.9	32.0	30.3	27.9	23.5	22.0	19.1	18.3	17.7	16.9	16.3
Black or African American female[d]	31.8	35.6	30.5	30.9	20.8	20.7	17.1	16.6	15.2	14.2	14.9
18 years and over, crude											
All persons	42.4	37.1	33.5	30.1	25.5	23.2	20.9	19.3	19.0	18.1	17.8
Male	51.9	43.1	37.5	32.6	28.4	25.6	23.9	21.5	21.6	20.5	20.5
Female	33.9	32.1	29.9	27.9	22.8	20.9	18.1	17.3	16.5	15.8	15.3
White male[d]	51.1	41.9	36.8	31.7	28.0	25.7	23.6	21.4	21.6	20.3	20.3
Black or African American male[d]	60.4	54.3	44.1	39.9	32.5	26.2	26.5	24.3	23.8	22.0	21.9
White female[d]	34.0	31.7	30.1	27.7	23.4	21.4	18.7	17.9	17.2	16.6	15.9
Black or African American female[d]	33.7	36.4	31.1	31.0	21.2	20.8	17.3	17.0	15.3	14.7	15.1
All males											
18–44 years	57.9	47.9	40.4	35.2	31.4	29.2	27.1	23.9	23.6	24.0	22.9
18–24 years	54.1	42.1	35.0	28.0	26.6	28.1	28.0	22.8	21.3	20.1	21.9
25–34 years	60.7	50.5	43.9	38.2	31.6	28.9	27.7	26.1	27.5	28.0	24.4
35–44 years	58.2	51.0	41.8	37.6	34.5	30.2	26.0	22.5	21.2	22.8	22.1
45–64 years	51.9	42.6	39.3	33.4	29.3	26.4	25.2	23.2	24.4	20.2	21.9
45–54 years	55.9	46.8	42.0	34.9	32.1	28.8	28.1	25.2	27.0	21.4	21.4
55–64 years	46.6	37.7	36.4	31.9	25.9	22.6	21.1	20.7	21.4	18.8	22.6
65 years and over	28.5	24.8	20.9	19.6	14.6	10.2	8.9	9.7	8.9	10.6	10.6
All females											
18–44 years	42.1	37.5	34.7	31.4	25.6	24.5	21.2	19.1	18.8	16.9	16.6
18–24 years	38.1	34.1	33.8	30.4	22.5	24.9	20.7	17.4	16.4	14.5	15.4
25–34 years	43.7	38.8	33.7	32.0	28.2	22.3	21.5	20.6	19.5	19.4	17.9
35–44 years	43.7	39.8	37.0	31.5	24.8	26.2	21.3	19.0	19.9	16.1	16.3
45–64 years	32.0	33.4	30.7	29.9	24.8	21.7	18.8	19.1	18.5	18.9	18.1
45–54 years	37.5	36.0	32.6	32.4	28.5	22.2	20.9	21.3	21.6	21.3	20.6
55–64 years	25.0	30.4	28.6	27.4	20.5	20.9	16.1	16.5	15.0	16.2	15.2
65 years and over	9.6	12.0	13.2	13.5	11.5	9.3	8.3	9.3	7.1	7.5	7.5

*Estimates are considered unreliable.

[a]Data prior to 1997 are not strictly comparable with data for later years due to the 1997 questionnaire redesign.
[b]Estimates are age-adjusted to the year 2000 standard population using five age groups: 18–24 years, 25–34 years, 35–44 years, 45–64 years, and 65 years and over. Age-adjusted estimates in this table may differ from other age-adjusted estimates based on the same data and presented elsewhere if different age groups are used in the adjustment procedure.
[c]Starting with 1993 data (shown in spreadsheet version), current cigarette smokers were defined as ever smoking 100 cigarettes in their lifetime and smoking now every day or some days.
[d]The race groups, white and black, include persons of Hispanic and non-Hispanic origin. Starting with 1999 data, race-specific estimates are tabulated according to the 1997 Revisions to the Standards for the Classification of Federal Data on Race and Ethnicity and are not strictly comparable with estimates for earlier years. The single-race categories shown in the table conform to the 1997 Standards. Starting with 1999 data, race-specific estimates are for persons who reported only one racial group. Prior to 1999, data were tabulated according to the 1977 Standards. Estimates for single-race categories prior to 1999 included persons who reported one race or, if they reported more than one race, identified one race as best representing their race. Starting with 2003 data, race responses of other race and unspecified multiple race were treated as missing, and then race was imputed if these were the only race responses. Almost all persons with a race response of other race were of Hispanic origin.

SOURCE: Adapted from "Table 52. Current Cigarette Smoking among Adults Aged 18 and over, by Sex, Race, and Age: United States, Selected Years 1965–2013," in *Health, United States, 2014: With Special Feature on Adults Aged 55–64*, National Center for Health Statistics, May 2015, http://www.cdc.gov/nchs/data/hus/hus14.pdf (accessed May 22, 2015)

FIGURE 7.12

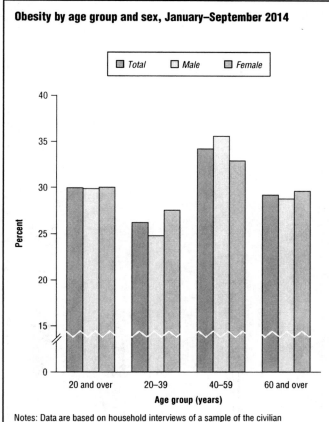

Obesity by age group and sex, January–September 2014

Notes: Data are based on household interviews of a sample of the civilian noninstitutionalized population. Obesity is defined as a body mass index (BMI) of 30 kg/m² or more. The measure is based on self-reported height (m) and weight (kg). Estimates of obesity are restricted to adults aged 20 and over for consistency with the Healthy People 2020 (3) initiative. The analyses excluded the 4.0% of persons with unknown height or weight.

SOURCE: "Figure 6.2. Prevalence of Obesity among Adults Aged 20 and over, by Age Group and Sex: United States, January–September 2014," in *Early Release of Selected Estimates Based on Data from the National Health Interview Survey, January–September 2014*, Centers for Disease Control and Prevention, National Center for Health Statistics, March 2015, http://www.cdc.gov/nchs/data/nhis/earlyrelease/earlyrelease201503_06.pdf (accessed June 1, 2015)

FIGURE 7.13

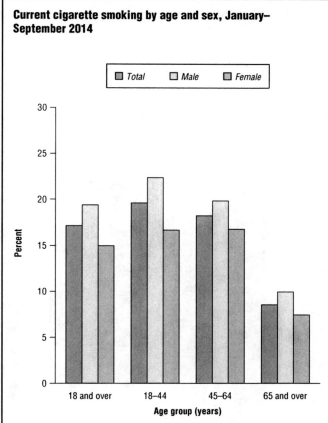

Current cigarette smoking by age and sex, January–September 2014

Notes: Data are based on household interviews of a sample of the civilian noninstitutionalized population. Current cigarette smokers were defined as those who had smoked more than 100 cigarettes in their lifetime and now smoke every day or some days. The analyses excluded the 0.5% of persons with unknown cigarette smoking status.

SOURCE: "Figure 8.3. Prevalence of Current Cigarette Smoking among Adults Aged 18 and over, by Age Group and Sex: United States, January–September 2014," in *Early Release of Selected Estimates Based on Data from the National Health Interview Survey, January–September 2014*, Centers for Disease Control and Prevention, National Center for Health Statistics, March 2015, http://www.cdc.gov/nchs/data/nhis/earlyrelease/earlyrelease201503_08.pdf (accessed June 1, 2015)

least likely to be current smokers—just 8.5%, compared with 19.7% of adults aged 18 to 44 years and 18.3% of those aged 45 to 64 years. (See Figure 7.13.)

The U.S. surgeon general explains that even older adult smokers realize health benefits from quitting. For example, a smoker's risk of heart disease begins to decline almost immediately after quitting, regardless of how long the person smoked.

Physical Activity

Regular physical activity comes closer to being a fountain of youth than any prescription medicine. Along with helping older adults to remain mobile and independent, exercise can lower the risk of obesity, heart disease, stroke, diabetes, and some cancers. It can also delay osteoporosis and arthritis, reduce symptoms of depression, and

improve sleep quality and memory. Despite these benefits, older adults are less likely to exercise than younger adults. In 2014 about one-quarter (27.9%) of adults aged 75 years and older met the 2008 federal physical activity guidelines for aerobic activity (150 minutes a week of moderate-intensity aerobic physical activity, or 75 minutes a week of vigorous-intensity aerobic physical activity, or an equivalent combination of moderate- and vigorous-intensity aerobic activity) through leisure-time activity. (See Figure 7.14.) Increasing evidence suggests that behavior change, even late in life, is beneficial and can improve disease control and enhance quality of life.

Use of Preventive Health Services

More widespread use of preventive services is a key to preserving and extending the health and quality of life

FIGURE 7.14

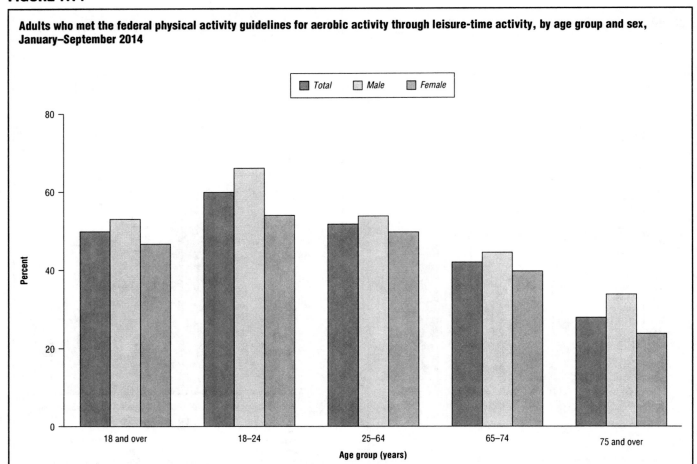

Adults who met the federal physical activity guidelines for aerobic activity through leisure-time activity, by age group and sex, January–September 2014

Notes: Data are based on household interviews of a sample of the civilian noninstitutionalized population. Estimates in this figure are limited to leisure-time physical activity only. This measure reflects an estimate of leisure-time aerobic activity motivated by the 2008 federal Physical Activity Guidelines for Americans, which are being used for Healthy People 2020 Objectives (3). The 2008 guidelines refer to any kind of aerobic activity, not just leisure-time aerobic activity, so the leisure-time aerobic activity estimates in this figure may underestimate the percentage of adults who met the 2008 guidelines for aerobic activity. This figure presents the percentage of adults who met the 2008 federal guidelines for aerobic activity. The 2008 federal guidelines recommend that for substantial health benefits, adults perform at least 150 minutes a week of moderate-intensity aerobic physical activity, or 75 minutes a week of vigorous-intensity aerobic physical activity, or an equivalent combination of moderate- and vigorous-intensity aerobic activity. The 2008 guidelines state that aerobic activity should be performed in episodes of at least 10 minutes and preferably should be spread throughout the week. The analyses excluded the 1.9% of persons with unknown physical activity participation.

SOURCE: "Figure 7.2. Percentage of Adults Aged 18 and over Who Met the 2008 Federal Physical Activity Guidelines for Aerobic Activity through Leisure-Time Aerobic Activity, by Age Group and Sex: United States, January–September 2014," in *Early Release of Selected Estimates Based on Data from the National Health Interview Survey, January–September 2014*, Centers for Disease Control and Prevention, National Center for Health Statistics, March 2015, http://www.cdc.gov/nchs/data/nhis/earlyrelease/earlyrelease201503_07.pdf (accessed June 1, 2015)

of older Americans. Screening for early detection of selected cancers (such as breast, cervical, and colorectal) as well as diabetes, cardiovascular disease, and glaucoma can save lives and slow the progress of chronic disease. People with a regular source of medical care are more likely to receive basic medical services, such as routine checkups, which present the opportunity to receive preventive services, and in 2014, 96.8% of adults aged 65 years and older reported having a regular source of medical care. (See Figure 7.15.) Given that Medicare covers a comprehensive range of preventive services and screenings, such as screening for heart disease, cancer, diabetes, glaucoma, and depression, it seems unlikely that cost prevents older adults from obtaining these services. Data from the 2014 National Health Interview Survey reveal that just 2.6% of respondents aged 65 years and older

reported that they failed to obtain needed medical care because of cost during the 12 months preceding the interview. (See Figure 7.16.)

SEXUALITY IN AGING

Despite the popular belief that sexuality is exclusively for the young, sexual interest, activity, and capabilities are often lifelong. Although the growing population of older adults will likely spur additional research, to date there are scant data about the levels of sexual activity among older adults. The data that are available are often limited to community-dwelling older adults, so there is nearly no information about the sexual behavior of institutionalized older adults.

FIGURE 7.15

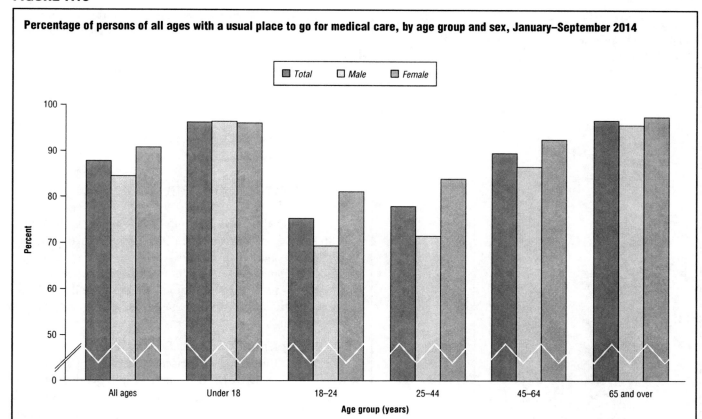

Percentage of persons of all ages with a usual place to go for medical care, by age group and sex, January–September 2014

Notes: Data are based on household interviews of a sample of the civilian noninstitutionalized population. The usual place to go for medical care does not include a hospital emergency room. The analyses excluded the 0.8% of persons with an unknown usual place to go for medical care.

SOURCE: "Figure 2.2. Percentage of Persons of All Ages with a Usual Place to Go for Medical Care, by Age Group and Sex: United States, January–September 2014," in *Early Release of Selected Estimates Based on Data from the National Health Interview Survey, January–September 2014*, Centers for Disease Control and Prevention, National Center for Health Statistics, March 2015, http://www.cdc.gov/ nchs/data/nhis/earlyrelease/ earlyrelease201503_02.pdf (accessed June 1, 2015)

After age 50 sexual responses slow; however, very rarely does this natural and gradual diminution cause older adults to end all sexual activity. More important, in terms of curtailing older adults' sexual activity is the lack of available partners, which limits opportunities for sexual expression, especially for older women. Another issue is the greater incidence of illness and progression of chronic diseases that occurs with advancing age. Medical problems with the potential to adversely affect sexual function include diabetes, hypothyroidism (a condition in which the thyroid is underactive—producing too little thyroid hormones), neuropathy (a disease or abnormality of the nervous system), cardiovascular disease, urinary tract infections, prostate cancer, incontinence, arthritis, depression, and dementia. Many pharmacological treatments for chronic illnesses have sexual side effects that range from diminished libido (sexual desire and drive) to erectile dysfunction. For example, some medications (e.g., antihypertensives, antidepressants, diuretics, steroids, anticonvulsants, and beta blockers) have high rates of sexual side effects.

Despite these changes, research reveals long-married couples still have active sex lives. In fact, couples married for 50 years actually experience a slight increase in their sex lives. In "Marital Characteristics and the Sexual Relationships of U.S. Older Adults: An Analysis of National Social Life, Health, and Aging Project Data" (*Archives of Sexual Behavior*, vol. 44, no. 1, January 2015), Samuel Stroope, Michael J. McFarland, and Jeremy E. Uecker explain this finding by observing that "relationship permanency may drive the greater sexual activity."

One of the biggest recent changes in the sex lives of older adults is older men's use of potency drugs for erectile dysfunction (Viagra, Cialis, and Levitra) to enhance their performance. Since the 1998 debut of Viagra, these pharmaceutical solutions to erectile changes affecting older men have enjoyed tremendous popularity.

Sexually Transmitted Infections

The article "Sex and the Older Woman" (*Harvard Women's Health Watch*, vol. 19, no. 5, January 2012) reports that more than 60% of women in their 50s, 45% of women in their 60s, and 28% of women in their 70s are sexually active. Because these women no longer require protection against

FIGURE 7.16

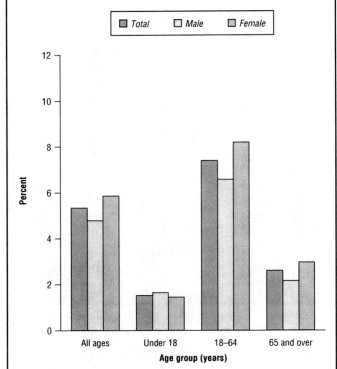

Percentage of persons of all ages who failed to obtain needed medical care due to cost, by age group and sex, January–September 2014

Notes: Data are based on household interviews of a sample of the civilian noninstitutionalized population. The analyses excluded the 0.1% of persons with unknown responses to the question on failure to obtain needed medical care due to cost.

SOURCE: "Figure 3.2. Percentage of Persons of All Ages Who Failed to Obtain Needed Medical Care Due to Cost at Some Time during the Past 12 Months, by Age Group and Sex: United States, January–September 2014," in *Early Release of Selected Estimates Based on Data from the National Health Interview Survey, January–September 2014*, Centers for Disease Control and Prevention, National Center for Health Statistics, March 2015, http://www.cdc.gov/ nchs/data/nhis/earlyrelease/earlyrelease201503_03.pdf (accessed June 1, 2015)

pregnancy, many do not practice safe sex. In one study just 13% of older women used condoms. As a result, there has been an increase in sexually transmitted infections among older women.

Data from the 2014 National Health Interview Survey reveal that adults aged 65 years and older were the least likely to have ever had an HIV test of any age group. Just 21.2% of men and 14.7% of women aged 65 years and older reported having had an HIV test. (See Figure 7.17.)

THE SHORTAGE OF SPECIALISTS IN GERIATRIC MEDICINE

In 1909 the American physician Ignatz L. Nascher (1863–1944) coined the term *geriatrics* from the Greek *geras* (old age) and *iatrikos* (physician). Geriatricians are physicians trained in internal medicine or family practice who obtain additional training and medical board certification in the diagnosis and treatment of older adults.

The American Geriatrics Society observes in "Who We Are" (http://www.americangeriatrics.org/about_us/who_we_are) that in 2015 there were more than 6,000 board-certified geriatricians, which is fewer than half of the estimated need. The shortage of specially trained physicians will intensify as the baby boom generation (people born between 1946 and 1964) joins the ranks of older adults. The American Geriatrics Society contends that financial disincentives pose the greatest barrier to new physicians entering geriatrics.

In "Doctor Shortage: Who Will Take Care of the Elderly?" (USNews.com, April 21, 2015), Magaly Olivero reports that there are 7,500 certified geriatricians and a projected need for 17,000 to care for the estimated 30% of the population age 65 and older that will need the care of a geriatrician.

FIGURE 7.17

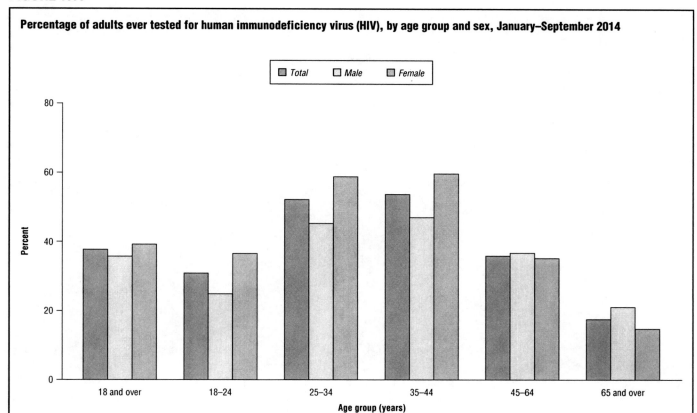

Percentage of adults ever tested for human immunodeficiency virus (HIV), by age group and sex, January–September 2014

Notes: Data are based on household interviews of a sample of the civilian noninstitutionalized population. Individuals who received HIV testing solely as a result of blood donation were considered not to have been tested for HIV. The AIDS Knowledge and Attitudes section of the National Health Interview Survey (NHIS) was dropped in 2011; only the HIV testing question was retained, and it was moved to the Adult Access to Health Care and Utilization section of the Sample Adult questionnaire. In 2013, the HIV testing question was moved to the Adult Selected Items section of the Sample Adult questionnaire and is not comparable with 2011–2012. Differences observed in estimates based on the 2010 and earlier NHIS and the 2011 and later NHIS may be partially or fully attributable to these changes in placement of the HIV testing question on the NHIS questionnaire. The analyses excluded the 4.4% of adults with unknown HIV test status.

SOURCE: "Figure 10.2. Percentage of Adults Aged 18 and over Who Had Ever Been Tested for Human Immunodeficiency Virus (HIV), by Age Group and Sex: United States, January–September 2014," in *Early Release of Selected Estimates Based on Data from the National Health Interview Survey, January–September 2014*, Centers for Disease Control and Prevention, National Center for Health Statistics, March 2015, http://www.cdc.gov/nchs/data/nhis/earlyrelease/earlyrelease201503_10.pdf (accessed June 1, 2015)

CHAPTER 8

MENTAL HEALTH AND MENTAL ILLNESS

Changes in mental capabilities are among the most feared aspects of aging. Mental health problems that impair functioning are among the most common age-related changes—and they are cause for concern because cognitive impairment (loss of intellectual functioning accompanied by memory loss and personality changes) is associated with increased risk for disability and progression to dementia (chronic disorder characterized by impaired reasoning, judgment, and language skills caused by damage to or death of nerve cells in the brain).

The aging population has spurred interest in age-related problems in cognition (the process of thinking, learning, and remembering). Cognitive difficulties much milder than those that are associated with organic brain diseases, such as Alzheimer's disease (a type of dementia), affect a significant proportion of older adults. Organic brain diseases, often referred to as organic brain syndromes, refer to physical disorders of the brain that produce mental health problems as opposed to psychiatric conditions, which may also cause mental health problems.

In "Screening for Cognitive Impairment in Older Adults: U.S. Preventive Services Task Force Recommendation Statement" (*Annals of Internal Medicine*, vol. 160, no. 11, June 3, 2014), Virginia A. Moyer of the U.S. Preventive Services Task Force in Rockville, Maryland, indicates that estimates of the prevalence (the total number of cases of a disorder in a given population at a specific time) of mild cognitive impairment among adults aged 65 years and older vary, ranging from 3% to 42%. Between 2.4 million and 5.5 million Americans suffer from dementia. The prevalence of dementia increases with age, from 5% in people aged 71 to 79 years, to 24% in those aged 80 to 89 years, and to 37% in those aged 90 years and older.

Because the number of people with cognitive impairments and dementia is anticipated to increase as the population ages, and older adults with cognitive impairment

are at risk for institutionalization, the economic burden for society is expected to escalate. As such, the mental health and illness of older adults is an increasingly important public health issue.

MENTAL HEALTH

Mental health may be measured in terms of an individual's abilities to think and communicate clearly, learn and grow emotionally, deal productively and realistically with change and stress, and form and maintain fulfilling relationships with others. Mental health is a key component of wellness (self-esteem, resilience, and the ability to cope with adversity), which influences how people feel about themselves.

When mental health is defined and measured in terms of the absence of serious psychological distress, then older adults fare quite well compared with other age groups. The 2014 National Health Interview Survey, conducted by the Centers for Disease Control and Prevention, questioned whether respondents had experienced serious psychological distress within the 30 days preceding the interview. Adults aged 65 years and older were the least likely to have experienced serious psychological distress (2.4%) in 2009–13, compared with adults aged 45 to 64 years (4.3%) and adults aged 18 to 44 years (3.1%). (See Figure 8.1.) However, of those with serious psychological distress, 27.3% of people aged 65 years and older had limitations in activities of daily living. (See Figure 8.2.)

Experience Shapes Mental Health in Old Age

One theory of aging, called continuity theory and explained by Robert C. Atchley in *The Social Forces in Later Life: An Introduction to Social Gerontology* (1985), posits that people who age most successfully are those who carry forward the habits, preferences, lifestyles, and relationships from midlife into late life. This theory has gained credence from research studies that find that traits

FIGURE 8.1

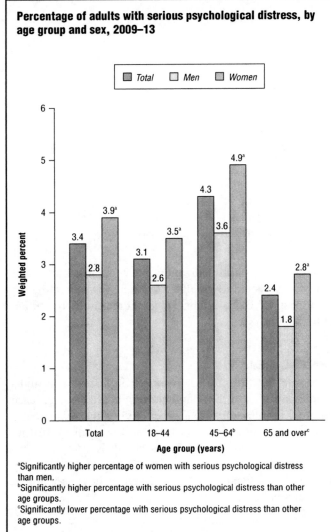

Percentage of adults with serious psychological distress, by age group and sex, 2009–13

Legend: ▨ Total ☐ Men ▨ Women

Y-axis: Weighted percent (0–6)

X-axis: Age group (years) — Total, 18–44, 45–64[b], 65 and over[c]

Values:
- Total: 3.4, 2.8, 3.9[a]
- 18–44: 3.1, 2.6, 3.5[a]
- 45–64: 4.3, 3.6, 4.9[a]
- 65 and over: 2.4, 1.8, 2.8[a]

[a]Significantly higher percentage of women with serious psychological distress than men.
[b]Significantly higher percentage with serious psychological distress than other age groups.
[c]Significantly lower percentage with serious psychological distress than other age groups.

SOURCE: Judith Weissman et al. "Figure 1. Percentage of Adults Aged 18 and over at Interview with Serious Psychological Distress, by Sex and Age: United States, 2009–2013," in "Serious Psychological Distress among Adults: United States, 2009–2013," *NCHS Data Brief*, no. 203, Centers for Disease Control and Prevention, National Center for Health Statistics, May 2015, http://www.cdc.gov/nchs/data/databriefs/db203.pdf (accessed June 2, 2015)

FIGURE 8.2

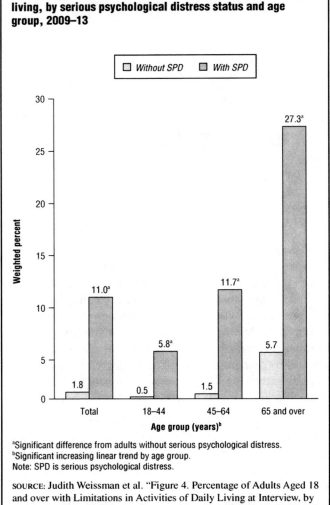

Percentage of adults with limitations in activities of daily living, by serious psychological distress status and age group, 2009–13

Legend: ☐ Without SPD ▨ With SPD

Y-axis: Weighted percent (0–30)

X-axis: Age group (years)[b] — Total, 18–44, 45–64, 65 and over

Values:
- Total: 1.8, 11.0[a]
- 18–44: 0.5, 5.8[a]
- 45–64: 1.5, 11.7[a]
- 65 and over: 5.7, 27.3[a]

[a]Significant difference from adults without serious psychological distress.
[b]Significant increasing linear trend by age group.
Note: SPD is serious psychological distress.

SOURCE: Judith Weissman et al. "Figure 4. Percentage of Adults Aged 18 and over with Limitations in Activities of Daily Living at Interview, by Serious Psychological Distress Status and Age: United States, 2009–2013," in "Serious Psychological Distress among Adults: United States, 2009–2013," *NCHS Data Brief*, no. 203, Centers for Disease Control and Prevention, National Center for Health Statistics, May 2015, http://www.cdc.gov/nchs/data/databriefs/db203.pdf (accessed June 2, 2015)

measured in midlife are strong predictors of outcomes in later life and that many psychological and social characteristics are stable across the life span. For most people, old age does not represent a radical departure from the past; changes often occur gradually and sometimes unnoticeably. Most older adults adapt to the challenges and changes associated with later life using well-practiced coping skills that were acquired earlier in life.

Adults who have struggled with mental health problems or mental disorders throughout their life often continue to suffer these same problems in old age. Few personal problems disappear with old age, and many progress and become more acute. Marital problems, which may have been kept at bay because one or both spouses were away at work, may intensify when a couple spends more time together in retirement. Reduced income, illness, and disability in retirement can aggravate an already troubled marriage and can strain even healthy interpersonal, marital, and other family relationships.

Older age can be a period of regrets, which can lead to mutual recriminations. With life expectancy rising, married couples can now expect to spend many years together in retirement. Most older couples manage the transition, but some have problems.

Coping with losses of friends, family, health, and independence may precipitate mental health problems. Hearing loss is common, and close correlations have been found between loss of hearing and depression. Visual impairment limits mobility and the ability to read and watch television. Loss of sight or hearing can cause perceptual disorientation, which in turn may lead to depression, paranoia, fear, and alienation.

A constant awareness of the imminence of death can also become a problem for older adults. Although most older adults resolve their anxieties and concerns about death, some live in denial and fear. How well older adults accept the inevitability of death is a key determinant of satisfaction and emotional well-being in old age.

Memory

Because memory is a key component of cognitive functioning, declining memory that substantially impairs older adults' functioning is a major risk factor for institutionalization. In "Self-Reported Increased Confusion or Memory Loss and Associated Functional Difficulties among Adults Aged ≥60 Years—21 States, 2011" (*Morbidity and Mortality Weekly Report*, vol. 62, no. 18, May 10, 2013), Mary L. Adams et al. report that an analysis of data from the 2011 Behavioral Risk Factor Surveillance System survey finds that 12.7% of older adults reported increased confusion or memory loss in the 12 months preceding the survey. Of those reporting increased confusion or memory loss, more than one-third (35.2%) described experiencing functional difficulties. The percentage reporting confusion or memory loss was significantly higher among people aged 85 years and older (15.6%), compared with those aged 60 to 64 years (12%) and 65 to 74 years (11.9%) and retirees (12.3%).

ORGANIC BRAIN DISEASES—DEMENTIAS

Dementia refers to a range of mental and behavioral changes caused by cerebrovascular or neurological diseases that permanently damage the brain, impairing the activity of brain cells. These changes can affect memory, speech, and the ability to perform the activities of daily living.

Occasional forgetfulness and memory lapses are not signs of dementia. Dementia is caused by disease and is not the inevitable result of growing older. Many disorders may cause or simulate dementia, which is not a single disorder—dementia refers to a condition that is caused by a variety of diseases and disorders, a small proportion of which are potentially reversible.

Furthermore, research suggests that although people with cognitive impairment have an increased risk for dementia, not all people with mild cognitive impairment will progress over time to dementia. Alex J. Mitchell and Mojtaba Shiri-Feshki conducted a large meta-analysis (a review that looks at the findings of many studies) and published their findings in "Rate of Progression of Mild Cognitive Impairment to Dementia—Meta-analysis of 41 Robust Inception Cohort Studies" (*Acta Psychiatrica Scandinavica*, vol. 119, no. 4, April 2009). The researchers

show that only a minority (20% to 40%) of people developed dementia even after long-term follow-up and that the risk appeared to decrease slightly with time. The analysis also suggests that mild cognitive impairment is not necessarily a transitional state between normal age-related changes and dementia. Mitchell and Shiri-Feshki find that some patients do not progress and others actually improve.

Multi-infarct Dementia

The National Institute of Neurological Disorders and Stroke indicates in "NINDS Multi-infarct Dementia Information Page" (August 12, 2015, http://www.ninds .nih.gov/disorders/multi_infarct_dementia/multi_infarct_ dementia.htm) that multi-infarct dementia is a common cause of memory loss and progressive dementia. Multi-infarct dementia is caused by a series of small strokes that disrupt blood flow and damage or destroy brain tissue. Sometimes these small strokes are "silent"— meaning that they produce no obvious symptoms and are detected only on imaging studies, such as computed tomography (CT) or magnetic resonance imaging (MRI) scans of the brain. An older adult may have a number of small strokes before experiencing noticeable changes in memory, reasoning, or other signs of multi-infarct dementia.

Because strokes occur suddenly, the loss of cognitive skills and memory present quickly, although some affected individuals may appear to improve for short periods, then decline again after having more strokes. Establishing the diagnosis of multi-infarct dementia is challenging because its symptoms are difficult to distinguish from those of Alzheimer's disease. Treatment cannot reverse the damage already done to the brain. Instead, it focuses on preventing further damage by reducing the risk of additional strokes. This entails treating the underlying causes of stroke, such as hypertension (high blood pressure), diabetes, high cholesterol, and heart disease. Surgical procedures to improve blood flow to the brain, such as carotid endarterectomy (a surgical procedure that removes blockages from the carotid arteries, which supply blood to the brain), angioplasty (a procedure that opens narrowed or blocked blood vessels of the heart), or stenting (using wire scaffolds that hold arteries open), as well as medications to reduce the risk of stroke are used to treat this condition.

PEOPLE WITH DIABETES ARE AT INCREASED RISK. Kristine Yaffe et al. reveal in "Association between Hypoglycemia and Dementia in a Biracial Cohort of Older Adults with Diabetes Mellitus" (*Journal of the American Medical Association*, vol. 173, no. 14, July 22, 2013) that people with type 2 diabetes may be at an increased risk for developing dementia. The researchers find that people with dangerously low blood sugar levels, called hypoglycemia, which is caused by excess insulin, had a twofold increased risk of developing dementia than people with normal blood sugar levels. Yaffe et al. also find that people with dementia were at higher risk for hypoglycemia, possibly because their cognitive impairment hinders their efforts to effectively manage their diabetes.

Alzheimer's Disease

Alzheimer's disease (AD) is the most common form of dementia among older adults. It is characterized by severely compromised thinking, reasoning, behavior, and memory, and it may be among the most fearsome of age-related disorders because it challenges older adults' ability to live independently. The disease was named after Alois Alzheimer (1864–1915), the German neurologist who first described the anatomical changes in the brain—the plaques and tangles that are the characteristic markers of this progressive, degenerative disease.

According to the Alzheimer's Association, in *2015 Alzheimer's Disease Facts and Figures* (2015, https://www.alz.org/facts/downloads/facts_figures_2015.pdf), an estimated 5.3 million Americans were afflicted with AD in 2015. The overwhelming majority (5.1 million) of AD sufferers were aged 65 years and older. An estimated 11% of people aged 65 years and older and nearly one-third (32%) of those aged 85 years and older had AD.

The Alzheimer's Association projects that the number of people aged 65 years and older with AD will reach 7.1 million in 2025 and that new AD cases each year will likely increase from 454,000 in 2010, to 615,000 in 2030, to 959,000 in 2050. The association asserts that if a cure or preventive measure is not found by 2050, then the number of Americans aged 65 years and older with AD will reach 13.8 million.

SYMPTOMS AND STAGES. In general, AD has a slow onset, with symptoms such as mild memory lapses and disorientation that may not be identified as problematical beginning between the ages of 55 and 80. As the disease progresses, memory loss increases and mood swings are frequent, accompanied by confusion, irritability, restlessness, and problems communicating. AD patients may experience trouble finding words, impaired judgment, difficulty performing familiar tasks, and changes in behavior and personality.

In "Stages of Alzheimer's" (2015, http://www.alz.org/alzheimers_disease_stages_of_alzheimers.asp), the Alzheimer's Association describes how AD progresses. In the early stage there is no and then little apparent cognitive decline, with mild lapses of memory, which are often discernible to family, friends, and coworkers. During moderate or middle-stage AD, cognitive decline is apparent. For example, AD patients may have diminished recall of recent activities or their own address or telephone number.

Ultimately, the disease progresses to severe or late-stage AD, when patients are entirely unable to care for themselves. In their terminal stages, AD victims require around-the-clock care and supervision. They no longer recognize family members, other caregivers, or themselves, and they require assistance with daily activities such as eating, dressing, bathing, and using the toilet. Eventually, they may become incontinent, blind, completely unable to communicate, and have difficulty swallowing.

According to the Alzheimer's Association, in *2015 Alzheimer's Disease Facts and Figures*, in 2010 an estimated 600,000 people died with AD, and it was the sixth-leading cause of death in people of all ages and the fifth-leading cause of death among adults aged 65 years and older.

GENETIC ORIGINS OF AD. AD is not a normal consequence of growing older. It is a disease of the brain that develops in response to genetic predisposition and nongenetic causative factors. Scientists have identified some genetic components of the disease and have observed the different patterns of inheritance, ages of onset, genes, chromosomes, and proteins that are linked to the development of AD.

In "The *mec-4* Gene Is a Member of a Family of *Caenorhabditis elegans* Genes That Can Mutate to Induce Neuronal Degeneration" (*Nature*, vol. 349, no. no. 6310, February 14, 1991), Monica Driscoll and Martin Chalfie of Columbia University reported their discovery that a mutation in a single gene could cause AD. The defect was in the gene that directs cells to produce a substance called amyloid protein. The researchers also found that low levels of acetylcholine, a neurotransmitter that is involved in learning and memory, contribute to the formation of hard deposits of amyloid protein that accumulate in the brains of AD patients. In healthy people, the protein fragments are broken down and excreted by the body.

In 1995 three more genes linked to AD were identified. Two genes are involved with forms of early-onset AD, which can begin as early as age 30. The third gene, known as apolipoprotein E (apoE), regulates lipid metabolism and helps redistribute cholesterol. In the brain, apoE participates in repairing nerve tissue that has been injured. According to the National Institute on Aging (NIA), in the press release "Cortex Area Thinner in Youth with Alzheimer's-Related Gene" (April 24, 2007, http://www.nimh.nih.gov/science-news/2007/cortex-area-thinner-in-youth-with-alzheimers-related-gene.shtml), 40% of late-onset AD patients have at least one apoE-4 gene, whereas only 10% to 25% of the general population has an apoE-4 gene. The NIA notes in "Alzheimer's Disease Fact Sheet" (July 20, 2015, http://www.nia.nih.gov/Alzheimers/Publications/adfact.htm) that research confirms that the apoE-4 gene increases the risk of developing AD, but it is not yet known how it acts to increase this risk. The NIA observes that inheriting the apoE-4 gene does not necessarily mean that a person will develop AD and that the absence of the gene does not ensure that an individual will not develop AD.

In April 2011 two studies published in *Nature Genetics* (vol. 43, no. 5)—Adam C. Naj et al.'s "Common Variants at MS4A4/MS4A6E, CD2AP, CD33, and EPHA1 Are Associated with Late-Onset Alzheimer's Disease" and Paul Hollingworth et al.'s "Common Variants at ABCA7, MS4A6A/MS4A4E, EPHA1, CD33, and CD2AP Are Associated with Alzheimer's Disease"—identified five additional genes that are implicated in increasing the risk of developing the disease and the course of the disease. However, it should be noted that none of the recently identified genes play as important a role as apoE—the newly identified genes increase risk by just 10% to 15%, compared with apoE, which confers a 400-fold increase in risk of developing AD.

In January 2012 two groups of researchers—Harold Neumann and Mark J. Daly, in "Variant *TREM2* as Risk Factor for Alzheimer's Disease," and Rita Guerreiro et al., in "*TREM2* Variants in Alzheimer's Disease" (both published in *New England Journal of Medicine*, vol. 368, no. 2, January 10, 2013)—identified mutations in the TREM2 gene, which is thought to interfere with the brain's ability to prevent the buildup of plaque. This discovery is important because it identifies a potential way to alter the course of AD.

Paola Piscopo et al. report in "SORL1 Gene Is Associated with the Conversion from Mild Cognitive Impairment to Alzheimer's Disease" (*Journal of Alzheimer's Disease*, April 16, 2015) that the sortilin-related receptor gene (SORL1), which is known to increase susceptibility for AD, may also be useful for identifying which people with mild cognitive impairment are at high risk for developing AD.

As of August 2015, there were two ongoing, long-term NIA initiatives: the Alzheimer's Disease Genetics Study, which began in 2003 and collects blood samples and deoxyribonucleic acid for researchers to use, and the Alzheimer's Disease Genetics Consortium, which began in 2007 and aims to compare genetic material from 10,000 people with AD to genetic material from 10,000 people without the disease. In "Alzheimer's Disease Genetics Fact Sheet" (July 20, 2015, http://www.nia.nih .gov/alzheimers/publication/alzheimers-disease-genetics-fact-sheet), the NIA reports that these initiatives have helped identify "key steps in the formation of brain abnormalities typical of Alzheimer's disease" and the variation in the age at which the disease begins. This research has spurred development of imaging tests that detect accumulation of amyloid and tau in the brain. The NIA also participates in the Dominantly Inherited Alzheimer Network, an international research project that studies early-onset AD in adult children of a parent with a mutated gene.

DIAGNOSTIC TESTING. Historically, the only sure way to diagnose AD was to examine brain tissue under a microscope. The brain of a patient who has died of AD reveals a characteristic pattern that is the hallmark of the disease: tangles of fibers (neurofibrillary tangles) and clusters of degenerated nerve endings (neuritic plaques) in areas of the brain that are crucial for memory and intellect.

Evaluation of people with cognitive changes involves obtaining a thorough medical history and a physical examination to rule out cognitive changes that may result from an underlying illness such as diabetes, a psychiatric disorder such as depression, or a reaction to medication. Physicians ask patients a series of questions to assess their memory, thinking, reasoning, and problem-solving capabilities. Although a complete medical history, physical examination, and psychiatric and neurological assessment do not provide as definitive a diagnosis of AD as an examination of the brain, they can usually produce an accurate diagnosis by ruling out other potential causes of cognitive impairment. Diagnostic tests for AD may also include analysis of blood and spinal fluid as well as the use of brain scans (CT and MRI) to detect strokes or tumors and to measure the volume of brain tissue in the areas used for memory and cognition. Brain scans assist to accurately identify people with AD and predict who may develop AD in the future.

Osama Sabri et al. describe in "Florbetaben PET Imaging to Detect Amyloid Beta Plaques in Alzheimer Disease: Phase 3 Study" (*Alzheimer's and Dementia*, March 28, 2015) the successful use of positron emission tomography (PET) imaging to detect the amyloid beta deposits that form in the brains of AD patients. In "Alzheimer-Signature MRI Biomarker Predicts AD Dementia in Cognitively Normal Adults" (*Neurology*, vol. 76, no. 16, April 19, 2011), Brad C. Dickerson et al. used MRI to measure the thickness of the cerebral cortex (the outer portion of the brain that is responsible for higher-order functions such as information processing and language) to help predict which cognitively normal people would develop AD. The researchers hypothesized that the cortical thinning observed in patients with mild AD might be present in cognitively normal adults who will develop AD before they have any symptoms of the disease. Dickerson et al. find that cognitively normal adults who went on to develop AD had thinner cortical areas and those in the highest third of cortical thickness never developed AD. The researchers conclude that "this measure [is] a potentially important imaging biomarker of early neurodegeneration."

The NIA explains in "Alzheimer's Disease Fact Sheet" that apoE testing is used as a research tool to identify research subjects who may have an increased risk of developing AD. Investigators are then able to look for early brain changes in research subjects and compare the effectiveness of treatments for people with different apoE profiles. Because the apoE test does not accurately predict who will or will not develop AD, it is useful for studying AD risk in populations but not for determining any one individual's specific risk.

Simon Lovestone of the University of Oxford observes in "Blood Biomarkers for Alzheimer's Disease" (*Genome Medicine*, vol. 6, no. 8, 2014) that progress has been made in the identification of biomarkers for AD in cerebrospinal fluid and that "prospects for identifying blood-derived markers for early diagnosis and prognosis are very good." He is less certain that blood biomarkers will be able to be used to monitor the progression of AD. Instead, Lovestone suggests that this will be done using multiple assessments, including imaging studies such as PET and MRI, electrophysiology (electrical activity in the brain), clinical cognitive measures, and molecular tests of cerebrospinal fluid and blood.

At the 28th International Conference of Alzheimer's Disease International (http://www.adi2013.org/docs/conference-documents/adi-2013-abstract-document.pdf?sfvrsn=2) in April 2013, Shieh-Yueh Yang et al. presented in "Risk Evaluation for Alzheimer's Disease by Assaying Biomarkers in Plasma Using Immunomagnetic Reduction" another new test that may determine the presence of AD using biomarkers for amyloid beta and tau proteins in plasma. The new test is described as able to detect AD more than 90% of the time and will cost as little as $50. In July 2014 Tafu Chen et al. confirmed the utility of this new test in "Blood Biomarker for Diagnosing Mild Cognition Impairment and Alzheimer's Disease Using Bio-functionalized Magnetic Nanoparticles" (*Alzheimer's and Dementia*, vol. 10, no. 4). The researchers note that the results of further research provide evidence for the feasibility of using blood testing for distinguishing between mild cognitive impairment and AD.

A simple and accurate test, such as a blood-based biomarker, that distinguishes people with AD from those with cognitive problems or dementias arising from other causes will prove useful for scientists, physicians, and other clinical researchers. However, because advances in detection have outpaced treatment options, the availability of tests to predict who may develop AD raises ethical and practical questions: Do people really want to know their risks of developing AD? Is it helpful to predict a condition that is not yet considered preventable or curable?

DIAGNOSTIC GUIDELINES AND CRITERIA FOR AD. In 2011 the NIA and the Alzheimer's Association established new guidelines for diagnosing AD, and Guy M. McKhann et al. summarize the details in "The Diagnosis of Dementia Due to Alzheimer's Disease: Recommendations from the National Institute on Aging and the Alzheimer's Association Workgroup" (*Alzheimer's and Dementia*, vol. 7, no. 3, May 2011). The guidelines update diagnostic criteria that were developed in 1984 and aim to detect and treat the disease earlier than ever before. They also acknowledge that imaging and biomarkers should not "be used routinely in clinical diagnosis without further testing and validation."

The updated guidelines explain AD as a continuum of mental decline that may begin many years before the first symptoms arise. Furthermore, they describe the first of three phases: preclinical, which occurs absent symptoms; mild cognitive impairment, which involves noticeable memory problems without loss of ability to function independently; and Alzheimer's dementia, with its characteristic decline in reasoning and function.

New criteria for determining cognitive impairment caused by AD were also created, and Marilyn S. Albert et al. outline the details in "The Diagnosis of Mild Cognitive Impairment Due to Alzheimer's Disease: Recommendations from the National Institute on Aging and Alzheimer's Association Workgroup" (*Alzheimer's and Dementia*, vol. 7, no. 3, May 2011). Two sets of new criteria were developed: one for use by health care providers without access to advanced imaging techniques or blood and cerebrospinal fluid analysis and one for use by clinical researchers. The second set of criteria describe the use of biomarkers that are based on imaging and blood and cerebrospinal fluid measures and establish four levels of confidence, depending on the presence and character of the biomarker findings.

TREATMENT. There is no cure or prevention for AD, and treatment focuses on managing symptoms. Medication may slow the appearance of some symptoms and can lessen others, such as agitation, anxiety, unpredictable behavior, and depression. Physical exercise and good nutrition are important, as is a calm and highly structured environment. The objective is to help the AD patient maintain as much comfort, normalcy, and dignity for as long as possible.

According to the Alzheimer's Association, in "Current Alzheimer's Treatments" (http://www.alz.org/research/science/alzheimers_disease_treatments.asp), in 2015 there were five prescription drugs—Aricept, Razadyne, Namenda, Exelon, and Cognex—for the treatment of AD that had been approved by the U.S. Food and Drug Administration, and National Institutes of Health (NIH) affiliates and pharmaceutical companies were involved in clinical trials of new drugs to treat AD. All the drugs being tested were intended to improve the symptoms of AD and slow its progression, but none was expected to cure AD. The investigational drugs aim to address three aspects of AD: to improve cognitive function in people with early-stage AD, to slow or postpone the progression of the disease, and to control behavioral problems such as wandering, aggression, and agitation of patients with AD.

In 2011 a new method of drug delivery, a transdermal patch that delivers the drug through the skin, compared favorably with oral drug administration. Pam Harrison reports in "Transdermal Patch for Alzheimer's Gets Caregiver Thumbs-Up: Delivery Method May Reduce Caregiver Stress, Enhance Patient Response" (Medscape.com, March 30, 2011) that Pablo Martinez-Lage et al. said that some patient caregivers felt the patch slowed, or even stopped, the deterioration that is the hallmark of AD. They opined that the continuous drug delivery offered by the patch might account for the reported improvement in the patients' behavior. Martinez-Lage et al. also observed that AD caregivers found administering the patch easier and less stressful than administering oral medication to potentially combative or uncooperative patients.

As use of the transdermal patch continued to increase, Steven Ferris, Xiangyi Meng, and Drew Velting wondered whether caregivers' preferences for this easy-to-administer treatment would improve AD patients' functional and cognitive outcomes. In "Caregiver Treatment Preference/Satisfaction and Efficacy among Patients in the Optimising Transdermal Exelon in Mild-to-Moderate Alzheimer's Disease (OPTIMA) Study" (*Aging, Dementia, Cognitive, and Behavioral Neurology: Clinical Trials*, vol. 84 no. 14, Suppl. P7.104, April 6, 2015), the researchers conclude, "Caregiver treatment preference/satisfaction is associated with positive functional and cognitive outcomes in mild-to-moderate AD; this highlights the importance of easy-to-use therapies that aid effective AD management."

CARING FOR THE AD PATIENT. AD affects members of the patient's family. Although medication may suppress some symptoms and occasionally slow the progression of the disease, eventually most AD patients require constant care and supervision. In the past, nursing homes and residential care facilities were not equipped to provide this kind of care, and if they accepted AD patients at all, they admitted only those in the earliest stages of the disease. Since 2000 a growing number of nursing homes have welcomed AD patients, even though they are more difficult and costly to care for than older adults without AD. This change is primarily financially motivated, because nursing home occupancy rates have been dropping in response to the growth of alternative housing for older adults.

The Alzheimer's Association indicates in *2015 Alzheimer's Disease Facts and Figures* that in 2014 more than 15 million caregivers provided nearly 18 billion hours of unpaid care valued at $217.7 billion. Many relatives of AD patients care for the affected family member at home as long as possible because they cannot afford institutional care or they feel an obligation to do so. No matter how devoted the caregiver, the time, patience, and resources required to provide care are immense, and the task is often overwhelming. As the patient's condition progresses, caregivers often find themselves socially isolated. Caregiving has been linked to increased rates of depression, compromised immune function, and a greater use of medication, particularly medications that are used to relieve symptoms of mental distress.

Caregivers who participate in support groups and make use of home health aides, adult day care, and respite care (facilities where patients stay for a limited number of days) not only feel healthier but also are better able to care for AD patients and maintain them at home longer than those who do not.

In *2015 Alzheimer's Disease Facts and Figures*, the Alzheimer's Association describes the growing burden that AD imposes on families, caregivers, and the U.S. health care system. The total cost of health and long-term care for people with AD was an estimated $226 billion in 2015 and is expected to exceed $1 trillion in 2050.

MENTAL ILLNESS

Older people with mental illnesses were once considered senile—that is, mentally debilitated as a result of old age. Serious forgetfulness, emotional disturbances, and other behavioral changes do not, however, occur as a normal part of aging. They may be caused by chronic illnesses such as heart disease, thyroid disorders, or anemia; infections, poor diet, or lack of sleep; or prescription drugs, such as narcotic painkillers, sedatives, and antihistamines. Social isolation, loneliness, boredom, or depression may also cause memory lapses. When accurately diagnosed and treated, these types of problems can frequently be reversed.

Mental illness refers to all identifiable mental health disorders and mental health problems. In the landmark study *Mental Health: A Report of the Surgeon General, 1999* (1999, http://www.surgeongeneral.gov/library/mentalhealth/home.html), the U.S. surgeon general defines mental disorders as "health conditions that are characterized by alterations in thinking, mood, or behavior (or some combination thereof) associated with distress and/or impaired functioning." The surgeon general distinguishes mental health problems from mental health disorders, describing the signs and symptoms of mental health problems as less intense and of shorter duration than those of mental health disorders, but acknowledges that both mental health problems and disorders may be distressing and disabling.

The surgeon general observes that nearly 20% of people aged 55 years and older experience mental disorders that are not part of normal aging. The most common disorders, in order of estimated prevalence rates, are anxiety (11.4%), severe cognitive impairment (6.6%), and mood disorders (4.4%) such as depression. The surgeon general also points out that mental disorders in older adults are frequently unrecognized, underreported, and undertreated.

Diagnosing mental disorders in older adults is challenging because their symptoms may be different from that of other adults. For example, many older adults complain about physical as opposed to emotional or psychological problems, and they present symptoms that are not typical of depression or anxiety disorders. Accurately identifying, detecting, and diagnosing mental disorders in older adults is also complicated by the following:

- Mental disorders often coexist with other medical problems.

- The symptoms of some chronic diseases may imitate or conceal psychological disorders.

- Older adults are more likely to report physical symptoms than psychological ones because there is less stigma associated with physical health or medical problems than with mental health problems.

The Growing Mental Health Needs of Older Adults

Stephen J. Bartels and John A. Naslund of the Dartmouth Institute for Health Policy and Clinical Practice in Lebanon, New Hampshire, report in "The Underside of the Silver Tsunami—Older Adults and Mental Health Care" (*New England Journal of Medicine*, vol. 368, no. 6, February 7, 2013) that between 5.6 million and 8 million adults aged 65 years and older have mental health or substance-use disorders and that by 2030 their ranks will grow to between 10.1 million and 14.4 million. Older adults with mental health disorders are more disabled than those with physical illness alone, and they make more hospital and emergency department visits, resulting in costs that are between 47% and 200% higher than their age peers without mental illness.

Depression

Symptoms of depression are an important indicator of physical and mental health in older adults, because people who experience symptoms of depression are also more likely to report higher rates of physical illness, disability, and health service utilization.

The prevalence of clinically relevant depressive symptoms (as distinguished from brief periods of sadness or depressed mood) increases with advancing age. According to the Centers for Disease Control and Prevention, in "Depression Is Not a Normal Part of Growing Older" (March 5, 2015, http://www.cdc.gov/aging/mentalhealth/depression.htm), an estimated 1% to 5% of healthy older adults living in the community are depressed, and 13.5% of older adults who require home health care and 11.5% of older hospital patients are depressed.

Often, illness itself can trigger depression by altering the chemicals in the brain. Examples of illnesses that can touch off depression are diabetes, hypothyroidism (a condition in which the thyroid is underactive—producing too little thyroid hormones), kidney or liver dysfunction, heart disease, and infection. In patients with these ailments, treating the underlying disease usually eliminates the depression. David M. Clarke and Kay C. Currie find in "Depression, Anxiety, and Their Relationship with Chronic Diseases: A Review of the Epidemiology, Risk, and Treatment Evidence" (*Medical Journal of Australia*, vol. 190, no. 7, April 6, 2009) not only strong evidence for the association of physical illness, depression, and anxiety but also their effects on outcomes (how well patients fare). The researchers indicate that people with disabling chronic illnesses such as arthritis, stroke, and pulmonary diseases are likely to become depressed. Furthermore, Clarke and Currie note that some prescription medications, as well as over-the-counter (nonprescription) drugs, may also cause depression.

Depression causes some older adults to deliberately neglect or disregard their medical needs by eating poorly and failing to take prescribed medication or taking it incorrectly. These may be covert acts of suicide. Actual suicide, which is frequently a consequence of serious depression, is highest among older adults relative to all other age groups. In 2013 the death rate for suicide among people aged 75 to 84 years was 17.1% and among adults aged 85 years and older was 18.6%. (See Table 8.1.) Older men had the highest rates—34.7% for those aged 75 to 84 years and 48.5% for those aged 85 years and older.

TREATMENT OF DEPRESSION. According to the surgeon general, in *Mental Health*, despite the availability of effective treatments for depression, a substantial fraction of affected older adults do not receive treatment, largely because they either do not seek it or their depression is not identified or accurately diagnosed. For example, although many older patients respond well to antidepressants, some physicians do not prescribe them to older patients already taking many drugs for chronic medical conditions because they do not want to risk drug–drug interactions or add another drug to an already complicated regimen. As a result, only a minority of older adults

TABLE 8.1

Death rates for suicide, by selected characteristics, selected years 1950–2013

[Data are based on death certificates]

Sex, race, Hispanic origin, and age	1950[a]	1960[a]	1970	1980	1990	2000	2010	2012	2013
All persons					Deaths per 100,000 resident population				
All ages, age-adjusted[b]	13.2	12.5	13.1	12.2	12.5	10.4	12.1	12.6	12.6
All ages, crude	11.4	10.6	11.6	11.9	12.4	10.4	12.4	12.9	13.0
Under 1 year	...	...	...	...	...	...	...	...	...
1–4 years	...	...	...	...	...	...	...	...	...
5–14 years	0.2	0.3	0.3	0.4	0.8	0.7	0.7	0.8	1.0
15–24 years	4.5	5.2	8.8	12.3	13.2	10.2	10.5	11.1	11.1
15–19 years	2.7	3.6	5.9	8.5	11.1	8.0	7.5	8.3	8.3
20–24 years	6.2	7.1	12.2	16.1	15.1	12.5	13.6	13.7	13.7
25–44 years	11.6	12.2	15.4	15.6	15.2	13.4	15.0	15.7	15.5
25–34 years	9.1	10.0	14.1	16.0	15.2	12.0	14.0	14.7	14.8
35–44 years	14.3	14.2	16.9	15.4	15.3	14.5	16.0	16.7	16.2
45–64 years	23.5	22.0	20.6	15.9	15.3	13.5	18.6	19.1	19.0
45–54 years	20.9	20.7	20.0	15.9	14.8	14.4	19.6	20.0	19.7
55–64 years	26.8	23.7	21.4	15.9	16.0	12.1	17.5	18.0	18.1
65 years and over	30.0	24.5	20.8	17.6	20.5	15.2	14.9	15.4	16.1
65–74 years	29.6	23.0	20.8	16.9	17.9	12.5	13.7	14.0	15.0
75–84 years	31.1	27.9	21.2	19.1	24.9	17.6	15.7	16.8	17.1
85 years and over	28.8	26.0	19.0	19.2	22.2	19.6	17.6	17.8	18.6
Male									
All ages, age-adjusted[b]	21.2	20.0	19.8	19.9	21.5	17.7	19.8	20.4	20.3
All ages, crude	17.8	16.5	16.8	18.6	20.4	17.1	19.9	20.6	20.6
Under 1 year	...	...	...	...	...	...	...	...	...
1–4 years	...	...	...	...	...	...	...	...	...
5–14 years	0.3	0.4	0.5	0.6	1.1	1.2	0.9	1.1	1.2
15–24 years	6.5	8.2	13.5	20.2	22.0	17.1	16.9	17.4	17.3
15–19 years	3.5	5.6	8.8	13.8	18.1	13.0	11.7	12.5	12.4
20–24 years	9.3	11.5	19.3	26.8	25.7	21.4	22.2	22.0	21.9
25–44 years	17.2	17.9	20.9	24.0	24.4	21.3	23.6	24.5	24.1
25–34 years	13.4	14.7	19.8	25.0	24.8	19.6	22.5	23.4	23.4
35–44 years	21.3	21.0	22.1	22.5	23.9	22.8	24.6	25.7	24.8
45–64 years	37.1	34.4	30.0	23.7	24.3	21.3	29.2	29.5	29.0
45–54 years	32.0	31.6	27.9	22.9	23.2	22.4	30.4	30.2	29.6
55–64 years	43.6	38.1	32.7	24.5	25.7	19.4	27.7	28.7	28.3
65 years and over	52.8	44.0	38.4	35.0	41.6	31.1	29.0	29.5	30.9
65–74 years	50.5	39.6	36.0	30.4	32.2	22.7	23.9	24.1	26.0
75–84 years	58.3	52.5	42.8	42.3	56.1	38.6	32.3	34.2	34.7
85 years and over	58.3	57.4	42.4	50.6	65.9	57.5	47.3	46.9	48.5
Female									
All ages, age-adjusted[b]	5.6	5.6	7.4	5.7	4.8	4.0	5.0	5.4	5.5
All ages, crude	5.1	4.9	6.6	5.5	4.8	4.0	5.2	5.5	5.7
Under 1 year	...	...	...	...	...	...	...	...	...
1–4 years	...	...	...	...	...	...	...	...	...
5–14 years	0.1	0.1	0.2	0.2	0.4	0.3	0.4	0.4	0.7
15–24 years	2.6	2.2	4.2	4.3	3.9	3.0	3.9	4.5	4.5
15–19 years	1.8	1.6	2.9	3.0	3.7	2.7	3.1	3.9	3.9
20–24 years	3.3	2.9	5.7	5.5	4.1	3.2	4.7	4.9	5.2
25–44 years	6.2	6.6	10.2	7.7	6.2	5.4	6.4	6.8	6.8
25–34 years	4.9	5.5	8.6	7.1	5.6	4.3	5.3	5.9	6.1
35–44 years	7.5	7.7	11.9	8.5	6.8	6.4	7.5	7.7	7.6
45–64 years	9.9	10.2	12.0	8.9	7.1	6.2	8.6	9.1	9.4
45–54 years	9.9	10.2	12.6	9.4	6.9	6.7	9.0	10.2	10.0
55–64 years	9.9	10.2	11.4	8.4	7.3	5.4	8.0	8.0	8.7
65 years and over	9.4	8.4	8.1	6.1	6.4	4.0	4.2	4.5	4.6
65–74 years	10.1	8.4	9.0	6.5	6.7	4.0	4.8	5.2	5.4
75–84 years	8.1	8.9	7.0	5.5	6.3	4.0	3.7	3.9	3.9
85 years and over	8.2	6.0	5.9	5.5	5.4	4.2	3.3	3.2	3.3

diagnosed with depression receives the appropriate drug dose and duration of treatment.

Treatment for depression includes psychotherapy, with or without the use of antidepressant medications, and electroconvulsive therapy (ECT). Psychotherapy is most often used to treat mild to moderate depression and is prescribed for a limited, defined period, generally ranging from 10 to 20 weeks. ECT is used for life-threatening depression that does not respond to treatment with antidepressant drugs.

In "Long Term Effect of Depression Care Management on Mortality in Older Adults: Follow-Up of Cluster Randomized Clinical Trial in Primary Care" (*BMJ*, vol. 3, no. 10, June 2013), a five-year study of 1,226 older

[Data are based on death certificates]

...Category not applicable.
*Rates based on fewer than 20 deaths are considered unreliable and are not shown.
ᵃIncludes deaths of persons who were not residents of the 50 states and the District of Columbia (D.C.).
ᵇAge-adjusted rates are calculated using the year 2000 standard population. Prior to 2001, age-adjusted rates were calculated using standard million proportions based on rounded population numbers. Starting with 2001 data, unrounded population numbers are used to calculate age-adjusted rates.
Notes: Starting with *Health, United States, 2003*, rates for 1991–1999 were revised using intercensal population estimates based on the 1990 and 2000 censuses. For 2000, population estimates are bridged-race April 1 census counts. Starting with Health, United States, 2012, rates for 2001–2009 were revised using intercensal population estimates based on the 2000 and 2010 censuses. For 2010, population estimates are bridged-race April 1 census counts. Rates for 2011 and beyond were computed using 2010-based postcensal estimates. Figures for 2001 include September 11-related deaths for which death certificates were filed as of October 24, 2002. Age groups were selected to minimize the presentation of unstable age-specific death rates based on small numbers of deaths and for consistency among comparison groups. Starting with 2003 data, some states allowed the reporting of more than one race on the death certificate. The multiple-race data for these states were bridged to the single-race categories of the 1977 Office of Management and Budget standards, for comparability with other states.

SOURCE: Adapted from "Table 33. Death Rates for Suicide, by Sex, Race, Hispanic Origin, and Age: United States, Selected Years 1950–2013," in *Health, United States, 2014: With Special Feature on Adults Aged 55–64*, National Center for Health Statistics, May 2015, http://www .cdc.gov/nchs/data/hus/hus14.pdf (accessed May 22, 2015)

---

patients, Joseph J. Gallo et al. not only find that depression is independently associated with mortality risk in older adults but also confirm that treatment for depression reduces this risk. Of the total number of subjects, about 600 were determined to be suffering from major or minor depression. During the five-year follow-up, subjects who received treatment for depression were 24% less likely to die than those who were not treated.

Anxiety Disorders

Anxiety disorders (extreme nervousness and apprehension or sudden attacks of fear without apparent external causes) can be debilitating. Symptoms may include a "knot" in the stomach, sweating, or elevated blood pressure. If the anxiety is severe and long lasting, more serious problems may develop. People suffering from anxiety over extended periods may have headaches, ulcers, irritable bowel syndrome, insomnia, or depression. Because anxiety tends to create various other emotional and physical symptoms, a cascade effect can occur in which these new problems produce even more anxiety.

Unrelenting anxiety that appears unrelated to specific environments or situations is called generalized anxiety disorder. People suffering from this disorder worry excessively about the events of daily life and the future. They are also more likely to experience physical symptoms such as shortness of breath, dizziness, rapid heart rate, nausea, stomach pains, and muscle tension than people who are afflicted with other panic disorders, social phobias, or agoraphobia (fear of being in an open space or a place where escape is difficult).

The surgeon general estimates in *Mental Health* the prevalence of anxiety disorder as about 11.4% of adults aged 55 years and older. Phobic anxiety disorders such as social phobia, which causes extreme discomfort in social settings, are among the most common mental disturbances in late life. In contrast, some disorders have low rates of prevalence among older adults, such as panic disorder (0.5%) and obsessive-compulsive disorder (1.5%). Generalized anxiety disorder, rather than specific anxiety syndromes, may be more prevalent in older people.

Effective treatment for anxiety involves medication, primarily benzodiazepines, such as Valium, Librium, and Xanax, as well as psychotherapy. Like other medications, the effects of benzodiazepines may last longer in older adults, and their side effects may include drowsiness, fatigue, physical impairment, memory or other cognitive impairment, confusion, depression, respiratory problems, abuse or dependence problems, and withdrawal reactions.

Nondrug treatment may also be effective for older adults suffering from debilitating anxiety. In "Antidepressant Medication Augmented with Cognitive-Behavioral Therapy for Generalized Anxiety Disorder in Older Adults" (*American Journal of Psychiatry*, vol. 170, no. 7, July 1, 2013), Julie L. Wetherell et al. compare cognitive behavioral therapy (CBT; goal-oriented treatment that focuses on changing thoughts to solve psychological problems), drug treatment alone, a combination of the two, and a placebo (a pill that contains no active drug) as treatment for generalized anxiety disorder in older adults. The researchers find that although both drug treatment and CBT relieved anxiety and prevented relapse when compared with a placebo, CBT alone provided long-term relief from anxiety. Wetherell et al. conclude that although medication prevents relapse, CBT is able to prevent recurrences without the need for long-term drug treatment.

Schizophrenia

Schizophrenia is an extremely disabling form of mental illness. Its symptoms include hallucinations, paranoia, delusions, and social isolation. People suffering from schizophrenia "hear voices," and over time the voices take over in the schizophrenic's mind, obliterating reality and directing all kinds of erratic behaviors. Suicide attempts and violent attacks are common in the lives of schizophrenics. In an attempt to escape the torment inflicted by their brains, many schizophrenics turn to drugs. The National Institute of Mental Health indicates in *What Is Schizophrenia?* (2015, http://www.nimh.nih.gov/health/topics/schizophrenia/index.shtml) that most symptoms of schizophrenia emerge early in life—the late teens or 20s and rarely begin after age 45.

In *Mental Health*, the surgeon general notes that the prevalence of schizophrenia among adults aged 65 years and older is estimated to be 0.6%, less than half of the 1.3% that is estimated for the population aged 18 to 54 years. However, the economic burden of late-life schizophrenia is high.

Drug treatment of schizophrenia in older adults is complicated. The medications that are used to treat schizophrenia, such as Haldol, effectively reduce symptoms (e.g., delusions and hallucinations) in many older patients, but they also have a high risk of disabling side effects, such as tardive dyskinesias (involuntary, rhythmic movements of the face, jaw, mouth, tongue, and trunk). Even newer atypical antipsychotic medications that are used to treat the symptoms of schizophrenia, such as Abilify, can produce troubling side effects, including tremors, restlessness, shakes, muscle stiffness, or other involuntary movements.

MISUSE OF ALCOHOL AND PRESCRIPTION DRUGS

The surgeon general observes in *Mental Health* that older adults are more likely to misuse, as opposed to abuse, alcohol and prescription drugs. The surgeon general estimates that the prevalence of heavy drinking (12 to 21 drinks per week) in the cohort (a group of individuals that shares a common characteristic such as birth years and is studied over time) of older adults is 3% to 9%. The prevalence rates are expected to rise as the baby boomer (people born between 1946 and 1964) cohort, with its history of alcohol and illegal drug use, joins the ranks of older adults. In "Substance Use Disorder among Older Adults in the United States in 2020" (*Addiction*, vol. 104, no. 1, January 2009), Beth Han et al. forecast that the number of adults aged 50 years and older with substance use disorder (alcohol/illicit drug dependence or abuse) is projected to double from an average of 2.8 million per year in 2006 to 5.7 million in 2020. The current group of older adults is more likely to suffer substance misuse problems, such as drug dependence, arising from underuse, overuse, or erratic use of prescription and over-the-counter medications.

Figure 8.3 shows that adults aged 65 years and older had the lowest rate of excessive alcohol consumption—just 6.9%—of all age groups. Older men (10.5%) were much more likely than older women (4.1%) to have met the National Health Interview Survey criteria for excessive alcohol consumption (at least one heavy drinking day in the past year).

Prevalence of Types of Older Problem Drinkers

In *Module 10C: Older Adults and Alcohol Problems* (March 2005, http://pubs.niaaa.nih.gov/publications/social/Module10COlderAdults/Module10C.html), the National Institute on Alcohol Abuse and Alcoholism (NIAAA) describes the prevalence of three types of problem drinkers: at-risk drinkers, problem drinkers, and alcohol-dependent drinkers.

- At-risk drinking is alcohol use that increases the risk of developing alcohol-related problems and complications. People over the age of 65 years who drink more than seven drinks per week (one per day) are considered at risk of developing health, social, or emotional problems caused by alcohol.

- Problem drinkers have already suffered medical, psychological, family, financial, self-care, legal, or social consequences of alcohol abuse.

- Alcohol-dependent drinkers suffer from a medical disorder that is characterized by a loss of control over consumption, preoccupation with alcohol, and continued use despite adverse health, social, legal, and financial consequences.

Figure 8.4 shows the estimated prevalence rates of these different types of drinkers as well as the majority (65%) of older adults that abstains from alcohol consumption.

Types of Older Problem Drinkers

Another way to characterize older problem drinkers is by the duration and patterns of their drinking histories. The first group consists of those over the age of 60 years who have been drinking for most of their life. Members of this group are called survivors or early-onset problem drinkers. They have beaten the statistical odds by living to old age despite heavy drinking, but they are most likely to suffer from cirrhosis of the liver (a chronic degenerative disease of the liver marked by scarring of liver tissue and eventually liver failure) and mental health disorders such as depression.

The second group, intermittents, has historically engaged in binge drinking interspersed with periods of relative sobriety. These drinkers are at risk for alcohol abuse because they are more likely than others to self-medicate with alcohol to relieve physical pain and emotional distress or to assuage loneliness and social isolation.

Reactors or late-onset problem drinkers make up the third group. The stresses of later life, particularly the loss

FIGURE 8.3

Adults who had at least one heavy drinking day in the past year, by age group and sex, January–September 2014

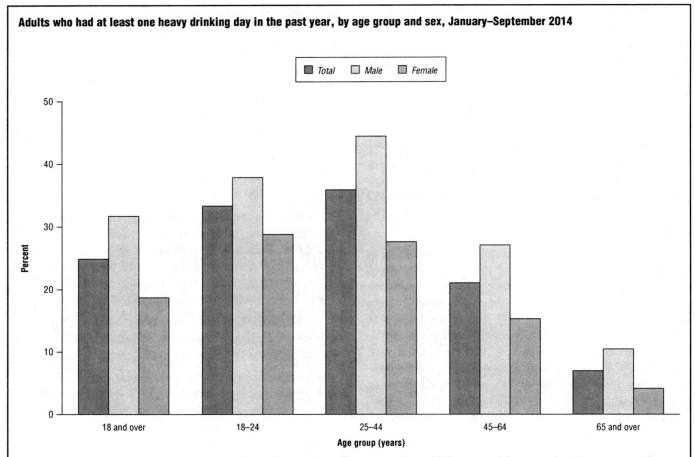

Notes: Data are based on household interviews of a sample of the civilian noninstitutionalized population. Heavy drinking days are defined as days in which men consumed five or more drinks and women consumed four or more drinks. The analyses excluded the 1.2% of adults with unknown alcohol consumption.

SOURCE: "Figure 9.2. Percentage of Adults Aged 18 and over Who Had at Least One Heavy Drinking Day in the Past Year, by Age Group and Sex: United States, January–September 2014," in *Early Release of Selected Estimates Based on Data from the National Health Interview Survey, January–September 2014*, Centers for Disease Control and Prevention, National Center for Health Statistics, March 2015, http://www.cdc.gov/nchs/data/nhis/earlyrelease/earlyrelease201503_09.pdf (accessed June 3, 2015)

of work or a spouse, may precipitate heavy drinking. These people show few of the physical consequences of prolonged drinking and fewer disruptions in their life.

Alcohol-Related Issues Unique to Older Adults

Older adults generally have a decreased tolerance to alcohol. Consumption of a given amount of alcohol by older adults usually produces higher blood-alcohol levels than it would in a younger population. Chronic medical problems such as cirrhosis may be present, but older adults are less likely to require detoxification and treatment of alcohol-withdrawal problems. One possible explanation is that few lifelong alcohol abusers survive to old age.

Because older adults usually take more medication than people in other age groups, they are more susceptible to drug–alcohol interactions. Alcohol reduces the safety and effectiveness of many medications and, in combination with some drugs, may produce coma or death. Adverse consequences of alcohol consumption in older adults are not limited to problem drinkers. Older adults with medical problems, including diabetes, heart disease, liver disease, and central nervous system degeneration, may also suffer adverse reactions from alcohol consumption.

SCREENING, DIAGNOSIS, AND TREATMENT. The NIAAA advocates screening to identify at-risk drinkers, problem drinkers, and dependent drinkers to determine the need for further diagnostic evaluation and treatment. Furthermore, in *Module 10C* it provides a screening protocol that recommends:

- All adults aged 60 years and older should be screened for alcohol and prescription drug use/abuse as part of any medical examination or application for health or social services.

- Annual rescreening should be performed if certain physical symptoms emerge or if the individual is undergoing major life changes, stresses, or transitions.

FIGURE 8.4

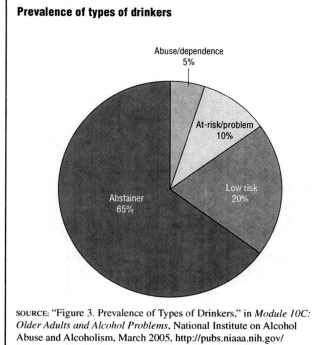

Prevalence of types of drinkers

Abuse/dependence
5%

At-risk/problem
10%

Low risk
20%

Abstainer
65%

SOURCE: "Figure 3. Prevalence of Types of Drinkers," in *Module 10C: Older Adults and Alcohol Problems*, National Institute on Alcohol Abuse and Alcoholism, March 2005, http://pubs.niaaa.nih.gov/publications/Social/Module10COlderAdults/Module10C.html (accessed June 4, 2015)

- These screening criteria apply to any health, social, work, or recreation setting that serves older adults and are not limited to medical care and substance treatment settings.

Diagnosis of problem drinking in the older population is complicated by the fact that many psychological, behavioral, and physical symptoms of problem drinking also occur in people who do not have drinking problems. For example, brain damage, heart disease, and gastrointestinal disorders often develop in older adults independent of alcohol use, but may also occur with drinking. In addition, mood disorders, depression, and changes in employment, economic, or marital status often accompany aging but can also be symptoms of alcoholism. Alcohol-induced organic brain syndrome is characterized by cognitive impairment (memory lapses, confusion, and disorientation). As a result, some older alcoholics may be incorrectly diagnosed as suffering from dementia or other mental illness.

Older problem drinkers make up a relatively small proportion of the total number of clients seen by most agencies for treatment of alcohol abuse. Little data about the effectiveness of intervention and treatment, which usually consists of some combination of counseling and education, in the older population exist. Nonetheless, the chances for recovery among older drinkers are considered good because older clients tend to complete the full course of therapy more often than younger clients.

There are indications that the number of older adults with alcohol and substance abuse problems will increase in the coming years. For example, in "Substance Abuse and Misuse in Older Adults" (Winter 2015, http://www.mhaofnyc.org/wp-content/uploads/2014/11/Substance-Abuse-BHN-Winter15.pdf), Michael B. Friedman and Kimberly A. Williams observe that as the baby boomers become "elder boomers," the number of older adults with substance use problems will at least double by 2030 and will likely outpace the growth of the older population. The researchers note that misuse of prescription and over-the-counter drugs is increasing, especially painkillers and sleep aids. There is also growing misuse of psychoactive medications, including antidepressants and antipsychotics. Because many substance abuse problems of older adults are not detected by family, friends, or health professionals, Friedman and Williams call for public education programs to increase awareness of the problem.

WHO WILL TREAT THIS GROWING PROBLEM? Just as there is a serious shortage of geriatricians (physicians who are specially trained to care for older adults), Bartels and Naslund assert that there is a comparable shortfall of geriatric mental health providers. More than half of the available training slots for geriatric psychiatrists go unfilled each year, and a scant 4.2% of psychologists focus on treating older adults. Friedman and Williams concur and add that other access problems exist. For example, providers and programs that do exist are overloaded or unavailable in some geographic areas or they are not affordable.

Bartels and Naslund suggest growing the geriatric mental health workforce by cultivating "health coaches and lay community health workers trained to provide screening and brief interventions for geriatric mental health and substance-use disorders." Other potential solutions might be Internet-based technologies, which may provide opportunities for screening and treatment for older adults who are unable to seek or access care because they lack transportation or have limited mobility. The relative anonymity and privacy of seeking and receiving care online might also reduce some of the stigma that is associated with mental health treatment.

CHAPTER 9

CARING FOR OLDER ADULTS: CAREGIVERS

In the United States most long-term care of older adults continues to be provided by families as opposed to nursing homes, assisted living facilities, social service agencies, or government programs. This continuing commitment to family care of older adults in the community is remarkable in view of relatively recent changes in the fabric of American society. American family life has undergone significant changes in the past three decades. Most households require two incomes, and greater numbers of women have entered the workforce. Delayed marriage and childbearing has produced a so-called sandwich generation of family caregivers that is simultaneously caring for two generations: their children and their parents. For the first time in U.S. history, adults may spend more years caring for a parent than for a child. Increased geographic separation of families further compounds the difficulties of family caregiving.

Another challenge is that the supply of caregivers is not keeping pace with the growth in the older population. The number of older adults for every 100 adults of working age (aged 20 to 64 years) is called the dependency ratio. Laura B. Shrestha of the Congressional Research Service notes in *Age Dependency Ratios and Social Security Solvency* (October 27, 2006, https://wikileaks.org/gifiles/attach/104/104779_Age%20Dependency.pdf) that in 2016 there will be an estimated 24.1 older adults for every 100 working-age adults. (See Table 9.1.) When the youngest members of the baby boomer generation (those born between 1946 and 1964) begin approaching retirement age in 2025, there will be 31.2 older adults for every 100 people of working age.

In *Occupational Outlook Handbook, 2014–15 Edition* (January 8, 2014, http://www.bls.gov/ooh), the U.S. Bureau of Labor Statistics (BLS) predicts changes in employment for all occupations. For example, the BLS projects that between 2012 and 2022 the number of home health aides will increase 48% and the number of personal care aides will increase 49%. In 2022 an estimated 1.3 million home health aides and 1.8 million personal care aides will be employed.

Furthermore, the Institute of Medicine's Committee on the Future Health Care Workforce for Older Americans observes in *Retooling for an Aging America: Building the Health Care Workforce* (2008, http://www.nap.edu/openbook.php?record_id=12089&page=R1) that about 80% of older adults rely exclusively on unpaid help from family and friends for assistance at home and that less than 10% receive all their care from paid workers. The committee also notes that an estimated 29 million to 52 million Americans—as many as 31% of all U.S. adults—provide some kind of unpaid help or care.

FAMILY CAREGIVERS

According to the Family Caregiver Alliance, in "Selected Caregiver Statistics" (December 31, 2012, https://caregiver.org/selected-caregiver-statistics), the majority of adults who receive long-term care at home rely exclusively on informal caregivers—family and friends. Every year, 65.7 million Americans devote billions of hours providing this care, which includes help with tasks such as bathing, meal preparation, and managing medications, enabling older adults to remain in the community and age in place (remain in their own home rather than relocating to an assisted living facility or other supportive housing). Forty-four million caregivers provide care for adults aged 50 years and older, and of this group 14.9 million care for an older adult suffering from dementia (loss of intellectual functioning accompanied by memory loss and personality changes).

Caregiving in the United States

In "Women and Caregiving: Facts and Figures" (February 2015, https://caregiver.org/women-and-caregiving-facts-and-figures), the Family Caregiver Alliance describes

TABLE 9.1

Age dependency ratios, 2016–30

Year	Population (in thousands)				Dependency ratio (number of dependents per 100 persons of working age)		
	Total	Children (0–19)	Working age (20–64)	Older persons (65–65+)	All dependents	Children (0–19)	Older persons (65–65+)
2016	329,662	86,106	196,245	47,311	68.0	43.9	24.1
2017	332,086	86,466	196,874	48,746	68.7	43.9	24.8
2018	334,497	86,859	197,405	50,233	69.4	44.0	25.4
2019	336,892	87,247	197,826	51,819	70.3	44.1	26.2
2020	339,270	87,547	198,213	53,510	71.2	44.2	27.0
2021	341,626	87,736	198,642	55,248	72.0	44.2	27.8
2022	343,958	87,883	199,059	57,016	72.8	44.1	28.6
2023	346,255	88,003	199,475	58,777	73.6	44.1	29.5
2024	348,514	88,233	199,736	60,545	74.5	44.2	30.3
2025	350,729	88,597	199,789	62,343	75.5	44.3	31.2
2026	352,871	88,942	199,847	64,082	76.6	44.5	32.1
2027	354,936	89,266	199,965	65,705	77.5	44.6	32.9
2028	356,946	89,574	200,139	67,233	78.3	44.8	33.6
2029	358,898	89,863	200,347	68,688	79.1	44.9	34.3
2030	360,794	90,133	200,644	70,017	79.8	44.9	34.9

SOURCE: Adapted from Laura B. Shrestha, "Appendix Table 1. Age Dependency Ratios, United States, 1950–2080," in *Age Dependency Ratios and Social Security Solvency*, Congressional Research Service, The Library of Congress, October 27, 2006, http://congressionalresearch.com/RL32981/document.php? study=Age+Dependency+Ratios+and+Social+Security+Solvency (accessed June 4, 2015)

the average caregiver as a 49-year-old, married, working woman who spends three or more years caring for a parent who does not live with her. Caregivers shop, prepare food, clean house, do laundry, provide transportation, and administer medication. They also assist with personal care, such as feeding, dressing, bathing, and toileting. In addition, caregivers research disease care and treatment as well as coordinate physician visits and manage finances.

Caregiving can take a toll on physical and mental health and well-being. Research reveals that caregivers may suffer a range of health problems, including:

- Elevated blood pressure and insulin levels, which in turn increase the risk of developing cardiovascular disease

- High levels of physical and emotional stress and impaired immune function, which renders them less able to defend against illness

- Depression, anxiety, anger, and other emotional problems

The Economics of Caregiving

Most of the costs and responsibility for long-term care for older adults rest with family caregivers. The shift toward increasing reliance on this informal system of care was spurred by changes in the health care financing system that resulted in shorter hospital stays, rising costs of nursing home care, older adults preferring home care over institutional care, and a shortage of long-term care workers. Taken together, these factors continue to increase the likelihood that frail, disabled, and ill older adults will be cared for by relatives.

In *The MetLife Study of Caregiving Costs to Working Caregivers: Double Jeopardy for Baby Boomers Caring for Their Parents* (June 2011, http://www.caregiving.org/ wp-content/uploads/2011/06/mmi-caregiving-costs-working-caregivers.pdf), the MetLife Mature Market Institute finds that the total estimated aggregate of lost wages, pension, and Social Security benefits of these boomers who serve as caregivers for their parents is nearly $3 trillion. For individual female caregivers, the cost in terms of lost wages and Social Security benefits is an estimated $324,044.

The Family Caregiver Alliance notes in "Women and Caregiving: Facts and Figures" that caregiving reduces paid work hours for women by about 41% and that its negative effect on caregivers' retirement funds is about $40,000 more for women than it is for men. Women caregivers are less likely than men caregivers to receive a pension, and of those who do receive a pension, they receive about half as much as what men receive.

Employers also shoulder many of the costs of caregiving. They spend about $3.3 billion to replace women who leave their job to become a caregiver, and absenteeism among women caregivers costs businesses nearly $270 million. Long lunch breaks and leaving work early or arriving late to accommodate caregiving has been estimated at $327 million, and interruptions during the workday add another $3.8 billion to the business tab.

A Slow and Uncertain Economy Affects Informal Caregiving

According to Susannah Fox, Maeve Duggan, and Kristen Purcell of the Pew Research Center, in *Family*

Caregivers Are Wired for Health (June 20, 2013, http://www.pewinternet.org/~/media//Files/Reports/2013/PewResearch_FamilyCaregivers.pdf), 39% of adults provided care for a loved one in 2012. More than one-third (36%) of U.S. adults served as a caregiver for one or more adults, and 47% of the adults being cared for were either a parent or parent-in-law. Interviewed by Yasmeen Abutaleb, in "Two-Fifths of U.S. Adults Care for Sick, Elderly Relatives" (Reuters.com, June 20, 2013), Susannah Fox, the study's lead author, explained that the number of family caregivers grew 10% between 2010 to 2012 and that the slow U.S. economy spurred this growth—families no longer have the resources to pay for professional caregivers.

The Effects of the Patient Protection and Affordable Care Act on Informal Caregivers

In 2010 President Barack Obama (1961–) signed the Patient Protection and Affordable Care Act (more commonly known as the Affordable Care Act [ACA] or Obamacare) into law. The law reformed health care delivery to improve access to care. In "Transforming the System of Care for Older Adults: The Affordable Care Act Five Years Later" (March 2015, http://www.thescanfoundation.org/sites/default/files/tsf_perspectives_aca5years.pdf), Bruce Chernof of the SCAN Foundation explains that the law recognizes the need for home care services and offers incentives for the states to provide these services through Medicaid for older adults with low incomes—up to 300% of the maximum Supplemental Security Income payment. One of the ways these services are provided is via the Community First Choice (CFC) option, which enables states to use Medicaid funds to provide community-based attendant services to older adults who meet Medicaid and level-of-care eligibility standards. In *Report to Congress Community First Choice: Interim Report to Congress as Required by the Patient Protection and Affordable Care Act of 2010 (P.L. 111-148)* (2014, http://www.medicaid.gov), the U.S. Department of Health and Human Services notes that as of December 2014, eight states (Arizona, California, Maryland, Minnesota, Montana, New York, Oregon, and Texas) were participating in the CFC. The SCAN Foundation exhorts in the policy brief *System Transformation in California: Coordinating Health Care and Long-Term Services and Supports* (July 2015, http://www.thescanfoundation.org/sites/default/files/tsf_policy_brief_ca_ltss_transformation_july_2015.pdf) that the "importance of family caregivers needs to be acknowledged, with corresponding strategies to support their needs in the community," and observes that many states have already "established legal and system supports for family caregivers in addition to existing federal policies."

According to Lynn Feinberg and Allison M. Reamy, in the fact sheet *Health Reform Law Creates New Opportunities to Better Recognize and Support Family Caregivers* (October 2011, http://assets.aarp.org/rgcenter/ppi/ltc/fs239.pdf), the ACA promotes new models of care that better recognize the family caregiver as a key partner in care and provides more support for family caregivers, especially those who are caring for people with multiple chronic conditions. This support includes Aging and Disability Resource Center initiatives, which serve as entry points for older adults in need of long-term care services, and geriatric education centers to offer free or low-cost training to family caregivers.

The Effects of the ACA on Paid Caregivers

The ACA redirects reimbursement to incentivize health professionals to care for people with chronic conditions in the community rather than in hospitals. It created the Community-Based Care Transitions Program to assist Medicare beneficiaries to return to their home following hospital discharge. It also created the Independence at Home Medical Practice Pilot Program that in 2012 began providing coordinated, primary care services to Medicare beneficiaries with multiple chronic conditions in their home.

According to the Commonwealth Fund, in "The Affordable Care Act's Payment and Delivery System Reforms: A Progress Report at Five Years" (May 7, 2015, http://www.commonwealthfund.org/publications/issue-briefs/2015/may/aca-payment-and-delivery-system-reforms-at-5-years), the ACA is providing ways to test new approaches to health care delivery and payment. For example, the Comprehensive Primary Care Initiative involves 29 payers, nearly 500 providers, and about 2.5 million patients and their caregivers in a program aimed at improving access to and coordination of care. Evaluation of this collaborative effort finds that during its first year the initiative reduced emergency department visits and hospital admissions.

ACA provisions aimed at increasing the numbers of health care workers include:

- Grant funding and other incentives to encourage students and health professionals to train in primary care, geriatrics, chronic care, and long-term care

- Funding to train health care workers who are direct-service providers such as home health aides and other providers of long-term and community-based services

- Establishing the Personal Care Attendants Workforce Advisory Panel to assess and advise on issues involving direct-care workers, including salaries, wages, and benefits

- Launching the National Health Care Workforce Commission to advise on ways to better meet the growing need for health care workers

In "Personal Care Aide Training Essential to Quality Care" (Hill.com, October 17, 2012), Jodi M. Sturgeon of the Paraprofessional Healthcare Institute reports that in 2012 the ACA awarded three-year grants to California, Iowa, Maine, Massachusetts, Michigan, and North Carolina to develop statewide competency-based curricula and credentialing standards, which will address the need for better training for personal care aides.

Although the ACA authorized the National Health Care Workforce Commission in 2010, as of August 2015 the commission had not yet become operational. In "The Dormant National Health Care Workforce Commission Needs Congressional Funding to Fulfill Its Promise" (*Health Affairs*, vol. 32, no. 11, November 2013), Peter I. Buerhaus and Sheldon M. Retchin urge Congress to fund the commission, explaining that it is necessary "to recommend policies that would help the nation achieve the goals of increased access to high-quality care and better preparation, configuration, and distribution of the nation's health workforce. In a climate where fiscal policy is dominated by spending on health care, the commission can also stimulate innovations aimed at reducing the cost of health care and achieving greater value and transparency."

THE CONTINUUM OF FORMAL SERVICES

As the older population increases, the segment of the population that is available to provide unpaid care, generally consisting of family members, has decreased. Because the availability of caregivers has diminished, increasing numbers of older adults in need of assistance will rely on a combination of family caregiving and paid professional services or on professional services alone.

Home Health Care

Home health care agencies provide a wide variety of services. Services range from helping with activities of daily living, such as bathing, housekeeping, and meals, to skilled nursing care. Home health care agencies employ registered nurses, licensed practical nurses, and home health aides to deliver the bulk of these services. Other personnel involved in home health care include physical therapists, social workers, and speech-language pathologists.

Home health care grew faster during the early 1990s than any other segment of health services. Its growth is attributable to the fact that in many cases caring for patients at home is preferable to and more cost effective than care that is provided in a hospital, nursing home, or other residential facility.

Before 2000 Medicare coverage for home health care was limited to patients immediately following discharge from the hospital. By 2000 Medicare covered beneficiaries' home health care services with no requirement for

prior hospitalization. There were also no limits to the number of professional visits or to the length of coverage. As long as the patient's condition warranted it, the following services were provided:

- Part-time or intermittent skilled nursing and home health aide services
- Speech-language pathology services
- Physical and occupational therapy
- Medical social services
- Medical supplies
- Durable medical equipment (with a 20% co-payment)

Since 2000 the population receiving home care services has changed. Although the ACA contains provisions to increase community-based chronic and long-term care, as of August 2015 much of home health care was associated with rehabilitation from critical illnesses, and fewer users were long-term patients with long-term conditions. This changing pattern of use reflects a shift from longer-term care for chronic conditions to short-term postacute care. Compared with postacute care users, the long-term patients are older, more functionally disabled, more likely to be incontinent, and more expensive to serve.

Respite Care and Adult Day Care

Respite care enables caregivers to take much-needed breaks from the demands of caregiving. It offers relief for families who may be overwhelmed and exhausted by the demands of caregiving and may be neglecting their own needs for rest and relaxation.

Respite care takes many forms. In some cases the respite worker comes to the home to take care of the older adult so that the caregiver can take a few hours off for personal needs, relaxation, or rest. Inpatient respite care, which is offered by some nursing homes and board-and-care facilities, provides an alternative to in-home care. Respite care is also available for longer periods, so that caregivers can recuperate from their own illnesses or even take vacations.

Adult day care programs, which are freestanding or based in hospitals, provide structured programs where older adults may receive the social, health, and recreational services they need to restore or maintain optimal functioning. Although they are not specifically intended to provide respite for caregivers, adult day care programs temporarily relieve families of the physical and emotional stress of caregiving.

Community Services

Besides home health care services, many communities offer a variety of services to help older adults and their caregivers:

- Home care aides assist with chores such as housecleaning, grocery shopping, or laundry, as well as with the activities of daily living

- Repair services help with basic home maintenance, as well as minor changes to make homes secure and safe, such as the installation of grab bars in bathrooms, special seats in the shower, or ramps for wheelchairs

- Home-delivered meal programs deliver nutritious meals to those who can no longer cook or shop for groceries

- Companion and telephone reassurance services keep in touch with older adults living alone (volunteers make regular visits or phone calls to check on and maintain contact with isolated older adults)

- Trained postal or utility workers spot signs of trouble at the homes of older people

- Emergency Response Systems devices allow older adults to summon help during emergencies (when the user pushes the button on the wearable device, it sends a message to a response center or police station)

- Senior centers offer recreation programs, social activities, educational programs, health screenings, and meals

- Communities provide transportation to help older adults run errands and attend medical appointments (these services are often subsidized or free of charge)

- Adult day care centers care for older adults who need supervised assistance (services may include health care, recreation, meals, rehabilitative therapy, and respite care)

Home and Community-Based Services

Home and community-based services refer to the entire array of supportive services that help older people live independently in their home and community. In 1981 federal law implemented the Medicaid home and community-based services (HCBS) waiver program. Before the passage of this legislation, Medicaid long-term care benefits were primarily limited to nursing homes. The HCBS legislation enabled states to offer services not otherwise available through Medicaid to serve people in their own home, thereby preserving their independence and ties to family and friends at a cost no higher than that of institutional care.

Seven specific services may be provided under HCBS waivers:

- Case management services
- Homemaker services
- Home health aide services
- Personal care services

- Adult day care/health care services
- Respite care services
- Rehabilitation services

Other services may be provided at the request of the state if approved by the federal government. Services must be cost effective and necessary for the prevention of institutionalization. States have flexibility in designing their waiver programs; this allows them to tailor their programs to the specific needs of the populations they want to serve.

In the fact sheet "Home and Community-Based Services" (January 10, 2014, https://www.cms.gov/Newsroom/MediaReleaseDatabase/Fact-sheets/2014-Fact-sheets-items/2014-01-10-2.html), the Centers for Medicare and Medicaid Services describes how the ACA provides new flexibility and enables expansion of HCBS. It details the key provisions and requirements for implementing HCBS under a final rule that was issued in January 2014. These provisions are intended to improve the quality of services delivered. For example, one provision requires that service planning for participants in Medicaid HCBS programs "must be developed through a person-centered planning process that addresses health and long-term services and support needs in a manner that reflects individual preferences and goals."

The National Aging Network

The National Aging Network (September 20, 2010, http://www.eldercare.gov/ELDERCARE.NET/Public/About/Aging_Network/Index.aspx), which is funded by the Older Americans Act (OAA), provides funds for supportive home and community-based services to 629 area agencies on aging, 246 Native American organizations, 56 state units on aging, and over 29,000 service providers. It awards funds for disease prevention/health promotion services, elder rights programs, the National Family Caregiver Support Program, and the Native American Caregiver Support Program. All older Americans may receive services through the OAA, but it specifically targets vulnerable older populations—those older adults who are disadvantaged by social or health disparities.

Eldercare Locator

The U.S. Administration on Aging sponsors the Eldercare Locator Directory (http://www.eldercare.gov/Eldercare.NET/Public/Index.aspx), a nationwide toll-free service that helps older adults and their caregivers find local services. The Eldercare Locator program connects those who contact it to an information specialist who has access to multiple databases, including the National Aging Network.

BenefitsCheckUp

The National Council on Aging offers the online BenefitsCheckUp program (http://www.benefitscheckup.org), which examines a database of more than 2,000 programs to determine older adults' eligibility for federal, state, and local private and public benefits and programs. Users respond to a few questions and then the program lists which federal, state, and local programs they might be eligible for and how to apply. It is the first online service that is designed to help older Americans, their families, and caregivers determine quickly and easily which benefits they qualify for and how to claim them.

In each state, there are approximately 70 programs available to individuals. Among the programs included are those that help older adults find income support, prescription drug savings, government health programs, energy assistance, property tax relief, nutrition programs, in-home services, veteran's programs, and volunteer, educational, and training programs. As of August 2015, the BenefitsCheckUp program had helped approximately 4.2 million people find benefits worth $15.2 billion to which they were entitled.

Women's Institute for a Secure Retirement

Founded in 1996 with a grant from the Heinz Family Philanthropies, the Women's Institute for a Secure Retirement (WISER; http://www.wiserwomen.org) works to help women understand and plan for retirement income. WISER publications help women navigate the complexities of Social Security, divorce, pensions, savings and investments, banking, homeownership, long-term care, and disability insurance. WISER also conducts research and workshops to identify opportunities for women to secure adequate retirement income.

Geriatric Care Managers Help Older Adults Age in Place

The increasing complexity of arranging care for older adults, especially when families live at a distance from the older adults in need of care, has given rise to a new service profession: geriatric care management. Geriatric care managers have varied educational backgrounds and professional credentials. They may be gerontologists (professionals who study the social, psychological, and biological aspects of aging), nurses, or social workers who specialize in issues that are related to aging and services for older adults. Geriatric care managers work with a formal or informal network of social workers, nurses, psychologists, elder law attorneys, advocates, and agencies that serve older adults.

Geriatric care managers work with families and increasingly with corporations wishing to assist employees to create flexible plans of care to meet the needs of older adults. They oversee home health staffing needs, monitor the quality of in-home services and equipment, and serve as liaisons for families at a distance from their older relatives.

Hired homemakers/caregivers, transportation services, home modifications, and other services are also available. The total monthly cost of services varies. An older adult who needs light housekeeping or companionship for three hours twice a week might spend around $300 per month, whereas someone who needs 24-hour-per-day supervision might pay $5,000 per month or more—much more if care from a certified home health aide or licensed vocational nurse is required.

Geriatric care management is especially important for older adults with dementia. Amy Benson et al. find in "Change in Burden and Distress among Caregivers of Community-Dwelling Older Adults with Dementia Enrolled in Care Management" (*American Journal of Geriatric Psychiatry*, vol. 21, no. 3, March 2013) that care managers help ease caregivers' distress, especially during particularly trying periods such as when medication is used to control troubling behavioral symptoms. The researchers suggest that caregiver access to education, support, and care management "may help improve caregiver well-being and ability to cope with patient symptoms, enabling caregivers to provide at-home care for longer periods prior to nursing home placement."

CHAPTER 10

HEALTH CARE USE, EXPENDITURES, AND FINANCING

Health care use and expenditures tend to be concentrated among older adults. Because older adults often suffer multiple chronic conditions, they are hospitalized more frequently, use the most prescription and over-the-counter (nonprescription) drugs, make the highest number of physician visits, and require care from more physician specialists and other health care providers—such as podiatrists and physical therapists—than any other age group.

Nearly all older Americans have health insurance through Medicare, which covers inpatient hospitalization, outpatient care, physician services, home health care, short-term skilled nursing facility care, hospice (end-of-life care) services, and prescription drugs. Historically, older adults' use of health care services has changed in response to physician practice patterns, advances in medical technology, and Medicare reimbursement for services. For example, advances in medical technology and physician practice patterns have shifted many medical procedures once performed in hospitals to outpatient settings such as ambulatory surgery centers.

Older adults are responsible for disproportionate health care expenditures. For example, the Centers for Medicare and Medicaid Services (CMS) notes in "NHE Fact Sheet" (July 28, 2015, http://www.cms.gov/Research-Statistics-Data-and-Systems/Statistics-Trends-and-Reports/NationalHealthExpendData/NHE-Fact-Sheet.html) that per person health care expenditures for adults aged 65 years and older was $18,424 in 2010, three times the spending of working-age adults ($6,125) and five times higher than health care spending for children ($3,628). (See Table 10.1.)

In "Healthy Aging: Helping People to Live Long and Productive Lives and Enjoy a Good Quality of Life—At a Glance 2011" (May 2011, http://www.giaging.org/documents/CDC_Healthy_Aging_AAG_508.pdf), the Centers for Disease Control and Prevention explains that these disproportionate expenses are in part attributable to the fact that 80% of older adults have one chronic health condition and 50% have at least two chronic conditions. The CMS projects that the national health expenditure will grow to $4.9 trillion by 2023. (See Table 10.2; note that because these numbers are projections, they differ from numbers presented in other tables and figures.) Medicare is projected to exceed $1.1 billion by 2023, accounting for 22.3% of all health care expenditures.

FINANCING HEALTH CARE FOR OLDER ADULTS

The Patient Protection and Affordable Care Act (more commonly known as the Affordable Care Act [ACA] or Obamacare) of 2010 contains about 165 provisions that affect Medicare. By reducing costs, increasing revenues, strengthening certain benefits, combating fraud and abuse, and conducting research to identify and strengthen provider payment mechanisms and health care delivery systems, these provisions are intended to improve the quality of health care for beneficiaries and reduce its costs.

By 2015, the ACA had expanded Americans' access to health care. It also addressed aspects of health care reform, including:

- Improving the quality and efficiency of health care—there is special emphasis placed on improving clinical outcomes (how patients fare as a result of treatment) for people receiving care through government entitlement programs

- Prevention of chronic disease and improving public health—the ACA established a national prevention and health promotion strategy; it also established the Prevention and Public Health Investment Fund to expand and support national investment in prevention and public health

TABLE 10.1

Per capita personal health care spending by age group and sex, selected years 2002–10

Age group	Levels				
	2002	2004	2006	2008	2010
Total	$4,768	$5,438	$6,065	$6,637	$7,097
0–18	2,369	2,770	3,117	3,361	3,628
19–64	4,098	4,670	5,273	5,749	6,125
19–44	3,104	3,496	3,845	4,179	4,422
45–64	5,707	6,452	7,312	7,893	8,370
65+	13,345	14,998	16,200	17,577	18,424
65–84	11,692	13,106	14,033	15,181	15,857
85+	25,192	28,252	30,661	33,124	34,783
Males	4,177	4,748	5,322	5,847	6,313
0–18	2,427	2,832	3,205	3,445	3,680
19–64	3,540	3,998	4,529	4,946	5,353
19–44	2,338	2,586	2,821	3,047	3,283
45–64	5,549	6,208	7,038	7,612	8,154
65+	12,665	14,175	15,290	16,686	17,530
65–84	11,716	13,103	14,048	15,217	15,920
85+	22,691	25,042	27,049	29,988	31,670
Females	5,343	6,109	6,789	7,407	7,860
0–18	2,308	2,706	3,026	3,273	3,572
19–64	4,654	5,340	6,014	6,548	6,892
19–44	3,887	4,425	4,888	5,331	5,579
45–64	5,859	6,687	7,576	8,163	8,577
65+	13,831	15,598	16,874	18,250	19,110
65–84	11,673	13,109	14,022	15,152	15,805
85+	26,237	29,648	32,299	34,603	36,296

SOURCE: "Table 7. Total Personal Health Care Per-Capita Spending by Gender and Age Group, Calendar Years 2002, 2004, 2006, 2008, 2010 Level (Dollars)," in "Age and Gender Tables," in *Health Expenditures by Age and Gender*, Centers for Medicare & Medicaid Services, December 2014, http://www.cms.gov/Research-Statistics-Data-and-Systems/Statistics-Trends-and-Reports/NationalHealthExpendData/Downloads/2010GenderandAgeTables.pdf (accessed June 5, 2015)

- Health care workforce—increasing the supply, training, and quality of health care workers

- Transparency and program integrity—providing public information and combating fraud and abuse

- Community living assistance services and supports—the ACA instituted the Community Living Assistance Services and Supports Independence Benefit Plan, a voluntary, self-funded long-term care (LTC) insurance program, to help older adults pay for community living assistance services

Of the many changes that have occurred under the ACA, several are particularly relevant to older adults. For example, the ACA eliminated lifetime and unreasonable limits on benefits, prohibited cancellation of health insurance policies, and enabled people with preexisting conditions to acquire insurance coverage. The act increased Medicare provider fees in rural areas and extended Medicare bonus payments for ground and air ambulance services in rural areas. It also created an independent Medicare Advisory Board to present Congress with proposals to reduce costs and improve quality for Medicare beneficiaries.

The Health Care and Education Affordability Reconciliation Act of 2010 amended the ACA. It contains a number of provisions that are important for older adults, including closing the Medicare prescription drug benefit known as the "donut hole." Jonathan Blum of the CMS explains in "What Is the Donut Hole?" (August 9, 2010, http://blog.medicare.gov/2010/08/09/what-is-the-donut%C2%A0hole) that the donut hole is a coverage gap in the Medicare Part D program that requires Medicare beneficiaries to pay 100% of their prescription drug costs from the time when their total annual drug costs reach $2,800 until their total prescription costs reach $4,550. The ACA, as amended by the Health Care and Education Affordability Reconciliation Act, retroactively provides a $250 rebate to each Medicare beneficiary who reached the donut hole by January 1, 2010. After January 1, 2011, the ACA began decreasing the donut hole by reducing beneficiaries' co-payments, with the intention of completely closing the hole by 2020.

In *Closing the Coverage Gap—Medicare Prescription Drugs Are Becoming More Affordable* (January 2015, https://www.medicare.gov/Pubs/pdf/11493.pdf), the CMS explains that Medicare beneficiaries will pay less in the coverage gap until it is closed by 2020. By 2020 they will pay 25% for covered brand-name and generic drugs during the gap—this is the same percentage they pay from the time they meet their health plan deductible (if any) until they reach the out-of-pocket spending limit, which was up to $4,700 in 2015. (See Table 10.3.)

MEDICARE

The spirit in which this law is written draws deeply upon the ancient dreams of all mankind. In Leviticus, it is written, "Thou shall rise up before the hoary head, and honor the face of an old man."

—Senator Russell B. Long (D-LA) at the original vote for Medicare in 1965

The major government health care entitlement programs are Medicare and Medicaid. They provide financial assistance for people aged 65 years and older, the poor, and people with disabilities. Before the existence of these programs, many older Americans could not afford adequate medical care. For older adult beneficiaries, the Medicare program provides reimbursement for hospital and physician care, whereas Medicaid pays for the cost of nursing home care.

The Medicare program, which was enacted under Title XVIII ("Health Insurance for the Aged") of the Social Security Act, was signed into law by President Lyndon B. Johnson (1908–1973) and went into effect on July 1, 1966. That year 19 million older adults entered the program. In 2015, 55.8 million people were enrolled in Medicare. (See Table 10.4.) By 2030 the Medicare population is projected to increase by 47%, to 81.8 million.

TABLE 10.2

National health expenditures by source of funds, 2013–23

Year	Total	Out-of-pocket payments	Health insurance[a]				Other health insurance programs[b]	Other third party payers[c]
			Total	Private health insurance	Medicare	Medicaid		
Historical estimates				Amount in billions				
2007	$2,158.7	$293.6	$1,611.8	$777.7	$432.8	$326.2	$75.1	$253.3
2008	2,257.3	300.7	1,703.2	807.8	467.9	344.9	82.6	253.4
2009	2,358.0	300.7	1,798.5	833.1	499.9	375.4	90.2	258.8
2010	2,449.6	305.6	1,873.9	859.6	520.2	398.1	96.0	270.2
2011	2,534.9	316.1	1,943.4	888.8	546.2	407.7	100.7	275.4
2012	2,633.4	328.2	2,014.4	917.0	572.5	421.2	103.8	290.8
Projected								
2013	2,735.1	338.6	2,094.1	947.5	591.2	449.5	105.9	302.3
2014	2,893.3	338.1	2,246.1	1,012.2	615.9	507.2	110.8	309.2
2015	3,040.8	345.7	2,372.5	1,082.4	632.7	541.1	116.2	322.7
2016	3,212.8	356.0	2,516.2	1,136.9	669.2	587.5	122.6	340.6
2017	3,395.5	372.1	2,662.2	1,191.3	714.1	626.5	130.2	361.2
2018	3,602.2	391.2	2,827.8	1,252.9	769.5	666.7	138.8	383.1
2019	3,834.0	413.5	3,015.2	1,330.4	825.3	711.3	148.2	405.3
2020	4,085.1	437.5	3,219.1	1,410.0	890.3	760.4	158.4	428.5
2021	4,340.9	461.1	3,427.5	1,489.3	958.9	810.3	169.1	452.3
2022	4,609.7	486.1	3,646.7	1,569.5	1,033.1	863.0	181.2	476.9
2023	4,891.3	512.2	3,875.9	1,653.2	1,111.3	918.8	192.6	503.2
Historical estimates				Per capita amount				
2007	$7,170	$975	d	d	d	d	d	d
2008	7,428	989	d	d	d	d	d	d
2009	7,693	981	d	d	d	d	d	d
2010	7,928	989	d	d	d	d	d	d
2011	8,150	1,016	d	d	d	d	d	d
2012	8,404	1,047	d	d	d	d	d	d
Projected								
2013	8,659	1,072	d	d	d	d	d	d
2014	9,083	1,061	d	d	d	d	d	d
2015	9,464	1,076	d	d	d	d	d	d
2016	9,912	1,098	d	d	d	d	d	d
2017	10,381	1,138	d	d	d	d	d	d
2018	10,912	1,185	d	d	d	d	d	d
2019	11,506	1,241	d	d	d	d	d	d
2020	12,146	1,301	d	d	d	d	d	d
2021	12,791	1,359	d	d	d	d	d	d
2022	13,466	1,420	d	d	d	d	d	d
2023	14,169	1,484	d	d	d	d	d	d
Historical estimates				Percent distribution				
2007	100.0	13.6	74.7	36.0	20.1	15.1	3.5	11.7
2008	100.0	13.3	75.5	35.8	20.7	15.3	3.7	11.2
2009	100.0	12.8	76.3	35.3	21.2	15.9	3.8	11.0
2010	100.0	12.5	76.5	35.1	21.2	16.3	3.9	11.0
2011	100.0	12.5	76.7	35.1	21.5	16.1	4.0	10.9
2012	100.0	12.5	76.5	34.8	21.7	16.0	3.9	11.0
Projected								
2013	100.0	12.4	76.6	34.6	21.6	16.4	3.9	11.1
2014	100.0	11.7	77.6	35.0	21.3	17.5	3.8	10.7
2015	100.0	11.4	78.0	35.6	20.8	17.8	3.8	10.6
2016	100.0	11.1	78.3	35.4	20.8	18.3	3.8	10.6
2017	100.0	11.0	78.4	35.1	21.0	18.5	3.8	10.6
2018	100.0	10.9	78.5	34.8	21.4	18.5	3.9	10.6
2019	100.0	10.8	78.6	34.7	21.5	18.6	3.9	10.6
2020	100.0	10.7	78.8	34.5	21.8	18.6	3.9	10.5
2021	100.0	10.6	79.0	34.3	22.1	18.7	3.9	10.4
2022	100.0	10.5	79.1	34.0	22.4	18.7	3.9	10.3
2023	100.0	10.5	79.2	33.8	22.7	18.8	3.9	10.3

The establishment of the Medicare program in 1966 served to improve equity in health care. Before the creation of Medicare about half of the older population was uninsured, and the insured population was often limited to benefits of just $10 per day. Furthermore, because poverty rates among older adults hovered at about 30%, some of the older population could not be expected to pay for private health insurance. The Medicare program extended health care coverage to a population that had growing health needs and little income.

TABLE 10.2

National health expenditures by source of funds, 2013–23 [CONTINUED]

Year	Total	Out-of-pocket payments	Health insurance[a]					Other health insurance programs[b]	Other third party payers[c]
			Total	Private health insurance	Medicare	Medicaid		
Historical estimates			Annual percent change from previous year shown						
2007	—	—	—	—	—	—	—	—
2008	4.6	2.4	5.7	3.9	8.1	5.8	9.9	0.0
2009	4.5	0.0	5.6	3.1	6.8	8.8	9.2	2.1
2010	3.9	1.6	4.2	3.2	4.1	6.1	6.4	4.4
2011	3.5	3.5	3.7	3.4	5.0	2.4	4.9	1.9
2012	3.9	3.8	3.7	3.2	4.8	3.3	3.1	5.6
Projected								
2013	3.9	3.2	4.0	3.3	3.3	6.7	2.1	4.0
2014	5.8	−0.2	7.3	6.8	4.2	12.8	4.7	2.3
2015	5.1	2.3	5.6	6.9	2.7	6.7	4.9	4.4
2016	5.7	3.0	6.1	5.0	5.8	8.6	5.4	5.6
2017	5.7	4.5	5.8	4.8	6.7	6.6	6.2	6.0
2018	6.1	5.1	6.2	5.2	7.8	6.4	6.6	6.1
2019	6.4	5.7	6.6	6.2	7.2	6.7	6.8	5.8
2020	6.5	5.8	6.8	6.0	7.9	6.9	6.8	5.7
2021	6.3	5.4	6.5	5.6	7.7	6.6	6.7	5.6
2022	6.2	5.4	6.4	5.4	7.7	6.5	7.2	5.4
2023	6.1	5.4	6.3	5.3	7.6	6.5	6.3	5.5

[a]Includes Private Health Insurance (employer sponsored Insurance and other private insurance, which includes marketplace plans), Medicare, Medicaid, Children's Health Insurance Program (Titles XIX and XXI), Department of Defense, and Department of Veterans' Affairs.
[b]Children's Health Insurance Program (Titles XIX and XXI), Department of Defense, and Department of Veterans' Affairs.
[c]Includes worksite health care, other private revenues, Indian Health Service, workers' compensation, general assistance, maternal and child health, vocational rehabilitation, other federal programs, Substance Abuse and Mental Health Services Administration, other state and local programs, and school health.
[d]Calculation of per capita estimates is not applicable.
Notes: Projections include effects of the Affordable Care Act and an alternative to the sustainable growth rate.
Per capita amounts based on estimates that reflect the U.S. Bureau of Census definition for resident-based population (which includes all persons who usually reside in one of the fifty states or the District of Columbia, but excludes (i) residents living in Puerto Rico and areas under U.S. sovereignty, and (ii) U.S. Armed Forces overseas and U.S. citizens whose usual place of residence is outside of the United States) plus a small (typically less than 0.2% of population) adjustment to reflect Census undercounts. Projected estimates reflect the area population growth assumptions found in the Medicare Trustees Report. Numbers and percents may not add to totals because of rounding.

SOURCE: Table 4. Health Consumption Expenditures; Aggregate and per Capita Amounts, Percent Distribution and Annual Percent Change by Source of Funds: Calendar Years 2013–2023, in *National Health Expenditures Projections 2013–2023*, Centers for Medicare and Medicaid Services, Office of the Actuary, September 17, 2014, http://www.cms.gov/Research-Statistics-Data-and-Systems/Statistics-Trends-and-Reports/NationalHealthExpendData/NationalHealth AccountsProjected.html (accessed June 5, 2015)

The Medicare program consists of several parts:

- Part A provides hospital insurance. Coverage includes physicians' fees, nursing services, meals, semiprivate rooms, special care units, operating room costs, laboratory tests, and some drugs and supplies. Part A also covers rehabilitation services, limited posthospital skilled nursing facility care, home health care, and hospice care for the terminally ill.

- Part B (Supplemental Medical Insurance) is elective medical insurance; enrollees must pay premiums to get coverage. It covers private physicians' services, diagnostic tests, outpatient hospital services, outpatient physical therapy, speech pathology services, home health services, and medical equipment and supplies.

- The third part of Medicare, sometimes known as Part C, is the Medicare Advantage program, which was established by the Balanced Budget Act of 1997 to expand beneficiaries' options and allow them to participate in private-sector health plans. The ACA restructured payments to the Medicare Advantage plans in response to geographic differences in fees and rewards plans that demonstrate quality with bonuses.

- Part D, the Medicare prescription drug benefit, was enacted after Congress passed the Prescription Drug, Improvement, and Modernization Act of 2003.

According to the Boards of Trustees of the Federal Hospital Insurance and Federal Supplementary Medical Insurance Trust Funds, in *2015 Annual Report of the Boards of Trustees of the Federal Hospital Insurance and Federal Supplementary Medical Insurance Trust Funds* (July 22, 2015, https://www.cms.gov/Research-Statistics-Data-and-Systems/Statistics-Trends-and-Reports/ReportsTrustFunds/Downloads/TR2015.pdf), in 2014, $613.3 billion was spent to provide coverage for the 53.8 million people who were enrolled in Medicare. The majority of Medicare recipients were aged 65 years and older.

Reimbursement under Medicare

Historically, Medicare reimbursed physicians on a fee-for-service basis (paid for each visit, procedure, or

TABLE 10.3

Percentage Medicare beneficiaries pay for prescription drugs in the coverage gap, 2016–20

	You'll pay this percentage for brand-name drugs in the coverage gap	You'll pay this percentage for generic drugs in the coverage gap
2015	45%	65%
2016	45%	58%
2017	40%	51%
2018	35%	44%
2019	30%	37%
2020	25%	25%

SOURCE: Adapted from, "What Additional Discounts and Savings Will I Have over Time in the Coverage Gap?" in *Closing the Coverage Gap— Medicare Prescription Drugs Are Becoming More Affordable*, Centers for Medicare and Medicaid Services, January 2015, https://www.medicare.gov/Pubs/pdf/11493.pdf (accessed June 5, 2015)

treatment delivered), as opposed to per capita or per member per month (PMPM). In response to the increasing administrative burden of paperwork, reduced compensation, and delays in reimbursements, some physicians opt out of Medicare participation—they do not provide services under the Medicare program and choose not to accept Medicare patients into their practice. Others continue to provide services to Medicare beneficiaries, but they do not "accept assignment"—that is, their patients must pay out of pocket for services and then seek reimbursement from Medicare.

The Tax Equity and Fiscal Responsibility Act of 1982 authorized a "risk managed care" option for Medicare, based on agreed-on prepayments. Beginning in 1985 CMS contracted to pay providers, such as health maintenance organizations (HMOs) or other prepaid plans, to serve Medicare and Medicaid patients. These groups were paid a predetermined amount per enrollee for their services. These became known as Medicare-risk HMOs.

During the 1980s and 1990s the federal government, employers that provided health coverage for retirees, and many states sought to control costs by encouraging Medicare and Medicaid beneficiaries to enroll in HMOs. HMOs kept costs down because, essentially, the federal government paid them fixed fees—a predetermined dollar amount PMPM. For this fixed fee, Medicare recipients were to receive a comprehensive array of benefits. The PMPM payment provided a financial incentive for HMO physicians to control costs, unlike physicians who were reimbursed on a fee-for-service basis.

Although Medicare recipients were generally satisfied with these HMOs (even when enrolling meant they had to change physicians and thereby end long-standing relationships with their family doctors), many of the health plans did not fare well. The health plans suffered

for a variety of reasons: some plans had underestimated the service utilization rates of older adults, and some were unable to provide the stipulated range of services. For other plans, the PMPM payment was simply not sufficient to enable them to cover all the clinical services and administrative overhead.

Regardless, the health plans providing these "senior HMOs" competed to enroll older adults. Some health plans feared that closing their Medicare-risk programs would be viewed negatively by employer groups, which, when faced with the choice of plans that offered coverage for both younger workers and retirees or that covered only the younger workers, would choose the plans that covered both. Despite losing money, most health plans maintained their Medicare-risk programs to avoid alienating the employers they depended on to enroll workers who were younger, healthier, and less expensive to serve than the older adults.

Approximately 10 years into operations, some Medicare-risk programs faced a challenge that proved insurmountable. Their enrollees had aged and required more health care services than they had previously. For example, a member who had joined as a healthy 65-year-old could now be a frail 75-year-old with multiple chronic health conditions requiring costly health care services. The PMPM had increased over the years, but for some health plans it was simply insufficient to cover their costs. Many health plans, especially the smaller ones, were forced to end their Medicare-risk programs abruptly, leaving thousands of older adults scrambling to join other health plans. Others endured, offering older adults comprehensive care and generating substantial cost savings for employers and the federal government.

Medicare Advantage

The Balanced Budget Act of 1997 replaced the Medicare-risk plans with Medicare+Choice, which later became known as Medicare Advantage. These plans offer Medicare beneficiaries a wider range of managed care plan options than just HMOs—older adults can join preferred provider organizations and provider-sponsored organizations that generally offer greater freedom of choice of providers (physicians and hospitals) than is available through HMO membership. Figure 10.1 shows the two ways to obtain Medicare coverage: through traditional, or original, Medicare or through a Medicare Advantage plan.

When older adults join the Medicare Advantage plans that have entered into contracts with the CMS, the plans are paid a fixed amount PMPM, which represents Medicare's share of the cost of the services. The attraction of these plans is that members no longer have to pay the regular Medicare deductibles and co-payments for covered services. Some plans charge modest monthly premiums

TABLE 10.4

Medicare enrollment, selected years, 1970–2085

| | HI | SMI | | | |
	Part A	Part B	Part D	Part C	Total[a]
Calendar year					
Historical data:					
1970	20,104	19,496	—	—	20,398
1975	24,481	23,744	—	—	24,864
1980	28,002	27,278	—	—	28,433
1985	30,621	29,869	—	1,271	31,081
1990	33,747	32,567	—	2,017	34,251
1995	37,175	35,641	—	3,467	37,594
2000	39,257	37,335	—	6,856	39,688
2005	42,233	39,752	1,841	5,794	42,606
2006	43,065	40,361	30,560	7,291	43,436
2007	44,010	41,093	31,392	8,667	44,368
2008	45,150	41,975	32,589	10,010	45,500
2009	46,256	42,908	33,644	11,104	46,604
2010	47,365	43,882	34,772	11,692	47,720
2011	48,549	44,917	35,720	12,383	48,896
2012	50,540	46,477	37,448	13,587	50,874
2013	52,145	47,942	39,103	14,842	52,481
2014	53,492	49,344	40,484	16,244	53,826
Intermediate estimates:					
2015	55,495	50,778	41,774	17,607	55,829
2016	57,071	52,159	43,238	18,650	57,404
2017	58,734	53,605	44,786	19,598	59,067
2018	60,485	55,132	46,037	20,237	60,818
2019	62,286	56,699	47,359	21,015	62,619
2020	64,137	58,333	48,755	21,920	64,471
2021	66,000	59,974	50,160	22,760	66,335
2022	67,910	61,660	51,601	23,589	68,246
2023	69,808	63,349	53,031	24,381	70,145
2024	71,662	64,989	54,429	25,069	72,001
2025	73,549	66,655	55,857	25,774	73,890
2030	81,660	73,894	61,992	28,541	82,005
2035	86,745	78,351	65,834	30,258	87,087
2040	89,328	80,663	67,783	[b]	89,666
2045	90,887	82,047	68,961	[b]	91,224
2050	93,027	83,982	70,582	[b]	93,368
2055	95,930	86,564	72,787	[b]	96,284
2060	99,531	89,838	75,525	[b]	99,907
2065	103,084	93,028	78,230	[b]	103,485
2070	107,021	96,581	81,231	[b]	107,454
2075	111,140	100,332	84,374	[b]	111,613
2080	113,735	102,684	86,363	[b]	114,244
2085	117,156	105,793	88,983	[b]	117,710

[a]Number of beneficiaries with HI and/or SMI coverage.
[b]The Trustees do not explicitly project enrollment in Part C beyond 2035.

SOURCE: "Table V.B4. Medicare Enrollment," in *2015 Annual Report of the Boards of Trustees of the Federal Hospital Insurance and Federal Supplementary Medical Insurance Trust Funds*, Centers for Medicare & Medicaid Services, July 2015, https://www.cms.gov/Research-Statistics-Data-and-Systems/Statistics-Trends-and-Reports/ReportsTrustFunds/Downloads/TR2015.pdf (accessed August 13, 2015)

and/or nominal co-payments as services are used, but there are no other charges by the plan for physician visits, hospitalization, or use of other covered services. However, members of the Medicare Advantage plans must continue to pay the Medicare Part B monthly premium. According to Gretchen Jacobson et al., in "Medicare Advantage 2015 Data Spotlight: Overview of Plan Changes" (December 10, 2014, http://kff.org/medicare/issue-brief/medicare-advantage-2015-data-spotlight-overview-of-plan-changes), more than 16 million Medicare beneficiaries were enrolled in about 2,000 Medicare Advantage plans in 2014. The researchers also note that federal payments to Medicare Advantage plans were grad-

ually reduced by the ACA to bring them into line with payments for traditional Medicare programs by 2017.

Insurance to Supplement Medicare Benefits

In 2012, 12 million (28.1%) older adults had private insurance obtained through the workplace to supplement their Medicare coverage. (See Table 10.5.) The most popular private insurance is supplemental insurance known as Medigap insurance. Federal regulations mandate that all Medigap policies sold offer a standard minimum set of benefits, but there are variations that offer additional coverage and benefits. As Table 10.5 shows, the percentage of older adults with Medigap insurance

FIGURE 10.1

Two ways to obtain Medicare coverage, 2015

WHAT ARE MY MEDICARE COVERAGE CHOICES?

There are 2 main choices for how you get your Medicare coverage. Use these steps to help you decide.

Step 1

Decide if you want Original Medicare or a Medicare Advantage Plan.

Original Medicare includes Part A (Hospital insurance) and/or Part B (Medical insurance)

- Medicare provides this coverage directly.
- You have your choice of doctors, hospitals, and other providers that accept Medicare.
- Generally, you or your supplemental coverage pay deductibles and coinsurance.
- You usually pay a monthly premium for Part B.

Medicare Advantage Plan (like an HMO or PPO)

Part C includes both Part A (Hospital insurance) and Part B (Medical insurance)

- Private insurance companies approved by Medicare provide this coverage.
- In most plans, you need to use plan doctors, hospitals, and other providers or you may pay more or all of the costs.
- You may pay a monthly premium (in addition to your Part B premium) and a copayment or coinsurance for covered services.
- Costs, extra coverage, and rules vary by plan.

Step 2

Decide if you want prescription drug coverage (Part D).

- If you want drug coverage, **you must join a Medicare Prescription Drug Plan.** You usually pay a monthly premium.
- These plans are run by private companies approved by Medicare.

Step 2

Decide if you want Medicare prescription drug coverage (Part D).

- If you want drug coverage, and it's offered by your Medicare Advantage Plan, **in most cases, you must get it through your plan.**
- In some types of plans that don't offer drug coverage, you can join a Medicare Prescription Drug Plan.

Step 3

Decide if you want supplemental coverage.

- You may want to get coverage that fills gaps in Original Medicare coverage. You can choose to buy a Medicare Supplement Insurance (Medigap) policy from a private company.
- Costs vary by policy and company.
- Employers/unions may offer similar coverage.

Note: If you join a Medicare Advantage Plan, you can't use Medicare Supplement Insurance (Medigap) to pay for out-of-pocket costs you have in the Medicare Advantage Plan. If you already have a Medicare Advantage Plan, you can't be sold a Medigap policy. You can only use a Medigap policy if you disenroll from your Medicare Advantage Plan and return to Original Medicare.

SOURCE: "What Are My Medicare Coverage Choices?" in *Medicare & You 2015*, Centers for Medicare and Medicaid Services, December 2014, http://www.medicare.gov/publications/pubs/pdf/10050.pdf (accessed June 5, 2015)

declined from 33.9% in 1992 to 18.9% in 2012, whereas the percentage with only Medicare rose from 9.9% to 15.5% over the same period.

Besides Medigap policies, older adults may also purchase Medicare supplement health insurance called Medicare SELECT, which offers essentially the same coverage as Medigap policies, but requires use of preferred providers (specific hospitals and in some cases plan physicians) to receive full benefits. Although Medicare SELECT policies restrict older adults' choices, they are generally less expensive than Medigap policies.

A less popular option is hospital indemnity coverage—insurance that pays a fixed cash amount for each day of hospitalization up to a designated number of days. Some coverage may have added benefits such as surgical benefits or skilled nursing home benefits. Most policies have a maximum annual number of days or a lifetime maximum payment amount.

The Prescription Drug, Improvement, and Modernization Act

Congress passed the Prescription Drug, Improvement, and Modernization Act of 2003, which represents the largest expansion of Medicare since its creation in 1965. The legislation established a Medicare prescription drug benefit. The benefit took full effect in January 2006. Among other things, it provides help for low-income beneficiaries and those with the highest drug costs.

Medicare Prescription Drug Coverage

Enrollees in the Medicare prescription drug program, called Part D, pay a monthly premium, which varies by plan, and a yearly deductible that in 2015 was no more than $320. They also pay part of the cost of their prescriptions, including a co-payment or coinsurance. Table 10.6 shows how the prescription drug plan works for Ms. Smith, a hypothetical Medicare drug plan member in 2015. Costs vary among the different drug plans—some plans offer more coverage and access to a wider range of drugs for a higher monthly premium. According to the Kaiser Family Foundation, in "The Medicare Prescription Drug Benefit Fact Sheet" (September 19, 2014, http://kff.org/medicare/fact-sheet/the-medicare-prescription-drug-benefit-fact-sheet), in 2015 the monthly Part D premiums ranged from $12.60 to $171.90, a 2% increase over 2014. Older adults with limited incomes may not have to pay premiums or deductibles for the drug coverage.

Medicare Faces Challenges

Like Social Security, the Medicare program's continuing financial viability is in jeopardy. The Social Security and Medicare trust funds are examined annually by the Social Security and Medicare Boards of Trustees, which publish annual reports on the current and projected financial status of the programs. This section reviews the origins of the challenges Medicare faces and the trustees' findings in *The 2015 Annual Report of the Board of Trustees of the Federal Old-Age and Survivors Insurance*

TABLE 10.5

Health insurance coverage for persons aged 65 and older, by type of coverage and selected characteristics, selected years 1992–2012

[Data are based on household interviews of a sample of noninstitutionalized Medicare beneficiaries]

Characteristic	Medicare Risk Health Maintenance Organization[a]					Medicaid[b]				
	1992	1995	2000	2011	2012	1992	1995	2000	2011	2012
Age					Number, in millions					
65 years and over	1.1	2.6	5.9	11.3	12.4	2.7	2.8	2.7	3.4	3.6
					Percent distribution					
65 years and over	3.9	8.9	19.3	28.4	29.1	9.4	9.6	9.0	8.6	8.5
65–74 years	4.2	9.5	20.6	28.5	29.1	7.9	8.8	8.5	7.8	7.6
75–84 years	3.7	8.3	18.5	30.0	30.1	10.6	9.6	8.9	9.4	9.2
85 years and over	*	7.3	16.3	24.4	26.3	16.6	13.6	11.2	10.3	10.3
Sex										
Male	4.6	9.2	19.3	27.9	28.9	6.3	6.2	6.3	5.7	5.6
Female	3.4	8.6	19.3	28.8	29.2	11.6	12.0	10.9	10.9	10.7
Race and Hispanic origin										
White, not Hispanic or Latino	3.6	8.4	18.4	25.9	26.9	5.6	5.4	5.1	5.4	5.1
Black, not Hispanic or Latino	*	7.9	20.7	33.1	30.3	28.5	30.3	23.6	18.9	19.0
Hispanic	*	15.5	27.5	46.3	45.5	39.0	40.5	28.7	20.2	20.2
Percent of poverty level[c]										
Below 100%	3.6	7.7	18.4	—	—	22.3	17.2	15.9	—	—
100%–less than 200%	3.7	9.5	23.4	—	—	6.7	6.3	8.4	—	—
200% or more	4.2	10.1	18.0	—	—	*	*	*	—	—
Marital status										
Married	4.6	9.5	18.7	28.4	28.6	4.0	4.3	4.3	3.9	3.9
Widowed	2.3	7.7	19.4	26.6	28.6	14.9	15.0	13.6	13.3	13.8
Divorced	*	9.7	24.4	32.9	32.4	23.4	24.5	20.2	16.8	15.7
Never married	*	*	15.8	25.5	27.4	19.2	19.0	17.0	17.7	14.5

Characteristic	Employer-sponsored plan[d]					Medigap[e]				
	1992	1995	2000	2011	2012	1992	1995	2000	2011	2012
Age					Number, in millions					
65 years and over	12.5	11.3	10.7	11.5	12.0	9.9	9.5	7.6	7.9	8.0
					Percent distribution					
65 years and over	42.8	38.6	35.2	28.8	28.1	33.9	32.5	25.0	19.8	18.9
65–74 years	46.9	41.1	36.6	30.6	29.8	31.4	29.9	21.7	18.4	17.5
75–84 years	38.2	37.1	35.0	26.7	25.9	37.5	35.2	27.8	20.0	20.2
85 years and over	31.6	30.2	29.4	26.1	26.1	38.3	37.6	31.1	25.3	22.1
Sex										
Male	46.3	42.1	37.7	31.1	30.2	30.6	30.0	23.4	18.8	17.2
Female	40.4	36.0	33.4	27.0	26.4	36.2	34.4	26.2	20.6	20.3
Race and Hispanic origin										
White, not Hispanic or Latino	45.9	41.3	38.6	31.5	30.6	37.2	36.2	28.3	23.1	22.4
Black, not Hispanic or Latino	25.9	26.7	22.0	23.8	27.4	13.6	10.2	7.5	6.5	5.7
Hispanic	20.7	16.9	15.8	13.6	13.1	15.8	10.1	11.3	7.5	6.3
Percent of poverty level[c]										
Below 100%	29.0	32.1	28.1	—	—	30.8	29.8	22.6	—	—
100%–less than 200%	37.5	32.0	27.0	—	—	39.3	39.1	28.4	—	—
200% or more	58.4	52.8	49.0	—	—	32.8	32.2	26.2	—	—
Marital status										
Married	49.9	44.6	41.0	34.2	32.9	33.0	32.6	25.6	20.5	20.1
Widowed	34.1	30.3	28.7	23.6	22.6	37.5	35.2	26.7	21.1	19.9
Divorced	27.3	26.6	22.4	17.8	19.7	27.9	24.1	16.9	14.6	13.0
Never married	38.0	35.1	28.5	23.5	24.3	29.1	26.2	21.9	18.2	16.7

and Federal Disability Insurance Trust Funds (July 22, 2015, http://www.ssa.gov/oact/tr/2015/tr2015.pdf).

A NATIONAL BIPARTISAN COMMISSION CONSIDERS THE FUTURE OF MEDICARE. The National Bipartisan Commission on the Future of Medicare was created by Congress in the Balanced Budget Act of 1997. The commission was charged with examining the Medicare program and drafting recommendations to avert a future financial crisis and reinforce the program in anticipation of the retirement of the baby boomers (people born between 1946 and 1964).

The commission observed that like Social Security, Medicare would suffer because there would be fewer workers per retiree to fund it. (See Figure 10.2.) It predicted that beneficiaries' out-of-pocket costs would rise and forecasted soaring Medicare enrollment. (See Figure 10.3.) Perhaps

TABLE 10.5

Health insurance coverage for persons aged 65 and older, by type of coverage and selected characteristics, selected years 1992–2012 [CONTINUED]

[Data are based on household interviews of a sample of noninstitutionalized Medicare beneficiaries]

Characteristic	Medicare fee-for-service only or other[f]				
	1992	1995	2000	2011	2012
Age			Number, in millions		
65 years and over	2.9	3.1	3.5	5.8	6.6
			Percent distribution		
65 years and over	9.9	10.5	11.5	14.4	15.5
65–74 years	9.7	10.7	12.6	14.7	16.0
75–84 years	10.1	9.9	9.9	14.0	14.6
85 years and over	10.8	11.3	12.1	14.0	15.1
Sex					
Male	12.2	12.6	13.3	16.5	18.0
Female	8.3	8.9	10.2	12.8	13.4
Race and Hispanic origin					
White, not Hispanic or Latino	7.7	8.7	9.6	14.2	15.1
Black, not Hispanic or Latino	26.7	25.0	26.1	17.7	17.6
Hispanic	18.3	17.1	16.7	12.4	14.9
Percent of poverty level[c]					
Below 100%	14.3	13.3	15.1	—	—
100%–less than 200%	12.9	13.1	12.7	—	—
200% or more	4.0	4.5	6.3	—	—
Marital status					
Married	8.5	9.0	10.5	13.0	14.6
Widowed	11.2	11.9	11.6	15.5	15.1
Divorced	15.7	15.1	16.1	17.9	19.3
Never married	*	13.1	16.8	15.1	17.2

*Estimates are considered unreliable if the sample cell size is 50 or fewer.
—Data not available.
[a]Enrollee has Medicare Risk Health Maintenance Organization (HMO) regardless of other insurance.
[b]Enrolled in Medicaid and not enrolled in a Medicare Risk HMO.
[c]Percent of poverty level is based on family income and family size and composition using U.S. Census Bureau poverty thresholds.
[d]Private insurance plans purchased through employers (own, current, or former employer, family business, union, or former employer or union of spouse) and not enrolled in a Medicare Risk HMO or Medicaid.
[e]Supplemental insurance purchased privately or through organizations such as American Association of Retired Persons or professional organizations, and not enrolled in a Medicare Risk HMO, Medicaid, or employer-sponsored plan.
[f]Medicare fee-for-service only or other public plans (except Medicaid).
Notes: Data for noninstitutionalized Medicare beneficiaries. Insurance categories are mutually exclusive. Persons with more than one type of coverage are categorized according to the order in which the health insurance categories appear in the table.

SOURCE: "Table 115. Health Insurance Coverage of Noninstitutionalized Medicare Beneficiaries Aged 65 Years and over, by Type of Coverage and Selected Characteristics: United States, Selected Years 1992–2012," in *Health, United States, 2014: With Special Feature on Adults Aged 55–64*, National Center for Health Statistics, May 2015, http://www.cdc.gov/nchs/data/hus/hus14.pdf (accessed May 22, 2015)

the commission's direst prediction was the determination that, without reform, the Medicare Part A fund would become bankrupt by 2008.

When the commission disbanded in March 1999, it was unable to forward an official recommendation to Congress because the plan it proposed fell one vote short of the required majority needed to authorize an official recommendation. The plan would have changed Medicare into a premium system, where instead of Medicare directly covering beneficiaries, the beneficiaries would be given a fixed amount of money to purchase private health insurance. The plan would have also raised the age of eligibility from 65 to 67, as has already been done with Social Security, and provided prescription drug coverage for low-income beneficiaries, much like the Medicare Prescription Drug, Improvement, and Modernization Act of 2003.

THE MEDICARE PRESCRIPTION DRUG, IMPROVEMENT, AND MODERNIZATION ACT AIMS TO REFORM MEDICARE. The Medicare Prescription Drug, Improvement, and Modernization Act of 2003 was intended to introduce private-sector enterprise into a Medicare model in urgent need of reform. Under the act, premiums and deductibles may rise quickly because they are indexed to the growth in per capita Medicare expenditures.

Older adults with substantial incomes face increasing premium costs. According to the CMS, in "Medicare 2015 Costs at a Glance" (2015, http://www.medicare.gov/your-medicare-costs/costs-at-a-glance/costs-at-glance.html), in 2015 older adults with annual incomes of $85,000 or less or couples earning $170,000 or less paid the standard premium, $104.90, for Medicare Part B. Individuals and couples with higher incomes paid additional income-adjusted amounts monthly, ranging from $209.80 to $335.70 per month.

TABLE 10.6

How Medicare Part D provides prescription drug benefits, 2015

[Ms. Smith joins the ABC Prescription Drug Plan. Her coverage begins on January 1, 2015. She doesn't get extra help and uses her Medicare drug plan membership card when she buys prescriptions.]

Monthly premium—Ms. Smith pays a monthly premium throughout the year

1. Yearly deductible	2. Copayment or coinsurance (what she pays at the pharmacy)	3. Coverage gap	4. Catastrophic coverage
Ms. Smith pays the first $320 of her drug costs before her plan starts to pay its share.	Ms. Smith pays a copayment, and her plan pays its share for each covered drug until their combined amount (plus the deductible) reaches $2,960.	Once Ms. Smith and her plan have spent $2,960 for covered drugs, she's in the coverage gap. In 2015, she pays 45% of the plan's cost for her covered brand-name prescription drugs and 65% of the plan's cost for covered generic drugs. What she pays (and the discount paid by the drug company) counts as out-of-pocket spending, and helps her get out of the coverage gap.	Once Ms. Smith has spent $4,700 out-of-pocket for the year, her coverage gap ends. Now she only pays a small coinsurance or copayment for each covered drug until the end of the year.

SOURCE: "Monthly Premium—Ms. Smith Pays a Monthly Premium throughout the Year," in *Medicare & You 2015*, Centers for Medicare and Medicaid Services, December 2014, http://www.medicare.gov/publications/pubs/pdf/10050.pdf (accessed June 5, 2015)

FIGURE 10.2

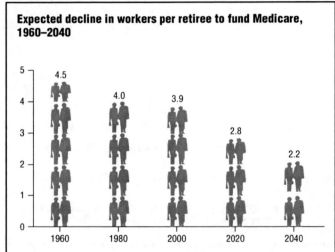

Expected decline in workers per retiree to fund Medicare, 1960–2040

SOURCE: "Fewer Workers per Retiree to Fund Medicare," in *The Facts about Medicare*, National Bipartisan Commission on the Future of Medicare, 1999, http://thomas.loc.gov/medicare/factpage4.html (accessed June 5, 2015)

FIGURE 10.3

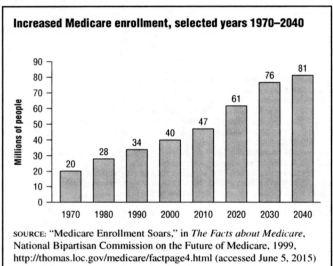

Increased Medicare enrollment, selected years 1970–2040

SOURCE: "Medicare Enrollment Soars," in *The Facts about Medicare*, National Bipartisan Commission on the Future of Medicare, 1999, http://thomas.loc.gov/medicare/factpage4.html (accessed June 5, 2015)

The act also expanded coverage of preventive medical services. According to the CMS, new beneficiaries receive a free physical examination along with laboratory tests to screen for heart disease and diabetes.

Medicare's Problems May Be More Urgent Than Those of Social Security

Forecasts of Medicare costs show them outpacing Social Security costs because it is anticipated that per capita health care costs will continue to grow faster than the per capita gross domestic product (GDP; the total value of goods and services that are produced by the United States) in the future. In *Status of the Social Security and Medicare Programs: A Summary of the*

2015 Annual Reports (2015, http://www.ssa.gov/oact/trsum), the Social Security and Medicare Boards of Trustees project that Medicare expenditures will increase from 3.5% in 2014 to 5.4% in 2035 and to 6% by 2089. (See Figure 10.4.) According to the trustees, Medicare paid out more in benefits than it collected in 2012 and by 2030 it will be insolvent (incapable of meeting financial obligations).

MEDICAID

Congress enacted Medicaid in 1965 under Title XIX ("Grants to States for Medical Assistance Programs") of the Social Security Act. It is a joint federal-state program that provides medical assistance to selected categories of low-income Americans: the aged, people who are blind and/or disabled, and families with dependent children.

FIGURE 10.4

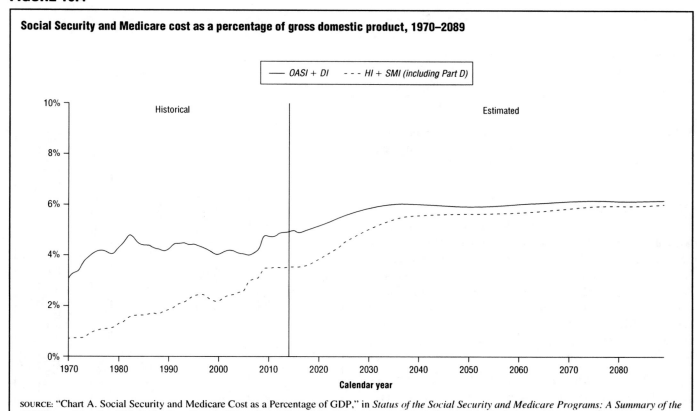

Social Security and Medicare cost as a percentage of gross domestic product, 1970–2089

SOURCE: "Chart A. Social Security and Medicare Cost as a Percentage of GDP," in *Status of the Social Security and Medicare Programs: A Summary of the 2015 Annual Reports*, U.S. Social Security Administration, Office of the Chief Actuary, 2015, http://www.ssa.gov/oact/trsum/ (accessed August 13, 2015)

Medicaid covers hospitalization, physicians' fees, laboratory and radiology fees, and LTC in nursing homes. It is the largest source of funds for medical and health-related services for the United States' poorest people and the second-largest public payer of health care costs, after Medicare. In 2015 Medicaid provided additional coverage for 4.6 million Medicare beneficiaries aged 65 years and older.

Medicaid covers services beyond those provided under Medicare, including nursing facility care beyond the Medicare 100-day limit, prescription drugs, eyeglasses, and hearing aids. Table 10.7 shows the 2015 Medicaid income eligibility requirements for Medicare beneficiaries.

Steve Eiken et al. report in *Medicaid Expenditures for Long-Term Services and Supports in FFY 2012* (April 28, 2014, http://www.medicaid.gov/medicaid-chip-program-information/by-topics/long-term-services-and-supports/downloads/ltss-expenditures-2012.pdf) that 2012 marked the second consecutive year with nearly no increase in national Medicaid spending for long-term services and supports. However, home and community-based services (HCBS) grew to 49.5% of total long-term services spending. Long-term services and supports expenditures reflect continuing efforts to shift expenditures from institutional services to HCBS.

TABLE 10.7

Medicaid income eligibility requirements for Medicare beneficiaries, 2015

[Based on percentage of federal poverty level]

All states and DC (except Alaska & Hawaii)	$1,001–individual	$1,348–couple
Alaska	$1,247–individual	$1,680–couple
Hawaii	$1,150–individual	$1,548–couple
Asset limits	$7,280–individual	$10,930–couple

Notes: Qualified Medicare Beneficiary (QMB):
Monthly income limits: (100% of the federal poverty level + $20.) Twenty dollars is the amount of the monthly social security insurance income disregard.

SOURCE: "2015 Dual Eligible Standards: Qualified Medicare Beneficiary (QMB)," in *Seniors & Medicare and Medicaid Enrollees*, Centers for Medicare & Medicaid Services, 2015, http://www.medicaid.gov/medicaid-chip-program-information/by-population/medicare-medicaid-enrollees-dual-eligibles/seniors-and-medicare-and-medicaid-enrollees.html (accessed June 5, 2015)

In "Economic Impact of the Medicaid Expansion" (March 23, 2015, http://aspe.hhs.gov/health/reports/2015/medicaidexpansion/ib_MedicaidExpansion.pdf) and "Insurance Expansion, Hospital Uncompensated Care and the Affordable Care Act" (March 23, 2015, http://aspe.hhs.gov/health/reports/2015/medicaidexpansion/ib_UncompensatedCare.pdf), the U.S. Department of Health and Human Services (HHS) analyzes the impact of Medicaid expansion and finds that:

- Increases in Medicaid coverage in 2014 led to a significant reduction in hospital uncompensated care.

- The volume of uninsured/self-pay emergency department visits has substantially decreased, largely in Medicaid expansion states.

- Medicaid expansion has had a positive impact on states' economies.

- Medicaid expansion generated federal revenue, increased jobs and earnings, increased state and local revenues, and reduced uncompensated care and hospital costs.

VETERANS' BENEFITS

People who served in the U.S. military are entitled to medical treatment at any veterans' facility in the nation. The U.S. Department of Veterans Affairs (VA) reports in "Trends in the Utilization of VA Programs and Services" (August 2014, http://www.va.gov/vetdata/docs/QuickFacts/ Utilization_quickfacts_FY2014.pdf) that in 2013 approximately 9 million veterans made more than 86.4 million outpatient visits, and patient expenditures were nearly $45 billion. (See Figure 10.5.)

The Veterans Millennium Health Care and Benefits Act of 1999 extended benefits and services for veterans. It enhanced access to and availability of an expanded range of health care programs and improved housing programs. Among the health care programs that were stipulated by the act, the requirement to provide extended care and LTC and a pilot program related to assisted living were especially relevant to older veterans.

The number of veterans aged 65 years and older who received health care from the Veterans Health Administration (VHA) increased steadily between 1990 and 2013. This increase may be attributable in part to the fact that VHA benefits cover services that are not covered by Medicare, such as prescription drugs (Medicare coverage began in 2006), mental health care, LTC (nursing home and community-based care), and specialized services for people with disabilities. Figure 10.5 shows the total growth in people served by the VHA and the growing utilization of outpatient services.

The VA offers many health services that are designed to meet older veterans' unique health care needs, such as post-traumatic stress disorder (PTSD; a mental health condition that is marked by severe anxiety, uncontrollable thoughts, and nightmares that are triggered by a terrifying event such as violence). Its National Center for PTSD (http://www.ptsd.va.gov/professional) trains practitioners how to diagnose and effectively treat this condition in older veterans who may have PTSD as well as other cognitive, emotional, and physical problems.

Benefits for older veterans also include job training and allowances to pursue higher education, vocational

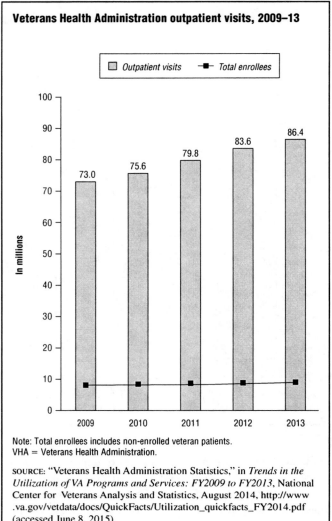

FIGURE 10.5

Veterans Health Administration outpatient visits, 2009–13

Note: Total enrollees includes non-enrolled veteran patients.
VHA = Veterans Health Administration.

SOURCE: "Veterans Health Administration Statistics," in *Trends in the Utilization of VA Programs and Services: FY2009 to FY2013*, National Center for Veterans Analysis and Statistics, August 2014, http://www .va.gov/vetdata/docs/QuickFacts/Utilization_quickfacts_FY2014.pdf (accessed June 8, 2015)

skills training, or apprenticeships. For example, monthly allowances help veterans to attend college—the allowances increase for veterans who have dependents, enabling them to care for their dependents while they attend school.

Veterans and their families can receive respite care to relieve family caregivers of veterans, nursing home services through three national programs (VA-owned and -operated community living centers, state veterans' homes owned and operated by the states, and the contract community nursing home program), home care services for veterans who require regular aid and assistance, home loan assistance, disability compensation for those with service-related disabilities, and nonservice-connected pensions for low-income, war-era veterans. Veterans and their dependents may qualify for education and training programs, and there is a college fee waiver for eligible dependents. In addition, surviving families of veterans who served during times of war may be helped by burial cost reimbursement and death pensions.

LONG-TERM HEALTH CARE

The options for quality, affordable LTC in the United States are limited but improving. Nursing home costs range from $50,000 to more than $200,000 per year, depending on services and location. In "Annual Median Cost of Long Term Care in the Nation" (2015, https://www.genworth.com/corporate/about-genworth/industry-expertise/cost-of-care.html), Genworth Financial notes that in 2015 nursing home care cost an average of $91,250 per year for a private room. Medicaid is the largest payer of long-term services, which includes home and community-based services.

In fiscal year 2012 Medicaid expenditures for nursing home care were nearly $52 billion. Figure 10.6 shows the growth in Medicaid expenditures for institutional and home-based services for older adults and people with disabilities between 1995 and 2012.

Although nursing home care may seem cost prohibitive, Genworth Financial reports that homemaker services can cost an average of $44,616 per year and that home health aide care has an annual cost of $45,760.

Medicare, Medicaid, and Long-Term Care

Medicare does not cover custodial or long-term nursing home care but, under specific conditions, it pays for short-term rehabilitative stays in nursing homes and for some home health care. (Custodial care is nonmedical care that helps individuals with their activities of daily living.) Medicaid is the only public program with LTC coverage.

Medicaid, however, does not work like private insurance, which offers protection from catastrophic expense. Medicaid is a means-tested program, so middle-income people needing nursing home care become eligible for Medicaid only after they spend down their own personal income and assets.

Even then, Medicaid will not necessarily pay the entire nursing home bill. Nursing home residents must

FIGURE 10.6

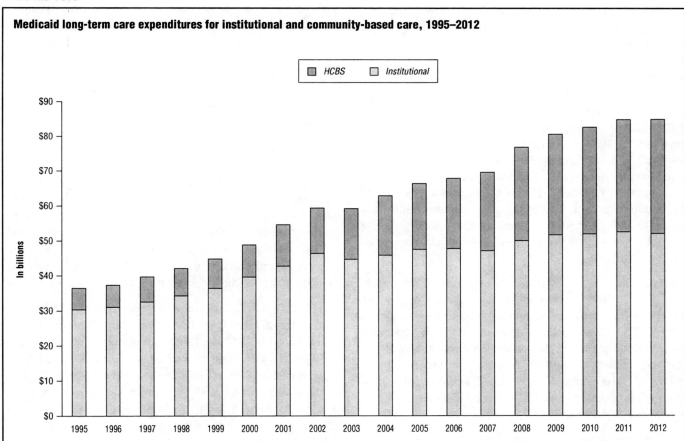

Medicaid long-term care expenditures for institutional and community-based care, 1995–2012

Notes: Institutional includes nursing facilities. Home and community-based services (HCBS) includes personal care, home health, community first choice, Program of All-Inclusive Care for the Elderly (PACE) private duty nursing, services authorized under Section 1915(j), and HCBS in Section 1915(c) waivers, Section 1915(a) programs, Section 1115 demonstrations, and Section 1932(a) programs targeting older people and/or people with physical disabilities.

SOURCE: Steve Eiken et al., "Figure 6. Medicaid LTSS Expenditures Targeted to Older People and People with Physical Disabilities, by Service Category, FFY 1995–2012 (in Billions)," in *Medicaid Expenditures for Long-Term Services and Supports in FFY 2012*, Centers for Medicare & Medicaid Services, April 28, 2014, http://www.medicaid.gov/medicaid-chip-program-information/by-topics/long-term-services-and-supports/downloads/ltss-expenditures-2012.pdf (accessed June 8, 2015)

also meet income eligibility standards. In some states older adults with incomes too high for regular Medicaid eligibility, but with substantial medical bills, are allowed to spend down to become income-eligible for Medicaid. They must incur medical bills until their income for a given period, minus the medical expenses, falls below the Medicaid threshold.

Although every state's Medicaid program covers LTC, each makes different choices about the parameters of its program. Eligibility rules and protection for the finances of spouses of nursing home residents vary, but federal law requires states to allow the community spouse to retain enough of the institutionalized spouse's income to maintain a monthly allowance for minimum living costs. The CMS indicates in "2015 SSI and Spousal Impoverishment Standards" (April 30, 2015, http://medicaid.gov/medicaid-chip-program-information/by-topics/eligibility/downloads/2015-ssi-and-spousal-impoverishment-standards.pdf) that the allowance is set by each state according to federal guidelines—in 2015 the allowance was no less than $1,991.25 and no more than $2,980.50 per month. The community spouse is also allowed to retain joint assets—an amount equal to half of the couple's resources at the time the spouse enters the institution, up to a federally specified maximum ($119,220 in 2015).

Private Long-Term Care Insurance

Another source of financing is LTC insurance. Private LTC insurance policies typically cover some portion of the cost of nursing home care and home health care services. The HHS explains in "What Is Long-Term Care Insurance?" (2015, http://longtermcare.gov/costs-how-to-pay/what-is-long-term-care-insurance) that the cost of a policy is based on the age of the purchaser, the maximum dollar amount the policy pays per day, the maximum number of days per year that the policy will pay for, and optional features such as benefits that increase to adjust for inflation.

According to the HHS, in "Long-Term Care Insurance Costs" (2015, http://longtermcare.gov/costs-how-to-pay/what-is-long-term-care-insurance/long-term-care-insurance-costs), in 2007, the most recent year for which data were available, the average LTC policy cost about $2,207 per year, covered 4.8 years of benefits, provided a daily benefit of $160, and covered LTC at home and in a facility. The average policy also included some provision to protect against the erosion of benefits by inflation.

The premiums for private LTC insurance are tax deductible. The American Association for Long-Term Care Insurance (AALTCI) notes in "Long-Term Care Insurance Tax-Deductibility Rules—LTC Tax Rules" (2015, http://www.aaltci.org/long-term-care-insurance/learning-center/tax-for-business.php) that in 2011 the Internal Revenue Service increased deductibility levels to encourage the purchase of LTC insurance. The amount that may be deducted increases with advancing age. For example, in 2014 people up to age 40 could deduct $370, whereas older adults aged 60 to 70 years could deduct up to $3,720 and adults aged 70 years and older could deduct $4,660. Many states offer tax incentives to promote the purchase of LTC insurance.

In "Long-Term-Care Insurance: Insurers Are Forced to Boost Premiums or Stop Selling Policies" (August 2012, http://www.consumerreports.org/cro/2012/08/long-term-care-insurance/index.htm), Consumer Reports states that between 2007 and 2012 half of the 20-leading insurance companies, including major companies such as MetLife, Unum, and Prudential, stopped selling new LTC policies. Insurance companies are abandoning the LTC market "because they overestimated how many people would stop paying for their policies over time and underestimated the costs of long-term care. And low interest rates have made it difficult to grow the reserves they need on hand to pay claims."

In addition, some companies that continue to offer policies have instituted steep rate hikes. For example, Consumer Reports notes that in 2012 some John Hancock policyholders' premiums increased 40% and Genworth Financial increased its rates 18% for a quarter of its policyholders. For policyholders who are hard pressed to pay higher premiums, some companies offer the option of paying a lower premium for a policy with reduced benefits.

To determine if a person needs LTC insurance, Consumer Reports cites the advice of the financial planner Ken Weingarten. Weingarten indicates that retired couples with $2.5 million or more in liquid assets probably do not need LTC insurance because they can afford to pay for care. Retired couples with less than $500,000 will probably not be able to afford the premiums. The retirees with assets between $500,000 and $2.5 million will probably be best served by LTC insurance.

The AALTCI reports in the press release "$7.8 Billion in Long Term Care Insurance Claim Benefits Makes National News" (AALTCI.org, February 24, 2015) that in 2014 LTC insurance companies paid a record $7.8 billion in claim benefits to 250,000 people. Jesse Slome, the director of the AALTCI, explained, "According to AALTCI research, half of all newly opened long term care insurance claims paid for care in the home," and advised consumers to view LTC insurance as "nursing home avoidance protection."

HOME HEALTH CARE

In *National Home and Hospice Care Survey: Home Health—Data Highlights* (February 13, 2012,

http://www.cdc.gov/nchs/nhhcs/nhhcs_home_highlights
.htm), the National Center for Health Statistics
describes home health care as "provided to individuals
and families in their places of residence for the purpose of promoting, maintaining, or restoring health or
for maximizing the level of independence while min-
imizing the effects of disability and illness, including
terminal illness."

Andrea Sisko et al. observe in "Health Spending Projections through 2018: Recession Effects Add Uncertainty
to the Outlook" (*Health Affairs*, vol. 28, no. 2, March–
April 2009) that between 2013 and 2018 home health care
spending growth is expected to remain steady, averaging
7.9% per year and reaching $134.9 billion in the next
decade. Although Medicare has been the principal payer
for home health care, Medicaid became the largest payer
for these services in 2010, as care continued to be redir-
ected from institutions to home and community-based services settings.

Community Housing with Home Care Services

Some older adults access home care services through
their place of residence. Assisted living facilities, retirement
communities, and continuing care retirement communities
are community housing alternatives that often provide services such as meal preparation, laundry and cleaning services,
transportation, and assistance adhering to prescribed medication regimens. In "Annual Median Cost of Long Term
Care in the Nation," Genworth Financial reports that in 2015
the annual cost of an assisted living facility was $43,200.

The Joint Center for Housing Studies of Harvard University indicates in *Housing America's Older Adults: Meeting the Needs of an Aging Population* (2014, http://www.aarp
.org/content/dam/aarp/livable-communities/documents-2014/
Harvard-Housing-Americas-Older-Adults-2014.pdf)   that
although just 2% of older adults live in group care settings,
37% of adults aged 65 years and older will receive care in an
institutional facility at some point during their life, with an
average stay of one year.

CHAPTER 11
CRIME AND ABUSE OF OLDER ADULTS

A serious human rights violation that too often goes ignored, elder abuse can include physical, psychological, or sexual abuse; neglect; and financial exploitation. Global data indicates 4 to 6% of adults over the age of 60 have experienced at least one of these types of abuse in the past month alone—a conservative estimate that amounts to 36 million cases worldwide. In a 2010 study, 1 in 10 community-residing older adults in the United States reported experiencing abuse the previous year.

—Caroline Bettinger-López, White House Adviser on Violence against Women, in "Supporting Survivors across the Lifespan: World Elder Abuse Awareness Day, 2015" (June 15, 2015)

In "What Is Elder Abuse?" (2008, http://www.preventelderabuse.org/elderabuse), the National Committee for the Prevention of Elder Abuse (NCPEA), a nonprofit organization that is dedicated to the prevention of abuse and neglect of older people and adults with disabilities, defines elder abuse as "any form of mistreatment that results in harm or loss to an older person" and explains that elder abuse encompasses physical and sexual abuse, domestic violence, psychological abuse, financial abuse, and neglect. The NCPEA (2015, http://www.preventelderabuse.org) asserts that financial exploitation of older adults is often associated with other forms of abuse and neglect and that it "threatens the health, dignity, and economic security of millions of older Americans."

CRIME AGAINST OLDER ADULTS

Older adults have lower rates of violent crime than other age groups, and their rate of serious violent crime (rape or sexual assault, robbery, and aggravated assault) stayed relatively constant during the first decade of the 21st century. The U.S. Department of Justice's Office for Victims of Crime notes in *2015 National Crime Victims' Rights Week Resource Guide* (April 2015, http://ovc.ncjrs.gov/ncvrw2015/pdf/FullGuide.pdf) that in 2012 older

adults made up 13.9% of the U.S. population and had the lowest rate of violent victimization. (See Figure 11.1.)

Jennifer L. Truman and Lynn Langton of the Bureau of Justice Statistics (BJS) indicate in *Criminal Victimization, 2013* (September 2014, http://www.bjs.gov/content/pub/pdf/cv13.pdf) that in 2013 victimization rates for violent crime declined with the advancing age of the victim, consistent with data that were reported in previous years. In 2013 the rate of violent victimizations of people aged 65 years and older was 5.4 per 1,000 people and the rate of serious violent crime was 1.1 per 1,000 people. (See Table 11.1.)

The Physical and Emotional Impact of Crime

According to the BJS, most older Americans who are the victims of violent crime are not physically injured. Physical injuries, however, do not tell the whole story. Victimization and fear of victimization can have far more serious effects on the quality of older adults' lives than they might for younger people.

Older adults are often less resilient than younger people. Even so-called nonviolent crimes, such as purse snatching, vandalism, or burglary, can be devastating. Stolen or damaged articles and property are often irreplaceable because of their sentimental value. Furthermore, nonviolent crimes leave victims with a sense of violation and heightened vulnerability.

Older People Are Considered Easy Prey

Because of their physical limitations, older adults are often considered easy prey. They are less likely than younger victims to resist criminal attacks. Their reluctance to resist may be based on awareness that they lack the strength to repel a younger aggressor and that they are physically frail and at risk of injuries that could permanently disable them. The BJS reports that crime victims over the age of 65 years who try to protect themselves most often use nonphysical actions, such as arguing,

FIGURE 11.1

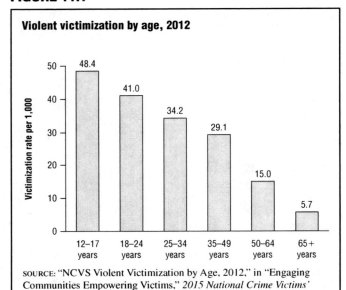

Violent victimization by age, 2012

SOURCE: "NCVS Violent Victimization by Age, 2012," in "Engaging Communities Empowering Victims," *2015 National Crime Victims' Rights Week Resource Guide*, U.S. Department of Justice, Office for Victims of Crime, April 2015, http://ovc.ncjrs.gov/ncvrw2015/pdf/FullGuide.pdf (accessed June 8, 2015)

reasoning, or screaming. Younger victims are more likely to use physical action, such as attacking, resisting, or running from or chasing offenders.

Besides physical limitations, there may be other factors that place older adults at increased risk of mistreatment or victimization. These risks include retirement or unemployment (80.9%), a prior traumatic event (62%), low household income (45.7%), low levels of social support (43.6%), use of social services (40.8%), requiring assistance with the activities of daily living (37.8%), and poor health (22.3%). (See Figure 11.2.)

FRAUD

Older adults are considered easy prey for fraud, deception, and exploitation. They are more readily accessible to con artists than other age groups because they are likely to be at home to receive visits from door-to-door salespeople or calls from telemarketers. Older adults who are homebound or otherwise isolated may not have regular contact with others who might help them to identify possible schemes or frauds. Law enforcement officials and consumer advocates assert that older people are targeted because:

- They are more likely than younger people to have substantial financial savings, home equity, or credit, all of which are tempting to fraud perpetrators.

- They are often reluctant to be rude to others, so they may be more likely to hear out a con's story. They may also be overly trusting.

- They are less likely to report fraud because they are embarrassed, they do not know how or to whom to report the crime, or they fear appearing incapable of handling their personal finances.

- Older adults who do report fraud may not make good witnesses. Their memories may fade over the span of time between the crime and the trial, and on the witness stand they may be unable to provide detailed enough information to lead to a conviction.

In "Is Psychological Vulnerability Related to the Experience of Fraud in Older Adults?" (*Clinical Gerontologist*, vol. 36, no. 2, April 25, 2013), Peter A. Lichtenberg, Laurie Stickney, and Daniel Paulson estimate that the prevalence of fraud among older adults is 4.5%. In a population study of 4,400 older adults, the researchers find that the most psychologically vulnerable older adults with the highest levels of depression and the lowest levels of socialization experienced more fraud than those who were not psychologically vulnerable.

The Federal Trade Commission (FTC) is the government's lead consumer protection agency. FTC authority extends over practically the entire economy, including business and consumer transactions via telephone and the Internet. The FTC's consumer mission includes prohibiting unfair or deceptive acts or practices.

The U.S. Food and Drug Administration (FDA) and the FTC actively work to prevent health fraud and scams. These agencies identify products with substandard or entirely useless ingredients as well as those with fraudulent or misleading advertising to prevent the dissemination of unsubstantiated or deceptive claims about the benefits of particular products or services.

Health Fraud

Older adults may be particularly susceptible to false or misleading claims about the safety and/or efficacy (the ability of an intervention to produce the intended diagnostic or therapeutic effect in optimal circumstances) of over-the-counter (nonprescription) drugs, devices, foods, and dietary supplements because the marketing of such products often relates to conditions that are associated with aging. Also, many of these unproven treatments promise false hope and offer immediate cures for chronic (long-term) diseases or complete relief from pain. It is understandable that older adults who are frightened or in pain might be seduced by false promises of quick cures.

Working together, the FDA and the FTC combat deceptive advertising for health products such as false and unsubstantiated claims for dietary supplements. One example of an FDA action is described in the press release "FTC Charges Marketers with Misleading Claims That Their Supplement Causes Weight Loss, Fat Loss, and Increased Metabolism in Women over Forty"

TABLE 11.1

Violent crime rates, by sex, race, Hispanic origin, and age of victim, 2004, 2012, and 2013

Victim demographic characteristic	Violent crime[a]			Serious violent crime[b]		
	2004	2012	2013	2004	2012	2013
Total	27.8	26.1	23.2	9.5	8.0	7.3
Sex						
Male	30.2	29.1	23.7	10.6	9.4	7.7
Female	25.5	23.3	22.7	8.4	6.6	7.0
Race/Hispanic origin						
White[c]	28.5	25.2	22.2	9.0	6.8	6.8
Black/African American[c]	30.2	34.2	25.1	16.3	11.3	9.5
Hispanic/Latino	20.1	24.5	24.8	6.5	9.3	7.5
American Indian/Alaska Native[c]	165.6	46.9	56.3	46.1!	26.2!	39.0!
Asian/Native Hawaiian/other Pacific Islander[c]	11.3	16.4	7.0	3.9	9.1	1.6!
Two or more races[c]	77.6	42.8	90.3	11.6!	9.5!	26.8
Age						
12–17	49.7	48.4	52.1	13.7	9.9	10.8
18–24	55.4	41.0	33.8	19.9	14.7	10.7
25–34	31.2	34.2	29.6	10.9	10.9	10.2
35–49	28.0	29.1	20.3	9.9	9.5	7.1
50–64	15.4	15.0	18.7	5.7	4.6	6.9
65 or older	2.5	5.7	5.4	0.8	1.6	1.1
Marital status						
Never married	46.2	40.7	36.3	16.5	11.9	9.6
Married	13.8	13.5	10.7	4.5	3.9	3.2
Widowed	9.3	8.3	8.6	1.8!	2.6	5.2
Divorced	36.7	37.0	34.4	11.8	10.9	16.0
Separated	110.7	83.1	73.2	38.9	39.5	33.3

[a]Includes rape or sexual assault, robbery, aggravated assault, and simple assault.
[b]Includes rape or sexual assault, robbery, and aggravated assault.
[c]Excludes persons of Hispanic or Latino origin.
!Interpret with caution. Estimate based on 10 or fewer sample cases, or the coefficient of variation is greater than 50%.
Note: Victimization rates are per 1,000 persons age 12 or older.

SOURCE: Jennifer L. Truman and Michael Planty, "Table 9. Violent Victimization, by Demographic Characteristics, 2004, 2012, and 2013," in *Criminal Victimization, 2013*, U.S. Bureau of Justice Statistics, September 2014, http://www.bjs.gov/content/pub/pdf/cv13.pdf (accessed June 8, 2015)

(May 12, 2015, https://www.ftc.gov/news-events/press-releases/2015/05/ftc-charges-marketers-misleading-claims-their-supplement-causes). The FTC explains that it moved to stop Lunada Biomedical, Inc., from advertising that its dietary supplement Amberen causes substantial weight loss for women over the age of 40 years and that the weight loss is clinically proven. Jessica Rich of the FTC explained that "Lunada marketed Amberen to women over 40 as 'clinically proven' to cause weight loss. But their own studies didn't support those claims." The FTC also objected to the company's claim that "Amberen is 'the ONLY product on the market today clinically proven to cause sustained weight loss for women over 40.'"

Financial Fraud, Abuse, and Exploitation

Financial crimes against older adults are largely underreported but are estimated to total losses of at least $2.9 billion each year. Of those who reported both crimes and their age to the FTC in 2014, adults aged 60 to 69 years made 18% of fraud complaints and those aged 70 years and older made 10% of complaints. (See Figure 11.3.)

This section presents findings from *The MetLife Study of Elder Financial Abuse: Crimes of Occasion, Desperation, and Predation against America's Elders*

(June 2011, https://www.metlife.com/assets/cao/mmi/publications/studies/2011/mmi-elder-financial-abuse.pdf), a study about reported instances of elder financial abuse in the media that was conducted by the MetLife Mature Market Institute, the NCPEA, and the Center for Gerontology at the Virginia Polytechnic Institute and State University.

The study's principal findings include:

- Approximately half (51%) of the reported fraud was committed by strangers. Financial abuse by family, friends, and neighbors was reported about one-third (34%) of the time, and 12% of reported fraud was perpetrated by businesses. Just 4% involved Medicare or Medicaid fraud; however, these represented the greatest financial losses to victims.

- Most victims were aged 80 to 89 years old, and women were twice as likely to suffer financial abuse. Victims were generally vulnerable as a result of having to rely on others to assist them with health care or home maintenance.

- Well over half (60%) of the perpetrators were male, aged 30 to 59 years, and were strangers who sought out vulnerable older adults—those with limited mobility, lived alone, or were visibly confused.

FIGURE 11.2

Mistreatment of older adults by risk factor, 2012

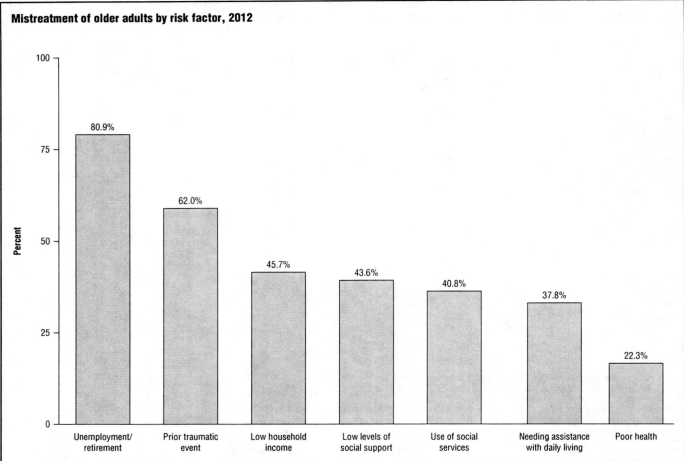

SOURCE: "Elder (Age 60 and Older) Mistreatment by Risk Factor," in "Engaging Communities Empowering Victims," *2015 National Crime Victims' Rights Week Resource Guide*, U.S. Department of Justice, Office for Victims of Crime, April 2015, http://ovc.ncjrs.gov/ncvrw2015/pdf/FullGuide.pdf (accessed June 8, 2015)

- News stories about elder abuse surged during the holiday season—between November 2010 and January 2011. Financial losses during this period attributable to family, friends, or neighbors were higher than losses sustained at other times.

- Financial abuse of older adults is more common than previously estimated and may be as high as 41 victims per 1,000 people.

- News stories cited deceit, threats, and emotional manipulation as well physical and sexual violence as the means that were used to perpetrate financial abuse.

The study concludes that in addition to financial ruin, elder financial abuse "engenders health care inequities, fractures families, reduces available health care options, and increases rates of mental health issues among elders. Elder financial abuse invariably results in losses of human rights and dignity. Despite growing public awareness from a parade of high-profile financial abuse victims, it remains underreported, under-recognized, and under-prosecuted."

Medicare Fraud

Every year Medicare loses millions of dollars due to fraud and abuse. The *MetLife Study of Elder Financial Abuse* reports that Medicare and Medicaid fraud totaled $306.1 million in a three-month period (April to June 2010), during which researchers monitored newsfeeds.

In "The Affordable Care Act and Fighting Fraud" (2015, http://www.stopmedicarefraud.gov/aboutfraud/aca-fraud), the U.S. Department of Health and Human Services (HHS) describes Affordable Care Act actions to prevent fraud, which have achieved "a record-breaking $10.7 billion in recoveries of health care fraud" in three years. The key provisions are:

- New rules and harsher sentences for crimes resulting in more than $1 million in losses.

- Providers and suppliers that may pose a higher risk of fraud or abuse will be given more scrutiny, including license checks and site visits.

- The Centers for Medicare and Medicaid Services will use state-of-the-art technology "to target resources to highly suspect behaviors."

FIGURE 11.3

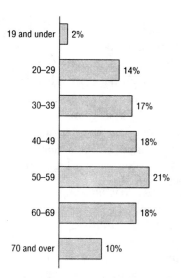

Federal Trade Commission Fraud complaints, by consumer age, 2014

[January 1 to December 31, 2014]

Age	Percentage
19 and under	2%
20–29	14%
30–39	17%
40–49	18%
50–59	21%
60–69	18%
70 and over	10%

Note: Percentages are based on the total number of Consumer Sentinel Network (CSN) fraud complaints for each calendar year where consumers reported the company's method of initial contact: calendar year-2012 = 611,960; calendar year-2013 = 568,631; and calendar year-2014 = 710,366. Of the total, 46% reported this information during calendar year-2014, 47% in calendar year-2013 and 55% for calendar year-2012.

SOURCE: "Consumer Sentinel Network Fraud Complaints by Consumer Age, January 1–December 31, 2014," in *Consumer Sentinel Network Data Book for January–December 2014*, Federal Trade Commission, February 2015, https://www.ftc.gov/system/files/documents/reports/consumer-sentinel-network-data-book-january-december-2014/sentinel-cy2014-1.pdf (accessed June 8, 2015)

- $350 million over 10 years to intensify Centers for Medicare and Medicaid Services antifraud efforts.

To combat Medicare fraud at the beneficiary level, the Administration on Aging (AoA) provides grants to local organizations to help older Americans become more vigilant health care consumers so that they can identify and prevent fraudulent health care practices. The Senior Medicare Patrol (SMP) program trains community volunteers, many of whom are retired professionals, such as doctors, nurses, accountants, investigators, law enforcement personnel, attorneys, and teachers, to help Medicare beneficiaries become better health care consumers.

Brian P. Ritchie of the HHS indicates in *Performance Data for the Senior Medicare Patrol Projects: June 2012 Performance Report* (June 13, 2014, https://oig.hhs.gov/oei/reports/oei-02-14-00140.pdf) that in 2013 there were 54 SMPs and their 5,406 volunteers conducted 148,235 one-on-one counseling sessions and 14,924 group education sessions. Medicare and Medicaid recoveries attributable to the projects were $9.1 million in 2013, which was a 50% increase over 2012.

ABUSE AND MISTREATMENT OF OLDER ADULTS

Domestic violence against older adults first gained publicity during the late 1970s, when Representative Claude Denson Pepper (1900–1989; D-FL) held widely publicized hearings about the mistreatment of older adults. Since those hearings, policy makers, health professionals, social service personnel, and advocates for older Americans have sought ways to protect the older population from physical, psychological, and financial abuse.

Magnitude of the Problem

It is difficult to determine exactly how many older adults are victims of abuse or mistreatment. As with child abuse and domestic violence, the number of actual cases is larger than the number of reported cases. There is consensus among professionals and agencies that deal with issues of elder abuse that it is far less likely to be reported than child or spousal abuse. The challenge of estimating the incidence (the rate of new cases of a disorder over a specified period) and prevalence (the total number of cases of a disorder in a given population at a specific time) of this problem is further compounded by the varying definitions of abuse and reporting practices used by the voluntary, state, and federal agencies, as well as by the fact that comprehensive national data are not collected. Furthermore, research suggests that abuse often occurs over long periods and that only when it reaches a critical juncture, such as instances of severe injury, will the neglect or abuse become evident to health, social service, or legal professionals.

Although the magnitude of the problem of abuse of older adults is unknown, its social and moral importance is obvious. Abuse and neglect of older individuals in society violate a sacred trust and moral commitment to protect vulnerable individuals and groups from harm and to ensure their well-being and security.

High-profile cases of elder abuse and the media's spotlight on the problem have helped increase Americans' awareness that it is a pervasive problem that occurs among people of all races, ethnicities, incomes, and educational attainment. For example, in 2009 the media chronicled the trial of Anthony D. Marshall (1924–2014), the son of the wealthy socialite and philanthropist Brooke Astor (1902–2007), who was charged with stealing millions of dollars from his mother's estate. In October 2009 the 85-year-old Marshall was found guilty of draining his mother's fortune as she suffered from Alzheimer's disease and was sentenced to up to three years in prison. In June 2013, after years of legal appeals, Marshall surrendered to begin his prison term. He died in November 2014.

Greater Efforts Are Needed to Combat Elder Abuse

In her testimony *Elder Justice: Stronger Federal Leadership Could Help Improve Response to Elder Abuse* (March 2, 2011, http://www.gao.gov/new.items/d11384t.pdf) before the U.S. Senate's Special Committee on Aging, Kay E. Brown of the U.S. Government Accountability Office (GAO) stated that in 2009 the prevalence of elder abuse was approximately 14.1% among noninstitutionalized older Americans (people who are not in the U.S. military, school, jail, or mental health facilities) and suggested that this was probably a low estimate of prevalence. During the same committee hearing Mark Lachs (March 2, 2011, http://www.aging.senate.gov/imo/media/doc/hr230ml.pdf) of Weill Medical College noted that a study conducted in New York State revealed that for every reported instance of elder abuse as many as 24 remain unreported. The committee was advised that although family members and staff are largely responsible for abuse and neglect of older adults in nursing homes and other facilities, older adults might also be victimized by fellow nursing home residents.

The committee also heard testimony from Mickey Rooney (1920–2014; http://www.aging.senate.gov/imo/media/doc/hr230mr.pdf), an American actor and World War II (1939–1945) veteran, who suffered from elder abuse. Rooney described the loss of control he experienced:

> In my case, I was eventually and completely stripped of the ability to make even the most basic decisions in my own life. Over the course of time, my daily life became unbearable. Worse, it seemed to happen out of nowhere. At first, it was something small, something I could control. But then it became something sinister that was completely out of control. I felt trapped, scared, used, and frustrated. But above all, I felt helpless. For years I suffered silently. I couldn't muster the courage to seek the help I knew I needed. Even when I tried to speak up, I was told to be quiet. It seemed like no one believed me.

His testimony underscored the observation that any older adult can fall victim to abuse and that this problem is not limited exclusively to older adults in nursing homes or those who suffer from cognitive impairments.

Brown concluded in her testimony that many state adult protective service programs charged with addressing elder abuse have struggled to keep pace with growing caseloads because they lack the funding and leadership to effectively fulfill their responsibilities. She called for stronger and more effective federal guidance for adult protective service programs. Among the many actions to combat such abuse, Brown recommended that the HHS develop an effective method for national surveillance of elder abuse and the collection of data as well as a system for compiling and disseminating these data nationwide.

A National Strategy to Combat Abuse

The GAO explains in *Elder Justice: National Strategy Needed to Effectively Combat Elder Financial Exploitation* (November 2012, http://www.gao.gov/assets/660/650074.pdf) that although combating financial abuse of older adults is primarily the responsibility of state and local social service, criminal justice, and consumer protection agencies, the federal government also has an important role. To identify the issues surrounding this problem, the GAO interviewed state and local social service, criminal justice, and consumer protection officials in California, Illinois, New York, and Pennsylvania (states with large populations of older adults); officials in federal agencies; and elder abuse experts. It also reviewed relevant research and legislation.

The GAO finds that although the states are largely responsible for combating elder financial abuse, the federal government could circulate information and assist to enhance public awareness of the problem. The Elder Justice Coordinating Council, which consists of officials from federal agencies that coordinate elder justice activities, was proposed as a group that could lead development and implementation of a coordinated national strategy. Coordination is important because even though countering elder abuse is the stated mission of just one federal agency—the Consumer Financial Protection Bureau—as Figure 11.4 shows many other agencies also work to prevent and identify elder abuse, to protect consumers, or to respond to consumer inquiries.

In July 2014 the Department of Justice and the HHS released *The Elder Justice Roadmap: A Stakeholder Initiative to Respond to an Emerging Health, Justice, Financial and Social Crisis* (July 2014, http://ncea.acl.gov/library/gov_report/docs/ejrp_roadmap.pdf). Among other things, the road map lists the results of an initiative that asked 750 stakeholders to complete, with as many ideas as they wished, the following statement: "To understand, prevent, identify or respond to elder abuse, neglect, or exploitation, we need...." It also delineates the top-five priorities for understanding and combating elder abuse and promoting health and justice for older adults:

- Increase public awareness of elder abuse.

- Conduct research on cognitive loss and mental health, which are critical factors for both victims and perpetrators.

- Determine the costs of elder abuse, which involves financial incentives and exacts huge fiscal costs to victims, families, and society.

- Provide better support and training for paid and unpaid caregivers who play a critical role in preventing elder abuse.

FIGURE 11.4

Federal agencies involved in combatting elder abuse

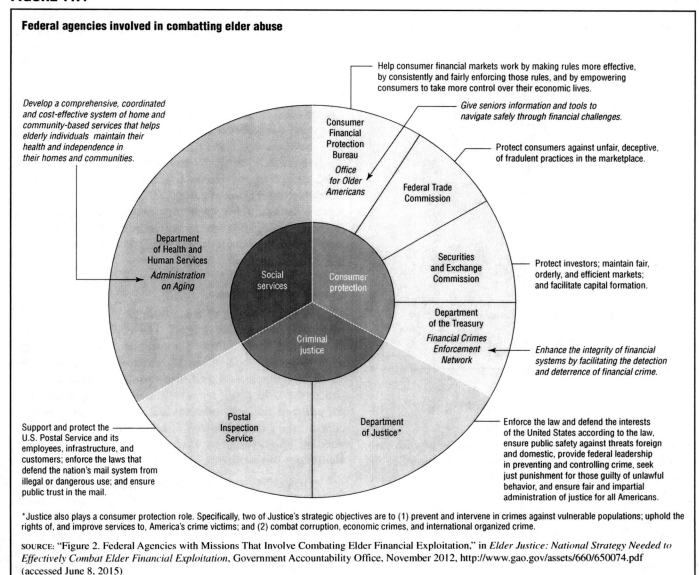

Help consumer financial markets work by making rules more effective, by consistently and fairly enforcing those rules, and by empowering consumers to take more control over their economic lives.

Develop a comprehensive, coordinated and cost-effective system of home and community-based services that helps elderly individuals maintain their health and independence in their homes and communities.

Give seniors information and tools to navigate safely through financial challenges.

Protect consumers against unfair, deceptive, of fradulent practices in the marketplace.

Protect investors; maintain fair, orderly, and efficient markets; and facilitate capital formation.

Enhance the integrity of financial systems by facilitating the detection and deterrence of financial crime.

Support and protect the U.S. Postal Service and its employees, infrastructure, and customers; enforce the laws that defend the nation's mail system from illegal or dangerous use; and ensure public trust in the mail.

Enforce the law and defend the interests of the United States according to the law, ensure public safety against threats foreign and domestic, provide federal leadership in preventing and controlling crime, seek just punishment for those guilty of unlawful behavior, and ensure fair and impartial administration of justice for all Americans.

*Justice also plays a consumer protection role. Specifically, two of Justice's strategic objectives are to (1) prevent and intervene in crimes against vulnerable populations; uphold the rights of, and improve services to, America's crime victims; and (2) combat corruption, economic crimes, and international organized crime.

SOURCE: "Figure 2. Federal Agencies with Missions That Involve Combating Elder Financial Exploitation," in *Elder Justice: National Strategy Needed to Effectively Combat Elder Financial Exploitation*, Government Accountability Office, November 2012, http://www.gao.gov/assets/660/650074.pdf (accessed June 8, 2015)

• Devote more resources to services, education, research, and enhancing knowledge to reduce elder abuse.

Types of Mistreatment

Most documented instances of elder abuse involve maltreatment of an older person by someone who has a special relationship with the older adult, such as a spouse, sibling, child, friend, or caregiver. Until recently, most data indicated that adult children were the most common abusers of older family members, but Pamela B. Teaster of the University of Kentucky indicates in *A Response to the Abuse of Vulnerable Adults: The 2000 Survey of State Adult Protective Services* (June 2003, http://www.ncea.aoa.gov/ Resources/Publication/docs/apsreport030703.pdf) that the landmark 2000 National Center on Elder Abuse (NCEA) survey found that spouses are the most common perpetrators of abuse and mistreatment. Figure 11.5 shows that after

partners/spouses, acquaintances, children/grandchildren, and other relatives are perpetrators of physical mistreatment of older adults.

The major types of elder abuse and mistreatment include:

• Physical abuse—inflicting physical pain or bodily injury

• Sexual abuse—nonconsensual sexual contact of any kind with an older person

• Emotional or psychological abuse—inflicting mental anguish by, for example, name calling, humiliation, threats, or isolation

• Neglect—willful or unintentional failure to provide basic necessities, such as food and medical care, as a result of caregiver indifference, inability, or ignorance

FIGURE 11.5

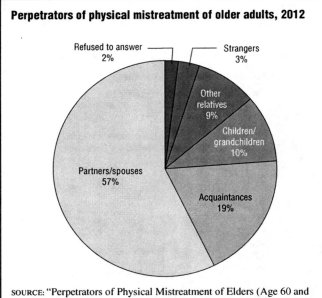

Perpetrators of physical mistreatment of older adults, 2012

Refused to answer 2%

Strangers 3%

Other relatives 9%

Children/ grandchildren 10%

Partners/spouses 57%

Acquaintances 19%

SOURCE: "Perpetrators of Physical Mistreatment of Elders (Age 60 and Older)," in "Engaging Communities Empowering Victims," *2015 National Crime Victims' Rights Week Resource Guide*, U.S. Department of Justice, Office for Victims of Crime, April 2015, http://ovc.ncjrs.gov/ncvrw2015/pdf/FullGuide.pdf (accessed June 8, 2015)

- Material or financial abuse—exploiting or misusing an older person's funds or assets

- Abandonment—the desertion of an older adult by an individual who has physical custody of the elder or who has assumed responsibility for providing care for the older person

- Self-neglect—behaviors of an older person that threaten his or her own health or safety

Reporting Abuse

Like child abuse and sexual assault crimes, many crimes against older adults are not reported because the victims are physically or mentally unable to summon help or because they are reluctant or afraid to publicly accuse relatives or caregivers. Loneliness or dependency prevents many victims from reporting the crimes, even when they are aware of them, because they are afraid to lose the companionship and care of the perpetrator. When financial abuse is reported, the source of the information is likely to be someone other than the victim: a police officer, ambulance attendant, bank teller, neighbor, or other family member.

The AoA estimates in "Protect Seniors in the Year of Elder Abuse Prevention" (December 2012, http://www.co.lucas.oh.us/DocumentCenter/View/11015) that 2.1 million older Americans suffer abuse, neglect, or exploitation each year. According to the agency, this number is only part of the picture: "Experts believe that for every reported case of elder abuse or neglect, as many as five cases go unreported."

In "Examining Barriers to Self-Reporting of Elder Physical Abuse in Community-Dwelling Older Adults" (*Geriatric Nursing*, vol. 35, no. 2, March–April 2014), Carolyn E. Ziminski Pickering and Veronica F. Rempusheski explain that although one out of 10 older adults experiences elder abuse during their lifetime, less than one-third of cases are reported. The researchers interviewed older adults to identify barriers to reporting abuse. They find that older adults' perceptions of abuse vary by both the abusive act and their relationship to the perpetrator. For example, acts by a paid caregiver were more likely to be viewed as abusive than the same acts committed by an adult child serving as caregiver. Other fears that prevent some older adults from reporting abuse is their perception that their caregiving needs are increasing and that they have limited options for caregivers and worry about being placed in a nursing home.

Causes of Elder Abuse

According to the NCEA, no single theory can explain why older people are abused. The causes of abuse are diverse and complicated. Some relate to the personality of the abuser, some reflect the relationship between the abuser and the abused, and some are reactions to stressful situations. Although some children truly dislike their parents and the role of caregiver, many others want to care for their parents or feel it is the right thing to do but may be emotionally or financially unable to meet the challenges of caregiving.

STRESS. Meeting the daily needs of a frail and dependent older adult is demanding and may be overwhelming for some family caregivers. When the older person lives in the same household as the caregiver, crowding, differences of opinion, and constant demands often add to the strain of providing physical care. When the older person lives in a different house, the pressure of commuting and managing two households may be stressful.

FINANCIAL BURDEN. Caring for an older adult often places a financial strain on a family. Older parents may need financial assistance at the same time that their children are raising their own families. Instead of an occasional night out, a long-awaited vacation, or a badly needed newer car, families may find themselves paying for ever-increasing medical care, prescription drugs, special dietary supplements, extra food and clothing, or therapy. Saving for their children's college education, for their children's weddings, or for retirement may be difficult or impossible.

CYCLE OF ABUSE. One theory of the causation of abuse of older adults posits that people who abuse an older parent or relative were themselves abused as children. The National Council on Child Abuse and Family Violence confirms this pattern of abuse in "Elder Abuse

Information" (2015, http://www.nccafv.org/elder.htm), stating, "In a family where there is a tendency to physically harm members who are weak or dependent, the aging members of society, who are among the most vulnerable, become the next victims in the cycle of intergenerational family violence." The council cautions that "it is important to remember that violence and its related behaviors are learned and often passed from one generation to the next. A child who is abused by a parent may become an adult who uses violence toward a spouse or child then, as caretaker for an aging parent, extends the abuse to his/her parent or relative."

INVASION OF PRIVACY. Trevor John Mills of the University of California, Davis, School of Medicine indicates in "Elder Abuse" (February 15, 2015, http://emedicine.medscape.com/article/805727-overview) that a shared living arrangement is a major risk factor for mistreatment of older adults, with older people living alone at the lowest risk for abuse. A shared residence increases the opportunities for contact, conflict, and mistreatment. When the home must be shared, there is an inevitable loss of a certain amount of control and privacy. Movement may be restricted, habits may need to change, and rivalries between generations may follow. Frustration and anxiety may result as both older parent and supporting child try to suppress anger, with varying degrees of success.

SOCIAL ISOLATION. Mills notes that social isolation is linked to abuse and the mistreatment of older adults. It may be that socially isolated families are better able to hide unacceptable behaviors from friends and neighbors who might report the abuse. Although there are no data to support the corollary to this finding, it is hypothesized that mistreatment is less likely in families that are rooted in strong social networks.

ALZHEIMER'S DISEASE OR OTHER DEMENTIA. According to Xinqi Dong, Ruijia Chen, and Melissa A. Simon, in "Elder Abuse and Dementia: A Review of the Research and Health Policy" (*Health Affairs*, vol. 33, no. 4, April 2014), older adults may be at a greater risk for mistreatment. The researchers find that psychological abuse was the most common form of abuse among older adults, affecting 27.9% to 62.3%. Between 3.5% and 23.1% of older adults with dementia experienced physical abuse, and many older adults experienced multiple forms of abuse simultaneously. Dong, Chen, and Simon also find that the risk of death from abuse may be higher in older adults with greater levels of cognitive impairment.

REVERSE DEPENDENCY. Some sources believe that abusers may be quite dependent, emotionally and financially, on their victims for housing, financial assistance, and transportation than are nonabusing caregivers. They appear to have fewer resources and are frequently unable to meet their own basic needs. Rather than having power

in the relationship, they are relatively powerless. From these observations, some researchers speculate that abusing caregivers may not always be driven to violence by the physical and emotional burden of caring for a seriously disabled older person but may have mental health problems of their own that can lead to violent behavior. Several studies specifically point to depression as a characteristic of perpetrators of elder mistreatment.

Intimate Partner Violence: The Abusive Spouse

The U.S. Preventive Services Task Force indicates in "Screening for Intimate Partner Violence and Abuse of Elderly and Vulnerable Adults" (January 2013, http://www.uspreventiveservicestaskforce.org/Home/GetFileByID/890) that intimate partner violence (IPV) and abuse of older and vulnerable adults is common but often undetected. Nearly 31% of women and 26% of men report some form of IPV during their lifetime. As many as 25% of older adults experience abuse.

The high rate of spousal abuse among the older population is possibly because many older adults live with their spouse, so the opportunity for spousal violence is great. Violence against an older spouse may be the continuation of an abusive relationship that began years earlier—abuse does not end simply because a couple ages. Sometimes, however, the abuse may not begin until later years, in which case it is often associated with mental illness, alcohol abuse, unemployment, postretirement depression, and/or loss of self-esteem.

There are many reasons the problem of spousal abuse among older adults may be underestimated and underreported. For example, in "Perceptions of Intimate Partner Violence, Age, and Self-Enhancement Bias" (*Journal of Elder Abuse and Neglect*, vol. 23, no. 1, January 2011), Michael N. Kane, Diane Green, and Robin J. Jacobs find that students preparing for careers in human services such as social work, psychology, and criminal justice were less likely to take allegations of domestic violence between older adults seriously. The students mistakenly assumed that a 30-year-old couple was more likely to engage in conflict and violence than a 75-year-old couple. They also felt that the 30-year-old couple was more likely to change its circumstances than the older couple. Kane, Green, and Jacobs opine that these are ageist beliefs and call for increased awareness and sensitivity to the issue, stating that "raising awareness may help students to identify the possibility of intimate partner abuse when the bruises on the 70-year-old face of Aunt Rose are not attributable to being clumsy but are attributable to 72-year-old Uncle Frank."

Intervention and Prevention

All 50 states and the District of Columbia have laws that address abuse of older adults, but like laws aiming to prevent and reduce child abuse and domestic violence among younger people, they are often ineffective. The effectiveness of these laws varies from state to state and even from county to county within a given state. No standard definition of abuse exists among enforcement agencies. In many cases authorities cannot legally intervene and terminate an abusive condition unless a report is filed, the abuse is verified, and the victim files a formal complaint. An older adult could understandably be reluctant, physically unable, or too fearful to accuse or prosecute an abuser.

Clearly, the best way to stop elder abuse is to prevent its occurrence. Older people who know that they will eventually need outside help should carefully analyze the potential challenges of living with their family and, if necessary and possible, make alternate arrangements. Furthermore, older adults should take action to protect their money and assets to ensure that their valuables cannot be easily taken from them.

Families or individuals who must serve as caregivers for older adults, voluntarily or otherwise, must be helped to realize that their frustration and despair do not have to result in abuse. Health and social service agencies offer interventions including group support programs and counseling to help caregivers and their families. Many communities allocate resources to assist families to offset the financial burden of elder care, for example, through tax deductions or subsidies for respite care.

Medical Professionals Can Help Identify Elder Abuse

Medical professionals (physicians, nurses, and others) can play a key role in preventing and combating elder abuse if they recognize which of their older adult patients might be vulnerable or victimized. The Investor Protection Trust conducted a survey of physicians and nurses in 2013 and published the results in *Elder Investment Fraud and Financial Exploitation: Do Doctors Know the Symptoms?* (June 12, 2013, http://www.investor protection.org/downloads/IPT_EIFFE_Medical_Survey_06-12-13.pdf). In the press release "Survey: 1 in 5 Doctors, Nurses Aware They Are Often Dealing with Older Victims of Investment Swindles" (June 12, 2013, http://www .investorprotection.org/downloads/IPT_EIFFE_Medical_ Survey_ Release_06-12-13.pdf), the Investor Protection Trust lists some of the major findings from the survey, including:

- 92% of medical practitioners said "mild cognitive impairment often makes seniors more vulnerable to investment fraud/financial exploitation"

- 84% of medical practitioners "are willing to refer an elderly patient who may be the victim of investment fraud to those who may be able to help them with their financial affairs or to the proper authorities for help"

- 82% of medical practitioners said "investment fraud/ financial exploitation targeting the elderly is a serious problem"

- 61% of medical practitioners expressed interest "in continuing medical education ... credits to learn more about spotting the signs of investment fraud/ financial exploitation of the elderly"

- 21% of medical practitioners said "they are aware that they often are dealing with the elderly victims of investment fraud/financial exploitation"

INSTITUTIONAL ABUSE: A FORGOTTEN POPULATION?

Abuse of the older population can and does occur in the institutions (nursing homes, board-and-care facilities, and retirement homes) that are charged with, and compensated for, caring for the nation's older population. The term *institutional abuse* generally refers to the same forms of abuse as domestic abuse crimes but is perpetrated by people who have legal or contractual obligations to provide older adults with care. Although the Omnibus Budget Reconciliation Act of 1987 states that nursing homes must take steps to attain or maintain the "highest practicable physical, mental, and psychosocial well-being of each resident," too many residents are victims of neglect or abuse by these facilities or their employees.

Older adult residents of long-term care facilities or supportive housing are thought to be at higher risk for abuse and neglect than community-dwelling older adults. They are particularly vulnerable because most suffer from one or more chronic diseases that impair their physical and cognitive functioning, rendering them dependent on others. Furthermore, many are either unable to report abuse or neglect or are fearful that reporting may generate reprisals from the facility staff or otherwise adversely affect their life. Others are unaware of the availability of help.

There are federal laws and regulations that govern nursing homes, but there is no federal oversight of residential care facilities, such as personal care homes, adult congregate living facilities, residential care homes, homes for the aged, domiciliary care homes, board-and-care homes, and assisted living facilities. As a result, it is more difficult than with nursing homes to estimate the prevalence or nature of abuse or neglect in these facilities. Despite reports in recent years that have raised the specter of widespread and serious abuse of institutionalized older people, as of August 2015 there had never been a systematic study of the prevalence of abuse in nursing homes or other residential facilities.

Several studies of elder abuse in long-term care facilities—such as Lawrence B. Schiamberg et al.'s

"Physical Abuse of Older Adults in Nursing Homes: A Random Sample Survey of Adults with an Elderly Family Member in a Nursing Home" (*Journal of Elder Abuse and Neglect*, vol. 24, no. 1, 2012), Linda R. Phillips and Guifang Gao's "Mistreatment in Assisted Living Facilities: Complaints, Substantiations, and Risk Factors" (*Gerontologist*, vol. 51, no. 3, January 2011), and Radka Buzgová and Katerina Ivanová's "Violation of Ethical Principles in Institutional Care for Older People" (*Nursing Ethics*, vol. 18, no. 1, January 2011)—find that it is associated with high staff turnover, which in turn may reflect unsatisfactory working conditions or other organizational problems as well as the use of unlicensed or poorly trained personnel.

Types of Abuse and Neglect

Institutional neglect and abuse can take many forms. In *An Examination of Resident Abuse in Assisted Living Facilities* (March 2013, https://www.ncjrs.gov/pdffiles1/nij/grants/241611.pdf), Nicholas Castle of the University of Pittsburgh analyzes survey data from facility administrators and direct care workers to improve understanding of institutional abuse. Table 11.2 shows the estimated prevalence rates of various types of staff abuse of residents from Castle's analysis.

Resident Risk Factors

Although there has been scant research describing the factors that contribute to risk for abuse of institutionalized older adults, some studies indicate that the risk for abuse increases in direct relationship to the older resident's dependence on the facility's staff for safety, protection, and care. For example, Diana K. Harris and Michael L. Benson, in *Maltreatment of Patients in Nursing Homes: There Is No Safe Place* (2006), and Mark Miller, a New York State long-term care ombudsman, in "Ombudsmen on the Front Line: Improving Quality of Care and Preventing Abuse in Nursing Homes" (*Generations*, vol. 2, no. 4, July–August 2001), suggest that residents with Alzheimer's disease or dementia are at greater risk for abuse in the average nursing home population. In "Elder Abuse and Neglect in Long-Term Care" (*Clinics in Geriatric Medicine*, vol. 21, no. 2, May 2005), Seema Joshi and Joseph H. Flaherty of the St. Louis Veterans Administration Medical Center indicate that residents with behavioral symptoms, such as physical aggressiveness, appear to be at higher risk for abuse by staff; this finding is supported by interviews with the certified nursing assistants.

Castle observes that social isolation and powerlessness may also increase the risk for abuse. Residents who have no visitors are especially vulnerable because they lack family or friends who could oversee their care, bear witness to and report any abuses, and advocate on their behalf.

TABLE 11.2

Estimated rates of abuse in assisted living facilities, 2013

Category and item	Estimated prevalence rate per 1,000 residents per year
Verbal abuse from staff	
Yelling	131
Nasty remarks	152
Swearing	173
Humiliating remarks	203
Argumentative with resident	160
Physical abuse from staff	
Pushing, grabbing, or pinching	41
Pulling hair or kicking	24
Hurting resident	35
Throw things at resident	46
Hitting a resident	31
Bullying a resident	73
Aggressive behavior	50
Psychological abuse from staff	
Threatening remarks	127
Critical remarks	163
Threatening to stop caring	22
Caregiving abuse from staff	
Not giving food	31
Not giving fluids	25
Medication abuse from staff	
Not giving needed medication	43
Given excessive medication	32
Delayed giving medication	158
Material exploitation from staff	
Stealing things	44
Stealing money	22
Sign important documents without permission	12
Destroying things	36
Sexual abuse from staff	
Unwelcome touching	16
Unwelcome discussion of sexual activity	12
Exposure of private-body parts to embarrass	21
Digital penetration	<1

SOURCE: Nicholas Castle, "Table 6. Estimated Rates of Staff Abuse in Assisted Living (N = 12,555)," in *An Examination of Resident Abuse in Assisted Living Facilities*, U.S. Department of Justice, Office of Justice Programs, National Institute of Justice, March 2013, https://www.ncjrs.gov/pdffiles1/nij/grants/241611.pdf (accessed June 8, 2015)

Efforts to Identify and Reduce Abuse

In an effort to improve the quality of care and eliminate abuse in nursing homes, government regulations and laws have been enacted that require greater supervision and scrutiny of nursing homes. President Ronald Reagan (1911–2004) signed the Omnibus Budget Reconciliation Act of 1987, which included protections for patient rights and treatment. The law went into effect in 1990, but compliance with the law varies from state to state and from one nursing facility to another.

In 1987 the AoA established the Prevention of Elder Abuse, Neglect, and Exploitation program. This program trains law enforcement officers, health care workers, and other professionals about how to identify and respond to elder abuse and supports education campaigns to increase public awareness of elder abuse and how to prevent it.

Many states have adopted additional legislation to help stem instances of institutional abuse and neglect. For example, in 1998 the state of New York enacted Kathy's Law, which created the new felony-level crime of "abuse of a vulnerable elderly person." At the state level there are many agencies involved in identifying and investigating cases of abuse and neglect. These agencies differ across states but may include ombudsmen (offices that assist patients who have complaints), adult protective services, the state survey agency responsible for licensing nursing homes, the state agency responsible for the operation of the nurse aide registry, Medicaid fraud units in the attorney general's office, and professional licensing boards.

The NCEA asserts in "Raise Awareness" (2015, http://www.ncea.aoa.gov/Get_Involved/Awareness/index .aspx) that raising public awareness of the problem is vital for preventing it. It encourages adult children to discuss mistreatment, abuse, and exploitation with their parents and other older adults and to take specific steps to reduce the risk of abuse, such as by carefully screening prospective caregivers.

LONG-TERM CARE OMBUDSMAN PROGRAM. Long-term care ombudsmen are advocates for residents of nursing homes, board-and-care homes, assisted living facilities, and other adult care facilities. The Long-Term Care Ombudsman Program was established under the Older Americans Act of 1965, which is administered by the AoA.

In "Long-Term Care Ombudsman Program" (December 31, 2014, http://www.aoa.acl.gov/AoA_Programs/ Elder_Rights/Ombudsman/index.aspx), the AoA reports that 8,290 volunteers and 1,233 paid ombudsmen worked to resolve 190,592 complaints in fiscal year 2013. More than two-thirds (70%) of all nursing homes and more than a quarter (29%) of all board-and-care, assisted living, and similar homes were visited regularly by state and local ombudsmen.

IMPORTANT NAMES
AND ADDRESSES

AARP (formerly the American Association of Retired Persons)
601 E St. NW
Washington, DC 20049
1-888-687-2277
URL: http://www.aarp.org/

ACAPcommunity
PO Box 8278
Morganton, NC 28680
1-877-599-2227
URL: http://www.acapcommunity.org

Administration on Aging
One Massachusetts Ave. NW
Washington, DC 20001
(202) 401-4634
FAX: (202) 357-3555
E-mail: aclinfo@acl.hhs.gov
URL: http://www.aoa.gov/

Alliance for Aging Research
1700 K St. NW, Ste. 740
Washington, DC 20006
(202) 293-2856
FAX: (202) 955-8394
E-mail: info@agingresearch.org
URL: http://www.agingresearch.org/

Alzheimer's Association
225 N. Michigan Ave., 17th Floor
Chicago, IL 60601-7633
(312) 335-8700
1-800-272-3900
FAX: 1-866-699-1246
E-mail: info@alz.org
URL: http://www.alz.org/

American Association for Geriatric Psychiatry
6728 Old McLean Village Dr.
McLean, VA 22101
(703) 556-9222
FAX: (703) 556-8729
E-mail: main@aagponline.org
URL: http://www.aagponline.org/

American Geriatrics Society
40 Fulton St., 18th Floor
New York, NY 10038
(212) 308-1414
FAX: (212) 832-8646
E-mail: info.amger@americangeriatrics.org
URL: http://www.americangeriatrics.org/

American Heart Association
7272 Greenville Ave.
Dallas, TX 75231
1-800-242-8721
URL: http://www.americanheart.org/

ARCH National Respite Network and Resource Center
4016 Oxford St.
Annandale, VA 22003
(703) 256-2084
FAX: (703) 256-0541
URL: http://archrespite.org/

Arthritis Foundation
1330 W. Peachtree St., Ste. 100
Atlanta, GA 30309
(404) 872-7100
URL: http://www.arthritis.org/

Assisted Living Federation of America
1650 King St., Ste. 602
Alexandria, VA 22314
(703) 894-1805
FAX: (703) 894-1831
URL: http://www.alfa.org/

Boomer Project
2601 Floyd Ave.
Richmond, VA 23220
(804) 358-8981
FAX: (804) 342-1790
URL: http://www.boomerproject.com/

Caregiver Action Network (formerly the National Family Caregivers Association)
1130 Connecticut Ave. NW, Ste. 300
Washington, DC 20036
(202) 454-3970

E-mail: info@caregiveraction.org
URL: http://caregiveraction.org/

Centers for Disease Control and Prevention
1600 Clifton Rd.
Atlanta, GA 30329-4027
1-800-232-4636
URL: http://www.cdc.gov/

Centers for Medicare and Medicaid Services
7500 Security Blvd.
Baltimore, MD 21244
(410) 786-3000
1-877-267-2323
URL: http://www.cms.gov/

CNY Mature Workers Employment Alliance
826 Euclid Ave.
Syracuse, NY 13210
(315) 446-3587
URL: http://cnymwa.ning.com/

Eldercare Locator Directory
1-800-677-1116
URL: http://www.eldercare.gov/

Encore.org
PO Box 29542
San Francisco, CA 94129
(415) 430-0141
FAX: (415) 430-0144
URL: http://www.encore.org/

Family Caregiver Alliance
785 Market St., Ste. 750
San Francisco, CA 94103
(415) 434-3388
1-800-445-8106
E-mail: info@caregiver.org
URL: http://www.caregiver.org/

Gerontological Society of America
1220 L St. NW, Ste. 901
Washington, DC 20005
(202) 842-1275
FAX: (202) 842-1150
URL: http://www.geron.org/

Insurance Institute for Highway Safety
1005 N. Glebe Rd., Ste. 800
Arlington, VA 22201
(703) 247-1500
FAX: (703) 247-1588
URL: http://www.highwaysafety.org/

Justice in Aging (formerly the National Senior Citizens Law Center)
1444 Eye St. NW, Ste. 1100
Washington, DC 20005
(202) 289-6976
URL: http://www.justiceinaging.org/

LeadingAge
2519 Connecticut Ave. NW
Washington, DC 20008-1520
(202) 783-2242
FAX: (202) 783-2255
E-mail: info@leadingage.org
URL: http://leadingage.org/

Medicare Rights Center
1825 K St. NW, Ste. 400
Washington, DC 20006
(202) 637-0961
1-800-333-4114
FAX: (202) 637-0962
URL: http://www.medicarerights.org/

National Academy of Elder Law Attorneys
1577 Spring Hill Rd., Ste. 310
Vienna, VA 22182
(703) 942-5711
FAX: (703) 563-9504
URL: http://www.naela.org/

National Alliance for Caregiving
4720 Montgomery Ln., Ste. 205
Bethesda, MD 20814
(301) 718-8444
FAX: (301) 951-9067
URL: http://www.caregiving.org/

National Association for Home Care and Hospice
228 Seventh St. SE
Washington, DC 20003
(202) 547-7424
FAX: (202) 547-3540
URL: http://www.nahc.org/

National Caucus and Center on Black Aged
1220 L St. NW, Ste. 800
Washington, DC 20005
(202) 637-8400
FAX: (202) 347-0895
URL: http://www.ncba-aged.org/

National Center for Health Statistics Division of Data Services
3311 Toledo Rd.
Hyattsville, MD 20782
1-800-232-4636
URL: http://www.cdc.gov/nchs

National Center on Elder Abuse University of Southern California Keck School of Medicine Department of Family Medicine and Geriatrics
1000 S. Fremont Ave., Unit 22 Bldg. A-6
Alhambra, CA 91803
1-855-500-3537
FAX: (626) 457-4090
URL: http://www.ncea.aoa.gov/

National Consumer Voice for Quality Long-Term Care (formerly the National Citizens' Coalition for Nursing Home Reform)
1001 Connecticut Ave. NW, Ste. 425
Washington, DC 20036
(202) 332-2275
FAX: 1-866-230-9789
E-mail: info@theconsumervoice.org
URL: http://www.theconsumervoice.org/

National Hispanic Council on Aging
Walker Bldg.
734 15th St. NW, Ste. 1050
Washington, DC 20005
(202) 347-9733
FAX: (202) 347-9735
URL: http://www.nhcoa.org/

National Hospice and Palliative Care Organization
1731 King St.
Alexandria, VA 22314
(703) 837-1500
FAX: (703) 837-1233
E-mail: nhpco_info@nhpco.org
URL: http://www.nhpco.org/

National Indian Council on Aging
10501 Montgomery Blvd. NE, Ste. 210
Albuquerque, NM 87111
(505) 292-2001
FAX: (505) 292-1922
URL: http://www.nicoa.org/

National Institute on Aging
Bldg. 31, Rm. 5C27
31 Center Dr., MSC 2292
Bethesda, MD 20892
(301) 496-1752
FAX: (301) 496-1072
E-mail: nianews3@mail.nih.gov
URL: http://www.nih.gov/nia

National Osteoporosis Foundation
1150 17th St. NW, Ste. 850
Washington, DC 20036
(202) 223-2226
1-800-231-4222
FAX: (202) 223-2237
URL: http://www.nof.org/

National PACE Association
675 N. Washington St., Ste. 300
Alexandria, VA 22314

(703) 535-1565
FAX: (703) 535-1566
E-mail: info@npaonline.org
URL: http://www.npaonline.org/

National Society for American Indian Elderly
PO Box 50070
Phoenix, AZ 85076
(602) 424-0542
E-mail: info@nsaie.org
URL: http://www.nsaie.org/

OWL The Voice of Women 40+
1625 Eye St. NW, Ste. 600
Washington, DC 20006
(202) 450-8986
E-mail: info@owl-national.org
URL: http://www.owl-national.org/

Pension Benefit Guaranty Corporation
1200 K St. NW
Washington, DC 20005-4026
(202) 326-4026
1-800-736-2444
URL: http://www.pbgc.gov/

Pension Rights Center
1350 Connecticut Ave. NW, Ste. 206
Washington, DC 20036
(202) 296-3776
1-888-420-6550
URL: http://www.pensionrights.org/

SeniorNet
5237 Summerlin Commons Blvd., Ste. 314
Fort Myers, FL 33907
(239) 275-2202
FAX: (239) 275-2501
URL: http://www.seniornet.org/

Service Corps of Retired Executives
409 Third St. SW, Sixth Floor
Washington, DC 20024
1-800-634-0245
FAX: (202) 205-7636
URL: http://www.score.org/

U.S. Census Bureau
4600 Silver Hill Rd.
Washington, DC 20233
URL: http://www.census.gov/

U.S. Department of Veterans Affairs
810 Vermont Ave. NW
Washington, DC 20420
1-800-827-1000
URL: http://www.va.gov/

U.S. Social Security Administration Office of Public Inquiries
1100 W. High Rise
6401 Security Blvd.
Baltimore, MD 21235
1-800-772-1213
URL: http://www.ssa.gov/

RESOURCES

Many of the demographic data cited in this text were drawn from U.S. Census Bureau and U.S. Bureau of Labor Statistics publications, including "Older Americans Month: May 2015" (May 2015), *The Next Four Decades—The Older Population in the United States: 2010 to 2050* (Grayson K. Vincent and Victoria A. Velkoff, May 2010), and the 2014 American Community Survey. The Guinness World Records provided information about the growing number of centenarians.

The report *A Profile of Older Americans: 2014* (May 2015) by the Administration on Aging and the data collected by the Federal Interagency Forum on Aging-Related Statistics provided useful information about older adults, as did population data from *The World Factbook* (2014) by the Central Intelligence Agency. The Center for Immigration Studies report *U.S. Immigrant Population Record 41.3 Million in 2013* (Karen Zeigler and Steven A. Camarota, September 2014) described the foreign-born older population.

The U.S. Census 2014 Current Population Survey Annual Social and Economic Supplement (2014) and the *Survey of Income and Program Participation* provided data about older adults' income distribution and poverty. The Social Security Administration discussed public and private pensions in *Fast Facts and Figures about Social Security, 2014* (September 2014), as did the Milliman report *Milliman 2015 Pension Funding Study* (John W. Ehrhardt, Zorast Wadia, and Alan Perry, April 2015). *The 2015 Retirement Confidence Survey: Having a Retirement Savings Plan a Key Factor in Americans' Retirement Confidence* (Ruth Helman et al., April 2015) by the Employee Benefit Research Institute Associates provided information about pension plans and other employee benefits. The U.S. Department of Labor and the National Economic Council Interagency Working Group on Social Security described trends in labor force participation. The Equal Employment Opportunity Commission offered information about age discrimination

issues and claims. Peter Shapiro's *A History of National Service in America* (1994) details the establishment of a national senior service during the administration of President John F. Kennedy.

The Pew Research Center and the Pew Forum on Religion and Public Life offered insight into the opinions and concerns of older adults. For example, in *Older Adults and Technology Use* (Aaron Smith, April 2014), the Pew Research Center reported the rates of Internet use by older adults. The Boomer Project (2015) described the thoughts and behaviors of members of the baby boomer generation. In *Encore Careers: The Persistence of Purpose* (2014), Penn Schoen Berland and Encore.org reported that millions of Americans aged 50 to 70 years are interested in launching so-called encore careers to address social needs.

The National Highway Traffic Safety Administration, in *Older Driver Program: Five-Year Strategic Plan 2012–2017* (December 2010), documented the increasing numbers of older drivers. In *Transportation for Older Adults: Measuring Results Could Help Determine If Coordination Efforts Improve Mobility* (December 2014), the U.S. Government Accountability Office explored ways to improve transportation options for older adults. The Insurance Institute for Highway Safety reported in "Older Drivers: 2013" (2015) that although the oldest and youngest drivers have the highest fatality rates on a per-mile-driven basis, older drivers involved in crashes are less likely than younger drivers to hurt others. In "New Data on Older Adult Drivers" (April 2015), the Centers for Disease Control and Prevention reported that older drivers take fewer risks than younger drivers. The American Medical Association and the National Highway Traffic Safety Administration developed the *Physician's Guide to Assessing and Counseling Older Drivers* (2010), which details medical conditions and their potential effects on driving skills.

The U.S. Department of Housing and Urban Development's Office of Community Planning and Development described in *Annual Homelessness Assessment Report (AHAR) to Congress, Part 2* (October 2014) the plight of homeless older Americans. The "Housing America's Older Adults—Meeting the Needs of an Aging Population" (2014) by the Joint Center for Housing Studies of Harvard University detailed homeownership rates and older adults' housing needs. The National Low Income Housing Coalition documented in *Out of Reach 2013* (Althea Arnold et al., 2014) income and rental housing cost data for the 50 states, the District of Columbia, and Puerto Rico. The National Center for Health described in "Long-Term Care Services in the United States, 2013 Overview" (Lauren Harris-Kojetin et al., 2013) characteristics of long-term care facilities and residents.

The U.S. Social Security Administration provided information about the history and future of Social Security as well as benefits and eligibility in publications such as *Fast Facts and Figures about Social Security, 2015* (September 2014) and *2015 Annual Report of the Boards of Trustees of the Federal Hospital Insurance and Federal Supplementary Medical Insurance Trust Funds* (July 2015).

The Centers for Medicare and Medicaid Services provided information about the history, the beneficiaries, and the future of these entitlement programs. The Centers for Disease Control and Prevention provided vital health statistics in publications such as *Health, United States, 2014* (May 2015) and the 2014 National Health Interview Survey. The Kaiser Family Foundation reports on Medicare, Medicaid, and long-term care expenditures in many publications, including "The Medicare Prescription Drug Benefit Fact Sheet" (September 2014).

The Administration on Aging report "Data Highlight Extensive Services Provided to Persons Living in Long-Term Care Facilities" (December 2014) described the most frequent concerns at board-and-care facilities. The *Genworth 2015 Cost of Care Survey* (2015) reported on the costs associated with nursing homes and assisted living.

The AARP underwrites research about older Americans. One example of its research cited in this text is the report *A Business Case for Workers Age 50+: A Look at the Value of Experience* (April 2015), which dispels myths about older workers and describes their strengths.

Many organizations and publications provided information on specific health and medical problems of older adults. Among the many publications cited in this text were the American Heart Association's "Older Americans and Cardiovascular Diseases" (2015), the American Cancer Society's *Cancer Facts and Figures, 2015* (2015), and the Alzheimer's Association's *2015 Alzheimer's Disease Facts and Figures* (2015). The U.S. Department of Veterans Affairs provided demographic projections of the health and other needs of older veterans.

Similarly, many agencies, organizations, and professional organizations, notably the National Center for Education Statistics, the Mature Workers Employment Alliance, and the American Geriatrics Society, offered data and analyses of myriad issues of importance to older Americans.

Professional medical journals publish research findings and information about health and disease among older adults as well as health service utilization and financing. Articles from the following journals were cited in this text: *Acta Psychiatrica Scandinavica*; *Aging, Dementia, Cognitive, and Behavioral Neurology: Clinical Trials*; *Aging, Neuropsychology, and Cognition*; *Alzheimer's and Dementia*; *American Journal of Geriatric Psychiatry*; *American Journal of Psychiatry*; *Annals of Internal Medicine*; *Archives of Sexual Behavior*; *BMJ*; *Clinical Gerontologist*; *Clinics in Geriatric Medicine*; *Computers in Human Behavior*; *Disability Health Journal*; *Genome Medicine*; *Gerontologist*; *Harvard Women's Health Watch*; *Health Affairs*; *Health Psychology*; *Home Healthcare Nurse*; *International Social Science Review*; *Journal of Alzheimer's Disease*; *Journal of the American Medical Association*; *Journal of the American Medical Association Internal Medicine*; *Journal of Elder Abuse and Neglect*; *Journal of Personality and Social Psychology*; *Journals of Gerontology*; *Medical Journal of Australia*; *Nature*; *Neurology*; *New England Journal of Medicine*; *Nursing Ethics*; *Nursing Older People*; *Obesity*; *PLOS One*; *Proceedings of the National Academy of Sciences*; *Psychology and Aging*; and *Psychology Today*.

Because the aging population affects nearly every aspect of society, from employment and housing to health care and politics, consumer publications frequently feature articles about and of interest to older adults. Articles cited in this volume were drawn from Atlantic.com, ConsumerReports.org, Forbes.com, Huffingtonpost.com, NYTimes.com, TheHill.com, Time.com, USNews.com, WashingtonPost.com, and WSJ.com.

Information about abuse and mistreatment of older adults was found in "Screening for Intimate Partner Violence and Abuse of Elderly and Vulnerable Adults" (January 2013) by the U.S. Preventive Services Task Force; *The MetLife Study of Elder Financial Abuse: Crimes of Occasion, Desperation, and Predation against America's Elders* (June 2011) by the MetLife Mature Market Institute, the National Committee for the Prevention of Elder Abuse, and the Center for Gerontology at the Virginia Polytechnic Institute and State University; *Elder Justice: National Strategy Needed to Effectively Combat Elder Financial Exploitation* (November 2012) by the Government Accountability Office; and *The Elder*

Justice Roadmap: A Stakeholder Initiative to Respond to an Emerging Health, Justice, Financial and Social Crisis (July 2014) by the U.S. Departments of Justice and Health and Human Services. The Bureau of Justice Statistics' *Criminal Victimization, 2013* (Jennifer L. Truman and Lynn Langton, September 2014) and the *Journal of Elder Abuse and Neglect* provided data about fraud, abuse, and violent victimization of older adults.

We are very grateful to the Gallup Organization for permitting us to present the results of its renowned opinion polls and graphics.

INDEX

CPSIA information can be obtained
at www.ICGtesting.com
Printed in the USA
FFOW05n1851080516

9 781573 026697